AAT

INTERACTIVE TEXT

Foundation Unit 19

Data Processing

(Windows)

September 1998 edition

This Interactive Text has the following enhancements.

- It reflects the latest releases of Sage software (Line 50 and Payroll 4), with on-line Help for users of older versions

- The payroll assignments have been updated for the 1998/99 tax year

- The Blitz program has been redesigned for ease of use and now includes on-line Help

FOR 1998 AND 1999 ASSESSMENTS

BPP Publishing
September 1998

First edition 1995
Fourth edition September1998

ISBN 0 7517 6117 6 (previous edition 0 7517 6106 0)

British Library Cataloguing-in-Publication Data

*A catalogue record for this book
is available from the British Library*

Published by

*BPP Publishing Limited
Aldine House, Aldine Place
London W12 8AW*

*Printed in Great Britain by
WM Print Ltd
Frederick Street
Walsall
West Midlands WS2 9NE*

Windows is a registered trademark of Microsoft Corporation.

*We are grateful to the Sage Group plc for their support in the preparation of
this book. Both the book and the associated Blitz program were developed by
BPP Publishing Ltd.*

*We should also like to thank Steve Morris for his helpful suggestions for
improvements to the Blitz package.*

*We are grateful to the Lead Body for Accounting for permission to
reproduce extracts from the Standards of Competence for Accounting.*

		Page
PREFACE		(v)
INTRODUCTION		(vi)

How to use this book - Sage software - Standards of competence - Assessment structure

PART F: APPENDICES

ORDER FORM

REVIEW FORM & FREE PRIZE DRAW

HOW TO USE THIS BOOK

The purpose of this book is:

(a) to provide some background 'core' knowledge about data processing; and

(b) to provide a series of practical assignments for processing credit, cash and payroll transactions by computer.

The book and an associated program that unloads data for a case study (the BPP 'Blitz' program) have been designed for use with the Sage medium range Windows-based software package for credit and cash transactions, and the Sage medium range Windows-based payroll package for payroll transactions (see below).

The book therefore covers Unit 19 (Data Processing) in the AAT's Foundation Stage of units of competence, and creates a practical link, for the purpose of course assessment, between Unit 19 and

(a) Unit 1:   Recording and accounting for cash transactions;
(b) Unit 2:   Recording and accounting for credit transactions; and
(c) Unit 3:   Recording and accounting for payroll transactions.

Certain aspects of the business administration units, Units 21 to 25, are also reflected in the contents of this books and the tasks it asks you to perform.

The case study

The case study is explained in detail later. Basically, however, it is about a newly-established company of contract cleaners, Blitz Limited. The company has been operating for about one month when the assignments in the book begin. The BPP Blitz program unloads all the transactions that have occurred during this early period, and provides you with 'opening balances' on the accounts in the ledgers, for use with the first assignment.

The BPP Blitz program sets up the 'correct' data for the start of each subsequent assignment. This means, for example, that you can attempt Assignment 4 without having to do Assignments 1, 2 and 3 first, to bring your ledger files up to date.

The book contains:

(a) 6 assignments for credit and cash transactions; and
(b) 4 assignments for payroll transactions;
(c) a variety of simple word processing and spreadsheet exercises.

Guidance is given on how to carry out the tasks in each assignment using Sage software and other widely-used packages such as Microsoft Office. At the end of each assignment you will be required to produce a printout (for example a report) or display certain information on your computer screen. This allows you both to check the accuracy of your answers and also to show your competence in handling accounting software.

How much prior knowledge is needed?

Before starting this book, you will require some core knowledge in accounting. Ideally, you should have an understanding of how to process accounting transactions in a manual (ie non-computerised) system. The book therefore does not explain ledgers, accounts, invoices, credit notes and so on. It assumes some prior knowledge of what these are and what information they should contain.

On the other hand, careful explanations are given for each assignment about how the computerised accounting system is being used, and why. It is obviously important to relate the data processing aspect of the assignments to the accounting aspect. If your knowledge of accounting is still fairly weak, you should still be able to follow most of the explanations in the book, and attempt the assignments.

SAGE SOFTWARE

Sage software is produced by the Sage Group plc, the leading producer of accounting software in the UK. There are over 100,000 registered users of Sage products in Britain alone, ranging in size from large organisations such as British Telecom, BP Oil and the Ministry of Defence, to small businesses.

Sage produce a number of different packages for different sized businesses. The most popular package, **Line 50** (formerly called **Sage Sterling**) is aimed at small to medium-sized businesses. This is the package on which this book is based.

Sage is a flexible software package consisting of a number of separate modules. It is 'user-friendly' and well-suited for anyone wishing to gain 'hands-on' experience in accountancy work on computer systems. We should like to acknowledge the assistance we have received from the Sage Group in preparing this book, and for their permission to reproduce screen displays.

Which version of Windows is needed?

The Sage for Windows programs require Windows version 3.1 or above.

Which version of Sage software is needed?

To use the Blitz program and this book, you need access to a computer (either a stand-alone PC or a terminal into a network) which has the Sage software loaded and is able to run it.

(a) Ideally to attempt the assignments for **credit and cash transactions**, you need one of the following.

Sage **Line 50**

Sage **Sterling for Windows version 4**

Sage **Sterling for Windows version 3**

These are the most recently released versions. All of the illustrations **in Part B of this book** are based on the latest version, **Sage Line 50**, and the Blitz program contains data which is compatible with all three versions.

However, some users may be using the earlier version of this package which was called Sage **Sterling Plus2** (version 2.1). The Blitz program also contains data that owners of this version can use, and the main differences between Plus 2 and the more up to date software are explained in a **Help** file, which is accessible via the Blitz program.

(b) To attempt the assignments for **payroll transactions**, you need either **Sage Sterling Payroll version 4**, or the earlier **Sage Sterling Payroll Plus2** (version 2.3) software.

Part C of this book is based on the more recent **Sage Sterling Payroll 4**, but the Blitz program includes two sets of payroll data, one for each version.

Help for users of the Plus2 payroll program is again available via the Blitz program.

Queries

Appendix 3 in this book has some general advice about setting up the case study, and the BPP Blitz program has its own **online Help**. See **Chapters 2 and 3** for more details.

If you have any queries about setting up **Sage** software on your computer system, please contact:

> The Sage Group plc
> Sage House
> Benton Park Road
> Newcastle-upon-Tyne
> NE7 7LZ
> 0191-255 3000

STANDARDS OF COMPETENCE

The competence-based Education and Training Scheme of the Association of Accounting Technicians (AAT) is based on an analysis of the work of accounting staff in a wide range of industries and types of organisation. The Standards of Competence for Accounting which students are expected to meet are based on this analysis.

The Standards identify the **key purpose** of the accounting occupation, which is to operate, maintain and improve systems to record, plan, monitor and report on the financial activities of an organisation, and a number of **key roles** of the occupation. Each key role is subdivided into **units of competence**. By successfully completing assessments in specified units of competence, students can gain qualifications at NVQ/SVQ levels 2, 3 and 4, which correspond to the AAT Foundation, Intermediate and Technician stages of competence respectively.

Foundation stage key roles and units of competence

The key roles and unit titles for the AAT Foundation stage (NVQ/SVQ level 2) are set out below (note that due to revisions to the Intermediate and Technician Standards taking effect from December 1998, certain Foundation Units of Competence have been renumbered).

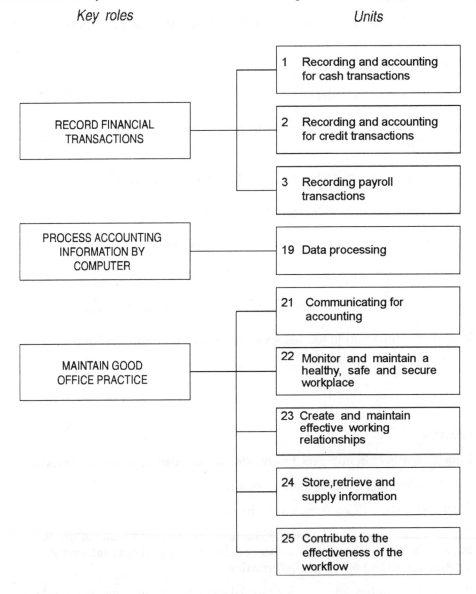

Key roles — *Units*

RECORD FINANCIAL TRANSACTIONS
- 1 Recording and accounting for cash transactions
- 2 Recording and accounting for credit transactions
- 3 Recording payroll transactions

PROCESS ACCOUNTING INFORMATION BY COMPUTER
- 19 Data processing

MAINTAIN GOOD OFFICE PRACTICE
- 21 Communicating for accounting
- 22 Monitor and maintain a healthy, safe and secure workplace
- 23 Create and maintain effective working relationships
- 24 Store, retrieve and supply information
- 25 Contribute to the effectiveness of the workflow

Units and elements of competence

Units of competence are divided into **elements of competence** describing activities which the individual should be able to perform.

Each element includes a set of **performance criteria** which define what constitutes competent performance. Each element also includes a range statement which defines the situations, contexts, methods etc in which the competence should be displayed.

Supplementing the standards of competence are statements of **knowledge and understanding** which underpin competent performance of the standards.

The elements of competence for Unit 19: *Data Processing* are set out below. The performance criteria and range statements for each element are listed first, followed by the knowledge and understanding required for the unit as a whole. Performance criteria and areas of knowledge and understanding are cross-referenced below to chapters in the *Cash Transactions Interactive* Text.

UNIT 19: DATA PROCESSING

Element 19.1 Input information from source documents into a computer system

Performance criteria		*Chapter in this text*
1	All vital fields are completed	4-9, 11-12
2	Incomplete or unauthorised source documents are referred for clarification	4, 6
3	All errors in inputting and coding are identified and corrected	3, 9, 11
4	Correct part of the computer system is used for inputting	2 onwards
5	New unique reference codes are generated as necessary	4, 5, 11
6	Inputting is completed to agreed deadline	2 onwards
7	Organisational procedures for filing source documents are followed	1 onwards
8	Risks to the information technology environment are minimised at all times	1, 3

Range statement

1   Information: words, numbers, information to be coded using reference codes

2   Source documents: complete and incomplete

3   Computer systems: databases, spreadsheets

4   Types of inputting: addition of new information (some of which require the generation of unique reference codes), modification of existing information, deletion/cancelling of existing information

5   Examples of databases are: stock control databases, customer databases, sales ledgers, purchase/bought ledgers, employee database and cash logs

6   Examples of unique reference codes are: stock codes, customer references, invoice numbers, employee numbers

Element 19.2 Locate and retrieve recorded details of requested items from a computer system

Performance criteria		*Chapter in this text*
1	Correct details are retrieved	4-9 ,11-12
2	Search facilities are used optimally	2, 4, 9, 10, 11
3	Confidential information is not disclosed to unauthorised people	1
4	Risks to the information technology environments are minimised at all times	1

Range statement

1 Methods of requesting items: specification of unique reference codes, specification of details

2 Methods of locating details: automatic searching, manual searching (browsing)

3 Computer systems: databases, spreadsheets

4 Examples of databases are: stock databases, customer databases, sales ledgers, purchase/bought ledgers, employee database and cash logs

5 Examples of recorded details of requested items are: cost codes for a cost heading, type of payment of an order, progress and status of an order, credit limit/status/worthiness of a customer, employee details and grant codes for courses

Element 19.3 Generate and print standard reports on a computer system

Performance criteria		*Chapter in this text*
1	Required range and report correctly specified	3 onwards
2	Printed information is correct and complete	2 onwards
3	Hard copy is clean, clearly printed and aligned correctly	1
4	Efforts are made to minimise the wastage of paper	1
5	Printer area is kept clean and tidy	1
6	Work is produced to agreed deadline	1
7	Documents are correctly collated and distributed as directed	1 onwards
8	Risks to the information technology environment are minimised at all times	1 onwards

Range statement

1   Generation: specification of the start and finish of the range and selection of the required report

2   Standard reports: bar charts, pie charts, histograms, standard database reports (some of which require special stationery)

3   Computer systems: databases, spreadsheets

4   Examples of standard database reports are: invoices, payments, pay runs, statements of accounts, infringement reports and flexitime reports

UNITS 1, 2 AND 3

Unit 19 is assessed within the framework of competences for Units 1, 2 and 3. The performance criteria for these units are set out below, indicating the chapter in this text where relevant performance criteria are covered.

Unit 1: Recording and accounting for cash transactions

Element 1.1 Record and bank monies received

Performance criteria		*Chapter in this text*
1	Monies are banked in accordance with organisation's policies, regulations, procedures and timescales	7
2	Incoming monies are checked against relevant supporting documentation	7
3	Cash is correctly counted and correct change given where applicable	-
4	Monies received are correctly and legibly recorded	7
5	Written receipts are correctly issued where required	7
6	Totals and balances are correctly calculated	7
7	Paying-in documents are correctly prepared and reconciled to relevant records	-
8	Documentation is correctly filed	-
9	Cash handling, security and confidentiality procedures are followed	-
10	Discrepancies, unusual features or queries are identified and either resolved or referred to the appropriate person	7

Element 1.2 Make and record payments

	Performance criteria	*Chapter in this text*
1	Payments are made and recorded in accordance with the organisation's policies, regulations, procedures and timescales	6
2	Payments are properly authorised	6
3	Cheques are prepared correctly and are signed by designated person(s) prior to despatch	-
4	Standing orders and other interbank transfers are correctly documented	-
5	Remittance advices are correctly prepared and despatched with payments	6
6	Totals and balances are correctly calculated and checked against documentation	6
7	Available cash discounts are identified and deducted	6
8	Documentation is correctly filed	-
9	Safety and security procedures for the handling of cash and cheques are followed	-
10	Discrepancies, unusual features or queries are identified and either resolved or referred to the appropriate person	6

Element 1.3 Maintain petty cash records

	Performance criteria	*Chapter in this text*
1	Transactions are accurately recorded and analysed to the correct expenditure heads	8
2	Cash withdrawals from the main cash account are accurately recorded	8
3	Claims are properly authorised, are within prescribed limits and are supported by adequate evidence	8
4	Totals and balances are correctly calculated	8
5	The balance of cash in hand is reconciled with the petty cash records at appropriate intervals	-
6	Documentation is correctly filed	-
7	Analysed totals of petty cash expenditure are transferred to the correct ledger accounts	8
8	Cash handling, security and confidentiality, procedures are followed	-
9	Any discrepancies, usual features or queries are identified and either resolved or referring to the appropriate person	-

Introduction

Element 1.4 Account for cash and bank transactions

Performance criteria		Chapter in this text
1	Entries in the cash book are accurately transferred to correct ledger accounts	5-8
2	Bank reconciliation statements are accurately prepared and are presented within specified timescales	8
3	Recorded transactions are supported by properly authorised primary documentation	7,8
4	Details for the relevant primary documentation are recorded in the cash book and analysed accurately	8
5	Totals and balances are correctly calculated	8
6	Security and confidentiality procedures are followed	-
7	The organisation's policies, regulations, procedures and timescales are observed	-
8	Any discrepancies, unusual features or queries are identified and either resolved or referred to the appropriate person	8

Unit 2: Recording and accounting for credit transactions

Element 2.1 Process documents relating to goods and services supplied on credit

Performance criteria		Chapter in this text
1	Invoices and credit notes are correctly authorised and coded, and despatched to customers	5
2	The calculations on invoices and credit notes, including discounts and VAT, are correct	5
3	Invoices and credit notes are correctly entered as primary accounting records in a form acceptable to the organisation	5
4	The analysis and totalling of the primary record is completed accurately	5
5	Documentation is correctly filed	-
6	The organisation's policies, regulations, procedures and timescales are observed	-
7	Discrepancies, unusual features or queries are identified and either resolved or referred to the appropriate person	9

Element 2.2 Process documents relating to goods and services received on credit

	Performance criteria	*Chapter in this text*
1	Suppliers' invoices and credit notes are correctly checked against ordering documentation and evidence that goods/services have been received	4
2	Suppliers' invoices and credit notes are correctly coded	4
3	All calculations on suppliers' invoices and credit notes are correct	4
4	Documents are correctly entered as primary accounting records in a form acceptable to the organisation	4
5	Documents are correctly filed	-
6	The organisation's policies, regulations, procedures and timescales are observed	-
7	Discrepancies, unusual features or queries are identified and either resolved or referred to the appropriate person	9

Element 2.3 Account for goods and services supplied on credit

	Performance criteria	*Chapter in this text*
1	Entries in the primary records are correctly transferred to the correct ledger accounts	5
2	Adjustments involving debtors' accounts are properly authorised and documented, and are correctly transferred to the correct ledger accounts	9
3	The control account in the general ledger is reconciled with the total of balances in the sales (debtors) ledger	-
4	Where required, statements of account are sent to debtors promptly	9
5	The organisation's policies, regulations, procedures and timescales are observed	-
6	Discrepancies, unusual features or queries are identified and either resolved or referred to the appropriate person	9
7	Communications with debtors regarding accounts are handled promptly, courteously and effectively	9

Element 2.4 Account for goods and services received on credit

Performance criteria		*Chapter in this text*
1	Entries in the primary records are correctly transferred to the correct ledger accounts	4
2	Adjustments involving creditors' accounts are properly authorised and documented, and are correctly transferred to the correct ledger accounts	9
3	The control account in the general ledger is reconciled with the total of balances in the purchases (creditors) ledger	-
4	The organisation's policies, regulations, procedures and timescales are observed	-
5	Discrepancies, unusual features or queries are identified and either resolved or referred to the appropriate person	9
6	Communications with creditors regarding accounts are handled promptly, courteously and effectively	6

Unit 3: Recording payroll transactions

Element 3.1 Operate and maintain a payroll accounting system

Performance criteria		*Chapter in this text*
1	Gross earnings are properly authorised, correctly calculated and coded	11, 12
2	The current, authorised payroll status of employees is accurately recorded	11
3	Records of gross employee earnings are correctly transferred to the payroll	11
4	Statutory and non-statutory deductions are correctly calculated and made in accordance with legal organisational requirements	10, 11
5	A summary and analysis of the payroll is accurately transferred to the correct ledger accounts	12
6	The organisation's procedures and timescales are observed	-
7	Confidentiality and security of information is maintained	-
8	Discrepancies, unusual features or queries are identified and referred to the appropriate person or resolved	-
9	Documentation is correctly filed	

Element 3.2 Make authorised payments to employees

Performance criteria	*Chapter in this text*
1 Payslip advice records are correctly prepared and reconciled with cash records	12
2 Due payments are correctly made within specified deadlines	-
3 Payroll information is clearly explained to employees, and enquiries from employees are handled courteously and confidentially	-
4 Annual tax records and other relevant documentation are made available to employees promptly	12
5 Defined procedures for dealing with unclaimed pay are strictly followed	-
6 Safety and security procedures for the handling of cash and cheques are always followed	-
7 Confidentiality and security of information is maintained	-
8 Discrepancies, unusual features or queries are identified and referred to the appropriate person or resolved	-
9 Documentation is correctly filed	

Element 3.3 Make authorised payments, claims and returns to external agencies

Performance criteria	*Chapter in this text*
1 Due payments, claims and returns are correct and made within specified deadlines	12
2 Relevant returns and documents are correctly prepared and submitted to external agencies in good time	12
3 The deduction records reconcile with the payroll system	-
4 Queries relating to external agencies are dealt with promptly, courteously and effectively	-
5 Documentation is correctly filed	-
6 Safety and security procedures for the handling of cash and cheques are followed	-
7 Confidentiality and security of information is maintained	-
8 The organisation's policies, regulations, procedures and timescales are followed	-
9 Discrepancies, unusual features or queries are identified and referred to the appropriate person or resolved	-

ASSESSMENT STRUCTURE

Devolved and central assessment

The units of competence at the Foundation stage are assessed by a combination of devolved assessment and central assessment.

Devolved assessment tests students' ability to apply the skills detailed in the relevant units of competence. Devolved assessment may be carried out by means of:

(a) simulations of workplace activities set by AAT-approved assessors; or
(b) observation in the workplace by AAT-approved assessors.

Central assessments are set and marked by the AAT, and concentrate on testing students' grasp of the knowledge and understanding which underpins units of competence.

The Foundation Stage

Units of competence at the AAT Foundation Stage (NVQ/SVQ level 2) are tested by central assessment (CA) and devolved assessment (DA) as follows.

Unit number		Central assessment	Devolved assessment
1	Recording and accounting for cash transactions	✓*	✓
2	Recording and accounting for credit transactions	✓*	✓
3	Recording payroll transactions	N/A	✓
19	Data processing	N/A	✓
21	Communicating for accounting	N/A	✓
22	Monitor and maintain a healthy, safe and secure workplace	N/A	✓
23	Create and maintain effective working relationships	N/A	✓
24	Store, retrieve and supply information	N/A	✓
25	Contribute to the effectiveness of the workflow	N/A	✓

* A single three-hour central assessment covers both the cash and credit units.

Part A
Introduction to data processing

Chapter 1   Introduction to data processing

Chapter topic list

1   Hardware

2   Software

3   Input of data

4   Keyboard, mouse and screen

5   Data retrieval

6   Output

7   Security and controls

8   Health and safety

Learning objectives

On completion of this chapter you will be able to:

	Performance criteria	Range statement
• describe the principle hardware and software elements that make up a typical business computer system		19.1.3, 19.2.3 19.3.3
• understand the principles of data input, data retrieval and data output	19.1, 19.2, 19.3	n/a
• understand how to risks to the computer environment can be minimised	19.1.8, 19.2.3, 19.2.4, 19.3.8	n/a

1   HARDWARE

1.1   It is common for a data processing system in business to be a computerised system. Accounting systems in particular are normally computerised, and anyone training to be an accountant should be able to work with them.

1.2   Computer systems consist of two integrated elements:

(a)   hardware - that is, equipment; and

(b)   software - that is, computer programs.

1.3   Hardware is the equipment that makes up a computer system. This consists of a central processor, devices for data input, storage (filing data) and output or data display, and the wiring, cables and telecommunications links that connect the hardware components to each other.

Central processor

1.4   Every system, from the smallest to the largest, has a central processor. In a typical desktop PC (personal computer) the central processor consists of several 'boards' of microchips, housed in a plastic box or container that also houses one or two disk drives, and perhaps a CD-ROM drive. The diagram below shows a typical PC configuration.

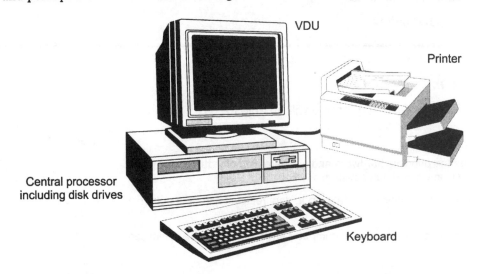

1.5   PCs can be used on their own as **'stand-alone'** computers, or they can be linked to other computers in a **network**, often via a **server** (a more powerful PC), or used as **'intelligent'** **terminals** for a mainframe computer system.

1.6   In a **network**, several users (each with their own keyboard and VDU screen) can share the same files, printers and other facilities and devices. Accounting systems are particularly well-suited to a network system, since several accounting staff can access the same data files from their own desktop keyboard and VDU screen. Larger networks may be run using what is still sometimes called a **minicomputer**, although the distinction between a minicomputer and a powerful **server** is now rather vague.

1.7   **Mainframe** computers are very powerful processors, normally used only by very large organisations such as banks. Older models are enormous and need to be located in a separate, environmentally-controlled-room. Newer mainframes are much smaller and more robust. In any case, the only hardware that users of a mainframe computer will normally see is their 'terminal' (keyboard and screen), and perhaps a printer.

Input, storage and output devices

1.8 Equipment is needed to **input** data to the computer for processing, to **store** data on **file** and for the **retrieval** of data or to produce **output** from the system. These are input, storage and output devices.

1.9 Some devices are used for **input only**. Input devices commonly used in office systems are the **keyboard** and the **mouse**. These are used in conjunction with a **VDU screen**, which displays the data that is being (or has been) entered for processing.

1.10 Some devices, such as printers, are for **data retrieval or output** only. **VDU screens** can be used to display data that has been retrieved from a file, without the need to print it out in '**hard copy**' form.

1.11 Some data is read into the main memory of the central processor. This memory is limited in capacity, and holds data and instructions that are needed all the time, and data that is currently being used by the computer. Most data is held on backing storage devices. The box containing the central processor usually includes one or more 'hard disks' as backing storage. These hold both software and some data for processing.

1.12 Data that is not needed for immediate processing can be held on files on other backing storage devices. The most common of these is the 3½ inch floppy disk. Other storage devices include magnetic tapes or cassettes, and compact discs (CD). Data can be put on to a backing storage file, held on file, retrieved or copied from file, or deleted from file. With CD-ROM, data can be read by the computer, but new data cannot be put on to the file. (ROM stands for Read-Only Memory and new data cannot be 'written' on to the file.) Disks and tapes can also be 'read-only' and prevent the computer user from adding new data to the file, or altering the data on file.

1.13 Computer storage devices, just like audio and video tapes and disks, hold data but need a 'player' - special equipment - to use them. Disks, for example, have to be inserted in a disk drive that can read data from the disk into the central processor or copy data from the central processor to disk. In PC-based systems with one floppy disk drive, the drive is usually called the 'A drive. When there are two floppy disk drives, these are usually called the 'A drive" and the 'B drive'. The hard disk in the central processor is usually the 'C drive'. Similarly, tapes need a tape unit or tape streamer, and CDs must have a CD unit.

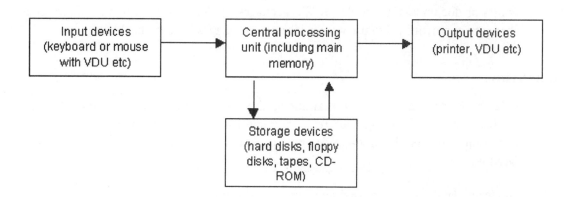

2   SOFTWARE

2.1   Hardware is useless without software. Software is the general name for all types of computer program. Two main types of software are:

(a)   operating system software; and

(b)   applications software.

2.2   *Operating system software* consists of programs that control the operation of the computer hardware and, quite simply, make the computer operate. PCs use different operating systems from larger computers. Similarly, stand-alone computers and networked computers use different operating systems. Older PCs generally use a Microsoft operating system called MS-DOS ; newer ones use Windows NT, Windows 95 or Windows 98. Similarly, there are widely-used operating systems for minicomputers that drive a network system. These include Unix.

2.3   *Applications software* is any program (or part of a program) that is written to perform a particular data processing job. Applications software can be written by a computer user for the user's specific needs. This is fairly common with large organisations that have complex data processing requirements. Alternatively, applications 'packages' or general purpose 'packages' can be purchased ready to install and use. A package is therefore an off-the-shelf program or group of inter-related programs. Computer games are just one example.

(a)   Other examples of applications packages are a sales order processing system, a payroll system, and a computer aided design (CAD) package. Packages might be modules that can either be linked together as part of a larger system, or used on their own. For example, packages for sales order processing, the sales ledger, the purchase ledger, the nominal ledger, stock control and payroll can be linked to form a complete, integrated accounting system.

(b)   General purpose packages are programs that have a broad purpose, but can be adapted to specific requirements of the user. They include word processing packages, spreadsheet packages, database packages and graphics packages.

Word processing packages

2.4   A word processing (WP) package has the general purpose of allowing the user to prepare documents. Specific applications of a WP package are writing letters, and producing reports or documents. Examples of WP packages are Microsoft Word and WordPerfect. There are opportunities to use word processing packages later in this book.

Databases

2.5   A database package is software that allows the user to create a file of data. The file (a 'database') can then be used for retrieving specific data at any time, according to the user's requirements. Examples of database packages are Microsoft Access, DBase IV and Paradox.

2.6   The term 'database' is also used more generally to mean any major file of data, such as a customer database (for example a file of customer records) a supplier database, a stock control database and an employee/payroll database.

Spreadsheets

2.7   Many accountants use *spreadsheet* packages. A computer spreadsheet can be compared to a large piece of squared paper, whose individual squares ('cells') can be filled with numbers, labels and formulae, to produce a table. When a user starts work on a spreadsheet it is 'blank' and contains no data.

2.8   The user constructs the table he or she wants on the spreadsheet template and sets the parameters for its use. The spreadsheet can be virtually any size with any column headings and row labels. (Each package does have a size limit for its spreadsheet tables, but this is very large.) Typical uses of spreadsheets are for preparing forecasts and budgets, since these, after all, are simply tables of figures with labels (column headings and row descriptions).

2.9   Examples of spreadsheet packages are Lotus 1-2-3 and Microsoft Excel. The use of spreadsheets is covered in depth at the AAT Intermediate stage, but you will have a chance to get some hands-on experience later in this book.

3   INPUT OF DATA

3.1   Data is input to a computer system for processing. When data is input, any of the following could happen.

(a)   The data might be processed immediately, and the results either output from the system or transferred to a file (perhaps to a floppy disk, or to file on the hard disk of the central processor).

(b)   The data might be put on to a file, for processing at a future time. Data can be copied from the main memory to a backing storage device. Data files are usually held on a backing storage device (a floppy disk or hard disk, say), or in the processor's own memory.

(c)   The data might be used to 'update' or amend other data already held on the file. For example, an item of data could be input to record the payment of an invoice by a customer, T Smith. This data would update the account for T Smith in the sales ledger file.

(d)   Input could simply be a 'file enquiry', to retrieve an item of data already held on file for displaying on a VDU screen or printing out in 'hard copy' form.

3.2   Data for input to a computer system can sometimes be 'captured' and input directly at the point where the transaction occurs. For example, laser readers or bar-code wands are used at many supermarket check-out points and in department stores and shops. These read the data on the price tag or the bar code on each item that customers buy. They record the sales and compute the total price payable by each customer. In many systems, however, data is first recorded on paper. The paper 'source document' is then used for copying the data into the computer system. Here are two examples.

(a)   A customer order is recorded on a sales order form. This is then used as the source document for input of the sales order transaction details into the sales order processing and accounts systems.

(b)   A goods received note, recording the delivery of goods by a supplier, and the supplier's purchase invoice are the source documents for recording the receipt and invoicing of goods purchased, for input to a stock control and purchase ledger system.

3.3 In many computer processing applications, it is usual to collect several source documents of a single type and input the data for all of them at the same time as a 'batch' of transactions. For example, it is usual to process several customer invoices at the same time, rather than process each invoice individually as soon as a copy of the sales order form is received in the accounts department. Processing similar items in batches ('batch processing') is generally more efficient and time-saving.

Example

3.4 Aston Barton Limited is a Midlands-based company that manufactures carpets for selling to department stores and wholesalers. In a typical week, the company receives ten payments by cheque from customers, and the average cheque amount is £8,000.

3.5 It is good financial practice to bank a cheque on the day that it is received. However, the accounts department can wait to input details of the receipts into the accounts system. It might be decided, for example, to process receipts once a week, and input the transaction details in a single batch (of about ten payment transactions each time).

Records and fields

3.6 The data that is input for a particular transaction is sometimes called a transaction *record* or input *record*. Similarly, all the data held on file for a customer, supplier, employee or stock item is called a customer record, supplier record, employee record or stock record.

3.7 The data in a record is divided into separate items, called *fields*. For example, when data is input to open a new customer account on the sales ledger, the input record will include fields for

(a) customer name;
(b) customer reference code;
(c) customer address;
(d) telephone number;
(e) contact name; and
(f) credit limit.

3.8 Applications packages are sometimes written in such a way that the computer user must input data one field at a time in a specific order. When there is no data for a particular field, the computer user then has to enter an instruction to leave the field blank. Modern Windows-based packages tend to be more flexible.

Data validation

3.9 A program might refuse to accept input data that it knows is invalid. Checks can be carried out by the program on any data field or combination of data fields. For example, if a record contains a 6 digit field for the date (such as 311298 = 31 December 1998) the program might refuse to accept:

(a) any letter instead of a figure in the date field;
(b) any number over 31 for the first two digits combined; and
(c) any number over 12 for the third and fourth digits combined.

3.10 Program checks on the validity of input data fields are known as 'data validation'.

Codes

3.11 Codes are widely used in computer systems, because they save time (and storage space on file). The meaning or identity of each code number has to be input initially in words or numbers and held on file. Having inserted the non-coded name once, however, the code can be used instead of the full name for all subsequent input of data.

3.12 For example, an accounts system might use codes to identify suppliers and customers, with, say, a 5-letter code for each supplier and a 10-digit code for each customer. The code ROBER could be used to represent a supplier, Robertson Castings Ltd of Great Mill Estate, Skelmersdale Road, Bolton, Lancashire. To process any transaction involving this supplier, the computer user could simply specify the code ROBER in the supplier reference code field, and the computer system will identify the supplier's name and address (and file record). Typically, as soon as the code is entered, the name (or name and address) will be displayed on the computer user's VDU screen.

Unique reference codes

3.13 In some cases, there must be a unique identification code or reference code for each record on file. In a sales ledger system, for example, there must be a unique code to identify each customer. Two different customers must never have the same code; otherwise invoices could be sent to the wrong person.

3.14 Similarly, there must be unique reference codes in a purchase ledger system for suppliers, in a stock control system for stock items, and in a payroll system for employees. The field in a record which contains a unique reference code is called the 'key field'.

3.15 Codes do not have to be unique. Two or more records on file can have the same code in a particular field. For example, in a payroll system, several employees can have the same tax code, and the same code for their department of employment.

Scheduling work

3.16 Many computer systems support office routines that are carried out regularly, day by day, week by week and month by month. It is often extremely important, particularly in accountancy, that work should be completed by certain deadlines, or as soon as possible after a 'cut-off' date. For example, in an accounting system, end-of-month routines are carried out as soon as all the relevant data has been input to the system. It can be important to make sure that all this data is input within just a day or so after the month end. Working to deadlines, for both input and output, is therefore a feature of many computer-based systems.

4   KEYBOARD, MOUSE AND SCREEN

4.1 Much input of data for accounting applications is done with a keyboard or mouse, in conjunction with a VDU screen. To work properly with computers, you must therefore be familiar with the main features of a computer keyboard, and how a keyboard or mouse should be used.

VDU screen

4.2 The VDU screen is a means by which the computer program can communicate with the computer user and the user communicates with the program. The screen displays messages or information, and often asks the user to give an instruction or to input data into a field that is indicated by a pointer or *cursor*. The cursor is highlighted on the screen, perhaps in a distinctive colour or as a flashing marker. Various kinds of screen message can be displayed.

(a) A screen can give 'prompts', instructing the user what to do next. The screen can also prompt the user to select from a choice of things to do next, by displaying a selection of different options.

(b) A screen can prompt the user to enter data for a particular field in a record, by displaying the fields on screen and indicating (with the cursor) which field should be entered next.

(c) The screen displays the data that the user keys in. The user can check that it is correct before 'entering' it into the system. Incorrect data can then be amended or abandoned before it is entered.

(d) A screen will often include header or trailer 'bars' at the top or bottom of the screen. These usually show a list of choices, that the user can select at any time, should he or she wish. For example, there could be an option to ask for guidance from the computer about what to do next (a 'help' facility), an option to call up a calculator on screen, an option to display a list of all the records on file, an option to exit the program, and so on.

Menus

4.3   Many applications packages provide prompts to the user by displaying a list of options for selection in a 'menu'. The user selects an option from the menu, and the screen then shows another display for further processing. In larger systems, there could be a hierarchy of menus, starting with a main menu at the top of the hierarchy and working down to sub-menus and sub-sub-menus. The program begins by prompting the user to make a selection from the main menu, and then lists a sub-menu for further selection, and so on until a specific processing option has been selected (for example for data input or file enquiry). This is the principle behind the Windows 95 'Start' button that was so widely advertised when it was introduced.

Example

4.4   A hierarchy of menus in an accounts system could include those shown in the diagram below.

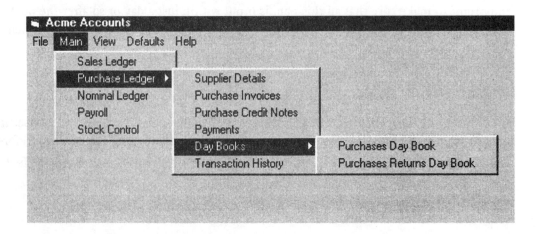

4.5   In this example, to produce a purchase day book listing, the user would specify 'Purchase Ledger' in the main menu, then 'Day Books' in the Purchase Ledger menu, and then 'Purchases Day Book' in the day books menu.

4.6   To get from a lower menu back to a higher menu, the user must enter a suitable instruction. In many systems, this is given by pressing the **Escape** key (Esc) at the top left hand corner of the keyboard, or selecting an Escape option on a menu bar at the top or bottom of the screen.

Tabs

4.7   More modern systems use not only menus but also screens that are laid out like index cards, one underneath another, with a series of **tabs** at the top giving the title of each 'card'. In the following example the tab showing the main **Details** of a supplier's account is uppermost.

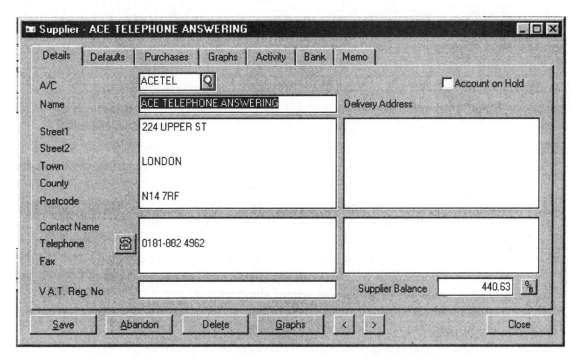

4.8   However, the user can simply click on any other tab to get a different information about this supplier. Here the user has click on the tab that says **Activity.**

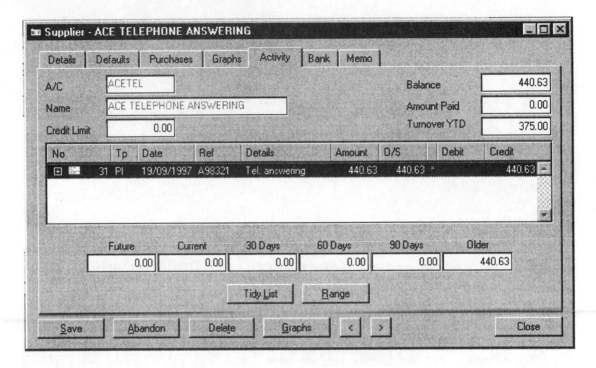

Keyboard

4.9 A typical computer keyboard is shown below.

4.10 Many of the keys are similar to those on an old-fashioned typewriter, and are used to enter letters, figures, punctuation and other items. Letters are usually displayed in lower case. To get a capital letter press one of the *shift* keys at the same time as the letter key. Similarly, to enter the top character where two are shown on the same key, for example to get a £ sign from the £/3 key, press the shift key at the same time as the £/3 key.

4.11 To input capital letters for everything, press the Caps Lock key. A light will probably show on the keyboard, to indicate that the Caps Lock key is on. However, even when Caps Lock is on, the program will record the *figures* for the 1, 2, 3 ... to 0 keys (the bottom character on the key, not the top one). This happens, for example, with Sage software packages.

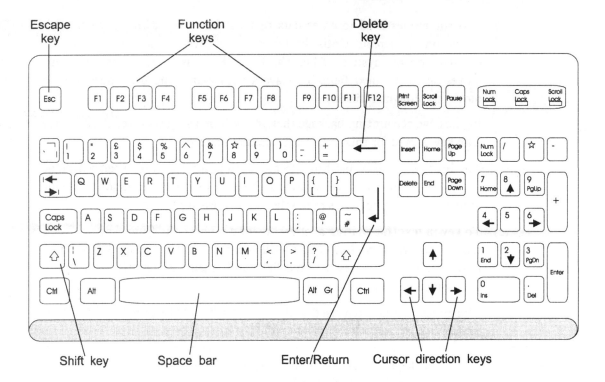

4.12 The space bar is usually for entering a space in text, but can be used with some programs to enter an instruction - for example 'move on to the next screen'.

4.13 The direction arrow keys ↑ ← ↓ and → can be used to move the *cursor* on the VDU screen in the direction indicated by the arrow. They are sometimes called the cursor up, cursor left, cursor down and cursor right keys. The cursor is a small flashing oblong or vertical line that indicates your current position on the screen.

4.14 The key with the longer arrowed line pointing left, below the F12 key, is a delete key. This deletes the character shown on screen to the *left* of the cursor. For example, a computer user might input 1234765, by mistake, when 1234567 was required. If the cursor is now to the right of the figure 5, the user can press the delete key three times, to delete 765, then enter the correct figures 567.

4.15 The Enter key, also called the Return key, is shown below. For convenience there is another Enter key next to the numeric keypad: this has exactly the same function.

4.16 This key (whichever of the two is pressed) has various uses.

(a) It is sometimes used to enter data that has been keyed in for a data field and is shown on the screen. Until the Enter key is pressed, the data has not been fully entered into the system. When the Enter key has been pressed, the cursor then moves on to the next field. To leave a field blank, the user must press Enter, to move on to the next field.

In the Sage accounting package that you will be using with this book, however, the **Tab** key is used for this important function instead.

(b) The Enter key can be used to select an option, for example to select an option from a menu. The direction arrow keys can be used to move the cursor to the menu item required, and the option is then selected by pressing Enter.

(c) To key in text (for writing a letter, say, or a report), the Enter key can be pressed to move down from one line of text to the next, and 'return' to the left hand side of the next line. The Enter key is also called the Return key for this reason, especially in word processing systems.

(d) The Enter key is often used with computer-based learning packages to move the screen display from one 'page' of text to the next.

4.17 There are five keys associated with looking through a list of items on screen; for example, to search through a list of customer names and reference codes. Such a list could be very long, and much too long to fit on the screen at the same time, or to search through line by line using the cursor direction keys $\downarrow$ and $\uparrow$. The computer user can search through the list by 'scrolling' down or up to find the record that he or she is looking for.

(a) The Page Down key takes the screen down the list.

(b) The Page Up key takes the screen back up the list.

(c) The End key takes the screen to the bottom items on the list.

(d) The Home key is for returning back to the top of the list.

(e) The Scroll Lock key is to stop the scrolling up or down, and 'lock' the display on screen at any point in the middle of the list.

4.18 There are 12 function keys F1 to F12 at the top of the keyboard. These can be used to give instructions to the computer. The nature of the instruction associated with each key varies from program to program.

4.19 Some keys on the main (left hand side) of the keyboard are duplicated on the right hand side in a number pad. These keys are for use with packages where most input is in figures rather than letters, and can be easier for right-handers to use than the number keys on the left hand side of the keyboard. Access to the use of these keys can be obtained by pressing the Num Lock key near the top right-hand side of the keyboard.

Mouse

4.20 Many application packages allow the user to enter instructions with a mouse as an alternative to using the keyboard. Moving a mouse on a flat surface moves the screen cursor in the same direction (that is, up and down, left and right). When the cursor is positioned over a desired option, such as a menu choice, clicking the left hand button on the mouse indicates the user's choice to the computer.

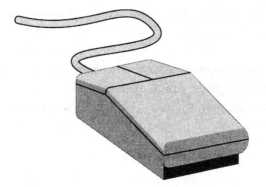

4.21   Some packages encourage the use of a mouse by presenting menus or other options in the form of a picture or icon. The mouse can be used to move the cursor to the appropriate icon, and clicking the left hand button makes the desired selection. Newer packages also have uses for the right hand button.

5   DATA RETRIEVAL

5.1   Once data has been input to a system and the source documents have been filed away, a user may wish to refer to the data, to look up an item of information. In most cases he will not want a printout of the data, but will simply want to check an item as quickly as possible. The most effective way of doing this is to call an item up on screen. Retrieving data on file is often necessary, for example, to answer queries from customers about their accounts, or from employees about their pay.

5.2   The method of retrieving data for display on screen (or for printing out) varies from one application package to another. A search facility (the ability to search through files quickly and easily to find data) is provided by many commercial packages. In a typical accounts system, for example, the computer user could check the details of a specific supplier's account by selecting:

(a)   the Purchase Ledger option on the main menu; and then

(b)   the Accounts Enquiries or Transactions History option on the purchase ledger menu.

5.3   A screen display might then prompt the user to specify the unique reference code for the supplier's account, and the account details will then be displayed on screen.

5.4   Searching for records by scrolling through a list on screen is sometimes known as *browsing*. There are two situations where this is commonly done.

(a)   A user might wish to locate an item in a long list, for example a customer account in a list of accounts, or an invoice in a list of invoices raised in the period.

(b)   A user might wish to look through several individual records in a list, such as a list of employee records. There should be no need to specify the unique reference code for every item in the list in order to make each selection; the computer will simply call up the next record when requested to do so.

5.5   Keyboard commands for browsing vary from one system to another. A user 'scrolling' through a list may well use Page Up and Page Down to move rapidly through the list, and the up and down arrow keys to move up or down one line at a time. Where the user wishes to browse through individual records, a system may use commands such as N for next page and P for previous page. Commands of this type are often shown on the bottom of the screen as a reminder.

5.6   Browsing is time-consuming when the user wants to locate a specific record on the file. Searching a file for the required data is speeded up if the user can specify search criteria. The more specific the request, the smaller the number of items which will satisfy it. For example if the user knows the relevant customer reference number, the system will retrieve instantly the details of the appropriate customer. Most systems allow searches to be made by name; clearly it is unreasonable to expect every user to know every relevant reference code, and so searching by name is often a more practical solution. Again, the more specific the user can be, the more limited the number of choices given. For example, criteria for a search of a payroll file could specify the department code (and the list will be quite long) or a specific name - for example SMITH - and the list will be much shorter.

6   OUTPUT

6.1   There are two important output devices in almost every computer system. One is the VDU screen, which allows the user to review an individual record or a small part of a file at any time. *Screen output* is for immediate viewing and is lost when the user turns off the computer, logs out or moves to another 'page'. The second important output device is the printer. Printed output (hard copy) is more permanent than screen displays. It can be reviewed and re-visited very easily, distributed to different recipients, written on by hand and filed away. Printed output is essential for much of the output from an accounts system, for example for statements and reminder letters in a sales ledger system, and payslips in a payroll system.

6.2   There are a number of different types of *printer* in widespread use. The most common are the dot matrix printer, the bubble jet printer and the laser printer.

(a)   Dot matrix printers are used with continuous computer stationery, and so are ideal for printing out long reports. The print quality is often not particularly good and the dots that form each character can be clearly seen. Dot matrix printers are used where reports are printed on *multi-part* stationery. Multi-part stationery allows more than one copy of a document, such as an invoice, to be printed at the same time.

(b)   Bubble jet printers are quicker and quieter. They are slightly more expensive than dot-matrix printers, but they give better quality.

(c)   Laser printers by comparison are much more expensive, much quieter and offer the best quality print. They are most commonly used with A4 paper rather than traditional continuous computer stationery. Laser printers are best suited to word processing and presentational applications such as producing reports, but are also used for other commercial applications, including accounting.

Types of paper

6.3   The type of printer that you are using dictates the type of paper you can use. Two types of paper are available:

(a)   continuous stationery; and
(b)   single sheet paper.

Continuous stationery

6.4   Continuous stationery is fed through the printer as a continuous sheet, like a paper concertina. Individual pages are separated by perforations. The length of page is set so that the printer starts each new page of text at the top of a new page of the paper. It is often multi-part stationery so that several copies of a document can be printed at the same time.

6.5   The multi-part stationery is held together by side strips. These have round holes which fit over the sprockets on the printer. The side strips must be torn off to separate the copies (*decollating*). The individual pages must also be separated for distribution (*bursting*).

6.6   Continuous stationery is very suitable for much of the printed output in accounting, where multiple copies of the same document are often required, for example invoices and purchase orders. For standard documents such as invoices and payslips a company will often use pre-printed stationery. The computer program specifies where the data output from the system should be printed on to the stationery. Software suppliers are usually able to provide a user with specially-formatted pre-printed stationery for use with their package.

6.7   Some businesses also produce cheques by computer. The stationery is supplied by the company's bank. They tend to be used with a purchase ledger package. When an accounts department produces its cheques by computer, it will usually try to print a large number of cheques all at the same time, for the sake of convenience and efficiency. The production of cheques in a large batch is known as a 'cheque run'.

Single sheet paper

6.8   When printed output is on to single sheet paper, the paper is usually placed in a special tray or feeder for the printer. The printer takes a fresh page as it requires one.

6.9   Most software packages give clear instructions to the user about printing selected output. Prompts on screen could ask the user:

(a)   to choose between screen display or printout; and

(b)   to specify the items for printing, or 'print range' (for example, a range of invoice numbers for printing invoices, a range of employee reference codes for printing payslips, or a range of dates to print out the details of all transactions that occurred between the specified dates).

6.10   The screen might then instruct the user about how to print - for example, by giving a reminder to check that the printer is switched on, and then a prompt to enter the print command (for example Press Enter, or Press Print Screen).

Print layouts

6.11   The layout of a printed document in an accounts system, such as list, letter or report, is specified within the program. A layout can be altered, and new layouts can be designed, but this will normally be the responsibility of a manager or supervisor in the accounts department.

6.12   The computer user might be required to insert details into a document before printing can take place. For example, it might be necessary to key in invoice details for an invoice production system. The screen should always provide sufficient prompts to allow the user to input the data required.

Using a printer

6.13   Before you use your printer, you should feel fairly confident that you know how to operate it. If necessary, read the operating manual carefully. In particular, be sure that you know how to:

(a)   switch the printer on;
(b)   check that the printer is *on-line* (ready to print);
(c)   align the paper properly in the printer;
(d)   move continuous stationery to the top of the next page;
(e)   stop the printer.

We shall encourage you to make a record of this information, as far as your college system is concerned, in the next chapter.

6.14   If you use a PC at work, say, check that you know how the printer is connected to the computer. You might at some time need to check the connection, if the printer is not working, to see if a faulty connection is the cause of the fault.

6.15   Printed output should be clean, clearly printed and properly aligned. If the alignment is incorrect (for example, if a single printed page is spread across two pages of continuous stationery because the paper was incorrectly positioned in the printer at the start of printing), you should print the output again. Don't ignore replacement parts. If the print quality is poor, for example, you might need a new ink cartridge in your printer.

6.16   Computer systems have a reputation for producing large and wasteful quantities of paper. There are two basic principles for keeping paper wastage to a minimum.

(a)   Take sensible precautions about aligning paper properly and keeping your printer properly supplied with replacement printing parts (cartridges).

(b)   Don't print long reports unless there are office routines and procedures that call for their production.

(c)   Use screen displays for output instead of a printout, where a screen display is sufficient.

(d)   When specifying the 'parameters' for a report, don't make reports unnecessarily long by specifying items for inclusion in the printout that you don't really need.

Print facilities

6.17   Printers spend a lot of time not in use, and it is often too expensive for an organisation to provide one printer per terminal or keyboard. A wages department is likely to have its own printer, so that confidential output is not produced where staff can see it. Other departments may not have their own printers, however, but may be linked to a central printing facility. Instead of a 'Report printing' message, users will be informed (on the computer screen) that their report has been sent to the print queue. Long reports such as a detailed nominal ledger printout or a printout of customer statements will be printed overnight so that the printer is not effectively taken out of circulation during working hours. The system itself will tell the staff in charge of the central printer which user has requested each printout. It will also notify them when pre-printed stationery is needed, for example for printing invoices and reminder letters.

Printing graphs and charts

6.18   Some software packages give the user an option to produce and print graphs or charts from numerical data. This is a facility with all graphics packages (software written specifically for the production of graphs and diagrams). It is also available with some other types of software, including spreadsheet packages.

Example

6.19   Carter Doyle Ltd had the following sales turnover in 19X7.

Quarter	Sales
	£000
1	75
2	100
3	175
4	150
Total	500

6.20   If this data were input into a program with a graph production facility, any of the following graphs or charts shown below could be prepared.

Pie chart: Annual sales

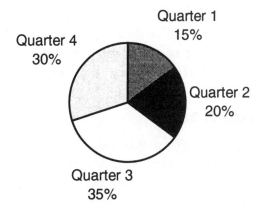

Graph: Time series

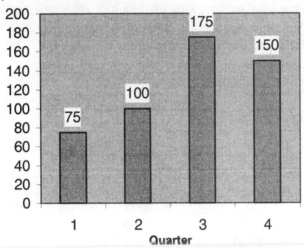

Histogram: Sales per quarter

Distribution

6.21 Computer reports should be distributed promptly to the individuals or departments that expect to receive them.

(a) Reports should not be late - managers could be waiting for them and wanting to use them. It is usual for regular reports such as monthly reports to be printed to a specified timetable and deadline. For the reports to be up-to-date, this means having to make sure that all the relevant data has been input and processed.

(b) Reports, once printed, should be distributed promptly. When data is confidential, the reports should be sent in sealed envelopes, with the recipient's name and the words 'STRICTLY CONFIDENTIAL' clearly shown.

7   SECURITY AND CONTROLS

7.1 Business data is often extremely confidential. This is particularly true of accounting data. Within any organisation, there must be strict controls over the processing and filing of financial and accounting data, and over the distribution of reports and other output. The opportunities for deliberate fraud or accidental errors must be prevented, or minimised as much as possible.

7.2 Many financial controls in computerised accounting systems are the same as the controls that should also be found in manual systems. For example, transactions should not be processed unless they have been properly authorised.

(a) A supplier's invoice must not be posted to the supplier's account in the purchase ledger unless a signature (or initials) of an authorised person has been added to either the invoice or a goods received note (if there is one), confirming that the goods have been received or the service has been provided, and the amount on the invoice is correct.

(b) An employee must not be paid for overtime hours worked without a document having been signed by an authorised supervisor, confirming that the hours have been worked.

7.3   Whenever you are asked to process a transaction that has not been properly authorised, or is missing some important details, you should consult your supervisor for instructions about what to do next.

7.4   Some problems of security and controls occur with computerised systems that do not occur (or are less serious) with manual systems. These problems relate to:

(a)   the physical protection of hardware; and

(b)   the protection of data on file, either in the hard disk of the central processor or on a backing storage device.

Hardware security

7.5   Computer equipment, like other electronic and electrical equipment, can easily malfunction and is easily damaged. Older mainframe computers need a special dust-free and controlled environment, and a secure power supply, to avoid malfunction. More modern computers are more 'robust' and can be used in an ordinary office environment, but even so, problems can occur.

(a)   Equipment can be knocked. Office cleaners who move a PC to clean a desk top can easily cause a malfunction when the computer is next switched on. Cleaners should be given clear instructions to avoid touching computer equipment.

(b)   The computer user should prevent the equipment from getting dirty or dusty. Dust can cause a malfunction. Office printers should be covered with a dust cover at the end of each day. Spilling a cup of coffee over a keyboard or a mouse is also a common danger to avoid.

(c)   Theft is not uncommon. Equipment should be locked away if it is valuable and easily moved. There should be rules about locking the office door, for example, at the end of each day.

Security of data

7.6   Data can get lost or damaged. It can also get into the possession of unauthorised individuals. Even more often, incorrect data can be input to a system without the error being spotted. Controls of various kinds can be established to reduce these risks. Here are just a few common examples.

(a)   Access into a system can be controlled by passwords. Unless the computer user can specify the correct password, he or she is refused access by the computer to the rest of the program and the data files. Different passwords can be used, with each password restricting access to a specific part of the system. All accounts packages make use of passwords.

(b)   Errors in data input to a system cannot be avoided. However, the number of errors can be reduced when the program includes data validation checks.

(c)   Access to printers (and printouts) can be restricted by locating the printer in a locked room to which only a few authorised personnel have access, and by applying strict controls over the distribution of printouts.

Back-up copies of files

7.7   A very common problem is that data held on file (that is, on tape or disk) is easily corrupted, and the file becomes unusable. Disks can also be lost or destroyed. All computer users should, as a matter of the utmost importance, maintain back-up copies of their files. If the original files are damaged or lost, the back-up files can be used to restore the data into the system.

7.8   In an accounts system, it is common practice to back up the files at the end of each day. In larger systems, the files are backed up on to tapes that can hold large quantities of data. In smaller systems, the files can be backed up on floppy disks. The back-up copies must then be held outside the office in the safekeeping of someone reliable. This means having to take new back-up files home every day. In addition to making daily back-up copies (which might be held for a week before re-using the disks), an organisation will often make a weekly back-up (which is held for a month) and a monthly back-up (which is held for a year before re-using the disk).

7.9   Back-up copies of files should be held away from the office premises because of the danger of damage to the building from accidents, such as fire or flooding. Many businesses, for example, were able to recover from the bomb damage at the World Trade Center in New York and at Bishopsgate in the City of London, both in 1993, because they held back-up data files away from their wrecked offices.

Care of disks

7.10   If you use floppy disks, you must take good care of them to protect the data on them. Both 3 ½" and 5 ¼" disks should be stored in a safe place, such as a disk box (this is a specially-designed plastic tray). Disk boxes are often kept in a fire-proof cabinet. Each disk should be labelled to show what data it contains. Stick-on labels are provided with the disks by disk suppliers.

(a)   5¼" disks have a protective casing, but this is thin. It is important to avoid bending the casing (with the disk inside) or touching the disk itself inside the casing. They should also be kept in their paper sleeves whenever they are not in use.

(b)   3 ½" disks have a thicker, rigid plastic cover, which makes them less prone to damage. However, they must still be cared for. Leaving a 3.5" disk on a hot window ledge in summer, in the sun's rays, for example, can wipe out the data on the disk.

Write-protection

7.11   It can be useful to compare computer disks to audio cassettes or video tapes. They can all be bought either with data already contained on them (for example an applications package) or blank, for recording data on to them. Disks are re-usable, and (like video tapes and audio cassettes) you can record fresh data on top of data they already contain.

7.12   When data is already held on a disk, however, the user might wish to keep it and prevent anyone from recording new data, and wiping out the old data. 3.5" disks have a tab in one corner which slides across a small square window. The computer will check the position of the tab before allowing the contents of the disk to be overwritten. If the window is 'open', data cannot be written on to the disk.

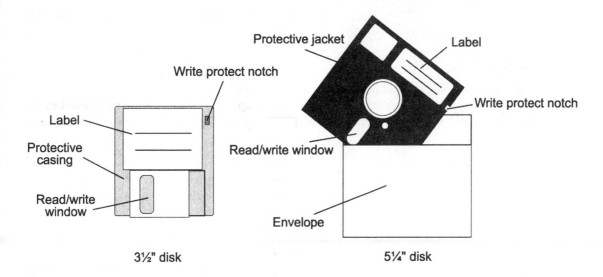

Protective jacket

Label

Write protect notch

Label

Protective casing

Read/write window

Write protect notch

Read/write window

Envelope

3½" disk   5¼" disk

8   HEALTH AND SAFETY

8.1   Computer equipment uses a lot of cable, plugs and connectors. It can generate a lot of heat, particularly when a large amount of equipment is located in the same small room. Computers can therefore create safety risks at work. If cables are lying across the floor of an office, someone will eventually trip over them. If the electrical wiring in an office is unsafe, a risk of electric shocks could exist. Staff in an office should always observe basic safety precautions. Cable should not be trailed across the office floor. Equipment should not be placed on surfaces where they can fall off. When you have any suspicions about the safety of the electrical wiring, inform your supervisor immediately. Remember that repairs to electrical equipment should only be carried out by a qualified electrician or a computer maintenance engineer.

8.2   Individuals who spend a large part of the working day at a VDU and keyboard can be exposed to health risk. The risks are more severe, for example, than watching TV for eight or nine hours a day. Risks include the possibility of eye strain, back problems and RSI (*Repetitive Strain Injury*). RSI affects the hands and arms, and can cause serious disability for regular keyboard users.

8.3   If you ever have any discomfort while working at a VDU or keyboard you must tell your supervisor, who should instruct you to take a break, or move on to a task that does not involve keyboard work.

8.4   Several things can be done to reduce the health risks.

   (a)   Keyboard users should sit on a swivel chair (preferably with an adjustable back rest) set at the correct height for working at the keyboard on the desk top.

   (b)   A screen can be fitted with a filter, to reduce the effects of the brightness of the screen on the eyes.

   (c)   Any computer user should break off regularly from keyboard work and avoid having to look at the screen for long periods of time at a stretch.

Chapter 2   Using PCs and Windows

Chapter topic list

1   Introduction

2   Using PCs

3   Windows: the basics

4   Windows: starting things up

5   More features of Windows

6   Filing with Windows

7   The BPP Blitz program

8   Using a word processor

9   Glossary of common terms

Learning objectives

On completion of this chapter you will be able to do the following, at a basic level, in a Windows environment:

	Performance criteria	Range statement
• complete all vital fields in an input screen	19.1.1	
• identify and correct errors in inputting and coding	19.1.3	
• use the correct part of a computer system for inputting	19.1.4	
• generate new unique codes as necessary	19.1.5	
• complete inputting to agreed deadlines	19.1.6	
• follow organisational procedures for filing source documents	19.1.7	
• retrieve correct details	19.2.1	
• use computer search facilities	19.2.2	
• correctly specify required ranges and reports	19.3.1	
• print out correct and complete information	19.3.2	
• print out clean, clear and correctly aligned hard copy	19.3.3	
• minimise the wastage of paper	19.3.4	
• keep the printer area clean and tidy	19.3.5	
• produce work to an agreed deadline	19.3.6	
• collate and distribute documents correctly	19.3.7	

1   INTRODUCTION

1.1   The chapter aims to teach you the basics of using a PC and Microsoft Windows software so that you can approach the Sage accounting and payroll packages, which are the main subject of this book, with some confidence.

1.2   We shall assume that you have never used a PC before and that, as far as you know, a window is something that lets in light and keeps out draughts.

1.3   For many students this won't be true. You may have been using PCs and Windows since you were at school. If so, you can skip the first few sections of this chapter. We suggest you start with sections 6 and 7, so that you understand how to use the BPP Blitz program. Then prove your Windows competence by doing Activity 2.9 in Section 8.

If you are new to computers and Windows it is worth spending some time on this chapter: it is a rather long one in any case. We suggest that you spend one complete session on sections 1 to 6, and another revising the basics and then working through sections 7 to 9.

Windows 3.x, Windows 95 and Windows 98

1.4   At college you may be using the older Windows 3.1 or 3.11 (referred to as Windows 3.x for convenience), instead of Windows 95 or Windows 98, which need more powerful PCs than many colleges possess at present. We describe the essential features of Windows 3.1 and Windows 95. Windows 98 works in the same way as Windows 95 for all practical purposes.

Alternative methods

1.5   There are usually at least two (and often more) different ways of doing the same thing in Windows. For the most part we only describe the options that we think are the easiest for a beginner to learn. If you can find a faster way to do something, or a way that you find easier to remember, or more comfortable for whatever reason, then use it.

1.6   We are also only going to describe those features that are useful in a very general sense, or in a particular sense for the operation of the *Sage* accounting package. This chapter does not pretend to be a comprehensive guide to Windows.

Activity 2.1

Find out whether you will be using Windows 3.x, Windows 95 or Windows 98 on your Unit 19 course.

---

2   USING PCS

Turning on your computer

2.1   If you really are new to computers, you are probably staring at a blank screen and wondering where the remote control is. Silly though it may seem in hindsight, when you first encounter a computer system it can take some time to build up the confidence simply to get a terminal going without someone holding your hand. This is often because the person introducing you to the system says alarming things about how easy it is to damage it, but does not give you clear guidelines on how to *avoid* damaging it.

Systems at college or at work

2.2 If you are using a larger system – the one at work or college, say – make sure that your supervisor shows you precisely what buttons to push/switches to switch to get the system going and how to turn it off again when you have finished. Maybe your tutor will always do this for you, but if not, ask to have a go yourself the first time you are told and *write down* the procedure for future reference.

2.3 Here is a handy blank space so that you have the necessary information with you whenever you are using this book.

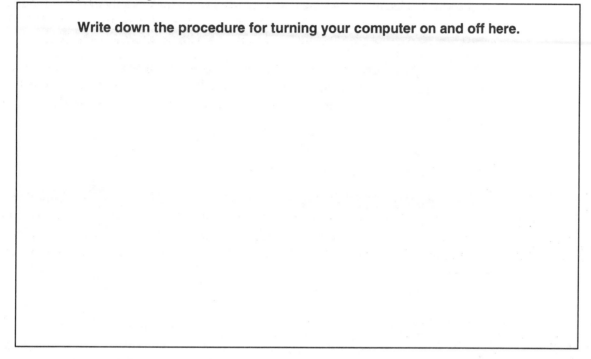

Write down the procedure for turning your computer on and off here.

PCs

2.4 With a 'stand alone' PC (one not connected to any other computers) it doesn't really matter how you turn it on. If you want a rule, first turn on the hard disk drive, then the VDU screen (but there is no reason not to do it the other way round). Only turn on the printer when you are ready to print out a document.

2.5 The *turning off* procedure needs a little care.

(a) *Windows 95 and Windows 98*

If you have Windows 95 or Windows 98 there is no need to worry about the C:\>. You just click on the **Start** button (even though what you want to do is stop!) and choose the option **Sh<u>u</u>t Down**... . When you have confirmed that this is what you want to do a message comes up on your screen telling you:

> It's now safe to turn off
> your computer

(b) *Windows 3.x*

Don't turn off your PC until you have exited from any programs that you have been using and the last line of the screen shows only the symbols **C:\>**. We shall tell you how to make sure about this shortly (see Activity 2.2 and the paragraphs that follow it). If you have C:\> as your last line you can turn off your equipment in whatever order you like.

3 WINDOWS: THE BASICS

3.1 A 'window' is a frame that appears on your computer screen. Several different frames may be visible at once, or a single window may occupy the whole screen. The screen shown below has five windows on it. One window contains the other four. You will see something like this within about a minute or less of turning on a PC that has Windows 3.x software loaded on it. (What you see certainly won't look exactly like this, though.)

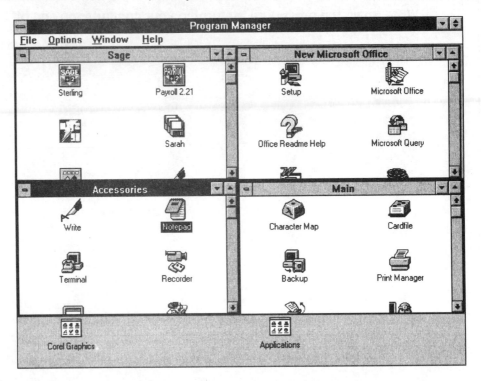

3.2 In Windows 95 and Windows 98 the initial screen is called the **Desktop**, but the Windows principle is still used. The next illustration shows the desktop (in the background) with a Window that has been called up using the Start button menus.

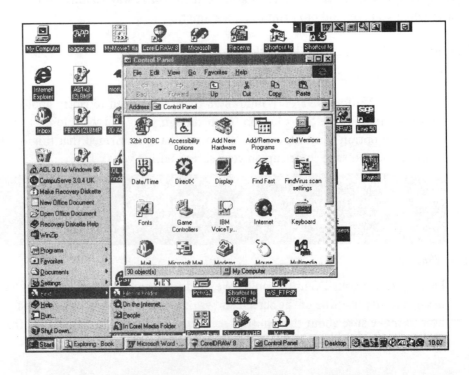

Features common to most windows

3.3   Nearly all windows have three common features

Title bar

3.4   A title, shown in a strip at the top the window. This is sometimes called the **title bar**.

Top left hand corner

3.5   Look up at the very top left-hand corner of the windows illustrated above.

(a)   In Windows 95/98 there is a symbol in the **top-left hand corner** [image]. You can use this to do a variety of things, but its main use is to *close* the window. (The symbol is different depending upon which program you are using.)

(b)   In Windows 3.x there is a flat-looking square in the **top left-hand corner** with a sort of minus sign in it. [image] Again the main use of this is to *close* the window.

Top left-hand corner

3.6   Now look up at the top **right hand** corner of a window. There are several shapes on little 3D squares that look like the **buttons** that you press on electrical equipment to make things happen (change channel, switch on and off and so on). In effect this is what they are, though you don't physically press them.

(a)   In Windows 95/98 you have three symbols in the top right-hand corner.

(i)   There is a line, which minimises the window, reducing it to a button on the 'task bar' at the bottom of the screen (where the Start button is).

(ii)   There are two squares, one on top of the other. This makes the window a little bit smaller so you can see what else there is on your screen or look at two different windows at once. If your window is already in its 'smaller' state only one square is shown and this makes the window bigger again.

(iii)   There is an **X.** This closes the window altogether.

(b)   In Windows 3.x there are upward and downward pointing triangles in the top right hand corner.

(i)   The down triangle (the 'minimise' button) makes the window as small as it can possibly be: typically one inch square and represented by a symbol called an 'icon'. The down triangle often makes your windows disappear 'behind' other windows. It is best *not to use it* until you are confident with Windows, because it just makes you lose things. We shall deliberately 'lose' a window later in this chapter to demonstrate this, and show you how to rescue it.

(ii)   The up triangle makes the window as big as it can possibly be, so that it fills the whole screen.

When a window fills the whole screen the up triangle is replaced by a square containing both up and down triangles in a sort of split diamond shape [image] . Sometimes there are two of these squares, one below the other. They make the window a little bit smaller so that you can see what else there is on your screen. Feel free to use the split diamond shape whenever you like.

3.7 You may be wondering *how* these things can be used, since nothing happens if you touch them with your finger. This is where the **mouse** and its buttons come in. If you are not already sitting at a PC with Windows loaded, please try to get access to one before continuing.

The mouse

3.8 If you slide the mouse connected to your computer from side to side (keep it in contact with the surface you are sliding it on) you will see a white arrow (or 'pointer') moving from side to side on your screen. Here is an Activity for the complete beginner.

Activity 2.2

If you have never used a mouse before you will probably find it very difficult to manoeuvre at first: most people do. With a little practice you will wonder why you ever had any problems.

Your first task, if you are a complete beginner, is to sit at a computer with a mouse and play with it for about five minutes. Don't at this stage press the buttons on the mouse. We shall come to this in a moment.

For now, practice getting the arrow on screen to the place where you want it to be. Trace round the edges of the screen. Position the *head* of the arrow on top of the different shapes and symbols and words you can see on the screen. See what happens to the arrow when you lift the mouse from the surface of the mouse mat and put it down in a different place. Can you make the arrow disappear right off the edge of the screen?

Clicking and selecting

3.9 If you did Activity 2.2, did you manage to resist pressing the buttons on the mouse, in spite of being told not to? Bet you didn't! It doesn't matter this time, but this is the last time you should ignore an instruction in this book.

3.10 Pressing a button on a mouse is called *clicking*. Make sure that your mouse arrow is not pointing at anything other than space on the screen and then press the left button once only. Unlike a real mouse, it makes a clicking sound. Every mouse is slightly different, but in general you should use a light, but definite, tap with the forefinger. Don't move the 'body' of the mouse as you do this.

3.11 If you point the head of your mouse arrow at a particular symbol or word on the screen and click the left mouse button once, the word or the symbol's 'label' is highlighted. (Typically this means it changes from black writing on a white background to white writing on a green background).

3.12 This is known as **selecting**. The thing that is highlighted is 'selected', in the sense that **the next action carried out on the computer will only be done to the thing or things that are selected**. This is a general rule in any Windows program and it is an important thing to remember.

3.13 The next activity gives you some clicking practice and shows you what a menu looks like. We talked about menus in Chapter 1.

Activity 2.3

Some people find it very difficult to take a photograph without their hand shaking. Some people find clicking very difficult at first.

(a) Being careful to click only once (otherwise you might start up a program that you don't want to start up), see if you can *select* each of symbols and words shown on your screen so that the label is highlighted.

Selecting some will result in a list of words springing out of the symbol. This is a menu. Ignore this and click with your mouse on the next symbol. The menu will disappear (or a different menu will appear: ignore this too). (Generally, to get rid of anything on the screen that you have called up and no longer want to see, press the **Esc** key on the keyboard.)

(b) (Windows 3.x only.) Click once on the white space inside the frame of one of the windows on your screen. What happens to the title bar? Click in another frame. Now what has happened to the title bars?

(c) Click on the little square with the minus sign in it or the symbol right at the very top left-hand corner of the screen. A menu will appear. Note down on paper the things listed in this menu and then click anywhere on the screen apart from on the menu to make it disappear.

(d) (Windows 95/98 only.) Click on the word Start and see what happens. Try clicking on things with the *right* mouse button.

3.14   The answer to part (c) of this activity is 'Restore , Move, Size, Minimize, Maximize, Close Alt + F4. Windows 3.x also has the option 'Switch To... Ctrl + Esc'.

Closing down Windows 95/98

3.15   You do this via the **Start** button and the **Shut Down** option. When you click on this you get the following message.

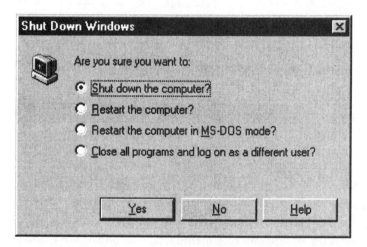

3.16   For now, however we don't want to shut down, so click on the **No** button (or **Cancel** in some versions) and the message will just disappear. Clicking on buttons to make things happen (or not happen) is something you do all the time in Windows.

Closing down Windows 3.x

3.17   The little square with the minus sign in the top left hand corner is actually called the 'Control-menu box'. In this book we avoid such terms where possible (because they are easily forgotten or confused) and instead tell you where to look for what you want on the screen. Click on the little square that produced this menu again. Then Click on the word Close. Two things will happen.

(a) Your mouse arrow will turn into an egg-timer shape. This often happens. It tells you that the computer is doing something, and you must wait until the egg-timer becomes an arrow again before you can do anything else.

(b) A box will appear on the screen as follows.

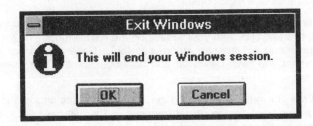

3.18 On this occasions click on the **Cancel** button, because you don't really want to end your Windows session. If you clicked on the **OK** button, the Windows screen would disappear and you would be left with a screen that was blank apart from the symbols **C:\>**. As mentioned earlier, when you get to this point it is safe to turn your computer off.

4 WINDOWS: STARTING THINGS UP

4.1 We are now going to see how to start up an application in Windows. We shall also learn about two more things that you can do with a mouse.

4.2 First you will need to find a symbol that looks like a notepad and is actually labelled Notepad.

In Windows 95/98 you find it by clicking on **Start**, moving your mouse pointer up the menu to **Programs**, then across to **Accessories**, then down to Notepad. Click on this to start up Notepad and move on to paragraph 4.8, since the next few paragraphs needn't bother you at all.

Windows 3.x only: finding the Accessories window

4.3 In Windows 3.x Notepad is likely to be in a window with the title **Accessories**. The Accessories window may well be on your screen already. If so, click on the downward pointing triangle within the frame of the Accessories window. It will disappear. We warned you about this earlier!

4.4 All is not lost, however. At the top of the main screen, just below the title bar, you will see the words **File**, **Options**, **Window** and **Help**. Click on the word **Window** and a menu will drop down from it.. You may wish to pause for a moment and experiment with the **Cascade** and **Tile** options on this menu. Click on one of them and see what happens to the items on your screen. Then click on the other and see what happens.

4.5 The second part of this menu, however, lists all the windows that you can look at from the main Windows program. These windows are, in fact, *groups* of programs (or 'applications'). Each program is represented by a symbol like the note pad that we are looking for.

4.6 Somewhere in this list should be the word **Accessories**. Click on this word and the Accessories window will instantly appear (or reappear if you made it disappear earlier). If it is too small, click on the up triangle in its right hand corner. Look through the symbols or 'icons' displayed in this window. You will probably see Notepad amongst them. (If not, and it is nowhere in sight use the **Window** menu to call up other windows that are not shown at present, until you do find it. Ask your tutor if you are completely unable to find it.)

4.7   Position the arrowhead of the mouse pointer right over the Notepad icon. Now press on the left mouse button twice in very quick succession. If this is the first time you have ever done this it is almost certain that nothing will happen! (you will probably manage to select Notepad, as in Activity 2.2, but nothing else will happen.) Try this *double-clicking* again, keeping the pointer right over the Notepad icon. After a few attempts your mouse pointer will turn into an egg-timer again, and very soon afterwards a window like the one shown below should appear.

Notepad

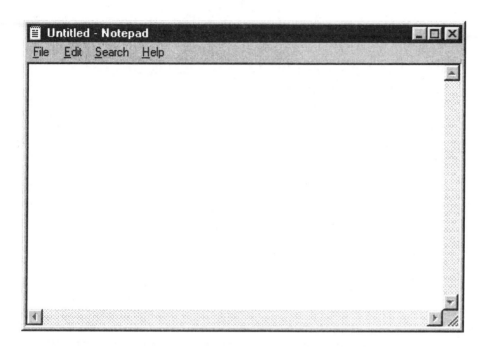

Untitled - Notepad

File   Edit   Search   Help

***Double-clicking* and making things happen**

4.8   What you have done is started up an application called Notepad – a very basic sort of word processor. As its name suggests it can be useful for making notes to yourself while you are using the computer because it is quick and easy to use. The window you see is an *application* window, not a program group window like the ones we have looked at so far. It works in much the same way, but has some additional features that we shall describe in a moment.

4.9   For now you need to practise *double-clicking*. Position the arrow head of the mouse pointer over the little square or symbol in the top left-hand corner of the Notepad window (not the main window). Then *double-click*. If all that happens is that a menu appears you weren't quick enough. Ignore the menu (or make it disappear by pressing Esc or clicking anywhere *within* the Notepad window) and try *double-clicking* again. Eventually the Notepad window will close and you will be back in the Accessories window.

4.10 Continue this exercise of opening and closing Notepad by *double-clicking* until you can do it at the first attempt every time. You will then have learned a skill that you will use every time you go near a computer in future.

5   MORE FEATURES OF WINDOWS

5.1   Start up the Notepad application. We are now going to use it to learn some more mouse skills and one or two keyboard tricks. First, though, some typing needs to be done.

For reference, here is the diagram of a typical keyboard from Chapter 1.

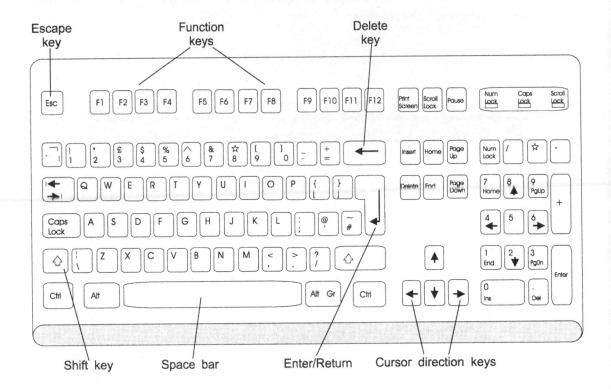

Activity 2.4

Having started up Notepad use the keyboard to type your name, then press the Return key to take you to the next line.

Now type the numbers 1 to 10, using the number keys above the letters. Each time you type a number press either the Return key or the Enter key. (This is just to satisfy you that they do exactly the same thing.)

You should have ten lines on screen numbered 1 to 10, and a line with your name in it.

Next key in the numbers 11 to 20 on consecutive lines, but this time use the numeric keypad at the right of the keyboard. This will only work if the Num Lock light (above the keypad) is lit. If it is not, press the Num Lock key. You will find it more convenient to use the Enter key this time, since it is next to the numeric keypad.

You should now have twenty lines on screen.

Next key in the letters A to Z, on consecutive lines. Key some in as small letters (lower case) and some as capitals (upper case) using the shift key.

You should now have typed 47 lines, but you won't be able to see the first ones you typed on screen any more.

Now find *three* different ways of getting back to the line you typed (with your name in it).

Scrolling and the cursor

5.2   *Six* ways are as follows. Try them all out.

(a)   Use the direction arrow keys. Press and hold down the upward pointing arrow key to the left of the numeric keypad. The black vertical line that flashes continuously on the screen and marks your place will move slowly back up the screen until you reach the first line.

The black vertical line is called the *cursor*. Moving it in this way is called *scrolling*. You can also move it within a line by using the left and right direction arrow keys.

(b)   To get to the last line again press the Page Down key several times. Then to get back to the beginning press the Page Up key several times. This is a form of scrolling in larger leaps.

(c)   T o get to the last line again hold down the Ctrl key and press the End key. Then to get to the *beginning* again hold down Ctrl and press Home. This takes you directly from one point to the other.

(d)   Press Ctrl + End to get to the last line again. Then use the mouse. At the right hand side of the screen is a grey strip with an arrow at the top and bottom.

Position your mouse pointer at the top of this strip over the upward pointing arrow. Press down the left mouse button and hold it down. You will see a little button-like marker gradually rising up the grey strip. Your screen will scroll back to the beginning. The grey strip is called a vertical scroll bar. Note that there is a similar scroll bar (a 'horizontal' one) along the bottom edge of the screen. This is used if the line you type is too long for the width of the screen to display it all at once.

(e)   Click once in the scroll bar just below the up arrow (assuming the cursor is at the last line). The little box in the scroll bar will jump about halfway up. Click in the same place again and you will be back to the beginning. This is like the Page Up/Page down option.

Note that with the scroll bar method the cursor stays where it was – only the screen display scrolls. However, if you click anywhere in one of your typed lines the cursor will instantly jump to that place.

(f)   Position the arrowhead of the mouse pointer directly over the grey button in the scroll bar. Press down on the left mouse button and hold it down. Keeping the mouse button held down, move the pointer up to the top of the scroll bar (or to the bottom if you are already at the top) and release the mouse button. You will see a ghostly outline of the little grey button whizzing along in the scroll bar. It will only appear again properly when you release the mouse button. This is the mouse equivalent of the Ctrl + Home and Ctrl + End option.

This use of the mouse is called *dragging and dropping*.

5.3   You may think we have dwelt on the topic of scrolling for too long. We have done so because there is an awful lot of scrolling to do in the Sage package, so you may as well know how to introduce a bit of variety into it at an early stage.

Holding down the mouse button

5.4 There are two ways in which holding down the left mouse button whilst moving the mouse can be useful.

(a) For dragging and dropping, as described. This is especially handy in, for example, a more sophisticated word processing package, where you can drag and drop sentences or even paragraphs of text from one position in a document to another.

(b) As a means of *selecting* items. For example, scroll back to first line of your Notepad screen. Notice that when the mouse pointer is in the white part of the screen it changes to an I shape. Position the pointer before (to the left of) the first character you typed (the first letter of your name) and press down the left mouse button. Keeping the button held down move the mouse downwards until you reach the last line. Then you can release it. All the characters you typed will now be highlighted.

As mentioned earlier, when something is highlighted it is *selected* as the object of the attention of all the actions that follow until it is deselected again. Press the Delete key. All your hard work will disappear! However, click on the word **Edit** at the top of the screen and then on the **Undo** option on the menu that drops down. All your hard work reappears, still highlighted!

Type the letter R. The letter R *replaces everything* that was highlighted. Undo this action in the same way as before.

Activity 2.5

How could you have 'undone' your deletion without using the mouse?

Moving and resizing windows

5.5 Position the mouse pointer arrowhead anywhere on the *title bar* of the Notepad window (the strip where it says Notepad). Hold down the left mouse button and move the mouse slightly as you do so. The edges of the window frame will go fuzzy and if you continue to move the mouse while keeping the button held down the whole window will move too. Take the Notepad window for a spin round the screen and drop it (by releasing the mouse button) in a different place to where you found it.

5.6 This may seem like a frivolous Activity, but is very useful in applications that show you a new window at the drop of a hat without the current one disappearing from the screen. You end up with lots of little windows covering up bits of each other that you want to see, so it is very useful to be able to move them around in this way. (It is a bit like shuffling pieces of paper around, a time-honoured office pastime!)

(If you accidentally click outside the Notepad window during this Activity, it will either vanish or the title bar will go dim. To re-activate Notepad, hold down the Alt key and press Tab repeatedly until you see a message saying Notepad, or the title bar goes bright again. Then release the Alt key.)

Resizing windows

5.7 It is sometimes (though not always) possible to change the shape and size of a window, too. You do this by moving your mouse pointer to one of the edges of the window. Just as it passes over the edge it changes shape and becomes a two-headed arrow, holding the frame in a vice-like grip. If you now click and hold down the left mouse button, you can pull out the side of the rectangle you are 'holding', elongating the window. Try it with the Notepad window: it is a bit tricky at first to get the point right on the edge so that it turns into a two-headed arrow, but persevere and you will get the knack.

5.8 You can resize a window in two dimensions at once if you point at one of the corners until the pointer turns into the two-headed arrow and then hold down the left button and drag.

5.9 Most people find these two features of Windows rather satisfying when they first encounter them, so don't be ashamed to play with them for a short while. As we have said, they are useful techniques.

6 FILING WITH WINDOWS

6.1 Without clearing your typing from the Notepad screen *double-click* on the symbol or n the square at the top **left-hand** corner of the window, just like you did when you were learning to double-click. Instead of the window disappearing instantly you get a message.

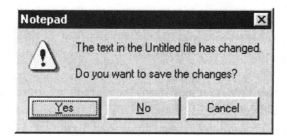

6.2 You are now going to have your first encounter with the Windows filing system. This section also contains important information for using the Sage package and the BPP Blitz program.

6.3 A 'file' in a computer system is a single document (or other collection of data) of a particular *type*. A word-processed letter would be one file. A spreadsheet would be another. It is not a file in the sense of something that you put pieces of paper into. In a computer system this sort of container is called a *directory*.

6.4 If you click on **Yes** when you get the above message a new window will appear.

Save As in Windows 95/98

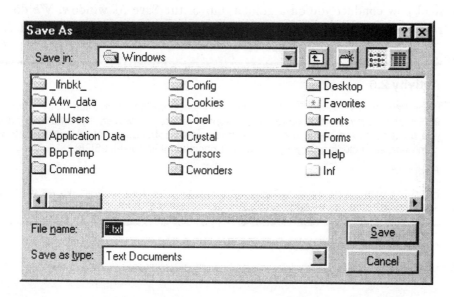

Save As in Windows 3.x

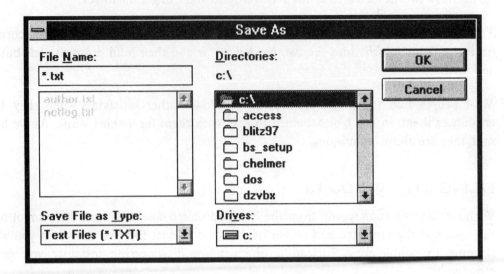

Saving files

6.5   The Save As window is common to all Windows-based applications that have a facility for storing data in a file.

6.6   If you haven't got the Save As window on your screen yet, open Notepad, type anything and then try to close Notepad. Click on the **Yes** button when you are asked if you want to save the changes. The window shown above will appear.

6.7   When the window first appears the File Name box is highlighted. Don't type anything here yet. You can move from section to section of this window by pressing the **Tab** key. This is the key above the Caps Lock key on your keyboard. Each time you press this, a different item in the window becomes highlighted (or is surrounded by a dotted line). Try this out.

You can move back and forward between consecutive items if you wish. To move back you hold down the **shift** key – the one you would use for capital letters – and press **Tab**. Try this out too.

6.8   This use of the Tab key is an important aspect of the Sage accounting package, so get some practice in now.

6.9   We shall now conduct you on a guided tour of the Save As window. We do so in the order in which you should make decisions or check things, not in the order of Tabbing.

Activity 2.6

If you have only Windows 3.x, you may prefer to ignore the information below about Windows 95/98, although you will need to know it sooner or later. However, if you have Windows 95/98 you must be aware of the methods of *both* systems, because not all packages that you will come across (including Sage) yet use the principles of Windows 95/98.

Required

Read the relevant paragraphs below and find out what part of the Save As window actually specifies where a file will be saved in Windows 3.x and Windows 95/98.

Drives

6.10   You must first decide what Drive you want to save your file in. This is like deciding what *filing cabinet* you are going to keep a paper file in. When we talked about storage of information in Chapter 1 we mentioned that computers put their data into different 'drives'. There is a hard drive, where the data is written onto a disk which is part of the computer equipment itself, and there is a 'floppy drive', where the data is written onto a disk that can be removed and carried about. The hard drive is usually called drive C, and the floppy drive is A. There can be more drives than this – there may well be on your systems at work and at college – but this is the usual set up for a stand-alone PC.

6.11   Typically your college is likely to prefer you to not to take up hard disk space, and you may therefore be told to save anything you want to save to the A drive on a floppy disk that is exclusively yours. If you have a floppy disk, put it in the A Drive and select the A Drive option in the Drive menu. When you click on A in the Drive box menu you will see the details in the Directories box above it change automatically. When you have done this change the drive back to C.

Windows 3.x

6.12   When the Save As window first appears in Windows 3.x the box labelled Drives will probably say C:\. However you can find out all the possibilities by clicking on the arrow at the right of the box. A menu will drop down and you can select the appropriate drive by clicking on its name in the menu.

Windows 95/98: Save in

6.13   Windows 95/98 works in much the same way as Windows 3.1 except that your first Save As window has a **Save in** box instead of a Drives box. This will probably say Desktop when the Save As window first appears. However you can find out all the possibilities by clicking on the arrow at the right of the box. A list of the drives available will then appear and you can select the appropriate drive by clicking on its name.

Directories: Windows 3.x

6.14   You must now decide what Directory you want to save your file to. This is like deciding what *folder* you are going to put it in.

6.15   The box above the Drives box (Windows 95/98: *below* the Save in box) can show the names of all the directories on the chosen drive.

6.16   When the Save As window first appears, the top line in the Directories box will show an icon like an open cardboard folder and the name of the C drive. Indented beneath this are sub-directories of the C drive and sub-directories of those sub-directories. At present your box is likely to show the following.

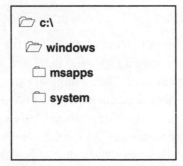

It shows this by default when the Save As window first appears because the program for the Notepad application is in the **windows** sub-directory of the C drive. However, you can change this. In practice you would almost always want to do so.

6.17   *Double-click* on the line 🗁 c:\. Two significant things happen.

(a)   The label above the Directories box (beneath the word 'Directories:') changes to **c:**. The label is important: it is *this line* that shows where the file will be saved.

(b)   The three sub-directories and sub-sub-directories of drive C shown above will disappear and be replaced by a list of *all* the sub-directories of the C drive.

6.18   Now *double-click* on the line 🗀 **msapps**. The label above the box will change appropriately and the details in the box will change again, to something   like the following. Note that the **msapps** icon is now an *open* folder.

> 🗁 **windows**
>   🗁 **msapps**
>   🗀 **artgalry**
>   🗀 **equation**
>   🗀 **grphflt**
>   🗀 **msdraw**
>   🗀 **msgraph**

6.19   If the directory you want is not here, click on the **windows** line again, to revert to the details shown in the first directories box you saw.

6.20   If you were going to save your file you would search for an appropriate directory and sub-directory by *double-clicking* in this way until you found one. You might have a directory on your floppy disk in the A drive called 'Notes', say. To save the file there, you would need to *double-click* on it in the directories box until the label above the box said **a:\notes**. Remember: in Windows 3.x it is the **LABEL** that specifies where the file will be saved, not the highlighting.

Windows 95/98

6.21   As already noted, use the arrow in the Save in box to change Desktop to (C:). The result will be something like this.

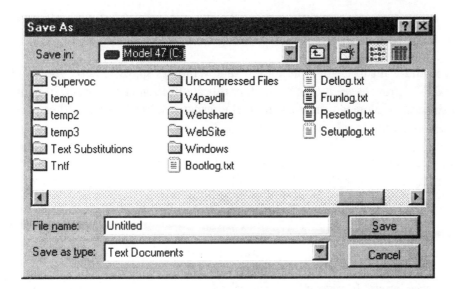

Double-click on any of the yellow folder like icons ☐ and the details in the box will change. For instance this is what happens if you double-click on the Windows directory folder.

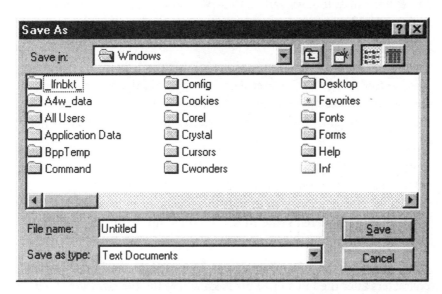

The Windows directory is now the one named in the Save in box and you have the option of 'drilling down' to further sub-directories of the Windows directory, as listed in the box below, just by clicking on their yellow folder. Notice that the folder currently open (Windows) actually *looks* like an open folder: ☐.

6.22   If you were going to save your file you would search for an appropriate directory and sub-directory by *double-clicking* in this way until you found one. You might have a directory on your floppy disk in the A drive called 'Notes', say. To save the file there, you would need to *double-click* in the Save in and directories boxes until the Save in box said 'Notes'. Remember: in Windows 95/98 it is the **SAVE IN** box that specifies where the file will be saved, not any highlighting anywhere else on the screen.

Save File as Type

6.23   As a rule you won't need to do anything with this box. It specifies the format in which the file will be saved, and it will always suggest the usual format for documents created in the application you are using. For the Notepad application the usual format is as a Text (.TXT) file. For a letter created in, say Microsoft Word, it is as a Word Document

(.DOC) file. For a spreadsheet created in Microsoft Excel it is as an Excel (.XLS) file, and so on.

6.24   If you did want to change the format that Windows suggests here, you would click on the down arrow to see if data created by this application can be saved in another format. In the case of Notepad there are no real alternatives, but there *are* other possibilities in, for example, the Sage accounting package.

6.25   The file type shown in the File Type box determines what files are listed in the box above it. In our example, there are no TXT files in the windows sub-directory, so there is nothing listed in this box.

File Name

6.26   When the window first appears this box is highlighted. It shows an asterisk, a full stop and three letters. In place of the asterisk you must choose a name for your file. You are not actually going to save it on this occasion (unless you want to), but you should know the basic rules for file names.

(a)   In versions of Windows earlier than Windows 95/98, file names must be **no more than eight characters long**. Characters can include numbers and letters but *not spaces*.

(b)   The name should be something sensible that will help to identify the file if you want to find it again at a later date. Try to avoid the names of applications in your file names: for example you *can* call a file 'WINDOW01', but the system already has hundreds of files with names something like this so it could easily get lost.

(c)   If you want to create a series of files of the same type and on similar subjects, it is helpful to number them sequentially. If you are sure there are going to be fewer than ten such files you can use 1, 2, 3, etc, but it is usually better to be safe and use 01, 02, 03, because the Windows filing system sorts numbers in order of the first digit. If you numbered some files 1, 2, 3, etc up to 10 they would be sorted in the order 1, 10, 2, 3, etc.

(d)   The format of the file must always be reflected in the file name by the three characters after the full stop. This is known as the file *extension*. There is no need for you to type an extension yourself. You can just type something like **NOTES01** in the file name box and Windows will automatically give the extension specified in the File Type box, in this case **.TXT**.

6.27   If there were existing files listed in the box below the File Name box you would be able to just click on one of them and it would appear in the box above where you could edit it. This can sometimes save a bit of typing. If you try to save one file with the name of another, however, it will overwrite the old file. Windows warns you about this and gives you a chance to change your mind.

Activity 2.7

You are going to save ten files using Windows 3.x. Devise a file name for each file incorporating part of your name (or your initials, or something that identifies you) and consecutive numbers.

Switching between applications

6.28 Before you close Notepad it is worth learning a very useful keyboard trick. You will come to use this all the time.

If you are using Windows 95/98 you will need to have two applications open before you can try this out. Without closing Notepad, click on the Start button, go to Accessories and start up the Calculator.

Alt + Tab

6.29 Now press and hold down the Alt key, then press the Tab key once, but do not let go of the Alt key. A grey box will appear in the centre of the screen with the name of another application on it (probably Program Manager). Now let go of the Alt key. You will instantly transfer to the application named in the grey box. Do this again, but this time before letting go of the Alt key press Tab several times. Each time you do so the name in the grey box changes, and if you release the Alt key you are taken to the application named in the box. If you had six applications running at once each would appear in the grey box in succession every time you pressed the Tab key. Use this trick to find your way back to Notepad.

Closing down

6.30 This concludes our guided tour of the Save As window. You can just click on the **Cancel** button, unless you want to save your Notepad file. (Save it onto a blank floppy disk if so. Pick an appropriate name and save it in the main A directory. Click on OK when you are ready to save the file. Unless there is *already* a file with the name you chose on the disk, the file will be saved.)

File Manager or Explorer

6.31 One of the most important applications in Windows 3.x is one called **File Manager**. Windows 95/98 has an equivalent called **Explorer** and an alternative called **My Computer**. Amongst other things, these allow you to see what directories and files are on a floppy disk, make copies of files and disks, move files around from one directory to another, look at the files in a directory in date order, or name order, or file type order, and to search for files.

6.32 It is quite possible, however, that your college system prevents you from using File Manager/Explorer. This will be to stop people messing about with files and directories that do not belong to them.

6.33 However, your tutor will probably be willing to give you a demonstration. They work in much the same way as the Drive and Directory and File list boxes that we have just been looking at, by means of menus and lots of *double-clicking*.

6.34 We are not going to describe File Manager/Explorer further, since this is an area best left to your college and its tutors and computer system administrators.

7   THE BPP BLITZ PROGRAM

7.1 Blitz is the name of the fictional company on which the Sage case study in the remainder of this book is based. Besides Microsoft Windows and Sage, Blitz also have some other Microsoft software: in particular Word for word processing and Excel for spreadsheets.

(One of the directors has WordPerfect and Lotus 1-2-3 on his PC at home, but finds that he can easily convert data from one package to the other.)

7.2   Several of the assignments in this book, therefore, ask you to perform simple tasks on a word processor or a spreadsheet. We are going to give you some hands on practice in the next section of this chapter, but first you need to be know how to unload the data that has been provided by BPP to your college for this purpose.

7.3   The data is stored in a form that enables it to be used over and over again without the risk of it being permanently overwritten. Unless your college has tailored its system to its own requirements you have to run a small program which converts the data into a form that is readable by your computer.

7.4   Below we describe how the Blitz program is used on a stand-alone PC or a small network. Your tutor will tell you if there is a different way of proceeding on your college's system.

Starting up the Blitz program

7.5   The Blitz program is represented by a yellow lightening icon on a green background , as shown below. This is probably located in the same group of programs, or near the same group of desktop icons, as the Sage package. Check with your tutor.

If your lightning icon does not say BLITZ98 you are looking at an old version which will not produce results compatible with the material in this book.

In Windows 3.x, when Windows starts up look for the relevant program group. It is probably called 'Sage'. (However it might be called **Plus2,** or **Sterling for Windows,** or **SFW3,** or **SFW4,** or **Line 50,** because the package has been through several different versions and name changes in recent years!).

If you cannot see the Sage group on your screen immediately, click on the word Window at the top of the screen and look though the full list until you find it. Click on it when you find it and the program group will appear.

In Windows 95/98 you may find the relevant option in the **Start ... Programs** menus.

7.6   Whatever the case, once you have found the Blitz icon or menu item double-click on it. The Blitz program will load up. The first time you use the program you will be taken through a Setup procedure. Follow the instructions on screen, or click on **Help** if you have difficulties. You will end up at the following screen.

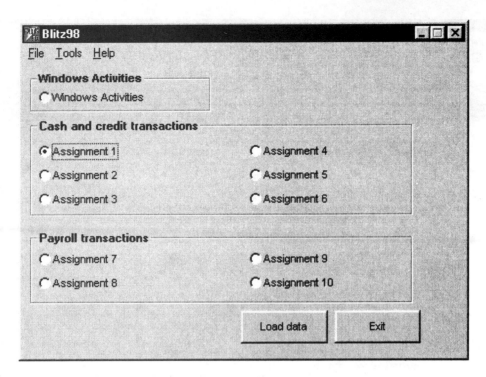

7.7   Choose **Windows Activities** and click on **Load data**. The files that you need will be copied into a **C:\Blitz98** directory.

Overwriting Blitz data

7.8   Whenever you load up Blitz data the Blitz program automatically **overwrites** any existing versions of the data that were unloaded previously. You cannot prevent it from doing this because that is what it is designed to do! If you make changes to the data and want to save them you need to save the files with new names (see the next section) or make a separate copy of them in a different directory or on a different floppy disk.

8   USING A WORD PROCESSOR

8.1   We could devote a whole book to the many facilities offered by a modern word processing package. All we are going to do here is give you a brief overview and then set you an Activity (using the Blitz program) that will give you a chance to see what a sophisticated Windows application is like and what it is capable of. This section also gives you a chance to practice your skills with the keyboard, before you start using the Sage accounting package. If this is old hat for you because you use such things every day, just make sure that you know how to find and open a file and be sure to do the Activity.

Word processing

8.2   We are going to tell you a bit about Microsoft Word, one of the most commonly used word processors. There is little difference between the main competitors these days: manufacturers are quick to copy each others' good features, and it is in their interests that users find it easy to transfer from another system to the one that they make.

8.3   If you start up Word you will be presented with a window something like (but not exactly like) the following.

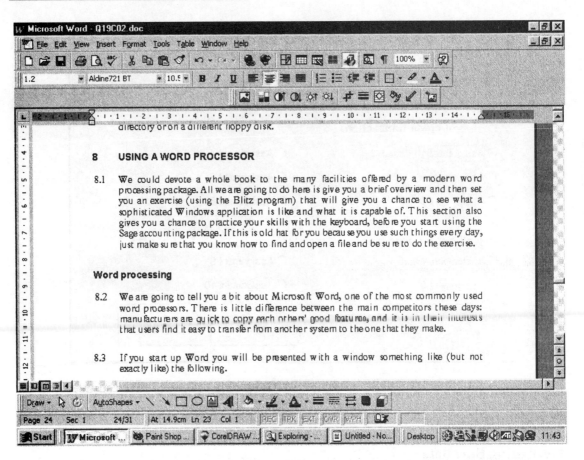

8.4 The main part of the screen is the area where you type, of course. At the top of the screen there is a bank of buttons and arrows that do useful things like **embolden** or *italicise* a word or words that you have selected, change the font style or size of selected text, or place text in the centre of the page, or set it to one side of the page. A host of other things can be done and you can create your own customised buttons to do them if you like.

In recent versions of Word, if you let the mouse pointer linger over a particular button (without clicking on it) a little label soon pops up telling you what it does. This is more fun than reading a book about it so we won't describe the buttons further.

Activity 2.8

Open your word processor, type in something (copy a paragraph of this book if you like) and then *select* a portion of text (see below if you can't remember how) and try clicking on different buttons.

8.5 The ruler below the buttons is used to set the left and right margins of the page and to indent paragraphs. You do this by dragging and dropping the triangular markers that you can see at either end of the ruler. The paragraphs on this page that you are reading now, for example, are indented by moving the lower of the two left-hand triangles in to the 1 mark.

8.6 The menu choices just below the title bar of the screen offer a huge range of further options. We are going to look at several of the most commonly used.

<u>F</u>ile: <u>O</u>pen

8.7 Click on the word <u>**File**</u> and a menu will drop down which includes the item <u>**Open.**</u> If you click on this, a window like the following will appear.

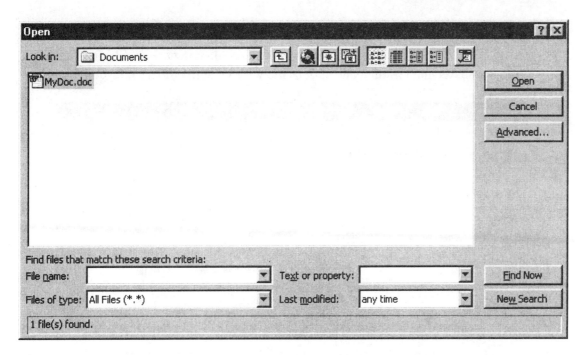

8.8   This is very much like the Save As window that we looked at earlier. To open a particular file you would click on the **Look in** box arrow (the Drive box arrow in Windows 3.x) to specify the drive (if it is not the one shown already) then *double-click* in the directories box to pick the directory. A list of all the Word type files in the chosen directory will appear. Click on the file name that you want and that name will appear in the File Name box. Alternatively, if you know the name of the file, you can type it in yourself. Then you click on OK to open the file and call it up on the screen.

Double-clicking on a file name has the effect of both selecting it and clicking on OK to open it.

File: Save As

8.9   This is menu option is the same as the one we looked at when we were experimenting with Notepad.

8.10   The important point to add here is that you can open a file that has one name, make some changes to it, and then save it with another name. The effect is that the file you originally opened reverts to its original form before you touched it, but the file with the new name retains all of your changes. Thus you could open a file containing a letter to Mrs Smith called Smith.Doc, change the name and address details, and save it as Jones.Doc. You would end up with *two* files – one called Smith.Doc and the other called Jones.Doc.

File: Close

8.11   Once you have finished with your file you must close it. This is not the same as closing down the whole application, so don't *double-click* in the box or symbol right up in the left-hand corner (or on the **X** in the top right-hand corner in Windows 95/98). Click on **File** and then on **Close** in the drop down menu. If you haven't already done so you will be asked if you want to save any changes you made. Once you have done so you get a new blank screen and can create another document.

File: Print

8.12   The **Print** option in the **File** menu brings up a window that you will often see. (The Windows 3.x version has the same options but with a slightly different layout.)

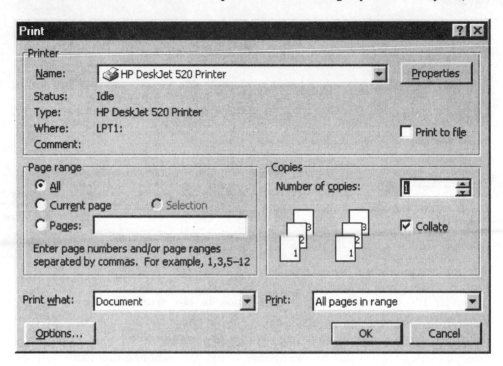

8.13   There are options to print more than one copy of the same document, to print only the page that your cursor was on when you clicked on the Print option or to print specific pages of your document. Just click in the relevant white spaces or on the arrows to make changes to any of the settings that come up when the window is first displayed.

8.14   An important point to check before you click on OK is the first line, which tells you which printer the document will be printed on. Printers often have very unfriendly names. It would be helpful if this line said something like 'the little Canon printer in the far corner by the window in the room next door', but it usually won't.

For the purpose of both this chapter and throughout the Blitz case study it will be helpful to know what printer should be specified here. (You may not have access to a printer, which will be a pity, though you will still be able to do all the important parts of the assignments and activities in this book.)

Ask your tutor now which printer or printers you should use and write the information down here so you have it with you when you are working from this book. You should also note any special instructions there may be for using the printers.

Write down the printer name and procedures for using it here.

Edit: Cut, Copy and Paste

8.15 The cut, copy and paste facilities are so useful that there are probably buttons for them as well as menu items. They are used as follows.

(a) Select some text. Do this by positioning the mouse pointer at the beginning of the first word, holding down the left mouse button and, keeping the button held down, moving the mouse to the end of the last word (not forgetting any punctuation marks) and then releasing the button. This portion of text will now be highlighted.

(b) Click on **Edit** at the top of the screen. A menu drops down.

   (i)   To retain the highlighted text in its current place and also to make a copy of it which is retained temporarily in the computer's memory, click on **Copy.**

   (ii) To remove the highlighted text from its current place, but also keep it temporarily in the computer's memory, click on **Cut.** The highlighted text will disappear.

(c) Move the cursor to the point in your document where you want to move the highlighted text or place a copy of it. Do this using the direction arrow keys or by pointing and clicking with the mouse.

(d) Click on Edit again and choose **Paste.** The text you highlighted will reappear in this new place.

8.16 Note that what you paste will be the last thing you cut or copied. If you cut out some text meaning to put it in later, but before you get there you cut or copy something else, the first thing you cut will be lost.

8.17 Note also that there are keyboard shortcuts for cutting, copying and pasting. These are listed on the **Edit** menu. In Word you can even *drag* the selected text and *drop* it in the new place. Try this with a sentence of the text you typed in at the beginning of this section.

Edit: Find and Replace

8.18 The **Find** and **Replace** options on the **Edit** menu are very useful. Suppose you had a document that included lots of references to a certain product made by your company: the 'Widget 9', say. If your company releases a new 'Widget 98' version of the product, it will be a slow process to scroll through the entire document and retype every instance of the product name when you see it. Fortunately you don't have to.

(a) Click on **Edit** and then on **Replace.**

(b) A window appears that allows you to type in one box 'Widget 9' and in another 'Widget 98'.

(c) You then have a choice of buttons to click.

    (i)   The **Find next** button will take you directly to each successive instance of 'Widget 9' in the document.

    (ii) The **Replace** button will replace a particular instance of 'Widget 9' with 'Widget 98'.

    (iii) The **Replace All** button will automatically replace *every* instance of 'Widget 9' with 'Widget 98'. This sounds better than option (ii), but there may be cases where you only want *some* of the examples of 'Widget 9' replaced.

You might think that it would be simpler still to find '9' and Replace All with '98', but give this some thought: there may be other instances of the number 9 in the document, such as 'Used by over 90 major UK companies' or 'costs only £19.99'.

Format: Paragraph

8.19 This item on the **Format** menu offers you (amongst other things) a better way of spacing out paragraphs than pressing return several times to leave blank lines.

8.20 Clicking on the **Paragraph** option in the **Format** menu brings up a window with a Spacing section which allows you to specify the number of 'points' (small units of vertical space) before paragraphs and after them. For example there are '18 pts' between this paragraph and the previous one.

Tools: Spelling

8.21 Finally we come to what is the best feature of word processors for bad spellers and clumsy typists. Click on **Tools** and then on **Spelling** in the drip down menu. Word will work right through your document seeing if the spelling matches the spelling of words in the computer's dictionary. If not it suggests alternatives from which you choose the correct one. For example, if you type 'drp', the choices you are offered include 'drip', 'drop', 'dry' and 'dip'. Do you think this paragraph has been spell-checked?

8.22 People sometimes forget that computer spell-checkers only recognise mistakes if they don't match a word in the computer's dictionary. For example, if you type 'form' instead of 'from' the computer will not realise you have made a mistake. It is also easy to make mistakes with a spell-checker if you are too eager to accept its first suggestion. The previous paragraph has a deliberate example.

Activity 2.9

Start up the word processor on your computer. Then use the Alt + Tab trick to get back to Program Manager, find the Blitz program icon and start the Blitz program. Unload the Blitz Windows activities onto a blank floppy disk in the way described earlier in this chapter.

(a) Open the file 0Ex01. If you are using a word processor other than Microsoft Word you may have to follow simple instructions on the screen for converting the document into another format. Accept all the default options offered: in other words just say yes to everything your computer suggests.

(b) Look through the document quickly and then *save* it with an appropriate new file name (but not with the name of any other file already on the disk).

(c) Embolden the subject heading 'New solutions from Good Solutions'.

(d) Type the following new paragraph at the beginning of the letter:

Widget users will be pleased to hear of the release of *Widget 98.* This is the new improved version of the well-loved Widget 9.

(e) Move the three lines 'The Widget 9 is based ... rest follow' to the end of the *current* first paragraph of the letter.

(f) Rearrange the features listed so that 'Same day delivery ...' comes first, and 'No leakage' comes before 'Stackable for easy storage'.

(g) Alter the font of the letterhead and make it stand out in some way. Reposition the letterhead as you think appropriate.

(h) Alter any other aspect of the layout of the letter that you think could be improved.

(i) Correct any mistakes that you can find.

(j) Make sure that the letter all fits onto one page.

(k) Replace Widget 9 with Widget 98 throughout the letter.

(l) Even if you have already done so, run a final spell check when you are satisfied that the letter is otherwise perfect.

(m) Save the letter and produce another copy to be sent to Ms Ann Richard, Spokes & Co Ltd, 99 Denton Drive, Mulcaster, Yorkshire, MS3 9RG. Save this second copy with a different filename.

(n) If you have access to a printer, print out a copy of both letters.

Finally close any open files and exit from your word processor.

8.23 There are several more activities like this in the Blitz case study assignments.

Using a spreadsheet

8.24 Spreadsheets are a topic at AAT Intermediate level, so we shall not jump the gun here. However, there are several activities involving simple spreadsheet tasks in the Blitz case study assignments.

9   GLOSSARY OF COMMON TERMS

9.1 You have now completed Part A of this Text. Before you move on to Part B make sure that you know what each of the terms listed on the next page means, or what it does. Write in the answer yourself to fix it in your mind. You can use the index to look up a word if you can't find the place in this chapter or the preceding one where it was explained. There are some spare boxes for your own use.

Application	
Button	
Click	
Cursor	
Directory	
Double-click	
Drag and drop	
Drive	
Enter or Return	
File	
Icon	
Menu	
Scroll	
Select	
Shift	
Tab key	
Window	

Answers to activities_____

Answer 2.5

You could have held down the Ctrl key and pressed Z. This is known as a keyboard shortcut. Most menus in Windows programs tell you what the keyboard shortcuts are: click on Edit again to bring up the menu and you will see Ctrl + Z alongside the Undo option.

Answer 2.7_____

Here are some suggestions for people named Steve Morris, John Smith and Jamie Lee Curtis.

SteveM01	SmithJ01	JLC_001
SteveM02	SmithJ02	JLC_002
SteveM03 etc	SmithJ03 etc	JLC_003 etc

Notice the use of the underscore (_) character in JLC_001. You can't have spaces in Windows 3.x.

Answer 2.9_____

Only the first letter is shown in our answer on the next page. Did you change the phone number? Did you keep 'Yours faithfully'?)

Good Solutions Limited
58 Alfriston Road
London
NW4 6SG

Mr P Wyzovski
Mulchester House
West Frintleigh
Devon
WF4 7QD

Date: As postmark

Dear Mr Wyzovski

New solutions from Good Solutions

Widget users will be pleased to hear of the release of *Widget 97*. This is the new improved version of the well-loved Widget 8.

Good Solutions has long been recognised as the premier supplier of widgets to meet every need of discerning manufacturers. The Widget 97 is based on industry-standard specifications and is used by many leading companies, such as ICI, GEC, Bosch, Ford Motors, and London Electricity. *Good Solution's* Widget 97s are still the only widgets that are compatible with hydraulic splinter technology. We lead, the rest follow.

The Widget 97 is a multi-purpose widget. Features include:

- Same day delivery in many areas
- Choice of finishes
- Light and transportable
- No leakage
- Stackable for easy storage
- Guaranteed for 12 months

Good Solutions won the Queen's Award for Industry in 1994.

If you would like a sample Widget 97 and further information, call Tim Davis on 0181-269 8246 or fill in the prepaid postcard enclosed.

Yours sincerely

Tim Davis
Marketing Director

Part B
Cash and credit transactions

Chapter 3   Introducing the case study

Learning objectives

On completion of this chapter you will be able to:

	Performance criteria	Range statement
• complete vital fields in an input screen	19.1.1	
• use the correct part of a computer system for inputting	19.1.4	
• generate new unique reference codes	19.1.5	
• use search facilities	19.2.2	
• print out correct and complete information	19.3.2	
• do the above in conjunction with customer databases, sales ledgers, purchase/bought ledgers		19.1.5, 19.2.5, 19.3.5

1   USING SAGE SOFTWARE

1.1   The Sage package is a 'user-friendly' software package and is designed to help you as much as possible. This first section describes some important features that you will use all the time.

Getting access to Sage

1.2   Check with your tutor or supervisor about how to gain access to the software package. The procedure is likely to be as simple as that described below for a stand-alone PC, but it may be different if your college has a larger system.

Windows 95

1.3   If you are using Windows 95, click on the Start button and search through the menus until you find Sage. Alternatively there may be a Sage **icon** like one of ones shown below on the 'desktop' (somewhere on the screen). If so, just **double-click** on it.

Windows 3.x

1.4   If you turn on a computer with Windows 3.1 or 3.11 loaded it will whirr and buzz for a short while and then come to rest at **Program Manager**. As we saw in the previous chapter, you are likely to be able to see lots of little pictures on the screen, and they will probably be grouped together into different boxes, or 'windows'.

1.5   If you can see a window headed **Sage** then there should be an icon like one of the ones shown above within that box. Move your mouse until the arrow is directly over the Sage icon and double click on it. The Sage package will start to load.

1.6   If you cannot see the Sage icon anywhere on your Program Manager screen the Sage group is probably hidden underneath one of the other windows. Just click on the word **Window** at the top of the Program Manager screen. A drop down menu will list all of the Program Groups available on your machine. One of these is probably called 'Sage'. Click on the appropriate menu option and the Sage group will appear. Now find the icon, *double click* on it and the program will start to load.

Line 50 and Sterling for Windows 3 and 4

1.7   This book is based on the most recent versions of the Sage medium-sized business accounting package at the date of preparation of this book. These are called *Sage Line 50* and *Sage Sterling For Windows version 4.0* (SFW4) and they are identical for all practical purposes.

Some BPP customers still have an older version of this package called *Sterling for Windows version 3* (SFW3). This looks slightly different, but in essence all these versions operate in the same way.

Sterling Plus 2

1.8   Some users have an older version of Sage still, called **Sage Sterling Plus 2**. This looks quite a lot different from the newer versions and, for some features, operates in a different way. For the sake of readability and space, features of the 'Plus2' package that differ from those of the more recent packages are **not covered** in this **book**. However, they are **fully covered** in the **on-line Help** that can be accessed using the BPP Blitz program.

Activity 3.1

(a)   Find out which version of Windows you are going to be using.

(b)   Find out which version of Sage you are going to be using.

(c)   Make sure that you can easily locate the Sage icon (or Start option) on your system (on whichever computers you are likely to use, if there is a choice of more than one).

You may wish to make notes of how to find Sage, in which case write them neatly in the space below so you always have this information with you when you are using this book.

....

....

....

....

....

....

....

Password

1.9   The software *may* have been set up by your college so that you have to enter a password before you can get into the package. BPP do not recommend this for the purposes of the Blitz case study, but if so, the first screen you see will tell you that the package is called something like Sage Line 50 or Sage Sterling version 4 and a box will appear labelled Password with a flashing vertical line in it (the 'cursor') and two buttons labelled OK and Cancel.

1.10 You will have to ask your tutor what the password is and **learn it**. Typically it might be something like LETMEIN. It doesn't matter whether you type in capitals or small letters. As you type the password you will see a series of tiny *'s appear in the box rather than the actual letters you type – there would be little point in having a password if the computer gave away what you were typing! Once you have typed in the password correctly you can either click on the OK button or press Enter. The first screen will disappear and you can start your Sage session.

If, when you are at the password stage, you decide not to proceed, click on Cancel or press Esc. This will return you to the opening Windows screen.

If you get the password wrong the computer will just beep at you or display a message telling you the password is invalid if you try to click on OK or press Enter. If you know you have made a mistake when typing the password use the Delete key to cross out the row of *'s and start again.

1.11 Once you have gained access to the package the Sage screen will look something like this. Notice the menu bar (File, Edit, View etc) and the row of icons or buttons beneath (Customers, Suppliers, Nominal, etc)

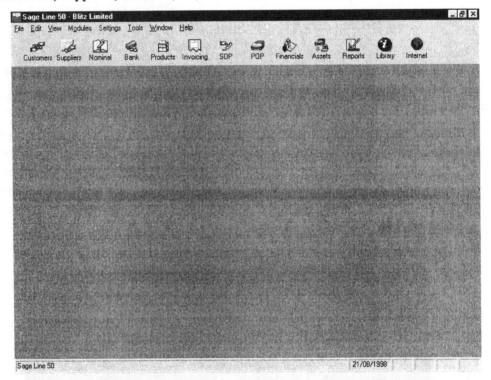

Activity 3.2

Don't be afraid to play with the Sage package. Use Blitz to load up any Assignment you like and then click on any of the buttons and menu options you fancy and look at what appears on screen. Each time you can press the **Esc** key to clear away what appeared and return to the main screen.

Buttons or icons

1.12   When you use Sage, the first task is to click on a button and choose the appropriate part of the program for the work you will be doing. When you click on a button a further window will then appear, specifying more detailed areas of work within your initial selection. Again you click on a button within this new window to select an option. The selection process goes on until you have reached the program or 'routine' that you wish to use.

1.13   When you have reached the program or routine you want to use, there will be a screen display and it should be fairly clear, from instructions on the screen or from the position of the cursor, what you are expected to do next. You might, for example, enter transaction details into the computer, or give instructions for extracting information from the files. You will be helped throughout by 'prompts' from on-screen messages and instructions. The cursor will show you at any time the position you have reached on the screen with entering data or instructions.

Using the keyboard and the mouse

1.14   The package can be used with a keyboard alone, but generally it is best to use a **mixture** of keyboard and mouse to enter transaction details and to give instructions to the computer.

1.15   When you are using a keyboard, you must be familiar in particular with the **Tab** key. The **Esc** (or Escape) key is also useful.

(a)   The **Tab** key is used to move on to the next item on screen. Using the **Shift** key and the **Tab** key together moves you back to the previous item on screen.

(b)   The Escape key (**Esc**) can be used to close the current window and move back to the previous window. It is just like the Close button described in the next paragraph.

Activity 3.3

Click on the button labelled **Customers** and then on the new button that appears labelled **Record**.

Find the cursor: it should be in a box labelled A/C. Press **Tab** several times (slowly) and watch the cursor move from one box to the next. At some times it will highlight a button such as Save instead of appearing in a box.

Now experiment with the Shift + Tab combination and watch the cursor move in reverse order.

What happens if you place your mouse pointer in a particular white space on the screen and click?

Press **Esc** when you are happy that you understand the tools you have available for moving the cursor around the screen.

Save, Abandon and Close

1.16   You must understand what will happen if you click on different buttons. The three most important buttons are the **Save, Abandon** and **Close** buttons.

(a)   If you click on a screen's **Save** button all the entries that you have made to that screen will be permanently recorded, overwriting any previous version of that data that there may have been. The part of the program you are using will remain open.

(b)   If you click on a screen's **Abandon** button any entries that you have made since you last clicked on the Save button will be cleared away and lost forever. The part of the program you are using will remain open.

(c) If you click on the **Close** button after making some entries but *without saving* them you will be asked if you are *sure* that you want to Exit that part of the program. If you click on **Yes** the entries you made will be lost forever. The part of the program you are using will close.

1.17 Therefore only use the **Save** button when you are sure that the entries you have made are correct; only use the **Abandon** button if you are sure that the entries you have made are incorrect (you will use this more often than you think!); and only use the **Close** button if you have already saved any entries you want to save.

Correcting errors

1.18 It is easy to make errors when data is input.

(a) If an error is spotted immediately, you will usually be able to wipe out the incorrect data using the **delete** key.

(b) If an error occurs whilst you are entering a transaction record, and you spot the mistake before the transaction is saved or posted, you can alter the details or cancel the transaction entirely and start again, using the **Abandon** option.

(c) If errors are spotted much later, you will need to make an appropriate input to correct the error. Correcting errors by this means is described in a later chapter.

Activity 3.4

(a) Click on **Customers**. If there are any customers listed note down the A/C code (eg ADAMSE) of the first one. Now click on **Record**, and type 000000 (six noughts) in the A/C box and press **Tab**. Now click on **Abandon**. What happens?

(b) Move back to the A/C box and type 000000 again and press Tab. Then click on **Close** and then on Yes to confirm that you are sure you wish to exit. What is the code of the first customer listed?

(c) Click on Record and enter 000000 in the A/C box and press Tab. Then click on Save and then Close. What is the code of the first customer listed?

Exiting from the Sage program

1.19 When you have finished working on Sage, you should exit from the system properly, to avoid the risk of corrupting data in the system. To exit the Sage programs, you should proceed as follows.

(a) Click on the word **File** in the top left-hand corner of the screen. One of the options on the menu that drops down when you do this is **Exit**. Click on this word.

(b) If you have Windows 95, click on the **x** button in the top right-hand corner of the screen or double-click on the Sage icon at the top left-hand corner.

(c) If you have Windows 3.x *double-click* in the little grey square in the top left hand corner. (If you click only once you will get another drop down menu and you should choose the Close option).

Do you wish to Backup your Data?

1.20 A message will then appear on the screen asking you whether you wish to back up your data. In a 'live' system, you should always take the Yes option. In a training system, your course supervisor might instruct you to select No. If you choose No (by clicking on the

No button or pressing N) you will exit from Sage, and you will be returned to the main Windows screen.

1.21   Note that any entries you may have made while in the Sage system are **saved** by this point, **whether or not** you make a back up copy, so even if you turn off the computer your work **will be preserved** until the Sage system is entered again (by you or somebody else) and more entries are made.

1.22   When you start doing the assignments in this book you may well want to make a copy of your work on a floppy disk. Procedures for **backing up** and restoring data are described at the end of this book in Appendix 3. Blitz98 has its own special options.

1.23   The whole of Section 1 of this chapter is very important. If you have not been doing so, you must work through it while sitting at a computer loaded with Sage.

2   THE CASE STUDY

2.1   The assignments in Part D of this workbook are based on a case study of a fictional North London company, Blitz Limited. The case study is set in late 1998 and early 1999.

2.2   Blitz Limited was established in August 1998 by two friends, Maria Green and Tim Nicholas. Each has put £20,000 into the company, and they are worker-directors.

2.3   The company provides cleaning services. Much of its business comes from office cleaning and other contract cleaning services (such as factory cleaning). However, the company also provides window cleaning services for businesses and domestic cleaning services for private individuals.

When does the case study begin?

2.4   The case study begins in October 1998, just over one month after the company has started operations. It has had a fairly busy September, and by 1 October, has received 27 invoices from various suppliers and has issued 35 invoices to customers. Apart from payments of wages and salaries, there were no cash transactions in September, and all invoices are as yet unpaid.

2.5   At the beginning of October 1998, Blitz Limited has 27 supplier accounts on its purchase ledger and 35 customer accounts on its sales ledger.

3   LOADING THE DATA FOR ASSIGNMENTS

3.1   The data for the assignments in this workbook has been arranged so that you can enter instructions to load the starting data for any assignment at any time and in any order.

3.2   You use the BPP Blitz program, as described in the previous chapter. If you skipped the previous chapter, please go back to it now and:

(a)   read section 7;
(b)   do Activity 2.9 in section 8.

Using the Blitz program

3.3   Ask your tutor to *show* you how your system is set up and how you should use it. The following instructions are aimed mainly at tutors and at the more adventurous students, but read them anyway so you know what is happening when you use the Blitz program.

Loading up data before you start Sage

3.4   Proceed as follows.

(a)   Click on the Blitz icon. In a few moments the main Blitz screen will appear.

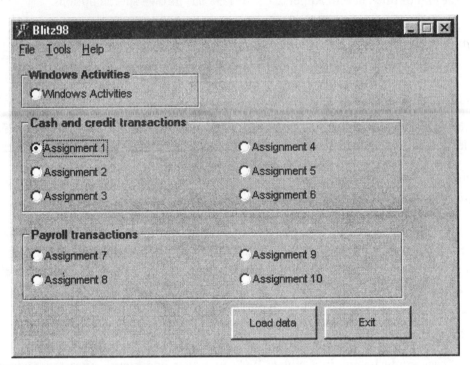

(b)   Choose an Assignment.

(c)   Click on the **Load data** button.

(d)   Soon you will get a message telling you which data has been unloaded. If this is the data you want click on **OK** . If not choose another assignment and click on **Load data** again.

(e)   If you want to use Blitz Help while you are working with Sage (eg for Plus 2 users), click on Help, choose the Help option you want, and then exit Blitz without closing the help file.

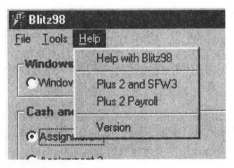

(f)   Click on the **Exit** button.

(g)   Start up the **Sage** package.

Click on **Help** and then **Help with Blitz98** if you have problems with Blitz.

Loading up data after you start Sage (F11)

3.5   With most (but not all) early versions of Sage it is possible to run the Blitz program *within* the Sage package, in other words *after* the package has been started up. See Appendix 3 if you want to do this. If the system is set up to do this you simply press function key F11 and then follow steps (b), (c) and (f) above.

Overwriting Blitz data

3.6   Every time you run the Blitz program a fresh copy of the data is loaded. The Blitz program overwrites any data that was there previously, so you can, for example:

(a)   load Assignment 1 and make any entries you like, even if they are complete nonsense, and then load assignment 1 again to get a fresh clean version of the assignment 1 data *without* the silly entries you made. In other words you can *experiment with the data* as much as you like without doing any permanent damage;

(b)   load Assignment 1, then load Assignment 2. The Blitz program will overwrite the data for Assignment 1 and replace it with the data for Assignment 2.

Activity 3.5

(a)   Load the data for assignment 1. Click on Suppliers. What is the code of the first supplier listed?

(b)   Load the data for assignment 2. Click on Suppliers. What is the code of the first supplier listed?

(c)   Create and save a supplier record with code 000000. Check that this is now the first account listed.

(d)   Load the data for assignment 1. Click on Suppliers. What is the code of the first supplier listed now?

Looking at the opening data

3.7   You can look at the opening data in the accounts for any assignment. For Assignments 1-6, one way of doing this is to use the Aged analysis and Activity options. There is an **Aged** button and an **Activity** button in the window for both the customers ledger and the suppliers ledger.

Suppliers ledger data

3.8   To look at the opening data in the suppliers ledger accounts, you should click on the **Suppliers** button in the main window (second from the left). The following window will appear.

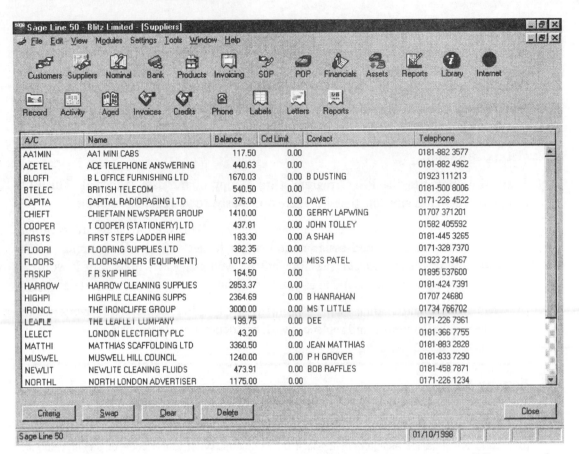

(If the screen you see is slightly different this is because you are using a different version of the Sage software than Line 50.)

3.13   In the Suppliers window you should then click on the **Aged** button (second row of icons, third from left). You will get a 'Defaults' date option. Just click on OK for now. The following window will appear.

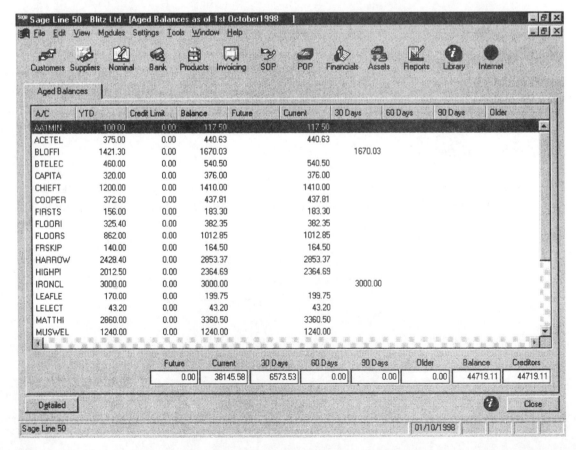

3.14 When you have had a look at this press the Esc key or click on **Close** to make this window disappear. Now click on the **Activity** button (next to the **Aged** button) and accept the date range you are offered by clicking on **OK** or pressing Enter. The next screen you see shows you details of how the balance on an account is made up. To see details for another account click on the *magnifying glass button* at the right of the box labelled A/C. A list of all the supplier accounts will drop down. Just scroll around and *double-click* on any account name to see the transaction history for that account.

Alternatively, if you prefer not to use the mouse, press the function key F4 when the Activity window first appears. This will bring down the menu of accounts. You can use the up and down cursor keys to scroll from one account to another and press the **Enter** key when the account you want is highlighted.

Customers ledger data

3.15 To look at the opening data in the customers ledger, you follow the same procedure. It is usually good practice to close any windows that you are not using. Do this by pressing the Escape key until you get back to the main window. When you get there, click on the **Customers** button.

3.16 From the Customers window, you should then select the **Aged** button or **Activity** button and follow the same procedures as above for the Suppliers ledger. The first customer account on the file for Assignment 1, for example, is for E T ADAMS.

4   ACCOUNT REFERENCE CODES

4.1 As you may already have realised, in our case study, Blitz Limited creates unique identification codes for suppliers and customers by taking the first six significant letters (or numbers) in the supplier's or customer's name. For initials and surname, the first six significant letters are taken from the surname. If there are less than six characters in the name (and initials), the code is made up to 6 digits with Xs.

Examples

Name	Account reference code
Matthias Scaffolding	MATTHI
Ace Telephone Answering	ACETEL
B L Office Supplies	BLOFFI
The Tomkinson Group	TOMKIN
R C Chadwick	CHADWI
A Wyche	WYCHEA
A Rose Ltd	ROSEAL
P Wood	WOODPX
C Fry	FRYCXX

4.2 You can use your Blitz data and the Activity facility to search quickly for a supplier's account details or a customer's account details when you have to answer a query. Try the following Activity.

Activity 3.6

Load the data for Assignment 1, then start up Sage. A customer of Blitz Limited, Mr E A Newall, telephones your office to say that he has not yet received an invoice for some domestic cleaning work. He would like to know how much the cost will be.

Can you answer his query?

---

5   THE NOMINAL LEDGER

5.1   Blitz Limited is using the 'default' accounts and codes for the nominal ledger that are provided in the Sage software. Only the sales account codes 4000, 4001, 4002 and 4100 have been renamed. A list of these nominal accounts and codes is given in Appendix 1 to this book.

5.2   At the beginning of October 1998, when Assignment 1 begins, the nominal ledger accounts (excluding those with zero balances) are as shown below.

Blitz Limited
25 Apple Road
London
N12 3PP

Nominal Ledger Trial Balance

Acct	Name	Debit	Credit
0020	PLANT AND MACHINERY	5731.60	
0030	OFFICE EQUIPMENT	1620.00	
0040	FURNITURE AND FIXTURES	1421.30	
0050	MOTOR VEHICLES	16220.80	
1100	DEBTORS CONTROL ACCOUNT	22620.43	
1200	BANK CURRENT ACCOUNT	33946.07	
2100	CREDITORS CONTROL ACCOUNT		44719.11
2200	Sales Tax Control		3369.03
2202	Purchase Tax Control	6022.38	
2210	P.A.Y.E.		1370.00
3000	ORDINARY SHARES		40000.00
4000	SALES - CONTRACT CLEANING		16597.40
4001	SALES - WINDOW CLEANING		1970.40
4002	SALES - DOMESTIC SERVICES		683.60
5000	MATERIALS PURCHASES	3703.83	
6201	ADVERTISING	2200.00	
6203	P.R. (LIT. & BROCHURES)	170.00	
7001	DIRECTORS SALARIES	1707.03	
7003	STAFF SALARIES	475.75	
7004	WAGES – REGULAR	4941.15	
7005	WAGES – CASUAL	480.00	
7100	RENT	3000.00	
7103	GENERAL RATES	1240.00	
7200	ELECTRICITY	43.20	
7400	TRAVELLING	100.00	
7500	PRINTING	500.00	
7501	POSTAGE AND CARRIAGE	89.50	
7502	TELEPHONE	1155.00	
7504	OFFICE STATIONERY	372.60	
7700	EQUIPMENT HIRE	296.00	
8202	CLOTHING COSTS	650.00	
		108709.54	108709.54

Looking at the opening data

5.3   You can look at this data on a screen display, if you wish.

5.4   If you have not already done so, you need to load the opening data for Assignment 1 into your computer using the BPP Blitz program.

5.5   The quickest option is to click on the **Nominal Ledger** button, which gives you the opening balances on all accounts.

5.6   If you want a trial balance report like the one above you need to click on the **Financials** button and then on the **Trial** (Balance) button. Choose a *period* Accounting Range of October 1998 and choose whether you want to print the report or preview it on screen. Then click on **Run**.

Activity 3.7

Your supervisor has asked you for details of cash received into the bank account and paid from the bank account since the company was established. With assignment 1 loaded, can you provide this information using the Activity facility? The nominal ledger code for the bank account is 1200.

---

6   CONCLUSION

6.1   You should now be able to do the following.

(a)   Use the BPP Blitz program to copy data into your computer or down load the data from the main files (the file server) in your network system.

(b)   Refer to individual accounts in the Suppliers ledger, Customers ledger or Nominal ledger (for assets, including cash, liabilities, expenses and income), in order to answer queries about transactions in the account.

(c)   Produce a Trial Balance.

(d)   Key in data at lightning speed!

Activity 3.8

If you have been reading through this Chapter while not sitting at a suitably equipped computer, make a note to do all of the activities **hands-on** as soon as you get the opportunity.

Answers to activities_____

Answer 3.4

(a)   The 000000 should disappear.

(b)   It should be the same as it was at the start of the Activity because you have not saved any changes.

(c)   It should be 000000. Click on the 000000 to highlight it and then click on Delete, if you don't want to keep this entry.

Answer 3.5_____

(a)   AA1MIN

(b)   3DTECH

(c)   Follow the instructions in Activity 3.4, except for Suppliers not Customers.

(d)   AA1MIN. You have a fresh copy of the assignment 1 data, free of any assignment 2 entries or any entries you made yourself.

This Activity is to encourage you to experiment with any entries you like, safe in the knowledge that you cannot damage the Blitz data.

Answer 3.6

The query is from a credit customer, so you begin by clicking on the Customers button. To find Mr Newall's account use the down arrow in the scroll bar to the right of the list of accounts. When you see NEWALL, click on that name to highlight it, then click on the Activity button. Accept the Defaults suggested by clicking on OK. The next screen will show you the current balance on Mr Newall's account.

The display on screen should show you that there is only one invoice outstanding, an amount for domestic cleaning invoiced on 22/09/98 for £77.55.

Answer 3.7

The supervisor's request is for the Transactions on the Bank Current account, nominal ledger code 1200. Select the Nominal button, scroll down to account 1200, highlight it, click on the Activity button. Accept the Defaults. You should see, on screen, the following information.

1200 Bank Current Account

No.	Tp	Date	Ref	Details	Amount	Debit	Credit
1	BR	190898		M Green - shares	20000.00	20000.00	
2	BR	190898		T Nicholas - shares	20000.00	20000.00	
8	JC	160998	xxxxx	Wages and salaries	6053.93		6053.93
						40000.00	6053.93
						33946.07	

The Tp column shows the type of transaction. BR is a bank receipt. JC is a journal entry (credit entry). The three figures at the foot of the display show total debits and credits and the balance.

Chapter 4   Supplier invoices and credit notes

Chapter topic list

1   The Suppliers window

2   New suppliers

3   Supplier details

4   Entering details of invoices received

5   Entering details of credit notes received

6   Reports

7   Conclusion

Learning objectives

On completion of this chapter you will be able to:

	Performance criteria	Range statement
• Set up accounts in the purchase ledger for new suppliers	19.1.1 to 19.1.7	
• Record invoices received from suppliers	19.1.1 to 19.1.7	
• Record credit notes received from suppliers	19.1.1 to 19.1.7	
• Post entries (for invoices or credit notes received) to the purchase ledger and the nominal ledger	19.1.1 to 19.1.7	
• Produce a listing of entries for invoices received and credit notes received	19.3.1 to 19.3.8	
• Check the current total balance for unpaid invoices from suppliers in the nominal ledger	19.2.1 to 19.2.4	

1   THE SUPPLIERS WINDOW

1.1   The Suppliers window, which is shown below, is displayed on screen when you click on the **Suppliers** button in the main window.

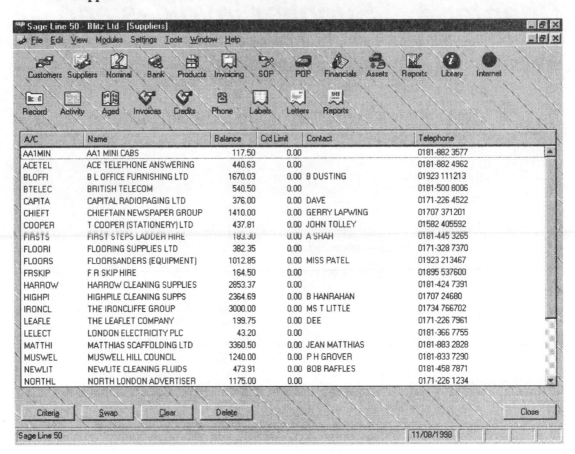

2   NEW SUPPLIERS

2.1   When an invoice is received from a new supplier, an account for the supplier must be set up. There are two ways of entering new supplier accounts.

(a)   Using the Supplier **Record** button.

(b)   Using the **Invoices** button

2.2   The **Record** button method is described here. However, the process is identical when the Invoices method is used.

3   SUPPLIER DETAILS

3.1   To set up an account for a new supplier, click on the **Record** button. This option allows you to insert details of a new supplier (that is, create a new supplier account) or to amend details of an existing account, for example to change the supplier's address or telephone number. Existing supplier accounts can also be deleted from the ledger in certain circumstances. When you click on the **Record** button, the following display will appear on screen.

Note that different aspects of supplier details are depicted as index cards (Details, Defaults, Graphs etc). You click on the index tab to get the section you want.

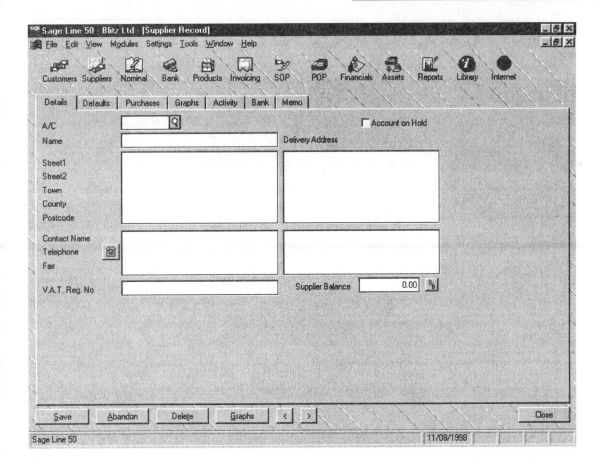

Details

3.2 The cursor starts at the **A/C box**. The supplier's reference code should be entered here. The maximum length for the code is six digits. The coding system used by Blitz Limited (in the case study) was described in Chapter 3, and will be explained in more detail later.

3.3 When you enter a code for a new supplier (a code not already in use) and press **Tab**, the words **New Account** will appear in the grey area next to the **A/C box**.

3.4 The cursor will have moved down to the next line, and you can insert the supplier's full name and address. Press **Tab** to move from one line of name and address down to the next. Press the **Shift** key plus **Tab** to move *up* to the previous line. If you want to leave a line blank just press **Tab** again to move on to the next line. However, never neglect to enter the post-code if you have it – not just to please the post office but because post-codes are very useful information for a business's marketing and distribution functions and provide an easy way for a computer to sort data.

Here is a typical set of entries that you might make.

Name	Lexington Supplies
Street 1	Billington House
Street 2	25-29 Dorchester Avenue
Town	London
County	
Postcode	W12 5TL

Activity 4.1

Load up Assignment 6 and using the A/C code LEXING enter all of these details as a new supplier account and save your entries. Between which two codes does the new account appear?

3.5   After you have entered the supplier's name and address, use the **Tab** key to move the cursor down the screen, from one item to the next. A contact name (in case of queries) and the supplier's telephone and fax numbers can be entered when the cursor has been moved down to these items.

3.6   In the assignments in this book *you will not be required* to enter any details in the box for **Vat Reg No** (it is not relevant at Foundation level). However, in practice these details would be entered in the box if required. You can just press **Tab** to leave the field blank and move on to the next field.

3.7   The next set of fields is headed **Delivery Address**. You would enter here the address to which the supplier in question normally delivers the goods you buy from him – a factory in Manchester, say. Blitz Limited has all its supplies delivered to its main address, so you will not need to enter anything here.

Defaults

3.8   Now click on the second index tab labelled **Defaults**. This gives you a new screen as shown below.

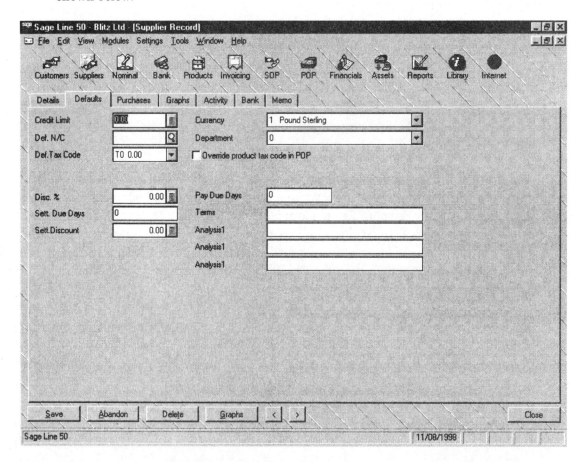

3.9   You would fill in the **Credit Limit** line if, say, the supplier had told you that they were only willing to supply you with goods up to a certain value before you paid them some money.

3.10   The Defaults index tab also allows you to specify certain details about how a transaction with the supplier will normally be posted. For example if one of your suppliers were Yorkshire Electricity you would probably be reasonably sure that all transactions you had with Yorkshire Electricity should be posted to the Electricity expense account in the nominal ledger.

If you make an entry in the **Def N/C** box when you first set up the Yorkshire Electricity account, then when you next have an invoice from Yorkshire Electricity the program will automatically suggest to you that it should be posted to the 'default' nominal account you specified when the account was set up. This means that you don't have to waste time thinking about it or typing in the same old account number yourself. (You can, however, choose a different nominal code at the time when you are posting the transaction if the default code is not the correct one for a particular invoice.)

3.11   This particular facility is *not used* in the Blitz case study because we want to make you *think* about nominal codes: you can leave the Def N/C box blank and press **Tab** to move on. However, note that at the right hand side of the Nominal box there is a button with a picture of a magnifying glass on it. This is the **Finder** button: a very useful facility which is described in more detail later in this chapter.

3.12   The **Def Tax Code** box will offer you a pull down list of possible VAT codes that apply to this supplier. In the assignments in the Blitz case study the default code is **T1 – 17.5%**, which is the standard rate of VAT at the time of preparation of this book. With the cursor in this box press the ↓ key or click on the arrow at the side of the box to change the default. We shall describe VAT tax codes in more detail later in this book.

3.13   Sage then has a box for **Disc%**. This is for discounts other than settlement discounts. It is not used in the Blitz case study.

3.14   The Due Days and Discount lines go together. A supplier might offer you a 10% discount if you pay an invoice within, say, 7 days. In this case you would enter the number 7 in the **Sett Due Days** box and 10.00 in the **Sett Discount** box.

3.15   The entry in the **Pay Due Days** box is the number of *days* (not months or weeks, note) that you have to pay an invoice: typically a supplier might expect payment within 30 days. The **Terms** box is for a narrative description: 'Pay by return of post or they'll send the boys round!', or 'Cash on delivery', or whatever is appropriate.

In the assignments in this book *you will not be required* to enter any details in these boxes.

3.16   At the top of the right half of the screen is a box labelled **Currency**. The default in the case study is '**1 Pound Sterling**'. If you click on this box and its downward pointing arrow you will be offered a number of other options such as French Francs or German Marks. The Blitz case study only uses UK currency, so you can just accept the default for this box.

3.17   In the assignments in this book *you will not be required* to enter any details in the boxes for **Analysis**. These are useful for management accounting purposes, but not part of the standards of competence at AAT Foundation level. In each case press **Tab** to leave the field blank and move on to the next field.

3.18   The other index tabs offer a number of ways of analysing transaction details. Some of them are updated automatically by the program when transactions are posted. They are not used in the assignments in this book, but you might find it interesting to have a look at them and see what happens when you click on various buttons. Don't be afraid of experimenting: you can always get a fresh copy of the data using the Blitz program.

Checking and saving your work

3.19 When you have entered all the details that need to be entered you should *check* what you have on screen against the document you are working from (against the details given in this book in the case of the assignments).

(a) If you have made just one or two errors just press **Tab** until the entry is highlighted and type in the correct entry. If just one character is wrong it is quicker to click on the entry, and move the cursor using the cursor keys until it is in the appropriate place, delete the wrong character and insert the correct one.

(b) If you have made a complete hash of the entries it may be better to start all over again and be more careful next time. In this case click on the button labelled **Abandon**. The screen will be cleared and you can start again.

(c) If you are happy that all your entries are correct click on **Save**. The new supplier will be added to the Suppliers ledger.

(d) If you click on Save and only then realise you have made a mistake in posting the details you can call up the details you posted again by selecting the supplier code from the main Suppliers window, click on **Record** and edit out your mistakes. Alternatively you can call up the account and click on **Delete** to remove it entirely. However you can only delete a supplier in this way if no transactions have yet been posted to that account.

Activity 4.2

(a)   What is the post-code for account AA1MIN?
(b)   What is the contact name for account TROJAN?
(c)   What is the full name and telephone number of the account COOPER?

Activity 4.3

Set up a supplier account for the following supplier in the same way as details have been entered for existing Blitz supplier accounts. Refer to the paragraphs above if you don't know whether you need to put an entry in a particular box or how to make the entry.

Lineker Leisurewear Limited
Bernard House
647 Spenser Street,
Birmingham, BH1 2OD
Contact: Frederic Ferinella
Phone: 0161 123 6543
Credit limit: £1,500

---

4   ENTERING DETAILS OF INVOICES RECEIVED

4.1   When invoices are received from suppliers, the details of each invoice must be entered in the Suppliers Ledger, in the appropriate supplier's account.

The Invoices option

4.2   To enter supplier invoice details, you should click on the **Invoices** button in the **Suppliers** window. The following window will be displayed.

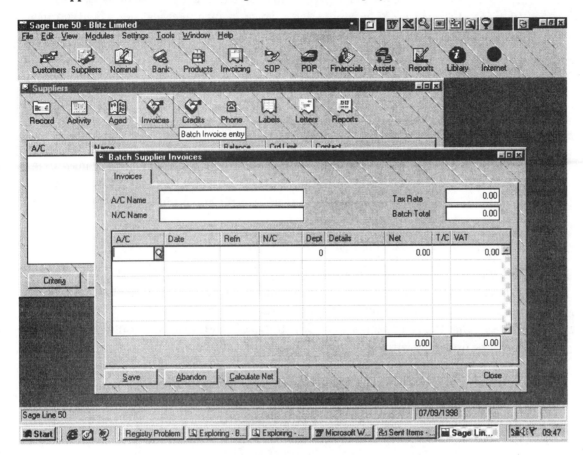

4.3   Suppose your company receives an invoice from a firm of public relations and marketing consultants as follows:

Invoice details	£	*Nominal ledger item*
Sales promotion expenses	2,000	Sales promotions
Advertising costs	1,500	Advertising
Public relations	600	PR
	4,100	

This invoice needs to be split into its three elements, £2,000 to charge to sales promotion expenses (nominal ledger account code 6200), £1,500 to advertising costs (N/C code 6201) and £600 to PR (N/C code 6203). You would enter three separate lines in the Batch Supplier Invoices window to post this invoice. Only nine (or less) lines are shown on the screen, but it will scroll down if you have more than nine items on your invoice.

You can enter as many lines as are necessary on each invoice. You can invoice *several different suppliers* on the same screen before saving, if you wish, or you can proceed as described above.

4.4   You can scroll back up and edit transactions if you realise you have made a mistake before you **Save** the invoice. If you want to delete an entire line, tab to it or click in it anywhere and then press function key F8. You can do this when you are in the middle of an entry, too, if you realise you have got something wrong.

Other function keys are useful too. See Appendix 2 for a list.

4.5   Once you have finished entering the details of an invoice you click on **Save** and the screen is cleared ready for the next supplier's invoice.

4.6   Entering the details of invoices received from suppliers is a repetitive process. You must go through the same procedures for each invoice in turn, *pressing Tab* when you have entered details for one item, to move on to the next item.

A/C

4.7   Initially the cursor will be in the box labelled **A/C.** If you know the *code* for the supplier you can just type it in and press Tab. If you know some of the details for the supplier but you can't quite remember the code, Sage offers you a handy tool for finding out what you need to enter. At the right of the A/C box is a button with a picture of a magnifying glass on it. This is called the **Finder** button. Sage provides this facility whenever you reach a point where you may have to do a search for the entry you need to make.

Searching for accounts: the Finder button (or F4)

4.8   When you are confronted with an empty box with the Finder button it will be because you have to choose one account code from many possibilities. Click on the button (or press **function key F4** if you prefer to use the keyboard). Another alternative if you know, say, that the code begins with G, is to type G and then press Enter. In each case you will be presented with a new little window as shown below.

4.9   If you can see the account you want in the list immediately just click on it to highlight it and then click on OK or press Enter. If not, use the scroll bar or the cursor keys to scroll up or down until you see the name you want, then click on it and click OK.

Activity 4.4

Click the relevant buttons until you reach the Supplier Invoices window and then press F4. What appears in the A/C *Name* box at the *top* of the window when you select the account code BLOFFI and click on OK or press Enter? What if you type in the code MUSWEL?

Searching for accounts: the Criteria button

4.10   The **Criteria** button at the foot of the Finder window offers you a means of searching for accounts that fulfil certain conditions. Let's say, for the sake of argument, that you are in charge of the purchase ledger for accounts of suppliers who come from Watford (unlikely in the case of Blitz Limited but a quite possible way of organising work for a larger company). Click on the Criteria button and you will see the following screen.

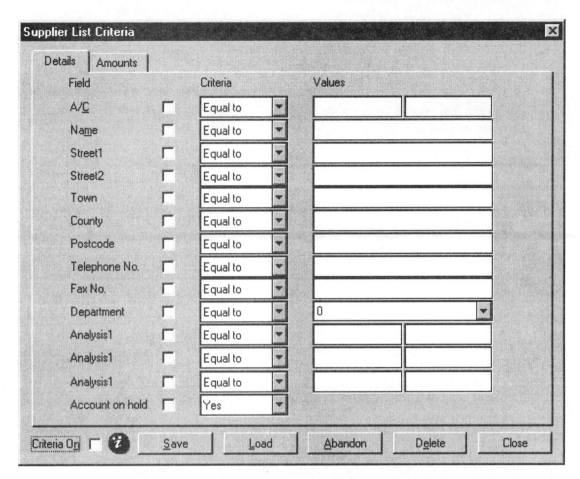

4.11 Click in the white square to the right of Town and an **x** will appear in it. Click in the 'Values' column alongside **Town** (after the 'equals' box) and a cursor will appear. Type 'Watford' and click in the white square labelled Criteria On. Then click on **Close**. You will be returned to a Finder list window which shows only the names of those suppliers whose records indicate that they are located in Watford. If you are trying this out using Blitz data there will be now be only three account names: BLOFFI, FLOORS and UNIFOR.

4.12 As you can see from the Supplier List Criteria screen there are numerous other options. For example the **Amounts** index tab gives you another screen on which you could choose all accounts with a balance of *more than* £1,000. When you click on the arrow to the right of 'equals' a menu of options drops down.

Equals	=
not equal to	!=
less than	<
greater than	>
Between	<>

4.13 The problem with this is that you need to have a pretty good idea of the criteria that you want to use to limit the number of accounts that you are given to choose from. If, for example, you have a vague idea that the post code for Watford begins with W it is no use just typing W in the postcode box. You can, however, type 'W*': the asterisk is a 'wildcard', standing for any other character or characters. Try it.

4.14 Beware also of the following pitfalls.

(a) Once you mark an **x** in the Criteria On square you will only ever get details for the accounts that fulfil those criteria, whatever window you are in. Click again to remove the **x** to stop this happening.

(b) If you want to change the search criteria you are using you must switch off any criteria that you no longer wish to apply. Do this by clearing the **x** in the box next to the criteria you don't want to apply: click on the **x** and it will disappear.

Activity 4.5

(a) Prove that what we say in paragraphs 4.11 and 4.13 is true, by trying out these techniques for yourself. Then turn the Criteria option off (see paragraph 4.14).

(b) With a fresh copy of Assignment 6 data loaded find the codes of all accounts with a balance greater than £1,000.

Date

4.15 When the right account code is entered the supplier's full name will be shown in the A/C Name box. Pressing Tab will highlight the **Date** box. This will show today's date, but you will usually have to change this. The date entered should be the date *on the supplier's invoice itself*, and not the current date when you are processing the invoices.

Sage has a delightful feature for entering dates. When the cursor enters the date field another Finder button appears. If you click on this or press F4 a little calendar appears and you just have to *double-click* on the date you want. Use the arrows at the top to scroll through the months and years if necessary.

The little calendar is fun, but as a rule it is probably just as quick, if not quicker, to *type in* the date using the numeric keypad. This is a matter of personal preference.

Activity 4.6

Enter any existing supplier code you like in the A/C box then press tab to get to the Date box. Use the calendar feature to enter today's date into the date field. Then use it to find out on what day of the week your birthday falls in the Year 2000. Enter this date. What warning message do you get?

Ref

4.16 Press Tab again and you are taken to a box headed **Ref.** You can leave this blank but it is best to use it for the supplier's invoice number for reference purposes

Entering the invoice details

4.17 Pressing Tab once more takes you to the parts of the invoicing screen that do what you would think of as the double entry in a manual system. The entries you make are as follows.

(a) The nominal ledger code (**N/C**). This is the account in the nominal ledger to which the purchase or expense relates. You will see the Finder button again beside this heading. This means that you can use the search facilities described above to find the nominal code you want.

A good shortcut here, if you have an approximate idea of the nominal account code, is to type in the approximate number and then press Enter, or function key F4, or click on the Finder button. This brings up the Nominal Accounts list starting from the number you typed. So, for example, if you know an invoice is an overhead and that overhead account codes are in the range 7000 to 7999 you can type in 7 and press F4. This saves you scrolling through lots of irrelevant accounts.

(b) The **N/C Name** box shows the name of the nominal account chosen. This will be filled in automatically when you enter a nominal code and press Tab.

(c) The **Dept** box can be used to analyse the information further. This is not used in the Blitz case study, so just press Tab again.

(d) In the **Details box** you type details of the goods or service supplied. Try typing *Lots of nice things to eat* and see how the text scrolls across as you reach the end of the box. You can edit your typing if you make a mistake.

(e) In the **Net** box key in the amount of the invoice item *excluding value added tax* (the net amount). Just key in figures, with a full stop between the pounds and the pence. Don't try to key in a £ sign. You don't need to key in zeros for pence at the end of a round figure amount.

    (i)   keying 123 gives you 123.00

    (ii)   keying 123.4 gives you 123.40

    (iii)   keying 1230 gives you 1230.00

(f) The code for the VAT rate (**T/c**) will automatically show T1, though you can alter this if necessary. The VAT codes used in the Blitz case study are:

T0   Zero-rated items (VAT = 0%)
T1   Standard-rated items (VAT currently = 17.5%)
T2   VAT-exempt items (No VAT)
T3   Discounted sales
T4   EU member states
T5   -
T6   -
T7   Purchases from an EU country
T8   EU purchases where the buyer must pay the VAT
T9   Transactions to which VAT does not apply

Of these, codes T0, T1, T2, T3 and T9 are used in this book. (EU stands for European Union - formerly the European Community or EC, but you need not worry about this in this book.) You will always be told what code to use, since you are not expected to know much about VAT at AAT Foundation level.

(g) The **Tax** is calculated automatically from the net amount of the invoice already entered and the VAT tax code.

The Calculate Net button

4.18   If you prefer, instead of entering the net amount of the invoice in the **Net** box, you can enter the total amount, *including VAT. Before* pressing Tab, click on the **Calculate Net** button or press function key F9. The program will now deduct VAT *at the standard rate* from the invoice amount you have keyed in, and display the VAT automatically in the **Tax** column.

4.19   When the VAT has been calculated and you have entered all the invoice details, press Tab again, and the cursor will move down to the next line of the screen. Details of another invoice item can then be entered on this line.

4.20   Note that running totals of your entries are shown at the foot of the Net column and the Tax column. You can compare the totals with the total shown on the invoice once you have posted all the items. If the totals are not the same there is a mistake somewhere. If it is your mistake you can scroll back up or tab to the error and correct it.

4.21   Remember that a whole line can be deleted by clicking on it or tabbing to it and pressing function key F8. Only use the **Abandon** button if you wish to scrap *all* the details you have just entered on the screen.

Activity 4.7

Load **Assignment 6** and enter the following invoice details, following the instructions given in paragraphs 4.17 to 4.21. You should not end up with any question marks, but use the features of the Sage package to calculate the correct figures for you.

A/C	Date	Refn	N/C	Details	Net	T/C	VAT
NEWLIT	01/10/98	SW369	5000	Materials	100.00	T1	??.??
IRONCL	04/10/98	214876	7701	Repairs	???.??	T1	??.??

The gross amount of the second invoice is £240.

Required

Find out the total amount of VAT for the two transactions, and what the N/C codes 5000 and 7701 stand for.

Save the details, once you have checked the answer.

Discounts and VAT

4.22   Sometimes suppliers offer an early settlement discount, for example 4% off if you pay the invoice within 7 days. The VAT on such a transaction *should* be calculated on the basis of the discounted net amount. For instance an invoice for £100 plus VAT and with the offer of 4% early settlement discount would be for a total of £100 + (£96 × 17.5%) = £116.80. If you took advantage of the discount you would pay £96 + (£96 × 17.5%) = £112.80, so you save £4.

4.23   If you received this invoice you might enter it in the normal way, with 17.5% VAT on the whole amount, at first and then find that the total calculated by Sage did not tally with the total on the invoice. To post this sort of invoice in the Blitz case study, you need to enter the Net amount, then Tab to the T/C box and replace the code T1 with code T3. Then press Tab and *type in* the VAT amount manually.

Posting the invoice details

4.24   When you have entered details for all the items on the invoice(s) you are processing and you are satisfied that they are correct, click on the **Save** button. A message will appear on the screen briefly to reassure you that the system is being updated. Then the screen will be cleared and you are ready either to process some more invoices or finish your work by clicking on **Close**.

4.25   When you post the details of an invoice, the program automatically:

(a)   updates the individual account of the supplier in the Suppliers Ledger;

(b)   updates the appropriate accounts in the Nominal Ledger. The accounts that are updated are the Creditors Control Account, the VAT Control account and the various purchases, expense or fixed asset accounts to which the invoices relate (as specified in the transaction details by your choice of N/C codes). The double entry posting to the nominal ledger will be:

Debit   Nominal Ledger Account selected
Debit   Purchase Tax Control, code 2202
Credit   Creditors Control Account, code 2100

Note that in Sage there are two VAT control accounts, one for VAT on purchases (debits), the other for VAT on sales (credits).

Activity 4.8

When you have done Activity 4.7 find out the debit or credit balances on the Nominal Ledger accounts 2100, 2202, 5000 and 7701 and the Suppliers ledger accounts NEWLIT and IRONCL and make a note of them.

Now reload a fresh copy of Assignment 6. How do the balances on the accounts differ? Explain each of the differences.

---

5   **ENTERING DETAILS OF CREDIT NOTES RECEIVED**

5.1   When a credit note is received from a supplier, the supplier is acknowledging that, for one reason or another, he has charged too much. Credit notes can be issued when goods are returned to the supplier as faulty or unwanted, or when there is a dispute about an invoice and the supplier agrees to reduce the bill.

5.2   Details of credit notes received from suppliers must be entered in the Suppliers Ledger, in the account of the appropriate supplier. The procedures are very similar to those for entering details of purchase invoices.

(a)   Click on the **Credits** button in the Suppliers window.

(b)   The screen will display a new window just like the Supplier Invoice window, except that the details of the credit note appear in red as you enter them.

5.3   The procedure is the same as that already described for entering details of purchase invoices. You must make sure, however, that:

(a)   the nominal ledger code you select (N/C) is the same as the code that was chosen for the original purchase invoice details;

(b)   the VAT code (T/C) is also the same as for the original purchase invoice.

5.4   Some other points should also be noted.

(a) Enter the **Date** on the credit note as the *date for the transaction*, not 'today's date'.

(b) The **Ref** item is for the credit note number, which you can copy from the credit note itself.

(c) The **Details** item can be used for recording brief details of the reason for receiving the credit note.

5.5 After you have entered the details of your credit note(s) click on **Save** as before. When you Save a credit note, the program:

(a) updates the account(s) of the individual supplier(s) in the purchase ledger; and

(b) updates the Creditors Control Account and the other relevant accounts in the nominal ledger.

Activity 4.9

With Assignment 6 data freshly loaded (from Activity 4.8) post the invoice for £240 to supplier IRONCL again and check the balance on the IRONCL account and on the nominal ledger accounts.

Then post a credit note for the same amount to the IRONCL account and check that the balances have reverted to their previous level.

---

6   REPORTS

6.1 When you have entered a day's batch of invoices you can print a list of the details, with totals. These listings are sometimes called 'Day Books'. In Sage, logically enough, they have names like 'Supplier Invoices' report, 'Supplier Credits' report and so on.

6.2 To produce a Supplier Invoices report or a Supplier Credits report, click on the Reports button in the Suppliers window.

A new window will appear as shown below.

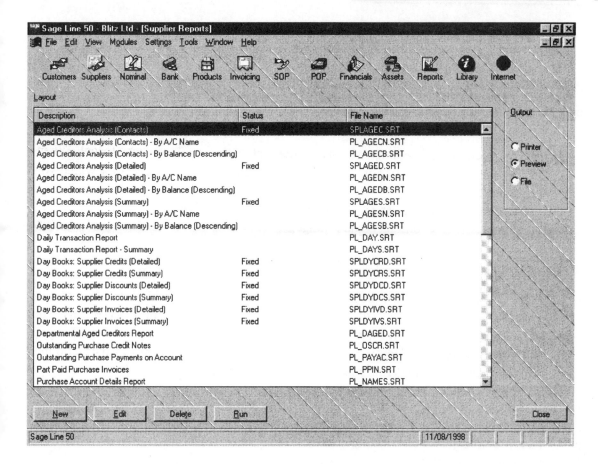

Output

6.3 In case you forget to do so later it is best to begin by choosing how you want your report to be output. There are always three or four alternatives, from which you choose *one* by clicking in the white circle next to the appropriate label in the Output section of the screen. A black bullet will appear in the circle when you do this.

(a) *Printer.* This sends your report straight to a printer to be printed out. The usual Windows Print window will appear, allowing you to choose what part of the document you want printed, what printer you want to send it to and so on. Printing things using Windows applications is explained in Chapter 2.

(b) *Preview.* This option brings up a screen display of the information that you can edit to some extent for printing purposes. For example you might want to change the font style or the width of the margins.

(c) *File.* This option allows you to save a copy of the report on disk. The usual Windows **Save As** window will appear and you will have to choose a name for report and specify the directory in which you want it to be saved. Again, see Chapter 2 if you have forgotten how to use the Save As window.

In the case study in this book you will use the Preview option mainly and the Printer option if you have access to a printer.

Report type

6.4 The main box on the screen contains a list of all the different types of report that the package is set up to produce. All you have to do is click on the type of report you want or scroll down to it, using the cursor keys ↓ or ↑ until it is highlighted. Pick Day Books: Supplier Invoices (Detailed), if you are trying this out on screen as you read (as you should be).

You now click on **Run**.

Which transactions?

6.5   You must now choose what transactions you want to appear in your listing. There are four main criteria for doing this.

(a)   By specifying a date range (the date or dates of the transactions you wish to list)

(b)   By specifying a transaction range (the range of transaction numbers for which you require a listing)

(c)   By specifying a supplier account range

(d)   By specifying a nominal account range

Specifying a date range

6.6   Press Tab if necessary until the first box in the date section is highlighted. As a default this may show the date 01/01/80, but it is unlikely that you will want to accept this. The second box will show today's date or a date like 31/12/99, and again it is unlikely that you will want to accept this. However, you must *always have a valid date range*, whatever other criteria you are using to define what appears in your report.

6.7   Instead you should key in the earliest date for transactions you wish to list and then the latest date. Key in each date using *two digits* for the day of the month, two digits for the month of the year and two digits for the year (there is no need to type slashes: the program will insert these automatically).

Examples	*Enter*
6th April 1998	060498
15th May 1998	150598
2nd November 1998	021198

6.8   Suppose today is 5 October and you have just entered invoices received from suppliers with various dates from 30 September to 2 October. In the first Date Range box enter 300998 then press Tab. In the second box type 021098. You can use the calendar button if you prefer.

6.9   You are now ready to produce your report. Just Click on **OK** and wait for the report to be output in the way you specified earlier.

Specifying a transaction range

6.10   Choosing the date range for a listing of purchase invoices or supplier credit notes can be a problem because the invoices or credit notes will have different dates. When an invoice has a date that is now several weeks old, it could be very difficult to be sure of including it in a report by specifying the date range, without listing other invoices you have already processed in the past.

6.11   You can specify the invoices (or credit notes) you wish to list by specifying their transaction numbers. These are unique numbers, automatically allocated to each entry into the system by the program. To specify a transaction range, you should remember to *take a note* of the first transaction number for the invoices and the credit notes when you start to process them. The second box in the Transaction section shows the total number of transactions entered so far on the system (purchase ledger, sales ledger and nominal ledger). Your next transaction will be the next number in the sequence. For example, if the box shows that 70 transactions have been processed (number of entries = 70) your next entry will be transaction 71.

You can find the last transaction number by clicking on **Financials** in the main window and jumping to the end of the list that appears.

6.12   The Transaction boxes on screen will display a transaction range from 1 to 9999999 (or to the most recent transaction number). You should alter the range, to specify the transactions you wish to list. The first number is the only item *you* need to get right, and you should enter the transaction number for the first entry you processed and want to include in the listing. Tab to the first box in the Transaction section, type in this number and press Tab. Then press Tab again to accept the transaction number already shown as a 'default' in the second box.

6.13   In a 'live' system this would be all you needed to do, but you might be doing the Blitz case study at any time it is quite possible that the real date when you are entering transactions will be different from the date of the transactions in the case study. You therefore need to check the second box in the Date Range section to make sure that it is the same as or later than 3 October 1998 (this is the fictional date when entries are made first made in the case study).

6.14   Don't worry about mixing purchase invoices and credit note transaction numbers. The report will contain only one type of transaction or the other (ie invoices only or credit notes only), depending on the type of report you have selected.

6.15   You are now ready to produce a report of transaction within the range specified. Just Click on **OK** and wait for the report to be output in the way you specified earlier.

Supplier range or Nominal range

6.16   The procedure is similar if you only want a report of transactions with suppliers in a certain range (A – D, say) or of transactions posted to specific nominal ledger account. If, for example, you had a query from a specific supplier about invoices sent to you in the last month you would specify the appropriate date range, leave the transaction range as it is (ranging from the first to the most recent transaction) and then enter the supplier code in *both* boxes in the **Supplier** section. Note that you can click on the Finder button (or press F4 when the cursor is in the appropriate box) if you are not sure of the account code. The Supplier Accounts list will shortly appear.

6.17   The procedure is the same if you wanted to know about all transactions posted, say, to nominal account codes 7000 to 7999, or code 1200 to 1200 (ie account 1200 only).

6.18   Again when you have specified the range you want you are ready to produce your report as before.

Activity 4.10

Load a fresh copy of Assignment 6 data. Run the report Day Books: Supplier Invoices (Detailed). Make sure that the data range covers the period from 1 August 1998 to 31 December 1998.

What are the totals shown and what is the number of the last transaction listed.

Running several reports: Report or File View windows

6.19   You can run several reports one after the other if you wish. If you use the Preview (or Display) option for Output, Sage will open a Report or 'File View' window for each of them and you can switch between them and the Sage package itself by clicking on the word **W**indow at the top of the screen and then clicking on whichever window you want.

Closing a Report or File View window

6.20   Buttons at the bottom of the screen give you a variety of options for moving about in the report, viewing it in different ways, saving it, printing it, or just closing the report window.

7   CONCLUSION

Experiment ...

7.1   This is an important chapter because it introduces many of the widely used features of the Sage package. Spend some time going over what you have read, ideally while sitting at a computer. Try calling up windows and making entries in the way we describe. You won't break the software by experimenting with its features and you can always call up a 'clean' copy of Blitz case study data, so don't worry about messing up the system by typing in and posting a few made up entries of your own.

... and try an Assignment!

7.2   If you think you can follow the instructions in this chapter, **you should now be able to attempt Assignment 1** at the end of this Interactive Text. If you haven't yet attempted the **Activities** in this and the previous chapter, you should do these first.

Answers to activities

Answer 4.1

It should appear between LERWIC and MATTHI.

Answer 4.2

(a)   N14 6TS

(b)   Candy Spicer

(c)   T Cooper (Stationery) Ltd, 01582 405592

Answer 4.3

Check the details you have entered on screen very carefully to make sure that all the spelling and numbers are exactly as you see them here. Have you got the right combination of letters and numbers in the post-code, for instance?

Answer 4.4

You should get BL OFFICE FURNISHING LTD and MUSWELL HILL COUNCIL.

Answer 4.5

(a)   This is a hands on activity.

(b)   FLOORI, HARDIN and LERWIC. This will only work if you follow the instructions given above and avoid the pitfalls.

Answer 4.7

You should get the answers £53.24, Materials Purchases and Office Machine Maintenance.

(Incidentally, unless we tell you otherwise, it does not normally matter whether you save information entered for activities or close without saving.)

Answer 4.8

These are the results you should get.

Account	With new transactions Dr	With new transactions Cr	Fresh Assignment 6 data Dr	Fresh Assignment 6 data Cr	Difference Dr	Difference Cr
2100		8034.78		7677.28		357.50
2202	7030.74		6977.50		53.24	
5000	6336.89		6236.89		100.00	
7701	204.26				204.26	
IRONCL		240.00		0.00		240.00
NEWLIT		789.63		672.13		117.50

The differences are entirely due to the transactions you posted in Activity 4.7. You should trace through each figure until you are happy about this, using your knowledge of double entry from Units 1 and 2. Ideally, write out all the T-accounts.

This Activity is to reassure you that Sage follows the same principles of double entry as a manual system and to highlight how much easier it is to use a computerised package.

Answer 4.10

The last transaction listed should be number 194. You should get the following totals.

Net	Tax	Gross
54,742.89	8,119.29	62,862.18

Chapter 5   Customer invoices and credit notes

Chapter topic list

1   Customers and Invoicing

2   New customers

3   Producing invoices

4   Invoicing for services provided

5   Invoicing for the sale of goods

6   Producing credit notes

7   Printing invoices and credit notes

8   Updating the ledgers

9   Updating the ledgers without producing invoices

10   Reports

11   Customer queries

12   Conclusion

Learning objectives

On completion of this chapter you will be able to:

	Performance criteria	Range statement
• Set up accounts in the customers ledger for new customers	19.1.1 to 19.1.7	
• Produce invoices for sending to customers	19.3.1 to 19.3.8	
• Produce credit notes for sending to customers	19.3.1 to 19.3.8	
• Post details of customer invoices and credit notes in the customers ledger and the Nominal ledger	19.1.1 to 19.1.7	
• Produce a listing of entries for the sales invoices and the sales credit notes	19.3.1 to 19.3.8	
• Deal with queries from customers about invoices or credit notes	19.2.1 to 19.2.4	

1   CUSTOMERS AND INVOICING

1.1   This time you will be using *two* buttons in the **main** window.

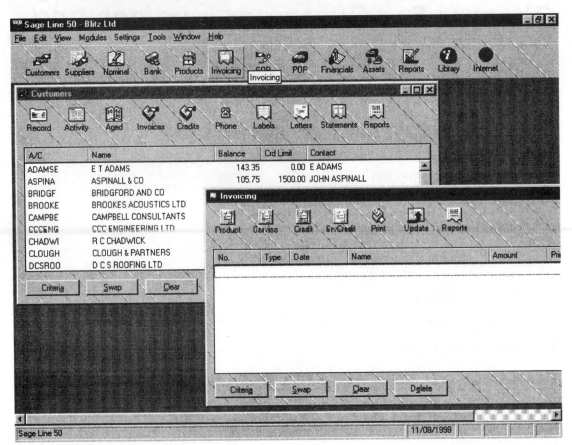

(a)   The **Customers** button brings up a Customers window which is very similar to the Suppliers window which we explored in the previous chapter.

(b)   The **Invoicing** button brings up a window that can be used to produce invoices and credit notes to send to customers, as well as to post sales invoices and credit notes to the accounting records.

2   NEW CUSTOMERS

2.1   When an invoice has to be produced for sending to a new customer (ie a customer who has not been invoiced before by your company), an account for the customer must be set up in the customers ledger. There is a choice of three ways of entering new customer accounts in the ledger:

(a)   using the **Record** button in the Customers window;
(b)   using the **Invoices** button in the Customers window; or
(c)   using one of the buttons in the **Invoicing** window.

2.2   The **Record** button option is not described here. It is similar to the Supplier Record option for entering details of new supplier accounts in the purchase ledger. This was described in the previous chapter. For the same reason, the option to set up new customer accounts from the **Invoices** button in the *Customers* window is not described here.

Activity 5.1

If you have forgotten what a 'record' looks like, or what details are needed, load up any Assignment you like, click on **Customers** and then on **Record** to remind yourself. Enter some imaginary details (for example your own name, address and so on) if you like.

Credit limits

2.3 The only extra point that you should note for the purpose of the case study and Assignment 2 is that you are more likely to be required to enter an amount for the maximum credit that will be allowed to the customer (ie the maximum value of goods or services that will be supplied on credit at any time). This amount should be entered as the 'Credit Limit' in the appropriate box on the screen.

2.4 Using one of the buttons in the **Invoicing** window to enter new customer accounts is described in the next section of this chapter.

3 PRODUCING INVOICES

3.1 The **Product** button and the **Service** button in the Invoicing window can be used to:

(a) set up accounts for a new customer in the customers ledger;

(b) record details of invoices for sending to customers; and

(c) print the invoices.

3.2 When you click on the **Invoicing** button, which is roughly the middle button in the main window, the following screen will be displayed.

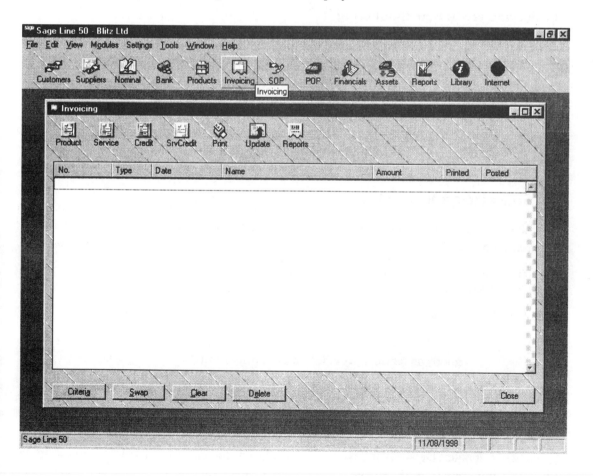

3.3   As you process invoices the blank space in this window will gradually be filled up with key details of each invoice, providing a handy numerical index of all invoices in the system. The **Criteria, Swap** and **Clear** buttons will be explained later in this chapter.

Invoicing for goods or services?

3.4   Invoices to customers can be for goods supplied on credit or services supplied on credit. Blitz Limited in the case study is a service company, and does not usually sell goods. However, to give you an opportunity to use as many features of Sage as are relevant at AAT Foundation level, Blitz will sell some cleaning materials on credit to customers.

3.5   The following options in the Invoicing window will all be explained.

	Pop-up Label	*Use*
(a)	Product Invoice	To invoice for the sale of goods or a product
(b)	Service Invoice	To invoice for the supply of services
(c)	Product Credit	To produce a credit note for goods
(d)	Service Credit	To produce a credit note for services
(d)	Print Invoices	To print invoices or credit notes either individually or in batches
(e)	Update Ledgers	To post invoices and credit notes to the ledgers
(f)	Reports	To produce lists of invoices in various stages of production

Invoice and credit note numbering

3.6   Invoices should be numbered sequentially. The program therefore allocates a number to each invoice automatically as you work, by adding 1 to the number of the previous invoice. You can set the number manually, however, for example if you are using Sage for the first time to continue a sequence of manually produced invoices.

3.7   When you process an invoice or credit note, or a batch of invoices or credit notes, it can be helpful to make a note of the invoice numbers or credit note numbers in the batch.

The Sage windows for Invoicing

3.8   Invoices (and credit notes) are built up in sections, and the appropriate details must be entered in each section.

(a)   There is a main input window, which is used to enter the customer's account reference code (and, for new customers, other details such as name and address).

(b)   Certain windows can be called up:

(i)   for entering line-by-line details for the invoice, such as the details of the goods or services provided and the price; and

(ii)   to specify the *nominal code* to which the transaction should be posted.

(c)   An Order Details screen can be displayed, for entering certain order details, such as specifying the delivery address, if this differs from the invoice address.

(d)   A Footer Details window can be displayed, for entering details to appear in the bottom part of the invoice, such as the price for carriage outwards (ie delivery cost), if any, and discounts. This needn't be used if there are no such details to add.

Activity 5.2

Familiarise yourself with the above by clicking on **Invoicing** in the main window and seeing what happens when you click on the various buttons and options available. Press **Esc** to get back to the initial Invoicing screen whenever you like.

4   INVOICING FOR SERVICES PROVIDED

4.1   Invoices for services can be produced using the **Service** button in the Invoicing window. When you click on this button, the window shown below will appear.

4.2   This window is used to enter the details for one invoice. Each invoice is for the sale of one or more services or items. There is a separate line for the details of each item, in the main (central) part of the screen.

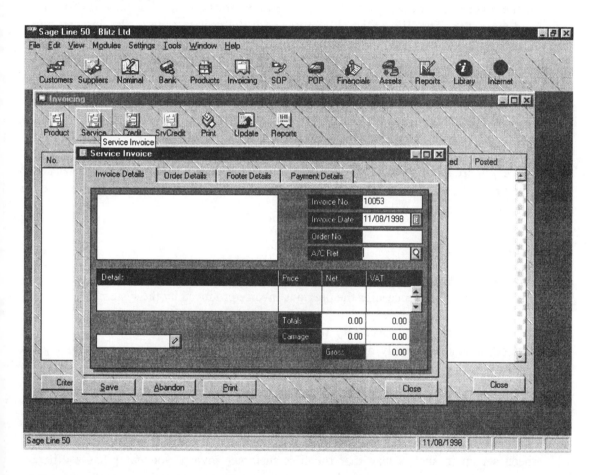

The customer account

4.3   The cursor begins in the **A/C Ref** box where you enter the customer's account reference. You can type in the code directly if you know it, or just type *part* of the code if you can make a good guess at it. If you type in your guess at the code and press Tab, a list of Customer Accounts will appear with the nearest code to the one you guessed at highlighted. If this is correct, click on OK or press Enter to accept the code. If not you will have to scroll up or down the list in the usual way to find the customer you want.

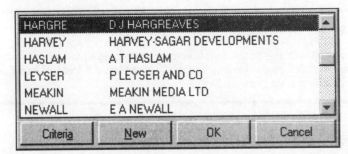

4.4   If you have no idea of the code, this first box has the Finder button beside it to help you find it. Click on this button or press function key F4 to display the list of Customer Accounts. Scroll down the list using the cursor keys or the scroll bar until you find the one you want then click on OK or press Enter. The customer code will appear in the A/C Ref box and the full name and address will appear in the box in the top left hand corner.

4.5   If the invoice is to be sent to a new customer, type in the code of the customer yourself and press Tab. The Finder list will appear with the nearest code to the one you typed highlighted. This time you ignore the highlighted code and click on the **New** button at the bottom of the Finder window. A screen will appear that is just like the one you met in the previous chapter for entering new Supplier records. Enter all the details for the new account and click on **Save** when you are happy that the details are correct. You will then be returned to the customer accounts list and the account that you have just set up will be highlighted. Press Enter or click on OK to accept this.

4.6   Once you are satisfied that you have the correct customer account code in the A/C Ref box press Tab. This will take you to the **Details** section of the screen, but before we proceed there are a couple of things to check.

Invoice number

4.7   The invoice number is already shown on the screen. This is automatically entered as the next number in sequence after the previous invoice produced by the system.

4.8   It should usually be unnecessary to alter this number. However, the number can be altered if required simply by typing in a new number. (If you do this you may get a message asking you to confirm the change (or you may not, depending which version of Sage you are using). Click on Yes if you are sure you want to make the change.) Unfortunately this will make the account code and details in the **A/C Ref** area of the screen disappear again! You will need to enter the account reference again if this happens, but your new invoice number will not then change. (The Blitz case study has been set up in such a way that the first customer invoice you enter has a different number to the one suggested by the Sage software, just so that you can see this happen.)

Invoice Date

4.9   The screen will display today's date (ie the date in the computer system). To accept this date, press Tab. Another invoice date can be entered, if required. Use the calendar button if you like. In the Assignments in this book, you will need to enter an appropriate date for every invoice.

Activity 5.3

Load up the data for **Assignment 1** and then enter these details in a service invoice, following the instructions above.

A/C Ref:	WRWCAT
Invoice number:	20000
Date:	25 November 1998

What are the full name and address details for the customer concerned?

The Details box

4.10 Having entered the date press Tab until you get to the main part of the screen. In the details box you can enter any description you like of the service that has been delivered. In the Blitz case study this will be something like 'Window Cleaning' or 'Domestic Services'. You can enter a much more wordy description if you wish, though this will probably not be necessary in the Blitz case study unless you get carried away.

4.11 It may have occurred to you that although you have told the computer the *Customer* account number and typed out details of the transaction, you have not entered a *Nominal* account code. How will the computer know which Sales account to post the transaction to?

4.12 It won't know unless you tell it (in fact it won't post the transaction at all unless you tell it what to do) and the way you do so is as follows.

4.13 Before tabbing on from the Details box to the Price box you *must* do one of two things (the choice is yours).

(a) Press function key F3.

(b) Click on the little button with a pencil symbol that you can see *below* the Details box next to the box that says 'Item 1 of 0'.

A third option is to Tab on to the Price box and then *double-click* in the Details line you have just entered. We do *not* recommend this because it is then too easy to forget about filling in all necessary details.

4.14 Whichever you do, the following window will appear.

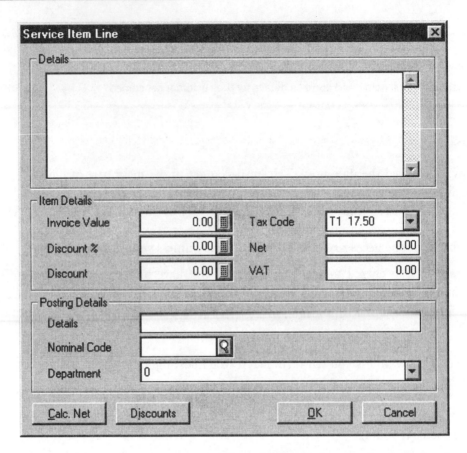

4.15   This window shows the text you entered in the details box in the main Service Invoice window. This is how the text will appear on the invoice and you can edit it or add to it if you like.

4.16   As mentioned above, this is the chance to change the Tax code if you need to do so. The VAT will be recalculated if you Tab down to the Tax Code box and specify a different code to the standard T1 (click on the arrow beside the Tax code box for other options). You won't normally need to do this.

4.17   You can also enter the Invoice Value and any *additional* Discount details (*not* settlement discount, which is handled automatically, if applicable) at this point if you wish. If you click on the buttons beside these boxes (or press F4) a little drop-down calculator appears.

This can be operated either with the mouse, or better, by using the *numeric keypad* on the keyboard. It is useful if, say, you are preparing an invoice for 7 items at £9.36 each and you don't trust yourself to do the maths in your head (!).

In fact you can also bring up a calculator window (with scientific facilities) at *any* time, just by pressing F2. To enter the result of a calculation into a field in a Sage screen you can sometimes press Ctrl + C, click on the field in question and press Ctrl + V.

Nominal code

4.18   Principally, however, this is the time to specify the nominal code for the invoice.

4.19   Each item on the invoice can have a different nominal ledger code if appropriate (in other words different items on the same invoice can be given different nominal ledger sales account codes). For each item (each line of Details you enter in the main Service invoice window) the code for the appropriate nominal ledger sales account should be entered using the Service Item Line screen.

4.20   In the Blitz Limited case study, the nominal ledger codes that are used are:

Code	*Customers account*
4000	Sales - Contract Cleaning
4001	Sales - Window Cleaning
4002	Sales - Domestic Services
4100	Sales - Materials

4.21   Rather than memorising this, an easy approach is to key in the number 4 alone and then press Tab (or use function key F4). This brings up the list of Nominal Accounts with number 4000 highlighted. If Contract Cleaning is not the account you want then just scroll around a little using the cursor keys to find Window Cleaning or whatever. Once the nominal account you want is highlighted press Enter or click on OK and this account number will be entered in the right box.

4.22   There is also the option of specifying a Department for management accounting analysis purposes. This facility is not used in the Blitz case study so once you have entered the nominal code you can just press Enter or click on OK to be returned to the main Service invoice window.

Price and VAT

4.23   Press Tab once you have entered the details for an item and its nominal code and you will be taken to the **Price** box. Enter the amount of the invoice *excluding VAT* and press Tab again. The Net and VAT amounts will be calculated automatically. By default VAT will be 17.5% of the Net Amount you entered. (If you need to change this you can return to the Service Item Line window and do so.)

4.24   You are now taken to the next line of Details and you can follow the same procedure to enter a second invoice item and a third, and so on.

Activity 5.4

Load up the data for **Assignment 6**. Prepare the following service invoices (you have to find out the Nominal code yourself). Click on **Save** when you have entered the details for each invoice.

No.	*Date*	*A/C*	*Details*	*N/C*	*Price*
10053	25/11/98	ADAMSE	Window cleaning	?	£100
10054	25/11/98	GARDEN	Contract cleaning	?	£100

When you have finished press **Esc** (or click on **Close**) to return to the initial Invoicing screen. Scroll down to the bottom and make a note of the amount of each of the invoices you entered.

Explain the results.

Order Details

4.25   Occasionally, you might want to include extra details about the order on the invoice, for example:

(a) to specify a delivery address when this differs from the invoice address;

(b) to specify payment terms (eg 'PAYMENT REQUIRED WITHIN 30 DAYS OF INVOICE DATE').

4.26 To add these details, you should click on the **Order Details** index tab. A new window will appear on screen, and you should use this to specify the details you wish to add or alter. Press Tab to move from one field (item) to the next, or when you do not wish to input any details for the field.

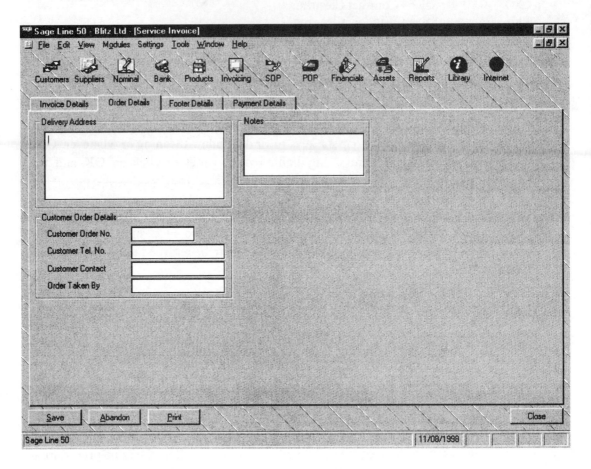

Customer Order No.

4.27 This box can be used to enter any customer reference for the order, such as the order number used by the customer when placing the order.

Customer Tel. No./Contact

4.28 The customer's telephone number and contact name will be displayed automatically.

Delivery Address

4.29 The delivery name and address can be entered here, when this is different from the name and address on the invoice (and in the records in the customer's account in the customers ledger).

Notes

4.30 Notes can be added, to appear on the invoice. These can be used, if required, to bring special information to the customer's attention; for example '5% DISCOUNT FOR SETTLEMENT WITHIN 7 DAYS OF INVOICE DATE'.

4.31   When you have inserted the special order details you require click on the next index tab at the top of the window.

Footer Details

4.32   If you wish, you can also add details to the bottom of the invoice for:

(a)   charging for the delivery of goods (Carriage); or

(b)   providing details of any discounts offered to the customer for early payment (Settlement Terms).

(c)   giving every item on the invoice the same tax code, nominal ledger code or department code (Global).

Of these, only (a) is described in this chapter.

4.33   If you wish to add footer details to an invoice, click on the **Footer Details** index tab. A new window will appear, as shown below.

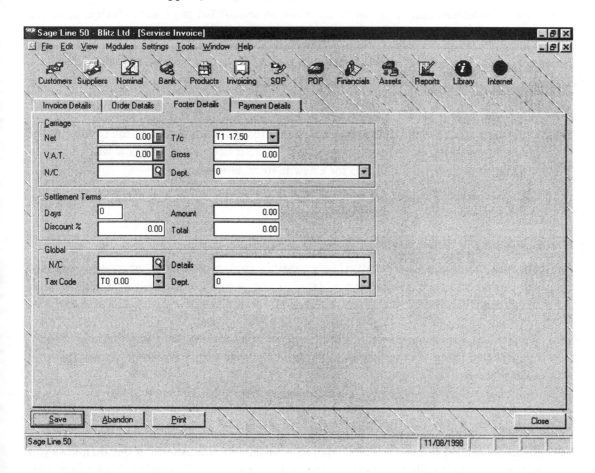

Carriage

4.34   The amount of charges for carriage outwards can be entered in the Net box at the top of the window. The charge for carriage, *excluding VAT*, should be keyed in.

Tax code (T/c)

4.35   Unless told otherwise use the same tax code for VAT as for the main invoice. It should usually be T1, meaning that VAT is chargeable at the standard rate of 17.5%.

Nominal code

4.36   Enter the nominal ledger code for the Carriage Outwards account in the nominal ledger. In the Blitz Limited system, this code is 4905. Otherwise you may need to click on the Finder button beside this box to find the right code.

Activity 5.5

Load up the data for Assignment 6. Enter the following details, referring back to the previous paragraphs for instructions if necessary.

No.	Date	A/C	Details	N/C	Price
10055	31/12/98	OWENLO	Sundry	4101	£100

Delivery address: 14 Woodgate Street, Barnet, N16 3BB
Order no.: 14879
Telephone number: 0171-734 2843
Customer contact: Jennifer
Carriage: £5
Settlement discount: 5% if settled within 30 days

What is the total amount of the invoice as shown on screen? Did any discrepancies arise as you were doing this activity, and if so what should you do about them?

Saving the invoice details

4.37   When you have entered all the details of the invoice (which might or might not include footer details) click on the **Save** button. This adds the main details of the invoice to the index shown in the main Invoicing window. The Service Invoice window will be cleared and you can start entering details for a new invoice. However:

(a)   the invoice you have saved is *not yet posted* to the customers ledger and nominal ledger; and

(b)   an invoice is not printed.

This feature of the Sage package very sensibly recognises that in practice you might realise that you want to change the details to be posted and printed at a slightly later stage than when you are doing the initial (draft) entries.

4.38   We shall see how to *print and post* invoices *later in this chapter*. It is important *not* be in a rush to post things to the ledgers. You have *saved* all your hard work, so none of it is wasted. Be patient for now.

Abandon

4.39   As an alternative to Saving the details you have entered, the **Abandon** button allows you to cancel all the details of the invoice you have just entered. You might think this is a bit desperate, but it is sometimes easier and safer to start again than trying to edit a hopelessly wrong set of entries.

Exiting the Service invoice window

4.40   You can exit the Service invoice window at any time you like, and return to it again later in the same session, so long as you have saved all the entries that you want to save. To do so just press **Esc** or click on the **Close** button. You will get a rather alarming message asking you, Yes or No, if you are *sure* you want to exit. There is no need to be alarmed (or to be particularly sure for that matter). Just click on Yes or press the Y key. If you do this and then realise that you want to enter details for another Service invoice just click on the **Clear** button at the bottom of the main Invoicing window (this ensures that you don't start editing an existing invoice) and then click on the **Service** button again.

Editing saved entries

4.41   You can change any of the entries you have made so far, so long as you haven't posted them (updated the ledgers). Click on the relevant invoice (which you will now see listed in the main Invoicing window) and then click on the **Service** button again.

Activity 5.6

(a)   Load Assignment 6 and find out the balance on the Customer account WOODPX.

(b)   Enter the following service invoice details (accept the invoice number offered by Sage and find out the nominal code for yourself). Then click on **Close** and respond **Yes** to the message that appears. Find the new invoice in the list in the Invoicing window.

Date	A/C	Details	Price
31/12/98	WOODPX	Domestic services	£60

(c)   Enter the details again, but this time click on **Save** and then **Close**. Find the new invoice in the list in the Invoicing window. Also, find out the balance on the customer account WOODPX now.

(d)   Edit the invoice you have just entered: the amount should have been £600. Click on **Save** and **Close** and find out the balance on the customer account WOODPX now.

---

5   INVOICING FOR THE SALE OF GOODS

5.1   To produce an invoice for the sale of goods on credit, you can use the **Product** button in the Invoicing window. When you click on this button, the screen will display windows similar to those that appear when you select the Service invoice option.

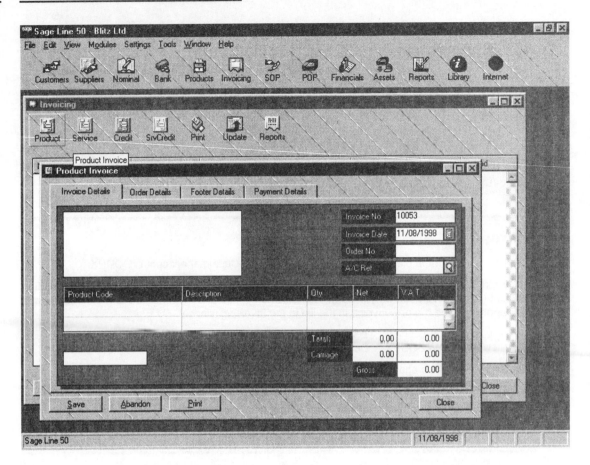

5.2   This operates just like the Service window with the following exceptions.

Product code

5.3   Once you have entered the A/C Ref and pressed Tab you will be taken to the **Product Code** box in the central part of the window. On each line of the screen, you can enter details of sales for a product. One line of details should be entered for each item sold.

5.4   Enter the code for the product. If you don't know what the code is you can use the Finder button beside the Product Code heading or press function key F4 when the cursor is flashing in the Stock Code column. A window will appear with a list of stock items and their codes. There is also the facility to set up a new stock item if you wish. This is much like setting up a new customer or supplier account. When the stock item you want is highlighted, press Enter or click on the OK button and this code will be shown in the Product Code field in the main screen, together with its description.

5.5   A company might not use product codes in its Sage system, perhaps because, like Blitz Ltd in the case study, selling materials is just a sideline, or because stock is set up on a different system. There may also be times when an item sold is 'non-standard' and does not have a stock code because it is not usually carried in stock. In this case you can make one of three entries in the Product Code field.

M   This simply allows you to type a message in the Description box. You might want to type something like '*Thank you for ordering the following items*' before listing out the items ordered with their prices.

S1   This code is used for a non-stock item to which VAT applies.

S2   This code is used for a non-stock item to which VAT does not apply.

5.6   You will only use the **S1** code in the Blitz case study. Type in S1 and press Tab. A window headed Product Item Line will appear. This is shown below.

5.7   If you think this is rather like the screen that appears when you press F3 when you are preparing a Service invoice, you are right. In fact this window will also appear if you *double-click* in the relevant line.

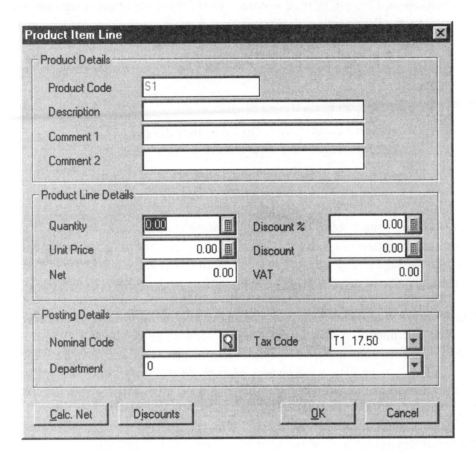

5.8   The entries to make are as follows.

(a)   *Description*. One line's worth of description can be entered. You can follow this with two lines of *Comments* which might describe the item further, or make it clear that it is a non-stock item, or explain how the item is packaged ('box of 12'), or whatever else you like.

(b)   Once you have entered your description and comments, Tab down to the *Quantity* box and key in the number of items you are selling. Note that if the item is sold and priced in, say, boxes of twelve you should key in the number of *boxes*, not the number of individual items.

(c)   Pressing Tab takes you to the *Unit Price*. This is the price of one unit of sale (eg a box), not of an individual item.

Suppose for example an item's price is £2 per can and cans are sold in boxes of 12. If you were selling somebody 36 cans you could enter this in two ways.

	Method 1		*Method 2*
Quantity	36	Quantity	3
Unit Price	2	Unit Price	24

Method 2 is generally preferable. To make things crystal clear on the invoice you might include the words 'box of 12 cans' in your description or comments

(d)   *Discount %*. This is zero, unless the customer is entitled to a trade discount on the net price; for example, a discount for bulk purchasing. You can simply Tab on to the next item when there is no trade discount. If you do offer a discount of, say, 2%, key in 2.

(e) *Nominal Code.* This is the nominal ledger code for the sales account to which the sales item relates. In the Blitz system, this will be the code for the Sales – Materials account, which is code 4100.

(f) *Department.* This can be used to enter a code for the department which has made the sale. In the Blitz system, department codes are *not used*, and you should leave this item blank simply by pressing Tab.

(g) The same *Tax Codes* apply as described previously. In the Blitz system, these are as follows.

T0   for zero-rated items
T1   for standard-rated items (with VAT currently at 17.5%)
T9   for items to which VAT does not apply

(h) *Net, Discount and VAT.* The total net amount payable for the item (Quantity × Unit Price), the amount of discount and the VAT payable are displayed automatically.

5.9   Once you have completed all the details you want to enter in this window click on OK. If you have forgotten to specify the Quantity, the Tax Code or the Nominal account you will get a message telling you so. Click on OK in the message box or press Enter to clear the message, type in the entry that you forgot, then click on OK.

5.10   This will take you back to the main Product invoice window. The details you have just specified will now be shown in the relevant boxes. The cursor will be flashing in the Description box and you add whatever details you like. Once you have done this and you are satisfied that the figures are correct (change them if not), press Tab until you reach the next line of the invoice.

5.11   The main invoice screen also gives you options for Order Details and Footer Details. These features were described in the previous section of this chapter.

5.12   When the invoice is complete and correct Save it by clicking on the **Save** button and the screen will be cleared ready for the next invoice. If you have entered details of all the invoices you have to process click on Close or press Esc to get back to the main Invoicing window.

Activity 5.7

On 21 October 1998 a customer R I Tepper Ltd purchased 4 cases of Gleamo. One case contains 12 tins and costs £10.68.

Load Assignment 5 and enter this transaction as a **Product** invoice number 10052, following the instructions given in the preceding paragraphs.

What is the total amount of the invoice? Which nominal code is used? What is R I Tepper Ltd's postcode?

---

6   PRODUCING CREDIT NOTES

6.1   The Invoicing window also offers you Credit Note options. Processing credit notes is similar to processing invoices.

6.2   Click on the **Credit** button or **SrvCredit** button in the Invoicing window and a new window will appear that looks and works exactly like the windows just described, except that headings are red.

6.3   To prepare a credit note for *goods* sold, proceed as described in the previous section of this chapter.

6.4   To produce a credit note for *services*, use the Service Credit (**SrvCredit**) button, which is just like preparing a Service invoice.

Activity 5.8

Load Assignment 3 and enter details for the following credit notes. You must decide whether to enter Product Credit notes or Service credit notes, and which nominal codes to use.

No.	Date	A/C	Details	Amount (gross)
4	14/09/98	BROOKE	Poor quality cleaning rebate	£500.00
5	15/09/98	ELITEC	Damaged goods	£23.50
6	16/09/98	CLOUGH	Window smashed while being cleaned	£58.75

Save your entries and Close down the credit note option(s). Then describe how what you have entered appears in the main **Invoicing** screen.

---

7   PRINTING INVOICES AND CREDIT NOTES

7.1   To print invoices and credit notes you have two main options.

(a)   At any time during the preparation of an invoice you can print out a hard copy to see what it looks like on paper. If you don't like what you see and *you have not yet updated the ledgers* (ie posted the invoice) you can make permanent changes to it. If you do like what you see, you can then Save the invoice and go on to the next one.

To print out a copy of the invoice while you are preparing it click on the **Print** button at the bottom of the Product invoice window or the Service invoice window. Further windows will appear as explained below.

(b)   You can Save each invoice or credit note until you have finished a batch. (This is what we have been recommending so far.) Then use the **Print Invoices** button in the main Invoicing window at a time of your choosing. An index of invoices will be shown in the main Invoicing window and from this you can select individual invoices to print or print the whole batch.

With either option you get the same series of windows taking you step by step through the printing procedure. The Print Invoices procedure is slightly more complex, so that is the one we shall describe.

The Print Invoices button

7.2   If you are going to use the **Print Invoices** button you must first select what sort of invoices you want to print out. One way of doing this is simply to highlight the invoice(s) concerned in the index list in the main Invoicing window by clicking on them. This is the easiest option if you only want to print one or two invoices. If you click on an invoice accidentally, just click on it again to clear the highlighting.

7.3   If you want to highlight *all* the invoices in an index list quickly, first use the **Clear** button at the bottom of the main invoicing window (this takes away any odd highlighting there might be) and then click on the **Swap** button (this will now highlight *all* the invoices). Every time the **Swap** button is clicked it changes highlighted invoices into unhighlighted invoices and vice versa.

If you want to practise this (as you should), you will need to load up one of Assignments 4, 5 or 6 using the Blitz program.

The Criteria button

7.4   You should *not* print out both service invoices and goods invoices in a single batch because, as we shall see in a moment, they are laid out differently. To cope with this problem you can use the **Criteria** button at the bottom of the main invoicing screen. Click on this and the following window will appear.

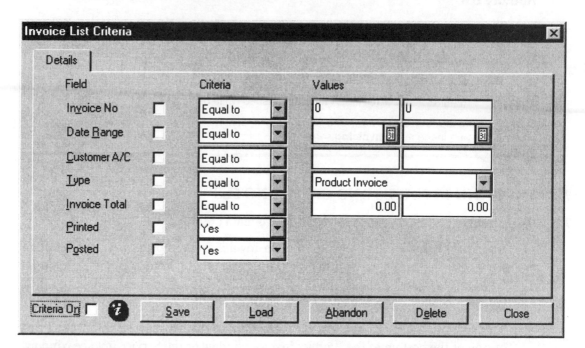

7.5   This gives you various options for specifying the range of invoices to print: by invoice number range, date range, customer account range, and so on. To make a criterion active click in the little white square so that an **x** appears in it (click in the box again to remove the **x**) and then, using the downward pointing arrow beside the 'equals' box, specify the condition that must be fulfilled. Here are some of the ways that you can specify conditions.

Criterion		Value	Value	Meaning
Invoice	Greater than (>)	10037		Picks only those invoices or credit notes with a number greater than 10037.
Date	Between (<>)	08/10/98	10/10/98	Picks only those invoices or credit notes with dates between 8th and 10th of October 1998.
Invoice total	less than (<)	1000.00		Picks only those invoices with a value of less than £1,000.
Customer a/c	Between (<>)	B*	G*	Picks only those invoices or credit notes that have been prepared for customers whose account code falls in the alphabetical range B-G. Note that the wildcard character * can be used to represent any number of characters.
Type	not equal to (!=)	Credit Note		Picks all items in the Invoicing window index list that *are not* credit notes
Printed	not equal to (!=)	Yes		Picks all those invoices that have *not* previously been printed
Posted	equals (=)	Yes		Picks only those invoices that have been posted.

7.6   When you have chosen your criteria click in the **Criteria On** square and then on the **Close** button and you will be returned to the main Invoicing window. Only those items that fulfil your criteria will be shown and you can click on the **Swap** button to highlight them all and select them for printing. To display all the invoices and credit notes again click on the **Criteria** button and then remove the **x** from the Criteria On square.

7.7   The **Type** criterion is of particular interest to us here. Since you cannot print both service invoices and goods invoices in the same batch you can use the Criteria button to select only one or the other type of invoice. It is possible to print credit notes and goods invoices in the same batch, however. The best way to do this is:

(a)   firstly to specify items that *are not equal to* (**!=**) Service invoices;

(b)   then, when you have printed these, specify items that *equal* Service invoices.

Activity 5.9

Load Assignment 5 and click on the Invoicing button. Use the criteria button as described above to produce the following lists in the Invoicing window.

(a)   A list of Service invoices only, with an invoice number less than 10040.
(b)   A list of invoices or credit notes that have not been posted.
(c)   A list of Product invoices with an invoice total greater than £250.
(d)   A list devised by you using the wildcard symbol (*).
(e)   A full list of all invoices and credit notes on the system.

Printing

7.8   If you click on the Print button in either the Product invoice window or the Service invoice window, or else click on the Print Invoices button in the main Invoicing window, another window will appear, like the following.

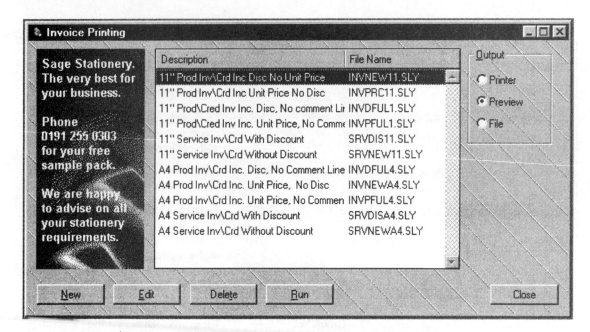

7.9 You are given the options of sending the invoice(s) straight to the Printer, seeing a Preview on screen (which you can edit for things like layout, font and so on) or creating a File copy of the invoice. (The file option has nothing to do with posting the invoice to the ledgers: it is a file copy of the invoice document.)

7.10 You get a list of possible layouts for your invoice in the Description box. You could also design your own layouts if you wished. We suggest you use the layouts with the codes:

(a) INVPFUL for Product invoices;

(b) SRVDIS for Service invoices.

You have two of each of these – one set for 11" paper and one set for A4 paper. Ask your tutor which your printer uses.

Alternatively your tutor might tell you to use a special layout designed by your college to suit its type of printers.

7.11 On the next page is an example of how an invoice might appear on headed paper using the format SRVDIS.

7.12 When you have selected your layout, click in the **Preview** circle and then click on **Run**. A screen display of your invoice will shortly appear. Click on **Zoom** and then Page Width to get a decent view of your invoice. If you are happy with what you see click on **Print.**

Managing the printer

7.13 When you click on the **Run** button the usual Windows Print window will appear. This gives you various options (number of copies, print quality and so on) partly depending on the type of printer(s) you have available. Look back at the section in Chapter 2 on printing if you are not sure what to do here.

7.14 When all the printing is finished a message *always* appears on the screen asking 'Do you want to update the ledgers with any outstanding entries?'. Click on Yes or No, depending upon which you want to do. You will get this message even if there is no updating to do. Updating the ledgers is the topic of the next section of this chapter.

Invoice	Page 1

BLITZ LTD

25 APPLE ROAD

LONDON

N12 3PP

D J HARGREAVES		Invoice No.	10042
6 COLLEGE PARK		Invoice/Tax Date	08/10/98
LONDON		Order No.	
NW10 5CD		**Account No.**	HARGRE

Service Details	Discount%	Net Amount	VAT Amount
Domestic services	0.00	43.50	7.61

Total Net Amount	43.50
Total VAT Amount	7.61
Carriage	0.00
Invoice Total	51.11

Extra copies

7.15   Once you have printed an invoice or credit note a Yes (or Y) will appear in the relevant row of the Print column in the main Invoicing window. This is a useful check if you are not sure whether or not an invoice has been printed, but *you can still print out a duplicate copy* of the invoice if you want to. An invoice might get lost in the post or damaged before it is sent, for example. To print another copy just select the invoice in the main Invoicing window, click on the **Print Invoices** button (even though you are not printing a batch), and proceed as usual.

Activity 5.10

Load Assignment 6 and print out your own copy of the invoice shown on the previous page.

---

8   UPDATING THE LEDGERS

8.1   When you inserted the invoice details, we told you to choose the Save option at the end of the input process for each invoice. When you click on the **Save** button after processing invoices (or credit notes), the details are *not* posted to the customers ledger or nominal ledger.

8.2   To post the details to the ledgers, you must click on the **Update Ledgers** button in the Invoicing window. Just like printing, you can post a batch of invoices (or credit notes) all at the same time, or you can select individual ones for posting. The following window will appear.

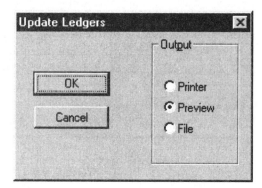

8.3   This procedure will generate a report telling you what has been posted. Decide whether you want a printed report or just a screen display or preview, or if you want a file copy of the report. Then click on OK or press Enter.

8.4   The Update Ledgers report is a list of the invoices or credit notes you have just posted to the ledger, showing details of each item posted. The listing shows:

(a)   the invoice number or credit note number;
(b)   the invoice date;
(c)   the customer's account code;
(d)   the transaction number given to the entry by the accounts;
(e)   the product code, if any;
(f)   the nominal ledger code for each transaction;
(g)   the department code (if any) for the transaction;
(h)   the description of the goods or services sold (and quantity);
(i)   the net amount of the invoice (or credit note);
(j)   the tax code for the VAT; and

(k)   the amount of the VAT;

(l)   the total of each invoice and a grand total for all invoices posted.

Activity 5.11

Load up Assignment 5 and confirm the balances on the following accounts.

GOODMA	0.00
HASLAM	0.00
Sales – Window cleaning (4001)	2,634.40

Now enter the following details exactly as instructed and **Save** each invoice.

Invoice.	Date	A/C	Details	Nominal code	Amount (net)
10053	25/10/98	GOODMA	Window cleaning	Delete any entry in the Nominal Code box so that it is left blank.	£100.00
10054	25/10/98	HASLAM	Window cleaning	4001	£100.00

(a)   What is the balance on the three accounts now?

(b)   In the Invoicing window click on **Clear** at the bottom of the screen and then on the option **Update Ledgers**. Say **Yes** to the message that appears and choose whether you want a print-out or just a screen preview.

What is the balance on the three accounts now?

(c)   Edit the invoice to GOODMA and insert the correct Nominal code. Update the ledgers for this invoice. What are the balances now?

---

9   UPDATING THE LEDGERS WITHOUT PRODUCING INVOICES

9.1   In some companies, invoices could be produced manually or by means of a different system, even when there is an accounting system capable of producing them. When this situation occurs, the accounting system is used to post invoice and credit note details to the customers ledger and nominal ledger, but not to produce invoices.

9.2   To update the ledgers without producing invoices, you should click on the **Customers** button in the main Sage window and then on the **Invoices** button in the Customers window. Entering and posting invoice and credit note details can then be done in the same way as entering and posting details of invoices and credit notes from suppliers. These procedures have already been described in Chapter 4.

10   REPORTS

10.1 When you have entered a batch of invoices or credit notes (or several batches of invoices or credit notes) you can print a list of the details, with batch totals. This is called a day book listing in a manual system. In Sage the relevant *Day Books* reports are called *Customer Invoices* and *Customer Credits*. These can be generated by clicking on the **Reports** button in the *Customers* window.

10.2 The procedure is exactly the same as the one described for producing Suppliers listings in the previous chapter. You can choose between detailed and summary reports, and specify a particular Date Range, Transaction Range, Customer Account Range or Nominal Account Range, just as before.

11   CUSTOMER QUERIES

11.1   Customers often telephone the accounts department of a company with queries about invoices or credit notes. These queries can often be answered by looking up the invoice details on the system. Typical queries could be:

(a)   I haven't received the credit note you promised. Have you sent it yet?

(b)   I haven't had an invoice from you yet. Can you tell me how much I will owe?

(c)   I haven't received your invoice yet. It might be lost in the post. Can you send me a duplicate copy?

Invoice or credit note details

11.2   You can look up the details of an invoice or credit note, to find out:

(a)   whether it is on the system; and
(b)   if so, whether the invoice or credit note has been printed (and so, presumably, sent) yet.

You can also obtain details of the invoice or credit note, if it is on the system. To look up these details, you can use **Invoicing** button to display a complete list of all invoices on the system and then, if you don't see the invoice you want immediately, use the **Criteria** button to specify the customer's account code as your condition (for example you would set your criterion as, say, Customer A/C = ADAMSE). You can narrow the field further by specifying additional criteria, such as a date range.

Example

11.3   You receive a telephone enquiry from T Roberts Ltd, asking about an invoice that had been expected but not yet received. You might know the customer's account reference number already. In the case study of Blitz Limited, the customer's code would probably be ROBERT. There are two ways of finding the details you want.

(a)   Call up the Invoicing window, set your criteria as Customer A/C = ROB★ and click in the **Criteria On** square and then the **Close** button. All accounts with codes beginning with the letters ROB will be shown and it should be a fairly easy matter to pick out and highlight the one you want. When it is highlighted click on the **Invoice** button or the **Service** button as appropriate. You will probably get a warning telling you that the invoice has been posted and that amendments will not be saved. You only want to *look* at the details, so just click on OK and the invoice window that you used to prepare the invoice will be displayed once more.

(b)   Alternatively click on the **Customers** button in the main Sage window. This too has a **Criteria** button and you might find it quicker to use this than to scroll right through the list until you find T Roberts' account. Once you find the account code click on it to highlight it and in successive windows click on **Activity**. You will see on screen details of all the invoices in T Roberts account. However this will not tell you whether the invoice has been printed yet. Take a note of the number and use the Invoicing window to find this information.

Duplicate invoices

11.4   We saw how to print extra copies of invoices in section 7 of this chapter.

12   CONCLUSION

12.1   If you can follow the instructions in this chapter, you should be ready to attempt **Assignment 2.**

12.2   Assignment 2 can be tackled in either of two ways:

(a)   using the Invoicing window for printing invoices and credit notes; or

(b)   using the Invoices options in the Customers window for entering and posting details of invoices and credit notes, but not for printing them.

Answers to activities

Answer 5.3

The screen should show the full details in the white box at the top left.

    W R W CATERING LTD
    11 STATION PARADE
    BARNET
    HERTS
    BT5 2KC

Re-read paragraph 4.8 if you don't have these details on screen. When you have managed to get all the details showing you can just click on Abandon.

Answer 5.4

You should have got an amount of £117.50 for ADAMSE (N/C 4001) and of £116.63 for GARDEN (N/C 4000). Although the net amount of both invoices is £100, GARDEN's record is set up to receive settlement discount of 5% and so the Sage package automatically charges VAT on the discounted amount (£100 − 5% = £95).

£95 × 17.5% = £16.63

Very well done if you were able to explain the results without looking at this solution. You can check the records of ADAMSE and GARDEN to confirm that one is set up to receive settlement discount and the other is not.

Answer 5.5

You should have got the amount £122.51. First, set up the customer's record to receive 5% settlement discount. Delivery address, order number, telephone number and contact name should be entered on the Order Details tab, but not before you have checked why the phone number shown above is different to the one contained in the customer record (0171-734 2043). The number may have changed, or it may have been entered into the system incorrectly, or it may just be an additional number. Likewise you should check whether the customer's record should be permanently amended to show the contact name Jennifer.

The other details are entered on the Footer details tab.

Answer 5.6

The initial balance should be £0.00. You should not have been able to find the invoice after doing (b), because you did not save it. The balance should be £0.00 throughout the activity, because you have not yet posted the invoice to any of the ledgers.

Answer 5.7

You should get the answer £50.20. The nominal code is 4100. The postcode is HA5 5DJ.

Answer 5.8

The three new credit notes should appear in red at the top of the Invoicing screen, following on from credit notes 1 to 3 (in spite of the dates).

Answer 5.9

(a)   Only invoices 10036 to 10039 should appear.
(b)   No invoices should appear.
(c)   Only 10043 and 10046 should appear.
(d)   Did you get the result you expected and wanted?
(e)   Credit notes 1 to 3 and invoices 10036 to 10052 should all appear.

Answer 5.11

(a)   It is the same as when you started because you have not posted anything yet.

(b)   GOODMA is still £0.00, because you did not include a nominal code and Sage did not know how to post the invoice. HASLAM has a balance of £117.50. The Sales – Window Cleaning account has increased by £100 to £2,734.40.

(c)   HASLAM remains the same as in (b). GOODMA now has a balance of £117.50 and the Sales – Window Cleaning account has increased by £100 to £2,834.40.

Chapter 6   Payments to suppliers

Chapter topic list

1   Source documents for recording payments

2   Locating invoices for payment. Aged analysis

3   Posting payments

4   Discounts

5   Credit notes

6   Payments on account

7   Payments when there is no invoice

8   Reports

9   Queries about payments

10   Conclusion

Learning objectives

On completion of this chapter you will be able to:

	Performance criteria	Range statement
• Identify the source documents you will need to process a payment to a supplier	19.1.2	19.1.2
• Locate unpaid invoices in the Suppliers ledger that are due for payment	19.2.1 to 19.2.3	19.2.1 to 19.2.5
• Post payments to suppliers in the appropriate Suppliers ledger accounts (and nominal ledger accounts)	19.1.1 to 19.1.7	19.1.1 to 19.1.6
• Record and post payments in full and part payments	19.1.1 to 19.1.7	19.1.1 to 19.1.6
• Record and post payments involving deductions for credit notes or early settlement discounts	19.1.1 to 19.1.7	19.1.1 to 19.1.6
• Record and post payments on account to suppliers (that is, payments in advance)	19.1.1 to 19.1.7	19.1.1 to 19.1.6
• Record and post cheque payments as bank transactions in the nominal ledger (for example, for cheque requisitions)	19.1.1 to 19.1.7	19.1.1 to 19.1.6
• Produce reports for payments	19.3.1 to 19.3.8	19.3.1 to 19.3.4
• Produce remittance advices	19.3.1 to 19.3.8	19.3.1 to 19.3.4
• Deal with queries from suppliers about payments	19.2.1 to 19.2.4	19.2.1 to 19.2.5

1   SOURCE DOCUMENTS FOR RECORDING PAYMENTS

1.1   Payments to suppliers should be recorded in the accounts after the cheque has been written, so that the cheque number can be entered as a transaction item. The main source document or documents you should have are:

(a)   a copy of the *invoice* or *invoices* for payment, and possibly a statement from the supplier listing all invoices still outstanding and unpaid;

(b)   a copy of any *credit note* or *credit notes* from the supplier; and

(c)   in the case of purchased goods, you might be required to check a copy of a *goods received note*, to confirm receipt of the goods that are being paid for.

1.2   The invoice must be signed or initialled by an *authorised* person, giving authority for the invoice to be paid. This signature could be written on the invoice itself, and dated. If any invoice has not been properly authorised, it should be referred to the supervisor in the accounts department.

1.3   A payment could be made for which there is an authorised *cheque requisition* form, instead of an invoice from a regular supplier with an account in the Suppliers Ledger. The procedures for recording such transactions in the accounts are different, and are explained later.

2   LOCATING INVOICES FOR PAYMENT. AGED ANALYSIS

2.1   If your supervisor tells you, say, to pay all invoices that have been outstanding for over one month, your first task would be to find the relevant source documents.

(a)   If your department keeps unpaid invoices in date order in a separate file, this is usually a simple manual task. You can take the invoices for payment out of the file.

(b)   Alternatively, you can identify which suppliers to pay by checking the records in the Suppliers Ledger. There are two ways of doing this.

Using the Criteria button

2.2   When you Click on the **Suppliers** button in the main window, you are presented with a screen listing the code, name, current balance, credit limit and contact name of all suppliers. At the bottom of the screen is a **Criteria** button. Click on this and then on the **Amounts** index tab and the following window appears.

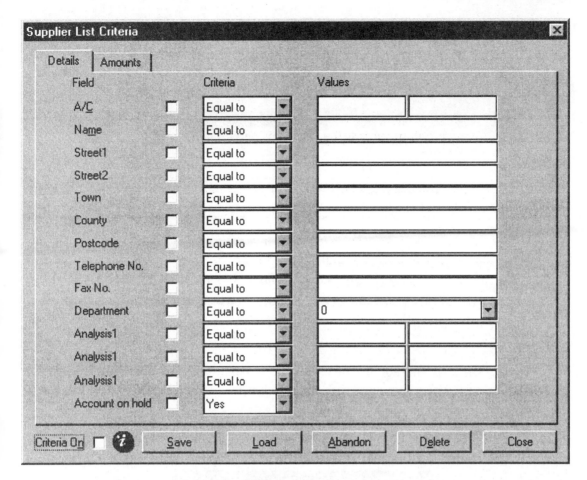

2.3   These options can be used to select only those accounts with specified amounts that have been outstanding for certain periods. For instance you might start by clicking in the Balance (Older) square, clicking in the Criteria On square and change 'equals' to 'greater than'. Leave Values as 0.00.

2.4   Click on **Close** and you are returned to the main screen where only those suppliers accounts containing invoices that have been outstanding for more than 120 days would be listed. You could make a note that these suppliers should be paid first. Then you could click in the 90 - 120 Days square and follow the same procedure to see what accounts had invoices more than 90 days old outstanding.

Changing the Program Date

2.5   The listing will calculate the number of outstanding days from the current date. Usually the 'current date' will be today's date according to the computer's internal clock and calendar. If you load up Sage it will show you the date towards the bottom right-hand corner. (If not, you don't have the Status Bar showing. Click on the **View** menu and then on Status Bar.)

2.6   However, suppose today's date was 7 November but you wanted to pay all invoices that had been outstanding for more than 120 days as at 31 October. You would need to make the computer think that it was 31 October to get the required information.

2.7   To do this click on the word **Settings** at the top of the screen. A menu drops down, the middle item of which is Change Program Date. Click on this and a window appears in which you can type the date you want – in our example 31/10/98. Then click on **OK** and note that the date shown at the foot of the screen has changed.

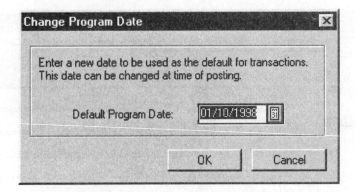

Activity 6.1

Load Assignment 1. Change the program date to 31/10/98.

Which suppliers have balances between £100 and £300?

Aged analysis

2.8   Alternatively (or in addition to) the criteria button approach you can obtain a listing of all accounts or selected accounts with the invoices analysed according to how long they have been outstanding.

2.9   Click on **Suppliers** and then on **Aged.** You will get the following dialogue box.

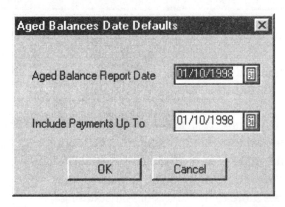

(a)   *Aged Balances Report Date.* This will show the Program Date which will be today's date unless you have changed it (see above).

You should enter the date you want to use to calculate the aged balances: the program will count back 30 days, 60 days, 90 days and so on from this date and analyse the balances accordingly. In the example above you would enter 311098 and you would get balances that were 30, 60, 90 etc days old as at 31/10/98.

(b)   *Include Payments Up To.* You might have paid lots of invoices in early November but this might not be relevant to your report on the state of affairs at the end of October. You might only wish to include payments made up to 31/10/98 (or another date): if so specify this here. This may seem a rather odd facility: it is useful for producing various management reports and for financial accounting reports that are beyond the scope of your studies at Foundation level.

Do not worry about this box. Unless told otherwise you should just enter the same date as you put in the box above.

2.10   Click on **OK** and the following report will appear.

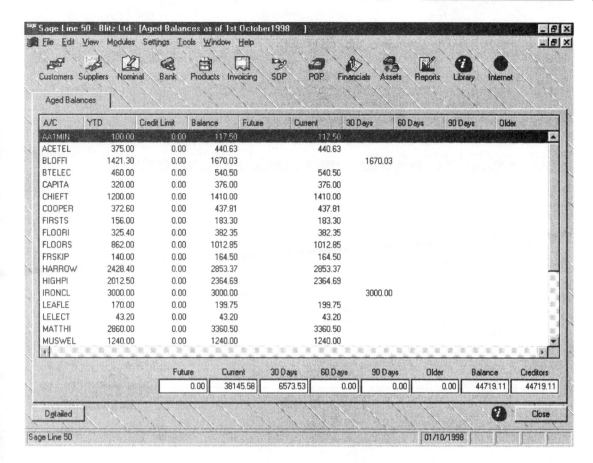

A/C	YTD	Credit Limit	Balance	Future	Current	30 Days	60 Days	90 Days	Older
AA1MIN	100.00	0.00	117.50		117.50				
ACETEL	375.00	0.00	440.63		440.63				
BLOFFI	1421.30	0.00	1670.03			1670.03			
BTELEC	460.00	0.00	540.50		540.50				
CAPITA	320.00	0.00	376.00		376.00				
CHIEFT	1200.00	0.00	1410.00		1410.00				
COOPER	372.60	0.00	437.81		437.81				
FIRSTS	156.00	0.00	183.30		183.30				
FLOORI	325.40	0.00	382.35		382.35				
FLOORS	862.00	0.00	1012.85		1012.85				
FRSKIP	140.00	0.00	164.50		164.50				
HARROW	2428.40	0.00	2853.37		2853.37				
HIGHPI	2012.50	0.00	2364.69		2364.69				
IRONCL	3000.00	0.00	3000.00			3000.00			
LEAFLE	170.00	0.00	199.75		199.75				
LELECT	43.20	0.00	43.20		43.20				
MATTHI	2860.00	0.00	3360.50		3360.50				
MUSWEL	1240.00	0.00	1240.00		1240.00				

	Future	Current	30 Days	60 Days	90 Days	Older	Balance	Creditors
	0.00	38145.58	6573.53	0.00	0.00	0.00	44719.11	44719.11

2.11 You can see at a glance how long each amount making up the current balance on each account has been outstanding.

Future

2.12 Sage is not clairvoyant, but if you are using dates for your reports that are prior to the real date it will know what transactions have been posted between your report date and the real date. Therefore an Aged Balances report will show you the total of such transactions in a **Future** box. For example, if you received and posted £5,000 of new invoices on 1 November, but ran a report on that day for 31 October the report would show an amount of £5,000 in the Future box. This *can* get a bit confusing: you need not worry about it for the purposes of the Case Study.

Print-outs

2.13 It may well have occurred to you that it would be handy to have a *print-out* of this information. If you scroll through the list you may also feel that accounts with nil balances may as well be excluded. Such a report can be obtained by using the **Reports** button in the Suppliers window. Get back to this by closing the Aged analysis window: just press Esc or click on Close.

2.14 First exclude any accounts with a nil balance. Do this by clicking on the Criteria button at the foot of the Suppliers window and setting the Balance option (on the Amounts index tab) as not equal to (!=) 0.00. Don't forget to click in the little square next to the Balance criterion. Then Click in the Criteria On square and then on **Close**. The only accounts listed will be those that have a balance other than 0.00. Select these by clicking on **Clear** and then **Swap**.

2.15 Now click on the **Report** button. A Supplier Reports window appears, as follows.

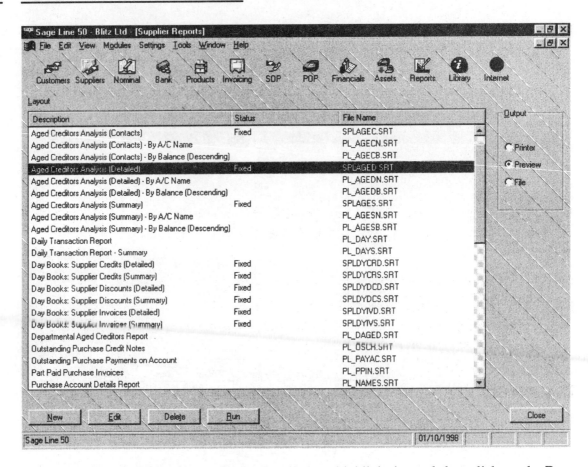

2.16 Click on Aged Creditors Analysis (Detailed) to highlight it, and then click on the **Run** button. Again you have to choose your 'report date' and 'payments up to' date as explained above. In a few moments an Aged Creditors report will be printed (or it can appear in preview for editing, or be sent to a file, depending on the Output choice you make).

2.17 You can of course get such a report for a variety of different selections of Suppliers. You just use the Criteria button to pick out those accounts you want included, select them and then proceed as described above.

Activity 6.2

It is a good idea to get some practice at using the Criteria button. Load up the data for, say, Assignment 2 in the Blitz case study and try getting listings of Suppliers' accounts according to a variety of criteria: all those with codes in the alphabetical range P to S, say, or all those with a balance over or under a certain amount, all those that do not have an address in London, or anything else you think of.

It is also a good idea to see what happens when you specify different dates for reports. Assignment 4 is a good one to use for this.

---

3   POSTING PAYMENTS

3.1 In the accounting system, payments to suppliers are posted to:

(a) the suppliers' individual accounts in the Suppliers Ledger;

(b) the creditors control account in the Nominal Ledger (there is a debit entry for payments in this account);

(c) the bank account in the Nominal Ledger (there is a credit entry in this account for cash payments).

3.2 To post a payment, you should have the following data:

    (a) the nominal ledger code for the bank account. In the Sage system case study, this is code 1200, which the program selects automatically as a default;

    (b) the supplier's account reference code;

    (c) the date of the payment;

    (d) if possible, the cheque number;

    (e) usually, the cheque amount.

3.3 If you want to check the previous transaction details on a supplier's account before recording the payment, you can use the **Activity** button.

Allocation of payments to invoices

3.4 Normally, a payment is made to pay off one or more outstanding invoices. Instead of just recording a payment in the supplier's account, the payment should be allocated to the invoice or invoices to which it relates.

How to post payments

3.5 If you Click on the **Bank** button in the main Sage window a bank accounts window will appear with a number of buttons and a list of all the company's bank accounts.

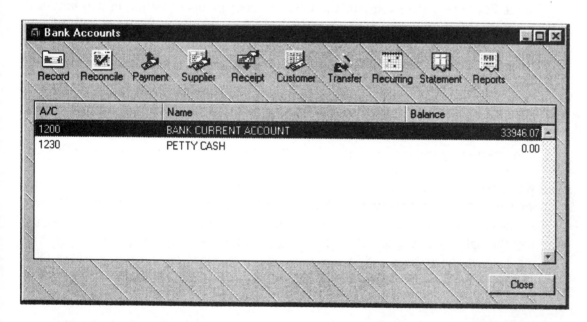

3.6 Click on the **Supplier** button and you will get a new window the top of which looks very much like a cheque book and the lower half of which tells you about outstanding invoices on a supplier's account.

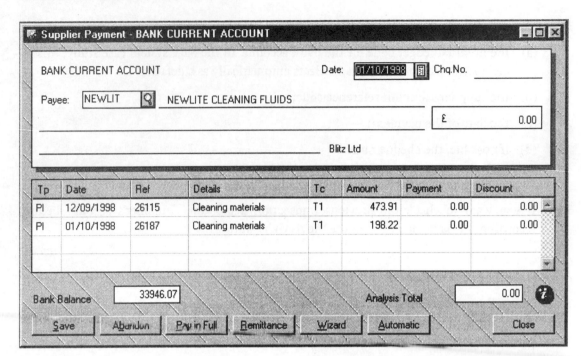

Most of the headings are self-explanatory. As you will see, the **Tp** column in the lower half of the screen identifies the type of transaction as a purchase invoice (PI), a purchase credit note (PC), or a purchase payment on account (PA).

3.7   When you first see this screen all the details will be blank and the cursor will be flashing in the **Payee** box. Here you type the supplier's code number (use the Finder button if you don't know the precise code). Press Tab. The supplier's full name will appear alongside the Payee box and the details of any outstanding invoices will appear in the lower half of the screen. The illustration above shows you what this will look like.

3.8   By default the **Date** box will show today's date (or the program date), but you can change this if you wish. If you do change it, the new date you enter will become the default date until you click on Close to shut down the window, so you probably won't have to change it for every entry you make.

3.9   When the date is the one you want, press Tab again and in the **Chq No.** box enter the number of the cheque you are posting. You will have to do this for *every* payment: after all, Sage will not know if you start a new cheque book with a new number sequence half-way through your postings. Do not neglect to enter the cheque number: it will then show up in the records and it is a very useful reference for keeping track of your company's money and for anybody else trying to make sense of your postings, such as your supervisor or an auditor.

3.10   Press Tab again and you are taken into a box with a pound sign. What you do next depends upon whether or not you have been told precisely *how much* to pay the supplier beforehand.

   (a)   If you know that the cheque you are entering is to be for, say, £500, *type in* 500 and press Tab.

   (b)   If you have been told to pay certain invoices, type nothing: just press Tab.

3.11   Look at the illustration above showing details for Newlite Cleaning Fluids. Two outstanding invoices are shown, one for £473.91 and the other for £198.22, a total of £672.18. The information and instructions you might have could be as follows.

   (a)   A cheque for £473.91 is to be sent to Newlite Cleaning Fluids. **OR**

(b) Any invoices received from Newlite Cleaning Fluids in September 1998 should be paid. **OR**

(c) The balance on the Newlite Cleaning Fluids account should be paid in full.

Predetermined cheque amount

3.12 If you have been told the amount of the cheque, type it into the box with the pound sign. Press Tab and two things will happen.

(a) Very satisfyingly, the amount that you typed in figures (eg '473.91') will appear in words ('Four hundred seventy-three Pounds and 91p'), just like on a real cheque.

(b) You will be taken to the first **Payment** box in the lower half of the screen. The amount shown (highlighted) in this box will at this point be 0.00. Look also at the Analysis Total box at the bottom of the window, which also shows 0.00 at this point.

3.13 Now click on the **Pay in Full** button at the bottom of the screen. The amount in the first Payment box (next to the invoice Amount box) will change to £473.91. The amount in the Analysis Total box will also change to £473.91. This, of course, is the total amount of the cheque you are paying.

3.14 The cursor, meanwhile will have moved down a line to the next Payment box and 0.00 will be highlighted. If you click on the Pay in Full button nothing will happen. Click on the Pay in Full button as much as you like but this will not change. This is because there is no difference between the amount in the £ sign box (the amount of the cheque) and the amount in the Analysis Total box: all the money available has already been allocated.

Remittance advices

3.15 If you want to print out a statement to send to the supplier indicating the invoices that are being paid you *must* do this now, before Saving the invoice. This is explained in more detail below.

Posting payments

3.16 So long as you have printed a remittance advice if you want to, you can now click on the **Save** button. The payment is then posted and the screen is cleared for the next payment. Payments will only be posted if the amount in the analysis total box equals the amount of the cheque.

Activity 6.3

(a) Load the data for Assignment 3. Change the program date to 31/10/98 if necessary. What is the balance on the Supplier account NEWLIT and the Bank account (1200)?

(b) Following the above instructions, enter the details for a cheque to NEWLIT for £473.91 dated 10 October 1998, cheque number 010203. Save your entry, then print out a remittance advice if you can.

(c) What is the balance on the account NEWLIT and the bank account now?

Paying specific invoices

3.17 Our second scenario suggested that you had been told to pay invoices with a September 1998 date only. If you look back to the illustration you will see that the only invoice that fits into this category is the one for £473.91. You proceed as follows.

   (a) When you reach the box with the pound sign, just press Tab, leaving the box blank.

   (b) The cursor will move to the September 1998 invoice's Payment box with an amount 0.00 highlighted.

   (c) Click on the Pay in Full button. The amount in the first Payment box will change to £473.91, and so will the amount in the box with the pound sign showing the amount that the cheque will be for, and the amount in the Analysis Total box.

   (d) The cursor will move to the next Payment box, beside the outstanding invoice amount of £198.22.

   (e) You *do not* want to pay this second invoice because it is not a September 1998 invoice. Therefore (unless you first want to print a remittance advice note) just click on the **Save** button. The payment is posted and the screen will clear for the next entry.

Activity 6.4

Load Assignment 3 again. Change the program date to 31/10/98 if necessary. Following the above, pay any invoices received from Newlite Cleaning Supplies in September 1998. Cheque number is 010203. Also pay any received from British Telecom in September 1998. Cheque number is 010204.

Paying off the balance

3.18 The final scenario suggested that you were told to pay off the balance on the account. The procedure is exactly the same as the procedure for paying specific invoices, except that instead of Saving at step (e) you click on Pay in Full. You continue to do this for each invoice listed until all the invoice Amount boxes on screen have an equivalent amount in the Payment box. The cheque amount and the amount in the Analysis Total box will increase by the amount of each invoice that you Pay in Full. When all the invoices shown are paid, print a remittance advice if you want to and then click on the **Save** button.

3.19 To finish processing payments click on the **Close** button or press Esc. You will see a message on screen asking if you are sure you wish to exit. Click on Yes or press Y to confirm that you do wish to close this window. (If you decide you *don't* wish to exit, press Enter or N or click on No.)

Part payments

3.20 If you had been instructed, say, to pay Newlite Cleaning Fluids an amount of only £150 (perhaps because of some dispute with the supplier) this would not cover either of the two invoices that are outstanding. In this case you make a part payment. The procedure is exactly as for any other predetermined cheque amount. Enter the amount of the cheque in the pound sign box then press Tab until you reach the Payment box of the invoice you want to part pay. Although you are not paying the invoice in full, click on the Pay in Full button and £150 will appear in the Payment box. Although you won't see it happen on screen, when you post the invoice the outstanding amount will be reduced by £150.

3.21 Another permutation might be if you wanted to pay the whole of some invoices but only a part of others. Tab through the box with the pound sign, leaving it blank. When you are in the Payment box for an invoice you want to pay in full, click on the Pay in Full button. When you are in the Payment box of an invoice you want to *part* pay, *type in* the amount you want to part pay yourself and press Tab. The amount of the total cheque, and in the Analysis Total box, will increase accordingly every time you do this.

Activity 6.5

Load Assignment 3 again. Change the program date to 31/10/98 if necessary.

Pay off the balance on the Newlite Cleaning Fluids account. Cheque number is 914785.

Pay Prairie Couriers Ltd £50.

What is the balance on these two accounts, now?

Remittances

3.22 A remittance advice can be sent with a payment to a supplier, indicating the invoices that are being paid, together with discounts taken and credit notes being used. It is, quite simply, a statement to show what the payment is for.

3.23 To produce and print a remittance advice, once you have entered (but *not saved*) the details of a payment click on the **Remittance** button. The following window appears.

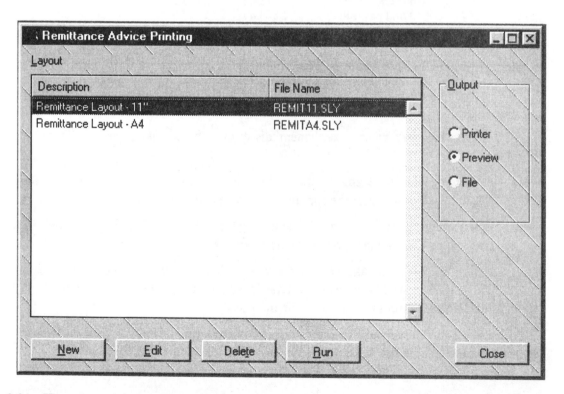

3.24 You must pick one of the default layouts, REMIT11 or REMITA4, depending on your printer's paper size, or use another one (perhaps one set up by your college). Choose what sort of Output you want – printed, preview or file – and then click on OK.

Activity 6.6

Load Assignment 3. Change the program date to 31/10/98 if necessary.

Pay Newlite Cleaning Fluids £198.22. Cheque number is 246264.

Print a remittance advice.

4   DISCOUNTS

4.1   As mentioned in Chapter 4, some suppliers offer a discount for early payment of an invoice. For example, payment terms of '30 days net, 3% discount 7 days' means that the invoice should be paid in full within 30 days, but a discount of 3% is available if payment is made within 7 days of the invoice date.

4.2   When such a discount (a 'settlement discount') is taken, you will need to calculate the amount of the discount. VAT rules stipulate that VAT should be charged on the discounted *net* amount (whether or not the discount is taken). Check that you can do the calculation accurately. For example, suppose that a supplier offers a 3% settlement discount for the following invoice.

	Taking the discount	Not taking the discount
	£	£
Net amount	1,600.00	1,600.00
Discount (3%)	(48.00)	
VAT-able amount	1,552.00	
VAT at 17.5%	271.60	271.60
Total payable	1,823.60	1,871.60

4.3   In other words, if you pay up within 7 days you can save your company £48. The VAT authorities are also happy, because your supplier's accounts show a VAT *output* (sales) tax amount of £271.60 and yours show a VAT *input* (purchases) tax amount of £271.60, whether you take the discount or not.

4.4   To record a payment when a settlement discount is being taken the procedure is as follows.

(a)   As before, click on **Bank** in the main window and then **Supplier** in the Bank Accounts window. Enter the supplier code, date and cheque number.

(b)   When you get to the box with the pound sign in it leave it blank by pressing Tab to take you on the Payment box. Make no entry here.

(c)   Press Tab again to take you to the Discount box. Type in the amount of the discount in pounds (for example type in 48.00). You may have to calculate this yourself, or it might be shown on the invoice already.

(d)   Press Tab. The amount in the Payment box will automatically be calculated as the amount of the invoice minus the discount. The cursor will move to the next payment line.

(e)   **Save** the payment as usual.

Activity 6.7

Load Assignment 3. Change the program date to 31/10/98 if necessary.

Pay off the full balance on the account SAMURA, taking a discount of 5% on the total amount owing. The cheque number is 222354

How much do you actually pay? What is the VAT element?

5   CREDIT NOTES

5.1   When a credit note has been posted to a supplier's account, this can be offset against an invoice that is being paid. For example, if a supplier has submitted an invoice for £100 and there is a credit note for £25, only £75 has to be paid to settle the account. Credit notes that have been posted to suppliers' accounts will appear with invoices in the list on the cheque screen.

5.2   To use a credit note, enter the details on the cheque in the usual way, leaving the cheque amount box with the pound sign blank by Tabbing through it. Press tab until you reach the *credit note's* Payment box. Click on the **Pay in Full** button. You will see the amount in the Payment box change to the amount of the credit note – in the example given it would be £25. However, look at the *Analysis Total* box. This will have changed to a *negative* amount equal to the amount of the credit note (–25, in the example). The amount in the cheque amount box will be 0.00 at this point.

5.3   Now Tab up or down to the Payment box of the invoice you want to pay. Click on **Pay in Full**. The amount in the invoice's Payment box will now be equal to the amount of the invoice (£100, say), but the Analysis Total box and the cheque amount box will show the amount of the invoice less the amount of the credit note: £75 in our example.

5.4   If the amount of the credit note is greater than the amount of any outstanding invoice, proceed as follows. Without entering a cheque amount, Tab down to the Payment boxes of the invoices in question and click on Pay in Full. Then Tab to the Payment box of the credit note and *type in* the amount shown in the Analysis Total box. Press Tab.

5.5   The cheque amount will then be nil – in other words no cheque needs to be sent. This will be relatively rare, but if it happens Tab back up to the cheque number box and clear any number you typed there by pressing Delete. When you click on **Save** this has the effect of clearing off the invoices that have been offset against the credit note, and reducing the amount of credit outstanding.

Activity 6.8

Load up Assignment 3. Change the program date to 31/10/98 if necessary.

Pay Trojan Secretarial Services £141. Cheque number is 147853.

---

6   PAYMENTS ON ACCOUNT

6.1   Occasionally, a payment might be made to a supplier 'on account', before an invoice is received. When this happens, the amount shown in the cheque amount box will still be greater than the amount shown in the Analysis Total box, even after you have paid any invoices you want to pay in full

6.2   To make a payment on account, enter the supplier, date and cheque number details and then *type into* the pound sign box the total amount of the cheque you want to pay, including both the amount of the payment on account and the amount of any outstanding invoices (less credit notes, if any). You may have to use the calculator beforehand to find out this total.

6.3   When the total cheque amount is entered Tab down to the Payment box and click on **Pay in Full** for each invoice in the normal way. When you have finished, assuming that you do not want to generate a remittance advice (see below), click on **Save**. A message like the one shown below will appear. Click on Yes (or key in Y or press Enter) to accept this, if appropriate.

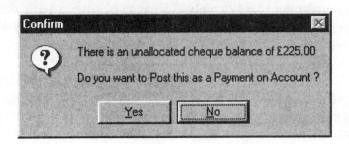

6.4   If you do want to send a remittance advice you must do this *before* you click on Save. Use the **Remittance** button in the way already described. You will not get a message about the payment on account, but it *will* be shown on the remittance advice in any case.

Offsetting payments on account against invoices

6.5   Later, when invoices have been received, the payment on account should be offset against them. This is done in the same way as using a credit note. Without entering a cheque amount, Tab down to the Payment boxes of the invoices in question and click on Pay in Full. Then Tab to the payment on account item, and *type in* the *smaller* of:

(a)   the total of the payment on account; and
(b)   the amount now shown in the Analysis Total box.

6.6   If the payment on account is not large enough to cover the newly-received invoices there will now be an amount shown on the cheque to make up the difference.

If the amount of the payment on account still exceeds the amount of any invoices received the cheque amount will be nil – in other words no cheque will be sent. Again, this will be relatively rare, but if it happens Tab back up to the cheque number box and clear it by pressing Delete. If you click on **Save** this has the effect of clearing off the invoices that have been offset against the payment on account, and reducing the amount of the outstanding payment on account.

Activity 6.9

Load up Assignment 6. Change the program date to 31/10/98 if necessary.

Pay the Leaflet Company £500 (cheque number 278400), part of which is a payment on account. Note down how much.

Post an invoice for leaflets dated 5 November 1998 (number WE4582) received from The Leaflet Company for £700 (gross). The Nominal account is the Printing account.

Change the program date to 15/11/98 and clear the balance on this supplier's account (cheque number 278487).

Required

(a)   How much was the payment on account?
(b)   What is the amount of the cheque needed to clear the balance?

---

7 PAYMENTS WHEN THERE IS NO INVOICE

7.1 Payments are sometimes made against a cheque requisition, not an invoice.

(a) If an invoice will be received in due course, the payment can be entered as a payment on account, as described above.

(b) If there will not be an invoice, *there should be no entry for the transaction in the suppliers ledger*, because the suppliers ledger is for credit transactions only.

7.2 A cheque payment for a bank transaction that will not be processed through the suppliers ledger should be recorded directly to the nominal ledger accounts. The payment should be processed as follows.

(a) Click on the **Bank** button in the main window.

(b) If different bank accounts are used for nominal ledger payments and Supplier payments, make sure the correct one is highlighted. (Only one account is used in the Blitz case study.)

(c) Click on the **Payment** button in the Bank Accounts window.

7.3 The following screen will appear.

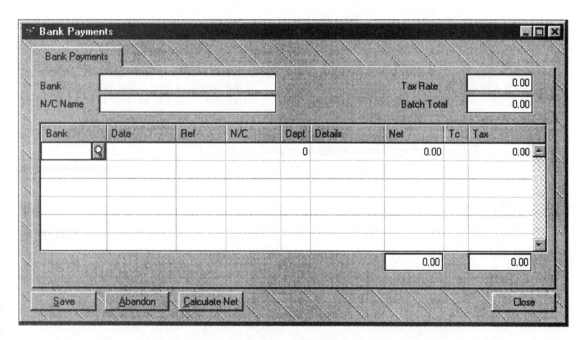

7.4 The cursor begins in the Bank column with the usual finder button. This is because many businesses make non-suppliers ledger payments from a separate bank account to the main one for purchases, although this does not apply in the case of Blitz, where you would simply choose A/C 1200 as usual.

7.5 Enter the **Date** in the usual way. The **Ref** should be the cheque number.

7.6 Press Tab again to take you to the **N/C** box. Here you enter the nominal ledger account code for the account to which the payment refers. For example, a cheque payment for the hire of a motor car should be given the nominal account code 7401 in the Sage system. This is the account code for Car Hire expenses. As usual, a list of codes can be displayed on screen by clicking on the Finder button or pressing the F4 function key.

7.7 In the Blitz case study you can Tab straight through the **Dept** box, but you should type in an appropriate brief description of what the payment is for in **Details**.

7.8   In the **Net** box you have two options.

(a)   Enter the *net amount of the payment (excluding VAT)* and press Tab. The cursor will move to the **T/c** (Tax code) box. The default code T1 for standard rate VAT will already be shown and the **Tax** box will already show VAT calculated at this rate. You can, however alter the tax code (usually to T0 for zero rated items). If you do this and press Tab the VAT will automatically be recalculated at the appropriate rate.

(b)   Alternatively you can enter the *total payment inclusive of VAT* in the **Net** box. Before pressing Tab click on the **Calc Net** button at the foot of the window. This will automatically calculate VAT at the standard rate and divide the total amount that you entered into net and VAT amounts. The tax code T1 will be shown in the **T/c** box. You can change this to another rate (in which case the figures will be recalculated) if necessary.

7.9   When you click on **Save** the transactions will be automatically posted to the appropriate nominal ledger accounts:

Credit: Bank Account (probably code 1200)
Debit: Nominal ledger account specified in the N/C field for the transaction.

Activity 6.10

Your supervisor has asked you, on 5 October 1998, to record a cheque payment to Goodtime Ltd for £1,410.00 (£1,200.00 net plus £210.00 for VAT at the standard rate.) The cheque is for UK Entertainment (nominal ledger code 7403). There is no invoice, and the request for payment has been submitted on a cheque requisition form. The cheque number is 345432.

Record this transaction, following the relevant instructions above for the version of Sage that you are using. (It does not matter which Assignment you have loaded.)

---

8   REPORTS

8.1   To see on screen a list of all the *transactions* on the bank account, click on **Nominal,** highlight account number 1200 and then click on **Activity**.

To get an equivalent print-out, click on **Nominal** as before, click on **Reports,** and choose Nominal Activity from the options you are offered. You will need to specify the relevant date range and account range (1200 to 1200).

8.2   To get reports on *payments* click on **Bank** in the main window, ensure the account you want is highlighted (A/c 1200 in the Blitz case study), and then click on **Reports**. The following window will appear offering you lots of options.

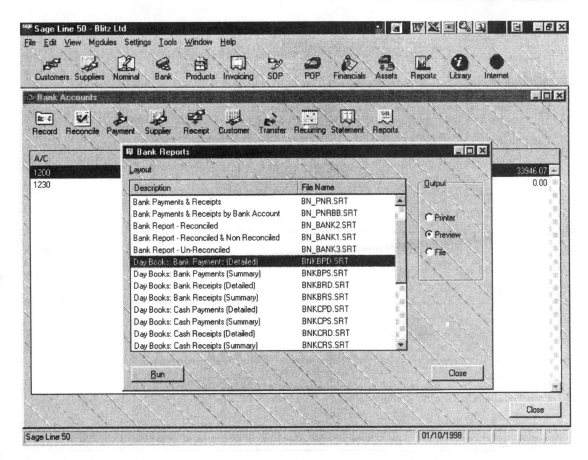

8.3   In the context of this chapter you would probably want Day Books: Bank Payments (Detailed). Highlight this, click on **Run** and (if necessary) specify the range(s) you want your report to cover. For a payments report the important specification is Date range.

9   QUERIES ABOUT PAYMENTS TO SUPPLIERS

9.1   You might be asked to deal with a query from a supplier who wants to know when you are going to pay an outstanding invoice.

9.2   Simply highlight the account in the main supplier window and click on Activity. this should show you how much is owed to the supplier, and for how long the payment has been outstanding or when invoices were paid.

10   CONCLUSION

10.1   If you think you can follow the instructions in this chapter, you should now be ready to attempt Assignment 3.

10.2   If you haven't yet done the exercises in this chapter, you can do so before you start the Assignment.

Answers to activities_____

Answer 6.1

AA1MIN, FIRSTS, FRSKIP, LEAFLE, PRAIRI, and TROJAN.

Clear the Criteria settings and turn them off when you have achieved this answer.

Answer 6.3

(a) The initial balances should be:

NEWLIT: £672.13
Bank   £33,946.07

(b) You cannot print out a remittance advice after you have saved a bank transaction.

(c) The balances should now be:

NEWLIT: £198.22
Bank   £33,472.16

Answer 6.5

The balances should be nil and £55.16.

Answer 6.7

The cheque is for £3,044.75. The discount has to be allocated between three separate items: £82.50 + £56.25 + £21.50 = £160.25. You should have used the (F4) calculator button.

There is no VAT on insurance. You could check this by finding the transaction numbers (Suppliers ... Activity), which are numbers 76, 77 and 78 and then looking up these numbers by clicking on Financials.

Well done if you got this activity completely right.

Answer 6.8

You should take advantage of the credit note, as explained above.

Answer 6.9

(a)   £300.25
(b)   £399.75

Could you remember how to post an invoice from a supplier?

Chapter 7   Receipts from customers

Chapter topic list

1   Receipts of invoice payments

2   Credit notes and customer receipts

3   Discounts

4   Returned cheques

5   Refunding paid invoices

6   Writing off small amounts

7   Account balances

8   Payments with order (bank receipts)

9   Reports

10   Conclusion

Learning objectives

On completion of this chapter you will be able to:

	Performance criteria	Range statement
• Record the receipt of payments from credit customers, and post the details to the relevant account in the Customers ledger (and the appropriate accounts in the nominal ledger)	19.1.1 to 19.1.7	19.1.1 to 19.1.6
• Take into account credit notes used by customers when making a payment	19.1.1 to 19.1.7	19.1.1 to 19.1.6
• Record early settlement discounts taken by customers	19.1.1 to 19.1.7	19.1.1 to 19.1.6
• Record payments on account by customers	19.1.1 to 19.1.7	19.1.1 to 19.1.6
• Deal with bounced cheques	19.1.1 to 19.1.7	19.1.1 to 19.1.6
• Deal with refunds for fully paid invoices	19.1.1 to 19.1.7	19.1.1 to 19.1.6
• Write off small unpaid balances on a customer's account	19.1.1 to 19.1.7	19.1.1 to 19.1.6
• Find the current unpaid balance on a customer's account by searching the sales ledger file	19.2.1 to 19.2.4	19.2.1 to 19.2.5
• Enter and post details of bank receipts other than payments by credit customers	19.1.1 to 19.1.7	19.1.1 to 19.1.6
• Produce reports for amounts received	19.3.1 to 19.3.8	19.3.1 to 19.3.4

1   RECEIPTS OF INVOICE PAYMENTS

1.1   When customers make payments for invoices, the receipt should be recorded in the Customers ledger. The information you will need to post a receipt is as follows.

(a)   The nominal ledger code of the bank account into which the payment will be made. In the Blitz case study, this code is 1200.

(b)   The name of the customer and the customer's account reference code, which must already be on the Customers Ledger.

(c)   The date of the receipt.

(d)   The cheque number (although this is not essential).

(e)   The cheque amount.

(f)   The amount of early settlement discount taken, if any.

1.2   You will also usually be given information about which invoice (or invoices) is being paid. The customer will possibly give the invoice reference number, or send a remittance advice note with the payment. The customer should also identify any credit notes that are being used.

1.3   Click on the **Bank** button in the main Sage window. As you learned in the previous chapter this gives a list of all the company's bank accounts. If there is more than one, highlight the one to which customer receipts are posted (probably account 1200, as in the Blitz case study) and then click on the **Customer** button. The following window will appear.

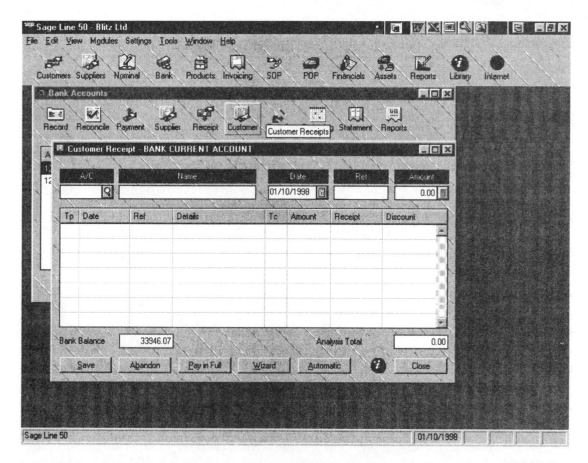

1.4   The cursor will be positioned at the box for A/C at the top left-hand side of the window. Here you enter the customer account code. Use the Finder button if you do not know this. When you enter a code and press Tab the full name of the customer appears automatically in the Name box and details of any outstanding transactions on the account appear in the lower half of the screen.

The Tp column shows the type of transaction on each line:

(a) SI means sales invoice;
(b) SC means sales credit note;
(c) SA means sales payment on account.

1.5 Enter the Date of payment as a six-digit code in the format DDMMYY or use the calendar button. By default this field will show today's date, as recorded in the computer system, but you can alter this. If you do so the new date will appear each time you start a fresh receipt until you close the window, so there is no need to change it every time.

1.6 Pressing Tab takes you to the Ref box. Here you can enter something like the customer's cheque number or the number of the customer's remittance advice or the number of the invoice being paid, or some other identifying reference. *Do not* leave this field blank: enter a unique reference of some kind.

Allocating receipts

1.7 When you reach the Amount box you have two options.

(a) If you can see at a glance that the amount of the cheque that you have received is the same as the amount of the outstanding invoice(s) shown in the lower half of the screen, leave the Amount box empty: just press Tab.

(b) If you are not sure what invoices are being paid it is safer to key in the amount of the cheque in the Amount box and press Tab. (A £ sign is not required.)

1.8 You must now allocate the receipt of the customer's payment to the outstanding invoice or invoices in the account, to indicate which invoice or invoices have been paid. The procedure is just like the procedure for allocating payments, as described in the previous chapter.

1.9 When you press Tab you will be taken to the **Receipt** box and an amount of 0.00 will be highlighted. If you click on the **Pay in Full** button this will change to the full amount of the invoice.

(a) If you left the Amount box blank this will also change to the amount of the invoice, as will the amount in the Analysis Total box. Press Tab again to move to the next line and repeat the procedure until the amount in the Amount box and the Analysis Total box equal the amount of your receipt. Click on **Save** and the screen will clear.

(b) If you did key in the amount of the receipt in the Amount box there are three possibilities.

(i) If the amount you entered was *less than* the amount of any invoice, it is a part payment by the customer. When you click on the **Pay in Full** button the amount you keyed in will appear in the Receipt box and in the Analysis Total box. There is no more money to allocate so you can just click on **Save**.

(ii) If the amount you keyed in was exactly the *same as* the amount of an invoice (or the same as the total of several invoices), then clicking on the **Pay in Full** button for the invoice or invoices will make an amount equal to the amount of the invoice(s) appear in the Receipt box and the Analysis Total box. Click on **Save** when there is no more money to allocate.

(iii)   If the amount you keyed in was *greater than* the total of all the outstanding invoices you have received a payment on account. Click on the **Pay in Full** button each time you Tab to the next Receipt box until any outstanding invoices are paid. The total will accumulate in the Analysis Total box, but when you have finished the Amount box will still show a greater total than the Analysis Total box. Click on **Save** and you will get a message telling you that there is an unallocated cheque balance of £X, and asking if you want to post it as a payment on account. Assuming that this is what you want, click on Yes.

1.10   This might sound complicated, but it is not really when you start using the system. The following table summarises what we have said so far.

Amount received	Amount(s) outstanding	Action
£254.31	£254.31	Leave the Amount box blank and Tab to the Receipt box beside the invoice amount £254.31. Click on Pay in Full then Save.
£500	£200 £300	You can see at a glance that what you have received is the same as the amount outstanding. Proceed as in the previous example for the two invoice amounts.
£193.46	£247.82 £193.46	The customer is clearly paying the second of the two invoices. Leave the Amount box blank and Tab to the Receipt box beside the amount £193.46. Click on Pay in Full and then Save.
£752.57	£466.18 £286.39	Key in the amount £752.57 in the Amount box and press Tab. Click on Pay in Full for each of the two invoices. The total in the Analysis Box will show £466.18 the first time you do this and increase to £752.57 the second time. The two invoices have been paid in full. Click on Save.
£200 (Part payment)	£350	Key in the amount £200 in the Amount box and press Tab. Click on Pay in Full. The amount in the Receipt box will show £200, as will the total in the Analysis Box. Click on Save. When you next call up the account it will show that £150 is still outstanding.
£500 (Payment on account)	£350	Key in the amount £500 in the Amount box and press Tab. Click on Pay in Full. The amount in the Receipt box will show £350, as will the total in the Analysis Box. However the Amount box will still show £500. Click on Save and respond Yes when you get a message asking if you want to post a payment on account of £150.

Activity 7.1

Load Assignment 6 and find out the balances on the bank account and the debtors ledger control account.

Post the following receipts from customers, all dated 15/11/98, following the procedures described above. Use the number of the first invoice that is being paid as your reference number.

ASPINA £211.50
BRADLE £500.00
DCSROO £200.00
ELITEC   £941.11
ROSEAL £146.00

What are the balances on the bank account and the debtors ledger control account now?

Print out a report of the activity on the ELITEC account.

2 CREDIT NOTES AND CUSTOMER RECEIPTS

2.1 When a customer has been given a credit note, the details of the credit note should be recorded already in the customer's account. The customer will probably deduct the value of the credit note from his next payment of an invoice. The payment will therefore cover the invoice less the credit note value.

2.2 The best way of recording a receipt in the customer's account where a credit note is being used is as follows.

(a) Enter the *actual cheque amount* in the Amount box.

(b) Tab down to the Receipt box of the credit note transaction and click on **Pay in Full**.

(c) Tab to the Receipt box of the other outstanding invoice or invoices and click on **Pay in Full** until the total amount of the cheque is used up.

Activity 7.2

Load up Assignment 3.

You have received a cheque for £1,762.50 from Royal Properties Ltd. Post this receipt as you think appropriate.

---

3 DISCOUNTS

3.1 A customer might take advantage of an early settlement discount, when this is offered. When a customer takes a discount, you will need to be informed of the amount of discount that has been taken. (You might also be asked to check that the customer has calculated the discount correctly. You can do this with the calculator buttons if you like.)

3.2 Recording a receipt net of discount is similar to recording a payment to a supplier net of discount.

(a) In the Discount box type in the amount of the discount in pounds. Press Tab.

(b) The Receipt box will automatically show the reduced balanced due.

Activity 7.3

Load up Assignment 3.

You have decided to offer Harvey-Sagar Developments a settlement discount of 2% on all future invoices.

(a) Amend the record of this customer accordingly.

(b) Post an invoice to Harvey-Sagar Developments dated 15 November 1998 for £850 (net) for Office Cleaning. (Accept the default invoice number offered by Sage.)

(c) Post a receipt dated 20 November 1998 from Harvey-Sagar Developments for £2,694.28, following the instructions above.

---

4 RETURNED CHEQUES

4.1 Occasionally, a cheque received from a customer might be 'bounced' and returned by the bank marked 'Refer to Drawer'. The customer's bank is refusing to pay over the money because there are insufficient funds in the customer's bank account.

4.2 When a cheque bounces, the receipt will already have been recorded in the customer's account. This must now be corrected.

4.3 Click on **Tools** at the top of the main window and choose the option **Write Off, Refund, Return** from the menu that drops down.

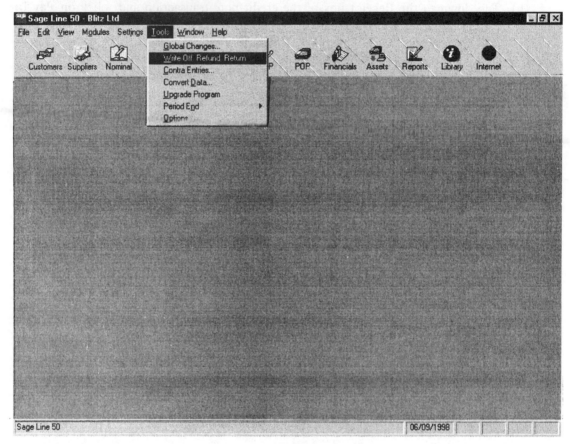

You are then asked to choose whether amendments will be made to the Sales ledger or the Purchase ledger. Click on **Next** when you have done so.

4.4 If you choose the Sales ledger you are given a list to scroll down. This includes the item Customer Cheque Returns. Highlight this and click on the **Next** button at the foot of the window. A list of customer accounts will appear. Highlight the one concerned and click on Next. This takes you to the following window.

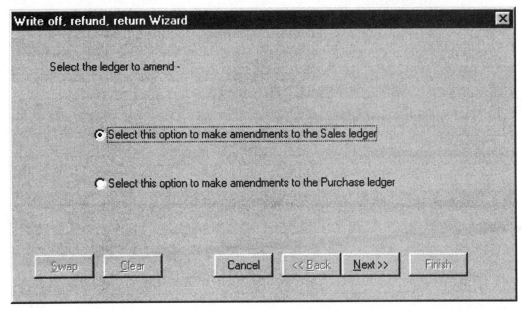

Look through the list displayed to find the appropriate transaction or transactions (the one(s) in respect of which the bounced cheque was received) and click on them to highlight them. Then click on Next and you will get a summary of what you are asking to be done. If you are happy with this you click on **Finish** to post the transaction. If not there is a **Back** option, allowing you to go back through these steps and change your decisions as necessary.

Activity 7.4

Load Assignment 6.

It is 31 October 1998. A cheque from A Wyche for £88.13 has bounced.

(a)   What is the initial balance on A Wyche's account and on the bank account?

(b)   Record the bounced cheque, following the instructions given above.

(c)   What is the balance on the two accounts now?

(d)   How is the transaction shown in A Wyche's customer's ledger account?

---

5   REFUNDING PAID INVOICES

5.1   To cancel an *unpaid* invoice, you should issue a credit note for the same amount.

5.2   However, when an invoice has been paid and it is subsequently decided that the customer should be given a refund in full, it is too late to issue a credit note and a different procedure is required to account for the refund.

5.3   Click on **Tools.** Then choose **Write Off, Refund, Return** and proceed exactly as described in the previous section, except that this time you choose **Customer Invoice Refunds**.

5.4   Details of all *fully-paid* invoices for the chosen customer will appear on screen. Click on the item to which the refund applies to highlight it and then click on the **Next** button. You are then asked which bank account you want to post the adjustment to. Choose 1200 for the case study. Then you get a summary of what you have said you want to do and are asked to confirm it by clicking on **Finish** (or Back if you are not happy).

5.5   The effect of this is as follows.

(a) A sales credit note is posted to the account in the Customers ledger, with the same reference as the refunded invoice, and showing 'Refund' in the details column. A dummy sales invoice is posted to the same account, and is automatically allocated in full to the credit note. The details column shows 'Allocation - Refund'. The sales turnover to date on the account is reduced by the amount of the refund.

(b) The appropriate Nominal ledger account for sales is reduced by (debited with) the amount refunded. The nominal ledger bank control account, out of which the refund is being paid, will be credited with the amount refunded (in other words the bank balance will be reduced).

Activity 7.5

Load Assignment 6.

What is the balance on the accounts for Bridgford and Co and Sales - Contract cleaning?

On 31 October 1998 it has been decided that Bridgford and Co should be given a refund for invoice number 10003.

Post this transaction. What is the new balance on Bridgford and Co's account and on the Sales - Contract cleaning account?

How does this transaction appear in Bridgford and Co's account?

Are any other accounts affected?

---

6   WRITING OFF SMALL AMOUNTS

6.1   It is quite common in practice for customers to pay less than they owe, but only by a small amount. Typically, a customer might ignore the amount in pence on an invoice. For example, a customer might remit a cheque for £76.00 to pay an invoice for £76.38.

6.2   When a company receives payments that are less than the invoiced amount, but only by a small amount, a decision might be taken to 'forget' about the unpaid amount, because it is too small to worry about. It would cost too much to chase the customer for payment and the effort wouldn't be worthwhile. The unpaid amount is therefore written off as a 'bad' or uncollectable debt.

6.3   Choose the **Tools** menu and then **Write Off, Refund, Return.** Pick the option *Write off Customer Transactions below a value* in the Sales ledger list.

6.4   A screen prompt asks you to 'Enter the value below which a transaction will be written off', and you must key in the amount below which the balance on any customer account will be written off as uncollectable. The value can be as little as 0.02 (ie. £0.02).

6.5   When you have keyed in this write-off and clicked on **Next**, the screen will automatically display every customer account and transaction for which the unpaid balance is currently less than the value you have entered.

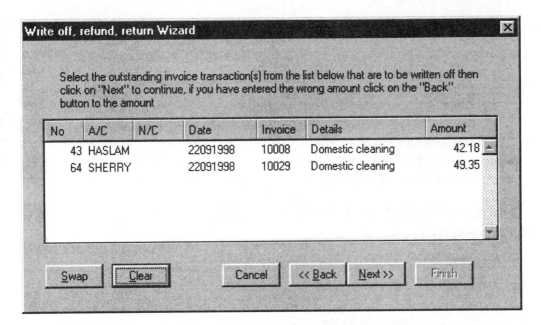

6.6   To write off the unpaid balance on any account displayed on the screen, highlight the account by clicking on it. To highlight all the transactions shown, click on the **Swap** button at the foot of the window.

6.7   When you have made your selection or selections, click on the **Next.** A further screen will ask you to confirm the write off. Click on Finish if you are happy with this.

   (a)   The account(s) in the Customers ledger will be credited with the amount written off, with 'Bad Debt Write Off' shown as the details.

   (b)   In the Nominal ledger, the debtors control account (code 1100) will be credited with the amount written off, and the bad debt write off account (code 8100) is debited.

Activity 7.6

Load up Assignment 5.

It is 31/10/98.

Post the following receipts from customers.

ASPINA   £105.00
CHADWI   £176.00
NORRIS   £1,087.27

Now, following the instructions above, write off any balances below £1.00.

What is the total amount written off?

Which nominal ledger accounts are affected?

---

7   ACCOUNT BALANCES

7.1   You might be asked to find out what is the unpaid balance on a customer's account. A customer might telephone, for example, and ask how much he owes. Or your supervisor might ask how much a particular customer still owes. The simplest way of finding the unpaid balance on an customer's account is to use the **Activity** button.

7.2   This gives a window similar to the Suppliers Ledger Activity window, which allows you to find the current unpaid balance on any supplier account in the Suppliers Ledger. Using this option was described earlier in Chapter 6.

8   PAYMENTS WITH ORDER (BANK RECEIPTS)

8.1   Customers might pay by cheque or credit card for goods or services when they make their order. There is no requirement for an invoice, and the customer is not asking for credit; therefore the transaction is not recorded in the Customers Ledger. Instead, it should be recorded as a sale and a bank receipt.

8.2   To record a cheque or credit card receipt for items that will not be processed through the Customers ledger, click on the **Bank** button in the main Sage window, and then (after selecting the appropriate bank account if there is more than one) on the **Receipt** button.

8.3   To enter the details of the receipt, you will need the following information:

(a)   the bank account to which the transaction will be posted (in the Blitz case study, this is the bank current account, code 1200);

(b)   the nominal account to which the credit will be posted (ie the account code of the sales account or other income account in the nominal ledger to which the receipt should be posted as income). The program allows you to create a new nominal ledger account if required. In the Blitz case study, bank receipts will be posted to existing sales accounts in the nominal ledger;

(c)   the department code, if any;

(d)   the transaction date;

(e)   the customer's cheque number, or other reference number such as your company's paying in slip reference (this is optional, however);

(f)   a description of the item for which the payment has been received (also optional);

(g)   the net value of the item (excluding VAT);

(h)   the VAT code for the item (in the case study, T0 or T1).

Entering bank receipt details

8.4   When you click on the **Receipt** button, the following window will appear.

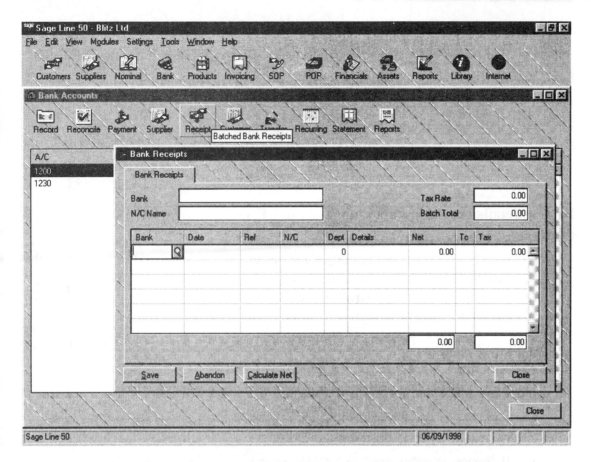

8.5   Enter the bank account code (1200 in Blitz) and the date as usual. For the **Ref** you can enter a reference for the transaction such as the customer's cheque number or your own paying-in slip number. Press Tab again.

8.6   Key in the code of the nominal ledger account (for sales or income) to which the receipt refers, then press Tab. In the Blitz case study, the code will be one of the following:

4000   Sales - contract cleaning
4001   Sales - window cleaning
4002   Sales - domestic services
4100   Sales - materials

8.7   When you key in the N/C code and press Tab, the N/C name will automatically appear in the N/C Name box at the top of the window.

8.8   In the Dept and Details boxes you can enter the code of the Department concerned if any and a description of the purpose of the payment from the customer.

8.9   You can enter either the net amount of the receipt (excluding VAT) or the gross amount (including VAT).

(a)   If you enter the net amount, press Tab and the cursor will move to the T/c column. This may show a default code such as T1, but you can alter it if you wish. In the Blitz case study, the codes are:

T0   for zero-rated items
T1   for standard-rate items (currently taxed at the rate of 17.5%)

(b)   If you key in the gross receipt in the Net column and click on **Calculate Net** (or press F9) this automatically deducts VAT at the standard rate (assuming tax code T1 applies). If you than press Tab you can change the tax code if you like and the amounts will be recalculated as appropriate. (If the code has to be altered from, say

T0 to T1, you may need to Tab back to the Net box, re-enter the gross amount and click on Calculate net again.

8.10 Whichever method you choose for entering the net payment and tax code, the amount of VAT will be calculated automatically and displayed in the Tax column.

8.11 Press Tab to move to the next line on screen, where you can enter further details of the receipt if necessary (for example if a single receipt is being posted to more than one Nominal code).

Posting details of bank receipts

8.12 When you have entered all the details of a bank receipts click on the **Save** button. This will only be active if the amount in the Amount box is equal to the amount in the Analysis Total box. Once you have saved an entry the screen will clear, ready for the next entry. If you have finished all your entries click on **Close** or press Esc. (You will be asked if you are sure you wish to Exit. If you are, click on Yes.)

Activity 7.7

Load Assignment 1.

It is 8 October 1998. You have received the following amounts from non-sales ledger customers.

Gleamo Prize for shiny windows:	£1,000 (N/C 4900; T/C T0)
D. Spenser, one-off payment for domestic services:	£100 (gross)

Post these transactions using the paying-in slip reference 123478.

What is the balance on the bank account after you have done this? What nominal ledger accounts are affected besides those beginning with a 4?

---

9   REPORTS

9.1 You can produce reports for receipts of money from customers.

(a) A listing of receipts from customers in settlement of invoices (and payments on account) and of bank receipts that are not recorded in the sales ledger can be produced using the **Reports** button in the **Bank** window.

(b) A listing of bank transactions can be produced using the **Report** button in the Nominal Ledger window.

Only (a) is described here, since we saw how to produce a report of bank transactions in the previous chapter.

9.2 To get a report on receipts click on **Bank** in the main window, ensure that the account you want is highlighted (A/C 1200 is the case study) and then click on **Reports.** As we saw in the previous chapter a window appears offering you lots of options.

9.3 This time you want Day Books: Bank Receipts (Detailed). You would typically want to obtain a listing of receipts for a particular day (or week). In the Date section specify the date or dates of the transactions for listing, using a six-digit code for date (eg 150299). Then choose what sort of Output you want – Printer, Preview or File. If you choose to print the listing, the screen will give you prompts for producing the printout.

10   CONCLUSION

10.1   If you think you can follow the explanations in this chapter, you should now be ready to attempt **Assignment 4**.

Answers to activities

Answer 7.1

The opening balance on the bank account is £4,616.49 and the closing balance is £6,615.10. the opening balance on the Debtors ledger control account is £25,486.83 and the closing balance is £23,488.22.

The receipt from ELITEC is likely to have been the most difficult to deal with: it does match up precisely to existing invoice amounts, however. Note that ROSEAL has underpaid by a small amount. You should be left with a balance of £0.88 on this account.

Here are the sort of details that your report on ELITEC should have contained. (This is an extract from a Customer Activity (Detailed) report.)

No	Tp	Date	Refn	N/C	Details	T/C	Value	O/S	Debit	Credit
56	SI	22/09/98	10021	4000	Kitchen cleaning	T1	756.70 p	556.70	756.70	
96	SI	08/10/98	10043	4000	KITCHEN CLEANING	T1	756.70		756.70	
97	SI	08/10/98	10043	4100	OVEN CLEANER	T1	71.68		71.68	
98	SI	08/10/98	10043	4100	FLAME DETERGENT	T1	84.60		84.60	
99	SI	08/10/98	10043	4100	BRUSHES	T1	28.13		28.13	
161	SR	10/10/98	10021	1200	Sales Receipt	T9	200.00			200.00
196	SI	16/10/98	10054	4000	Kitchen cleaning	T1	223.25 *	223.25	223.25	
246	SR	15/11/98	10043	1200	Sales Receipt	T9	941.11			941.11
							779.95	779.95	1,921.06	1,141.11

Answer 7.3

The customer should end up with £17 discount and a balance of £0.00 if you do all of this correctly.

Answer 7.4

(a)   £0.00 and £4,616.49.

(c)   £88.13 and £4,528.36.

(d)   As follows. The cheque receipt on 10 October is now shown as a cancelled cheque and the invoice from 22 September is reinstated.

No	Tp	Date	Refn	Details	Amount	O/S	Debit	Credit
70	SI	22/09/98	10035	Window cleaning	88.13		88.13	
150	SR	10/10/98	CANCEL	Cancelled cheque	88.13			88.13
246	SI	31/10/98	CANCEL	Cancelled cheque	88.13	88.13	88.13	

What other account in the nominal ledger is affected?

Answer 7.5

The initial balances are £0.00 and £27,167.80.

The new balances are £0.00 and £26,752.80.

Here is the activity as recorded in Bridgford's account.

No	Tp	Date	Refn	Details	Amount	O/S	Debit	Credit
38	SI	22/09/98	10003	Office cleaning	487.63		487.63	
94	SI	08/10/98	10041	Office cleaning at inv	493.50		493.50	
145	SR	10/10/98	10003	Sales Receipt	981.13			981.13
246	SC	31/10/98	REFUND	Refund - 10003	487.63			487.63
247	SI	31/10/98	REFUND	Allocation - 10003	487.63		487.63	

The Bank account (1200) is affected and so is the Sales Tax Control (2200) account.

Answer 7.6

The three amounts written off are £0.75, £0.43, and £0.25, a total of £1.43. This is debited to the Bad Debt Write Off account (8100) and credited to the Debtors Ledger Control account (1100). Check the activity on these accounts to see the transactions for yourself. (The memorandum accounts for the three customers are also credited, of course.)

Answer 7.7

It should be £35,040.07 (debit). The bank account is, of course, the only other nominal ledger account affected.

Chapter 8   Other cash transactions

Chapter topic list

1   Petty cash transactions

2   Journal entries and bank-cash transactions

3   Bank transactions not involving sales or purchases

4   Bank reconciliations

5   Conclusion

Learning objectives

On completion of this chapter you will be able to:

	Performance criteria	Range statement
• Make the accounting entries for petty cash transactions in a computerised system	19.1.1 to 19.1.7	19.1.1 to 19.1.6
• Make the accounting entries for bank-cash transactions in a computerised system	19.1.1 to 19.1.7	19.1.1 to 19.1.7
• Make the accounting entries for bank transactions not involving sales or purchases in a computerised system	19.1.1 to 19.1.7	19.1.1 to 19.1.7
• Use the Sage system to carry out a bank reconciliation	19.2.1 to 19.2.4, 19.3.1 to 19.3.8	19.2.1 to 19.2.5, 19.3.1 to 19.3.4

1   PETTY CASH TRANSACTIONS

1.1   A petty cash account is a record of relatively small cash payments and cash receipts. The balance on the petty cash account at any time should be the amount of cash (notes and coins) held within the business. Petty cash is commonly kept in a locked metal box, in a safe or locked drawer. The box will contain notes and coins, vouchers recording amounts of cash withdrawn (and the reasons for using the cash) and vouchers for petty cash receipts.

1.2   The accounting records for petty cash are often maintained in a book. Transactions are recorded from the vouchers into the petty cash account in the book. However, a petty cash account must also be maintained in the nominal ledger of any computerised accounting system. It is therefore common for the accountant responsible for petty cash to maintain the account in a book, and then from time to time to copy the entries from the book into the computer system.

1.3   For payments of cash out of petty cash, details must be entered of

(a)   the amount withdrawn; and

(b)   the purpose of the cash spending (ie the nominal ledger account to which the item of expense relates).

1.4   Similarly, for receipts of cash into petty cash, details must be entered of

(a)   the amount received; and

(b)   the reason for the receipt (ie the nominal ledger sales account or income account to which the item of income relates).

Recording petty cash transactions

1.5   The information you need to record a cash payment or cash receipt is as follows.

(a)   The code of the nominal ledger account to which the payment will be debited or the receipt credited

(b)   The transaction date

(c)   If appropriate, a reference number such as the petty cash voucher number (this item is optional)

(d)   A description of the reason for the payment or receipt (also optional)

(e)   Either the net value of the item (excluding VAT), or the gross amount of the item (including VAT)

(f)   The appropriate VAT code

1.6   The petty cash account is included in the list in the Bank Accounts window. Just select this account (code 1230) instead of the main bank account (code 1230).

1.7   Transactions are posted **exactly as for Bank receipts and payments**, using the same buttons. All you need do, therefore, is try an Activity.

Activity 8.1

Load up Assignment 3.

Post the following transactions to the petty cash account. Transactions are numbered consecutively, beginning at PC013. VAT receipts have not been obtained, so no VAT applies.

25 Oct Stationery: £5.26.
28 Oct Refreshments: £4.45
24 Oct Present for new baby: £27.99 (N/C 6202)
25 Oct Loan (Joan Davies): £50 (N/C 9998)
31 Oct Received from Joan Davies: £50.

What is the balance on the petty cash account and on account 7504 now?

2 JOURNAL ENTRIES AND BANK-CASH TRANSACTIONS

2.1 A journal is a 'book of prime entry' in an accounting system. It is not used frequently, but its purpose is to make the initial record of 'unusual' accounting transactions that will not be recorded in any other book of prime entry.

2.2 Although a journal can be thought of as a 'book' for recording transactions to be posted to the nominal ledger, it is common for journal transactions to be recorded on slips of paper, known as journal vouchers.

2.3 Entries in the journal must subsequently be posted to the appropriate accounts in the nominal ledger. For every journal transaction, there will have to be:

(a) a debit entry in one nominal ledger account; and
(b) a corresponding credit entry in another nominal ledger account.

2.4 In other words, two nominal ledger accounts must be specified in the transaction, one for the debit entry and one for the credit entry.

2.5 A transaction recorded in the journal, for example, could relate to a transfer between accounts in the nominal ledger. In the Sage system, a journal entry is used, for example, to record transfers of petty cash from the bank account to the cash account.

2.6 Movements of money between the bank account and petty cash (the 'cash account') are known as bank-cash transactions.

Recording bank-cash transactions

2.7 To record a movement of money from the bank account to cash (that is, a cash withdrawal) or to record the payment of cash (notes and coin) into the bank, click on the **Nominal** button in the main Sage window and then on the **Journals** button in the Nominal Ledger window. The window shown below will be displayed.

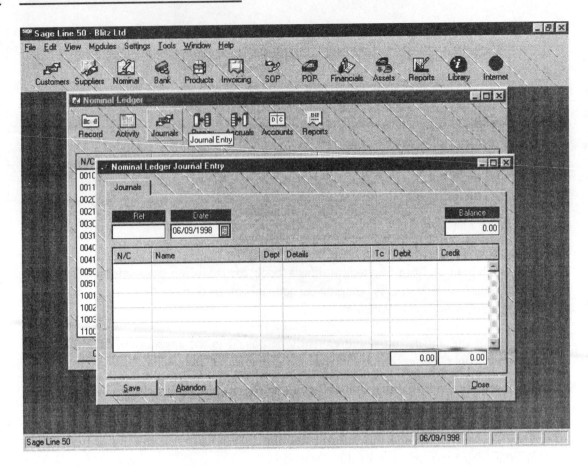

2.8   The cursor begins at the Ref box.

Ref

2.9   This is an optional item, which can be used to identify the transaction. The journal voucher number could be inserted here (up to a maximum of six characters).

Date

2.10   If necessary, enter the transaction date, as a six-digit code in the format DDMMYY or use the calendar button.

2.11   The cursor will now move past the box labelled Balance (which is updated automatically) straight down to the main part of the screen. Here, you must enter the details of the debit item and the credit item, one per line, for the transaction.

2.12   For a bank-cash transaction, the debit and credit entries are as follows.

(a)   When *cash is withdrawn* from the bank.

		Nominal ledger code
DEBIT	Petty cash	1230
CREDIT	Bank current account	1200

(b) When *cash is paid into* the bank from petty cash.

		Nominal ledger code
DEBIT	Bank current account	1200
CREDIT	Petty cash	1230

N/C and Name

2.13 Enter the nominal ledger code of the bank account (1200) or the petty cash account (1230). It does not matter which code you enter on the first line. You will need to enter both, one per line, to complete the input details. When you enter the code, the account name will appear in the Name box automatically. (To find other codes you can use the Finder button in the normal way: click on it or press function key F4 when the cursor is in this box.)

Details

2.14 You can enter brief details of the transaction. For example:

N/C	Name	Description	T/c	Debit	Credit
1230	PETTY CASH	Received from bank a/c	T9	100.00	
1200	BANK CURRENT A/C	To petty cash float	T9		100.00

2.15 The description for one side of the entry should always indicate the other nominal ledger account to which the transaction relates. In the example above, the details for the withdrawal of £100 from the bank (the credit of 100.00 for N/C 1200) refer to petty cash which is the recipient of the money.

T/c (Tax Code)

2.16 A bank-cash transaction does not involve VAT. Enter tax code T9.

Debit/Credit

2.17 Enter the amount of the transaction, in the debit or the credit column, according to whether the nominal ledger account should be debited or credited.

2.18 Remember that there must be two entries for a bank-cash transaction, one a debit and one a matching credit, to complete a journal entry. In fact the system will not allow you to post your journal until Debits equal Credits and the amount shown in the Balance box is nil.

2.19 When you have completed the entry, Click on **Save** as usual and the nominal ledger accounts will be updated with the transaction details.

Activity 8.2

Load Assignment 6.

A payment of £1200 has been incorrectly analysed as Legal Fees. In fact £500 of this related to consultancy fees and £300 was advertising. All figures are stated net.

Post a journal to correct this (reference J23) dated 6 November 1998. What is the balance on the advertising account now?

---

3   BANK TRANSACTIONS NOT INVOLVING SALES OR PURCHASES

3.1   A business will occasionally receive or make payments by cheque (that is, through its bank account, not in cash) that do not involve sales or purchases, receipts from customers or payments to suppliers. These cash payments or receipts should be recorded using the **Payment** and **Receipt** buttons in the **Bank** window. These options are described in Chapter 6 (payments) and Chapter 7 (receipts).

3.2   Examples of transactions you could be expected to record are suggested below.

   (a)   Payment of PAYE income tax to the Inland Revenue authorities
   (b)   Payment of a court fine (eg a parking ticket fine)
   (c)   Payment for a road vehicle licence (car tax)
   (d)   The receipt of a loan

4   BANK RECONCILIATIONS

4.1   Sage includes a facility for making a bank reconciliation - ie checking the bank account records in the nominal ledger against a bank statement sent by the bank.

4.2   If a transaction is the same in both the bank statement and the nominal ledger account it is said to be 'reconciled'. The reconciliation process therefore involves checking every item on the bank statement against the transactions listed in the nominal ledger bank account and matching the transactions. Any differences should then be identified, to complete the reconciliation.

Note that you always work *from* the bank statement *to* the nominal ledger account. *Unreconciled* (also called *uncleared*) items are those that have *not yet appeared in the bank statement*, even though they have been recorded in the nominal ledger account.

Documents for checking

4.3   You will obviously need a bank statement from the bank to carry out a reconciliation. Paying in slips will also probably be needed, as we shall see. You will also need a list of transactions in the nominal ledger bank account.

4.4   To produce a print-out of the bank transactions, you can click on the **Bank Statement** button (the simpler option), or else (in all versions) click on the **Nominal** button in the main Sage window and select the bank account (account 1200) by scrolling down to it and clicking on it to highlight it. Then click on the **Report** button in the Nominal Ledger window. The reason why you need this report is explained in a moment.

4.5   Four standard reports are listed – Day Books: Nominal Ledger, Nominal Activity, Nominal Balances and Nominal List. You want the one called *Nominal Activity*, so click on this to highlight it. If possible the Output option to choose is Printer, but if you do not have access to a printer, choose Preview. Then click on Run. Specify account code 1200 in the Report Criteria or Additional Report Filter window. You don't actually need to do this if you highlighted account 1200 before clicking on **Reports,** but it is good practice to do so.

4.6   If you are printing the report a series of windows will give you printing options and instructions.

Starting the bank reconciliation

4.7   Click on the **Bank** button in the main Sage window and (having highlighted the account you want to reconcile, if there is more than one account) then on the **Bank Reconciliation** button in the Bank Accounts window.

4.8   The program will display the window shown below.

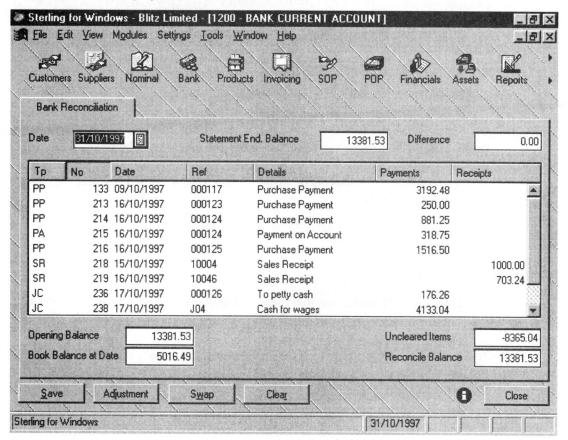

4.9   Key in the date of the *bank statement* and the closing balance shown at the end of the bank statement.

All versions

4.10   You can use the scroll bar or the cursor direction keys ↓ and ↑ to look through the list, and the Page Up, Page Down, Home and End keys to speed up the process.

4.11   Four boxes on the screen need some explanation.

Opening Balance

4.12   This is the bank Reconcile Balance brought forward from the last time a bank reconciliation was done using the Sage software. It should reflect the opening balance on the bank statement. If there has not been a previous bank statement, or if the procedure has never been carried out before, the balance brought forward will be 0.00.

Uncleared items

4.13   This is the net total (debits plus credits) of all items or receipts that are left unreconciled on the screen. Each time you reconcile an item listed in the bank statement with an item on the screen, you will find that the balance in this box changes.

Book Balance (at Date)

4.14 This is the current account balance for the bank account in the nominal ledger. The main reason why this balance is different to the bank Reconcile Balance is because, unlike the bank statement, it takes into account any receipts or payments that were in the process of clearing through the banking system when the bank statement was produced.

Reconcile Balance

4.15 When the bank reconciliation is finished, the balance shown in this box must match the ending balance on the bank statement. Each time an item is identified as being reconciled, the total in this box is increased (if it is a receipt) or decreased (if it is a payment). The first time you ever do a bank reconciliation the box will show 0.00; subsequently it will show the same amount as the Opening Balance box when you begin.

4.16 You will find that the Reconcile Balance plus the value of uncleared items is always equal to the book balance.

Reconcile Balance + Uncleared Items = Book Balance

Reconciliation procedures

4.17 In a bank reconciliation, you must match the transactions listed in the bank statement with the transactions in the nominal ledger bank account.

4.18 When you find a transaction on the bank statement is matched by a transaction in the nominal bank account click on it to highlight the transaction on the screen. The figures in the Reconcile Balance box and the Uncleared Items box will change by the amount of the transaction that you just highlighted.

4.19 If you make a mistake, and want to de-select a transaction, just click on it again.

Items made up of several transactions

4.20 You may have a problem in matching items because there may be some that are the total of several smaller transactions. This happens on both the bank statement and on the screen listing.

(a) If several receipts were paid into the bank on a single paying-in slip the bank statement will probably only show the total. You need to consult the paying-in slips to see how these items are made up, and match individual receipts.

(b) The reconciliation screen will lump together any transactions of the same type (eg five customer receipts) that were posted one after the other and had the same date, unless they were given a unique *reference* number when they were posted. A single total will then be shown for all of these individual transactions, making matching far more difficult. The details will just say 'Customer Deposit'.

You may remember that we emphasised the importance of giving receipts a unique reference number when we were describing how they should be posted. This is the reason why.

(A possible solution, that would make a *virtue* of these 'problems', would be to post receipts from paying-in slips, giving each batch of receipts the same reference as the paying-in slip number. In fact this would make it *easier* to match items on the bank statement and the reconciliation screen.)

Items in the bank statement but not in the ledger account

4.21   There could be some items in the bank statement that have not been entered in the nominal ledger bank account. For example, there could be some bank charges that have not yet been recorded in the account.

4.22   You can make an adjustment, and post the receipt or payment to the bank account in the nominal ledger. To do this click on the **Adjustment** button at the foot of the window. A new window will appear, as shown below.

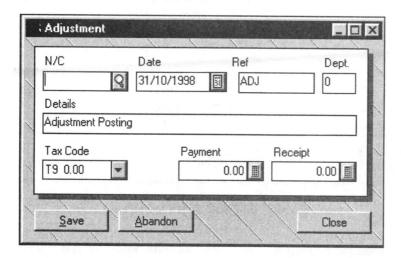

4.23   The entries to make are as follows.

(a)   *N/C (Nominal Code).* Enter the nominal ledger code for the account to which the item of income or expense relates. In the Blitz case study, for example, a deduction of bank interest would be coded 7900 and a deduction of bank charges would be coded 7901.

(b)   *Date.* Enter the date of the receipt or payment.

(c)   *Details.* By default this says 'Adjustment Posting but it is better to enter your own brief narrative details of the item.

(d)   *Tax Code.* The VAT code would be T9 for bank charges, but for other items (for example, some direct debits) it would be T1. Check with your supervisor if you are not sure.

(e)   *Payment / Receipt.* Enter the gross value of the receipt or payment, in the appropriate box. (The other box is left as 0.00.)

4.24   Click on **Save** when you are satisfied that your adjustment details are correct. The transaction will be posted in the appropriate nominal ledger accounts.

Completing the reconciliation

4.25   When you have checked the items in the bank statement against the nominal bank account, the value in the Reconcile Balance box should equal the balance on the bank statement itself. If it does not, you have made a mistake. Consult your supervisor.

4.26   If it does reconcile, click on the **Save** button. This will clear the reconciled transactions (ie the transactions that you have matched and highlighted in the nominal bank account and the bank statement). The unreconciled items will be displayed on screen the next time you do a bank reconciliation. The reconciled transactions will not be listed next time, provided you have cleared them.

4.27 To get a list of unreconciled payments and receipts use the Bank Reports option and find these reports in the list that appears.

Activity 8.3

Load Assignment 6. On 20 October you receive the following bank statement.

Date	Details	Withdrawals	Deposits	Balance
1998				
10-Oct	Balance from sheet no. **5**			**13,381.53**
11-Oct	000117	**3,192.48**		**10,189.05**
14-Oct	BGC		**1,000.00**	**11,189.05**
18-Oct	000124	**1,200.00**		
18-Oct	000125	**1,516.50**		**8,472.55**
20-Oct	BACS	**4,133.04**		**4,339.51**
20-Oct	Bank interest	**74.50**		**4265.01**

Perform a bank reconciliation as at 20 October 1998, following the procedures explained in the preceding section. What are the outstanding items, if any?

---

5 CONCLUSION

5.1 You may want more practice with a bank reconciliation. This is included in **Assignment 5**, which you can now attempt.

Answers to activities

Answer 8.1

You should get £262.30 (Dr) for petty cash and £415.10 (Dr) for account 7504.

Answer 8.2

The balance on the advertising account should be £3050.00

(Cr Legal Fees (7600) £800; Dr Consultancy (7602) £500, Dr Advertising (6201) £300.)

Answer 8.3

If you have ever performed a manual bank reconciliation you should find the computerised method a joy to use.

The outstanding items are as follows.

Cheque 000123	250.00
Cheque 000126	176.26
Receipt	(703.24)
Total	(276.98)

Chapter 9 Other credit transactions

Chapter topic list

1   Contra entries

2   Exceeding a credit limit

3   Writing off bad debts

4   Chasing customers for overdue payments

5   Correcting errors

6   Conclusion

Learning objectives

On completion of this chapter you will be able to:

	Performance criteria	Range statement
• Make the accounting entries for contra entries in a computerised system	19.1.1 to 19.1.7	19.1.1 to 19.1.6
• Deal with customers who exceed their credit limit in a computerised system	19.1.1 to 19.1.7	19.1.1 to 19.1.6
• Write off bad debts	19.1.1 to 19.1.7	19.1.4
• Delete supplier accounts and customer accounts from the ledgers	19.1.1 to 19.1.7	19.1.1 to 19.1.6
• Chase customers for payment, using an aged debtors list for analysis, statements and reminder letters	19.2.1 to 19.2.4	19.2.1 to 19.2.5
• Correct errors in computerised accounting entries	19.1.3	19.1.4

Italicised objectives are areas of knowledge and understanding underlying the elements of competence for Unit 19.

1   CONTRA ENTRIES

1.1   *Contra* is an accounting term that means against, or on the opposite side. A contra entry is made in the accounts of a business when a debit entry can be matched with a credit entry so that one cancels out the other. A common type of contra entry occurs when a supplier is also a customer. The amount owed as a supplier and the amount owing as a customer can be offset, to leave just a net amount owed or owing.

1.2   For example, suppose that ABC Limited is both a customer of your business, currently owing £1,000, and a supplier to your business who is currently owed £700. ABC Ltd pays £300 to settle the debt. The £700 owed has been offset against the £1,000 owing, and ABC Limited has simply paid the net debt of £300. This would be recorded in the accounts as a

(a)   a cash receipt of £300; and

(b)   a contra entry for £700, to cancel the debt to ABC as a supplier and the remaining £700 owed by ABC as a customer.

1.3   In the Sage system, the accounting that is done for a contra entry is as follows.

(a)   In the sales ledger, the customer's account is credited with the amount of the contra entry. This reduces the customer's outstanding debt.

(b)   In the purchase ledger, the supplier's account is debited with the same amount.

(c)   In the nominal ledger, the double entry transactions are:

CREDIT	Debtors Control Account (code 1100)
DEBIT	Bank Current Account (code 1200)
	(or any other specified bank account)
DEBIT	Creditors Control Account (code 2100)
CREDIT	Bank Current Account (code 1200)
	(or any other specified bank account)

Posting a contra entry

Post the payment or receipt first

1.4   Before you post a contra entry, you should record the actual cash payment (or receipt) in the purchase ledger (or sales ledger). For example, suppose that your company owes ABC Ltd £700, ABC Ltd owes your company £1,000 and ABC Ltd sends you a cheque for £300 to settle the difference. Your first step should be to record the £300 received as a part payment of an invoice in the account for ABC Ltd in the sales ledger. This will make the outstanding balance on the customer account (£700) equal to the outstanding balance on the supplier account (£700).

1.5   You can find out the balances on the two accounts by looking at them in the windows that appear when you click on the **Customers** button and the **Suppliers** button. Subtract one from the other to find out the amount due.

1.6   In Sage it is *not* essential that there are equal amounts owed and owing before you post a contra entry, but it is good accounting practice, so always post the payment (and/or) receipt that brings this about *first*.

Making the contra

1.7   Click on the word **Tools** at the top of the screen. A menu will appear from which you should select **Contra Entries.** A window will be displayed, for entering the details.

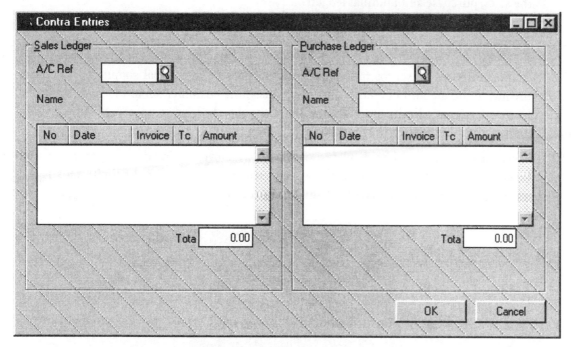

The cursor begins at the top left-hand side of the screen in the Sales A/C box, which will be blank.

Sales Ledger A/C (Customer Account)

1.8   Enter the customer's account reference code if you know it (or use the Finder button or press function key F4 if not). When you press Tab the customer's name will be displayed automatically, and a list of outstanding invoices on that customer's account will appear in the left-hand box below. (Credit notes and payments on account are not listed.)

Purchase Ledger A/C (Supplier Account)

1.9   Enter the supplier's account reference code. This would normally be the same as the customer's code, but not necessarily so – for instance, a customer might trade under a different name when making supplies. When the code is entered, pressing Tab brings up the supplier's name and a list of outstanding invoices appears in the right hand box below it. (Again, credit notes and payments on account are not listed.)

1.10   Now that the two accounts are shown side-by-side, you should be able to identify the matching transactions for which you want to make the contra entry.

1.11   To make the contra entry, select the appropriate transaction (sales invoice) in the customer account, by clicking on it. The amount in the Total box for sales invoices at the bottom of the screen is increased by the value of the transaction. (Note: you can de-select an invoice by clicking on it again.)

1.12   When you have selected the appropriate sales invoice find the appropriate purchase invoice in the other box, and select it by clicking. The amount in the Total box for purchase invoices at the bottom of the screen is increased by the value of the transaction you have selected.

1.13 So long as you first posted any payment that was due or receipt that had been received the two totals will now be equal.

1.14 Click on OK to save the transaction, which will be posted to the appropriate accounts in the sales, purchase and nominal ledgers.

2 EXCEEDING A CREDIT LIMIT

2.1 Credit limits can be set for individual customers (or by individual suppliers). These fix the maximum amount of credit (unpaid invoices) the customer should have at any time. In practice, credit limits are not always strictly observed, or customers will be given a higher credit limit when they exceed their current limit.

2.2 A warning message will be displayed on screen whenever an invoice you are processing takes the outstanding balance on the account above its current credit limit. This is the warning you see if you are using the **Invoicing** option.

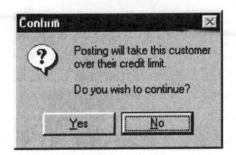

2.3 You should ask your supervisor what to do whenever you are not sure. If your supervisor is busy, and you want to get on with your work, you can choose not to proceed at the moment. Select the **No** option.

2.4 If you know that you should proceed, perhaps on instructions from your supervisor, you can select the **Yes** option. The program will then allow you to continue with the entry, despite the warning.

2.5 If your supervisor instructs you to increase the customer's credit limit, click on **No** and then (without closing the current **Invoice** window) click on the **Customers** button, select the Customer's account from the list and then click on **Record**. Tab to or click on the Credit Limit box, key in the new limit and then click on **Save**. Then press Esc twice to get back to the invoice window. If you try to save the invoice now it will be accepted without complaint by the system.

2.6 A customer who is over his credit limit is listed *in red* in the main Customers window.

Activity 9.1

Load Assignment 3.

Post an invoice for £400 (net) to School of Dance. The invoice is for Window cleaning, is numbered 21785, and is dated 14 November 1998.

By how much is School of Dance over its credit limit and what is the new balance on the Sales – Window Cleaning account?

---

3   WRITING OFF BAD DEBTS

3.1   Occasionally, a customer who has been invoiced will fail to pay, and the debt must eventually be 'written off' as uncollectable. There are various reasons why a debt could become a 'bad debt'. Three common reasons are:

(a)   the customer proves unreliable and is not creditworthy;

(b)   the customer goes out of business;

(c)   there is a dispute with the customer about whether a particular invoice should be paid, and it is eventually decided to write off the individual transaction as a bad debt.

3.2   When a debt is written off as uncollectable, one of two possible situations could apply.

(a)   The customer will not be granted credit ever again. The customer's entire debt is written off, and the customer's account will eventually be deleted from the sales ledger.

(b)   An individual transaction is written off, but the company will continue to sell on credit to the customer. A dispute about one transaction is not allowed to affect the long-term relationship with the customer.

Writing off an account

3.3   To write off all the outstanding debts in a customer's account, click on the word **Tools** at the top of the screen and then on **Write Off, Refund, Return**.

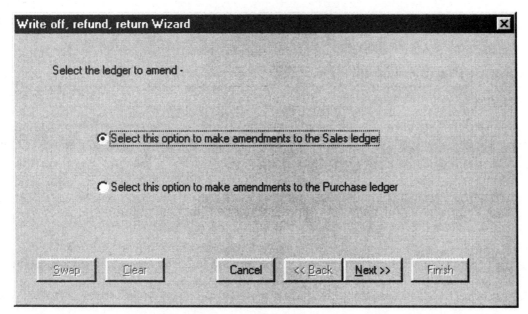

3.4   The option for amendments to the Sales ledger is selected when this window loads. You can click in the white circle and make amendments to the Purchase ledger if you like. If you accidentally pick the wrong option now or later you can click on the **Back** button to take you back to the previous step.

3.5   When you have this screen click on **Next** and another window will appear.

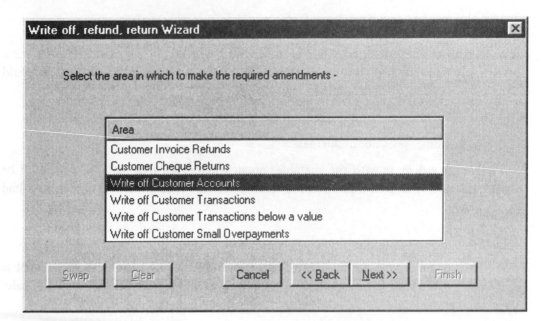

3.6   This gives you a number of options (a similar list appears if you select the Purchase ledger). The one we want on this occasion is **Write Off Customer Accounts.** Select this and then click on **Next.** A window appears very much like the one that drops down when you click on the Finder button or press F4 – you get a list of account names that you can scroll through. Select the account you want and then click on **Next.**

3.7   Read the instructions at the top of the next window carefully. Although only the first item is selected, clicking on **Next** will write off *all* the transactions listed.

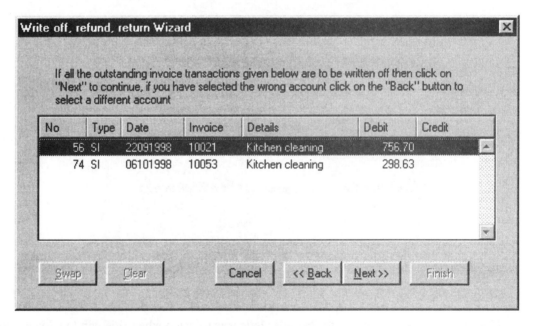

3.8   When you click on Next a window appears asking you to check 'all' the information shown. You don't actually get much information here and it is not very easy to check unless you have made a separate record of what you intended to do beforehand.

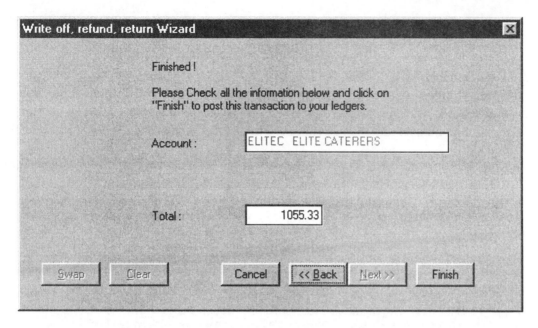

3.9 Click on **Finish** and you are returned to the main screen. The effect of all this is as follows.

(a) The customer's account in the Customers ledger will be updated automatically when you select the Yes option to write off the outstanding debts on the account. The account will remain, however, in the sales ledger and will not be deleted.

(b) The appropriate accounts in the nominal ledger will also be updated automatically:

CREDIT   Debtors control account (N/C code 1100)
DEBIT   Bad debt write off account (N/C code 8100)

If you check the Customers account and Nominal accounts Activity records you will see the entry that has been made.

Removing the account from the ledger

3.10 You might think that, having chosen the option **Write off Account,** the account will no longer appear in the ledger. Actually, however the customer record will not be completely removed. This is because it is needed for record keeping and auditing purposes. Since there have been some transactions with the customer during the year (even if the only 'transaction' has been your write-off of all outstanding amounts), the record must be kept on the system.

Activity 9.2

Load up Assignment 2,

It is 15 November 1998. Write off the account of the customer named Vice Versa.

What entries are shown in the customer's Activity record once you have done this?

What accounts are affected in the nominal ledger?

Writing off a transaction

3.11 To write off a single outstanding invoice, you may need to know how much it was for. If, for example, you are told to write off invoice number 10021 and are *given no other details,* one option is to click on **Financials** and scroll through the list looking at the Ref column until you see the invoice number 10021.

You should then make a note of the transaction number (56 in Blitz for this example) the account code (here, ELITEC).

3.12 A quicker approach if there are hundreds of entries on the system is to click on the **Nominal** button, select the Debtors control account (1100) and then click on Activity. You will see a display listing invoices in invoice number order. Make a note of the transaction number and then consult the **Financials** list as above to get the other details.

3.13 Now click on the word **Tools** at the top of the screen, then on **Write Off, Refund, Return** and select the Sales ledger options. The amendment you want this time is **Write Off Customer Transactions**. Select this, click on Next, then select the account (ELITEC in our example). Clicking on Next brings you this screen and instructions.

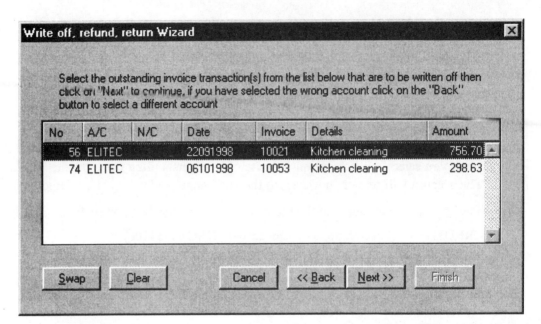

3.14 You want transaction number 56 so click on this to select it, then click on Next and then Finish.

Activity 9.3

Load Assignment 5.

It is 20 November 1998. Write off invoice number 10025, following the instructions above as appropriate.

What is the amount of the write off and the new balance on the Debtors Control account?

---

4 CHASING CUSTOMERS FOR OVERDUE PAYMENTS

4.1 It is an unfortunate fact of business life that many customers delay payment of invoices. They will pay eventually, and there will not be a bad debt. However, unless a determined effort is made to collect the unpaid invoice or invoices, the customer might continue to delay payment for as long as possible. In most businesses, there are procedures for:

(a) producing a regular list of unpaid invoices, analysing the length of time for which each invoice has been outstanding (an 'aged debtors list')

(b) producing statements of unpaid invoices for individual customers, for sending out to the customer as a reminder

(c)   producing and sending reminder letters to customers whose invoices are overdue for payment

Aged debtors list

4.2   To produce a list of unpaid debts, analysed by age, print out an Aged debtors analysis (Detailed) using the **Reports** option in the Customers window. The procedures for producing an aged debtors list have already been described in Chapter 7.

Statements

4.3   A statement of account is a printed statement of the amounts of unpaid invoices currently owed by a customer. Statements are sent to customers to assist with debt collection.

4.4   The layout of a statement can be adapted by each user of Sage. For the case study in this book, a standard layout provided by Sage (Statement With Tear Off Remit Advice, Individual) is used. This shows the following details.

(a)   Customer name, address and account code

(b)   Today's date

(c)   Brought forward figures at the beginning of the period covered by the statement

(d)   Details of transactions in the period covered by the statement (date, invoice number, description, amount)

(e)   An analysis of outstanding amounts by age

(f)   A total of the amounts outstanding

4.5   To produce statements, as you might guess, you use the **Statements** button in the **Customers** window. First however you have to select which customers you want to produce a statement for. To do this it is best to use the **Criteria** button in the main Customers window. For example you might set three criteria, as follows.

(a)   Only accounts with codes in the alphabetical range A to D should be included. This might be required in an accounts department where, to spread the workload, different individuals were made responsible for dealing with a different ranges of account codes.

(b)   Only balances greater than nought should be included.

(c)   Only accounts with balances greater than nought between 30 and 60 days old should be included (a separate batch might be printed for those that had been outstanding for longer, if there were any).

4.6   When you have chosen *and highlighted* the range of customers for whom statements will be produced, click on the **Statements** button in the Customers window. The window shown below will appear. You need to do the following.

(a)   Choose what type of output you want.
(b)   Pick your layout (as instructed by your tutor if you are getting a print-out).
(c)   Specify a date range.

4.7   Note that the dates you specify affect how the information is shown in the statement. If you specify, say 010180 as the Beginning Date and leave the Ending Date as the end of the current month you will get full details of all transactions in that period. If you leave the dates as the first and last day of the current month, all transaction dated before the first day of the current month will be lumped together in a single brought forward figure.

4.8   Click on **Run** when you are ready and your statements will be produced.

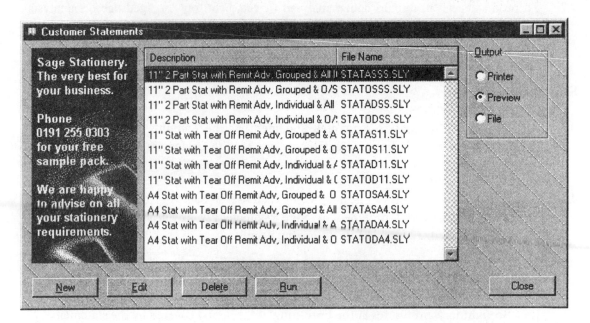

Reminder letters

4.9   Reminder letters can be sent to customers to urge them to settle invoices that are overdue for payment. The Sage package allows users to create 'standard' reminder letters (which can then be used for all reminder letters to customers).

Sage offers you a choice of three increasingly stern letters.

4.10   To print reminder letters, you must first choose which customers are to receive them in exactly the same way as described for choosing which customers will receive statements.

4.11   Then click on the **Letters** button in the Customers window. A Customer Letters window will appear that works just like the Customer Statements window. Use it in the same way.

Activity 9.4

Load Assignment 3. It is 31 December 1998.

Print out a statement and as stern a reminder letter as you can for Townend Angus Ltd.

How many days overdue is payment of the invoice?

---

5   CORRECTING ERRORS

5.1   Errors can easily be input to an accounts system, and spotted only after the input has been posted. They must be corrected. The appropriate procedure for correcting errors in the data on file depends on the nature of the error. Errors can be grouped into two types:

(a)   non-accounting errors
(b)   accounting errors

Non-accounting errors	Accounting errors
Errors in descriptive items, not affecting account code or money amounts Date Reference items Transaction details Department number Tax code (provided correcting the error does not affect the amount of VAT payable, eg. using tax code T0 instead of T2)	*Errors in* Account - ie input of the wrong account code Amount - ie the amount or value of a transaction, such as entering £1,100 instead of £1,000

5.2 Whichever type you are correcting, it will save time if you can note down the number of transaction concerned when you first become aware of the error. This may involve you looking through a list of sales invoices (call up the **Activity** of the Debtors Ledger Control Account or the Creditors Ledger Control Account), or looking through a particular customer or supplier account (again using the **Activity** option).

5.3 With an accounting error you will need to get full details of the transaction and it is best to do this before you start the correction procedure. Locate the transaction in the appropriate ledger and, if possible, select the relevant account and print out an Activity report for that account. If you cannot get a print-out, note down:

(a) the transaction number;
(b) the date;
(c) the account codes concerned (customer/supplier and nominal accounts);
(d) the invoice number or other reference number;
(e) the details; and
(f) the amount (net and VAT).

Correcting non-accounting errors

5.4 To correct a non-accounting error, first close any windows that are currently open until you have only the main Sage window in front of you.

5.5 At the top of the screen you will see the word **File.** Click on this and a menu appears. The item you want is **Maintenance.** If you click on this the following appears.

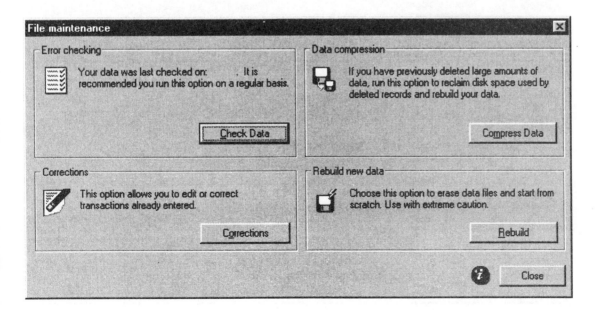

Posting error corrections

5.6   You only need use the **Corrections** button. If you click on this the following screen will appear. This lists all the transactions currently on the system, in transaction number order.

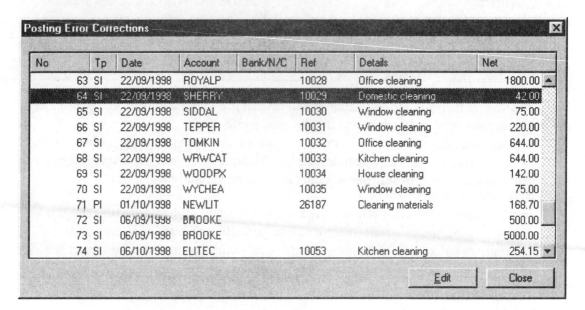

5.7   Your first job is to locate the transaction. If you noted down the transaction number this should be easy enough. If not, you will have to scroll through the list until you find the transaction you want to correct. When you find it, highlight it and click on the **Edit** button. A new window – Edit Transaction Header Record – will appear.

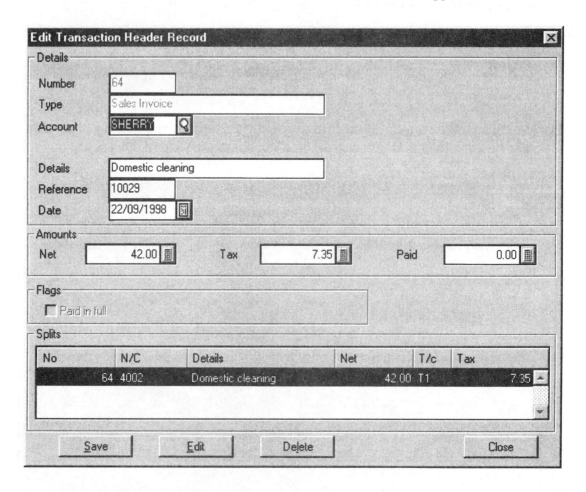

5.8   If you press Tab repeatedly you will find that only certain boxes are highlighted as you do so – others are skipped. This is because you cannot correct all the entries you see by this means. The only ones you can always correct are as follows.

(a)   Details
(b)   Reference

As we shall see in a moment you can also correct the Net and Tax fields, so long as the Paid in Full flag box does not have an **x** in it.

5.9   To correct an error in any of these fields simply Tab to the appropriate field and key in the correct details. Then click on **Save**. A message will appear asking you if you 'Do you wish to post these changes?' (even if there is only one change). So long as you *are* sure click on Yes. You are then returned to the Posting Error Corrections screen and you can select another transaction to correct if necessary. Otherwise click on Close.

Correcting errors in account code or amount

5.10   To correct an *accounting* error, you need to 'reverse' the transaction (cancel it out), and then post it again correctly.

5.11   You can only do this using the **Maintenance** option if the transaction has not already been settled: in other words if a receipt or payment relating to the invoice has not yet been recorded on the system.

5.12   Make your way to the Posting Error Corrections window again, select the transaction, and then click on Edit to bring up the Edit Transaction window.

What happens next depends on which version of the software package you are using.

5.13   You can correct accounting errors as follows.

(a)   Get to the Edit Transaction Header Record window as already described.

(b)   You cannot Tab directly into the Net and Tax fields. However, there is another **Edit** button at the foot of the window. Click on this.

(c)   A new window (Edit Transaction Split Record) appears. You can change things like the Nominal Code and the Net amount using this window.

(d)   Click on **Close**.

(e)   Click on **Save**.

The transaction will be 'reversed': the original transaction will be shown as 'Cancelled' on the screen and a new entry, equal and opposite to the first one, will have been posted.

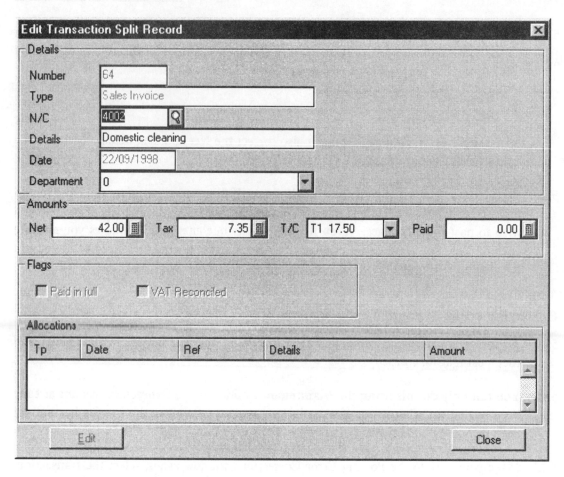

5.14 For example, if the original entry were:

DEBIT	Debtors control account	117.50	
CREDIT	Sales		100.00
CREDIT	Sales Tax Control (ie VAT)		17.50

then the reversing entry would be:

DEBIT	Sales	100.00	
DEBIT	Sales tax control	17.50	
CREDIT	Debtors control account		117.50

5.15 An entry would also have been posted in the individual customer's account. (Remember that Customer and Supplier accounts are 'memorandum' accounts only, represented in the trial balance by the single Debtor's control account)

5.16 In a manual system you would then need to input the correct entry as a 'new' transaction in the normal way. However, Sage does the reversal and the fresh posting all in one go. The correct details are posted in place of the original entry. A new transaction is recorded with the next transaction number *showing* the deleted entry for the record, but not including it in any balances.

Example

5.17 You have entered a purchase invoice transaction for an invoice from T Wilson (account reference WILSON). The invoice was entered for £200.00 + VAT of £35.00 as a materials purchase item (nominal ledger code 5000). The entry should have been for £300.00 plus VAT of £52.50.

5.18   To correct the mistake, you should find the transaction in the Posting Error Corrections window and select it, then click on **Edit**. When you get the Edit Transaction Header Record window click on **Edit** again. This will bring up the Edit Transaction Split Record window. Set the Net field to £300 and the Tax field to £52.50. Note that this is one place where the Tax field is not calculated automatically: there is a calculator button beside the box though, so you could press F4 and then tap in 300 * 0.175 if you didn't know the new VAT amount. When you have made your entries, click on **Close** and then **Save**.

5.19   The program will reverse the entry as follows.

   (a)   The original transaction number (say it was 234) will appear in all relevant accounts with the *corrected* figures.

   (b)   A new transaction will be listed in all the relevant accounts with the details 'Deleted - see tran 234' and showing the old figures. This is literally just for the records: the old figures are not include in any balances.

Settled transactions

5.20   The Maintenance (or Disk Doctor) option cannot be used if a transaction is already settled, as mentioned above. In this case any error must be corrected by means of two *journal* entries. The reversing entry would be done by the first journal, and the correcting entry by a second. This is more a test of manual accounting skills and understanding of debits and credits, so it is not part of Unit 19 and the Blitz case study. You will learn how to do it in your studies for Units 1 and 2, Cash and Credit Transactions.

Activity 9.5

Load the data for Assignment 3.

The details for a purchase invoice from the Ironcliffe Group posted on 26 August 1998 should have read 'Rent to 31 October 1998'.

Correct the details, as described above.

Activity 9.6

Still with Assignment 3 loaded, find the balance on each of the sales accounts. Then alter the amount of invoice number 10018 to £1000 plus VAT, and alter the details and nominal code to that for Window Cleaning.

What appears in the Activity record of the relevant customer's account after you have done this?

How have the balances on the sales accounts changed?

---

6   CONCLUSION

6.1   You should now be ready to attempt the last Assignment on cash and credit transactions, **Assignment 6**.

Answers to activities

Answer 9.1

School of Dance is £163.75 over the limit. The new balance on the Sales – Window Cleaning account is £2,920.40.

Answer 9.2

Here is what you should see in Vice Versa's account.

No	Tp	Date	Refn	Details	Amount	O/S	Debit	Credit
58	SI	22/09/98	10035	Window cleaning	52.88		52.88	
84	SC	15/11/98	BADDBT	Bad Debt Write Off	52.88			52.88

The write off affects the Debtors control account (1100) and the Bad Debt Write Off account (8100).

Answer 9.3

The write off is for £2,714.25. The new balance on the Debtors Control account is £17,235.19.

Answer 9.4

More than 90 days.

Answer 9.6

You should see the following activity.

No	Tp	Date	Refn	Details	Amount	O/S	Debit	Credit
53	SI	22/09/98	10018	Window cleaning	1175.00	1175.00	1175.00	
107	SI	22/09/98	10018	Deleted – see tran 53	940.00			

The balances change as follows.

Account	Before £	After £	Change £
4000	20,807.80	20,007.80	800.00
4001	2,520.40	3,520.40	1,000.00
4002	853.10	853.10	None
4100	980.14	980.14	None

Part C
Payroll transactions

Chapter 10 Introducing the payroll case study

Chapter topic list

1 Sage Payroll and payroll knowledge needed

2 The payroll case study

3 Company settings and pay elements

4 Government legislation

5 Selecting employees

6 Changing the process date

7 Quitting the program

Learning objectives

On completion of this chapter you will be able to:

	Performance criteria	Range statement
• open the Sage Payroll package	19.1.4	19.1.3
• understand how computerised payroll systems apply the rules of payroll		19.1.3
• locate an individual employee record	19.2.1, 19.2.2	19.2.1 to 19.2.5
• ensure that payroll details are processed in the correct period	19.1.1 to 19.1.7	19.1.1 to 19.1.5

1   SAGE PAYROLL AND PAYROLL KNOWLEDGE NEEDED

1.1   The aim of this chapter is to introduce the payroll case study, and explain the nature of the information that must be held on the data files, to carry out routine payroll procedures.

This part of this book is based on **Sage Payroll 4**. If you are using the old version of the package, Payroll + 2, which is very different from the new version, full guidance is available on-screen in the **Plus 2 Payroll Help file** that comes as part of the Blitz program.

Knowledge of payroll transactions

1.2   To follow the instructions in this part of the book, and attempt the associated assignments, you need to have some knowledge of payroll transactions. This book does not explain, for example, the rules about PAYE and National Insurance contributions.

1.3   If you are not reasonably familiar with payroll transactions, you should do some studying for Unit 3 of the AAT Foundation stage, which covers this subject.

2   THE PAYROLL CASE STUDY

2.1   The contract cleaning business of Blitz Limited, established in August 1997, expanded very quickly in the following months. In late October, the company won a large contract to supply daily cleaning services to a local government authority. To fulfil the contract, the company established a separate group of employees to do this work, the Blitz A Team, under the full-time management of one of the company directors, Tim Nicholas and his deputy, Sam Lynch.

2.2   Tim Nicholas was keen to computerise the payroll system for this new team, and has added the recently released Sage Sterling Payroll Version 4 module to the company's accounting software. The payroll system has already been converted to the Sage system.

2.3   The Blitz A Team, as at the end of December 1998, consists of the following members.

Basic pay		Name	Employee no	Tax code		Full time/ part time	Monthl weekly pa.
£							
36,000	pa	Timothy Andrew Nicholas (Director)	01	425L		Full	Month
25,500	pa	Samuel Moore Lynch	02	475H		Full	Month
19,800	pa	Arvind Patel	03	419L		Full	Month
18,000	pa	Joanna Louise Escott	04	345L		Full	Month
16200	pa	Norman John Hazelwood	17	K20		Full	Month
10,200	pa	Arthur Ben Cropper	05	419L		Full	Month
10,500	pa	Alice Elizabeth Vaughan	06	285L		Full	Month
10,800	pa	Katherine Muriel Knight	07	419T		Full	Month
13,000	pa	Lewis Robert Leroy	08	315T	Wk1Mth1	Full	Month
13,200	pa	Leyton Cargill Brown	09	550H		Full	Month
13,000	pa	Martin George Koretz	10	543H		Full	Month
13,000	pa	Neville Parker	11	543H		Full	Month
215.25	pwk	Gideon Turner	12	330L		Full	Week
240.00	pwk	Mahendra Kothari	13	543H		Full	Week
210.00	pwk	Nursat Farouk	14	419L		Full	Week
205.00	pwk	Linda Emily Farrow	15	404L		Full	Week
4.00 per hour		Ethel Parkinson	16	270L		Part	Week

2.4   Before you learn how to process the weekly or monthly payroll, you should know a little about the information that is already held on the computer files for:

(a)   company-wide settings
(b)   government legislation; and
(c)   employees.

Getting access to Payroll 4

2.5   Getting access to Sage Sterling Payroll 4 is just like getting access to the accounting package. When you start up Windows you must find the program group in which the package is installed. This is probably called Sage, or Payroll, or SFW3, or SFW4, or Line 50. With Windows 95 look at the icons on your desktop or search using the Start button. Your tutor will tell you where and how to find it on your college's system.

2.6   Find the yellow stopwatch icon (probably labelled Payroll v 4.00) and *double-click* on it. You may then be asked for the password (which might be LETMEIN, depending on the password system you are using). Shortly, the following screen will appear.

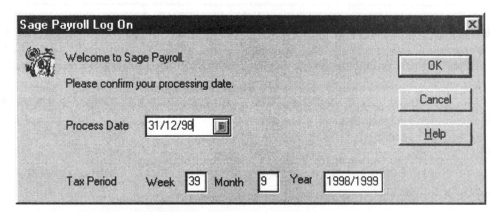

You can just accept the processing date for now, so just click on OK and this window will disappear. We shall explain about the Process Date later: it is an important feature.

You are left with the main payroll window.

(*Note.* If you have any experience of using the Internet and Websites you will be familiar with this type of layout. Tutors will note that it is very significantly different from the layout of the previous version of Sage Payroll. It will take some getting used to if you have experience of that version. However Payroll 4 offers several different methods of doing most tasks, and some of the methods are very similar to those used in older versions.)

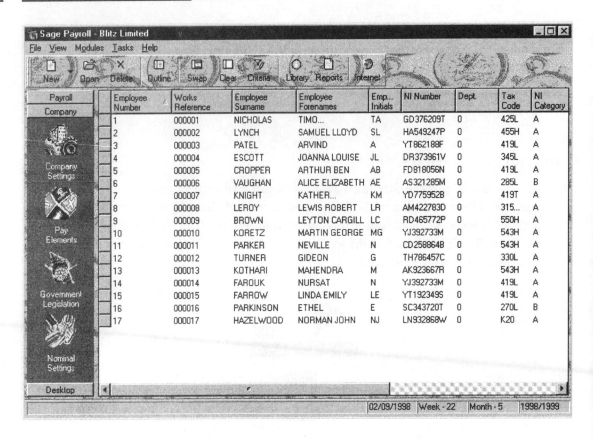

Activity 10.1

Find out now exactly how you should start up Sage Payroll and Blitz98 on the system you are using.

2.7   As you can see, the main part is a list of employees and their payroll details.

2.8   On the left is a set of icons which is called a *stacked toolbar*. In other words if offers you a different set or 'stack' of icons, depending upon which of the three buttons shown - Payroll, Company, or Desktop - you click. The Payroll stack is selected in the diagram above: this is the stack you will use most often.

2.9   At the top of the screen are menu items (File, View etc) and below these, a series of buttons (New, Open, Delete etc). The buttons labelled Open, Outline, Swap and Clear are the most useful.

2.10   Before we get to the detail of processing the pay of individual employees we shall take a brief look at how the program knows how to do so: how it knows what tax rates and rates of pay to use.

2.11   As you read on you should ideally be sitting at a computer with Sage Payroll 4 and some Blitz data loaded and you should try out all the buttons and so on that we describe. Use the BPP Blitz program to choose any of the Payroll assignments. Instructions for loading Blitz data are given in Chapters 2 and 3.

Activity 10.2

Load up Assignment 7. How many employees are listed?

3   COMPANY SETTINGS AND PAY ELEMENTS

3.1   Click on the **Company** button in the stacked toolbar. A set of buttons will appear.

Company settings

3.2   This allows you to enter details such as the following.

(a)   Banking information (the name, address, sort code and account details for the company)

(b)   Cash analysis (allowing the user to *exclude* certain notes and coins from the system's facility to determine how employees paid in cash will actually receive their money: no £50 notes, say)

(c)   Department names (for analysis purposes)

(d)   Pension schemes (allowing the user to set up percentages of pay to be contributed to a company pension scheme by employer and employee)

(e)   Statutory Sick Pay and holiday details

3.3   None of these options is of major relevance to the case study in this book.

Pay Elements

3.4   If you click on **Company** in the stacked toolbar, and then on the **Pay Elements** icon, you will see the following window. This shows the types of payment that the company might make to its employees.

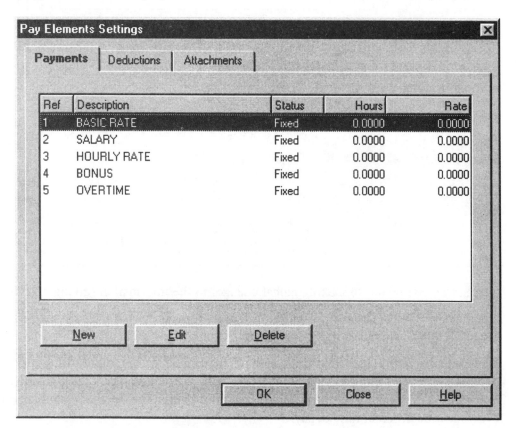

3.5   The table lists five Pay Elements that have been set up in the Blitz system.

Type

1	*Basic rate.*	This refers to weekly payments of a fixed wage.
2	*Salary.*	This refers to monthly fixed salary payments.
3	*Hourly rate.*	This refers to payments to staff at a rate per hour worked.
4	*Bonus.*	This refers to additional bonus payments that employees might receive.
5	*Overtime.*	This refers to overtime payments that employees might receive. In the Blitz system, overtime will be paid at a given rate per hour.

3.6 Every employee on the payroll receives payment by one or more of these methods. The payment type or types that are relevant to each employee are held on file within the Employee record part of the program.

3.7 Changes can be entered by highlighting a payment type by clicking on it, and then clicking on the **Edit** button, which brings up a further window.

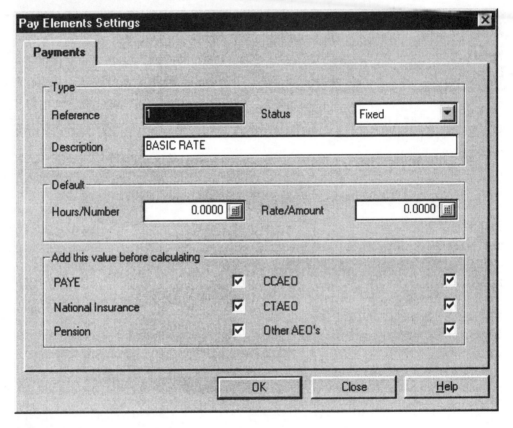

3.8 The **Status** box relates to making global changes to the information (giving everyone a 10% pay rise, for instance) and to the way information is reported. It is not used in the Blitz case study.

3.9 The **Defaults** can be used if there is a standard number of hours and rate of pay that applies to everyone who gets this pay element (this saves entering the same information every time a new employee starts). Defaults are not used in the Blitz case study because everyone is on different rates of pay.

3.10 Ticks in the PAYE, Nat Ins and Pension boxes indicate that income tax and National Insurance should be deducted from the selected payment type and that calculations of pension contributions should include this pay element.

3.11   For example, if Blitz Limited introduced a profit-related pay scheme (PRP scheme), approved by the Inland Revenue, pay under the scheme (up to a certain limit) would not be liable for PAYE. A new payment type, PRP, could be added, with no tick in the PAYE box.

3.12   The boxes CCAEO, CTAEO and Other AEO's refer to what are called Attachment of Earnings Orders. These are beyond the scope of AAT Foundation studies.

3.13   If any changes are made, of course, you must click on **OK**. If not, or when you have finished checking the details, click on **Cancel** or press Esc until you are back at the Company stacked toolbar.

Nominal Settings

3.14   This icon offers the option of linking up the Payroll 4 package to the Sterling for Windows 4 accounting package. It is not used in the Blitz case study, because it is not an option available to users of older versions of these packages.

Activity 10.3

Following the above explanations, set up a new payment type for Blitz called PRP, which is not liable for PAYE.

---

4   GOVERNMENT LEGISLATION

4.1   The **Government Legislation** icon in the company toolbar stack can be used to input, check or alter the rates for income tax, National Insurance contributions, SSP, SMP and Class 1a National Insurance.

4.2   Sage send out a disk at the beginning of each tax year with the new rates already entered and with alterations to the software for any changes in legislation that may have occurred. You can alter the rates yourself, but if you use this service this should not normally be necessary.

4.3   When you choose a payroll assignment, the Blitz program will automatically load up the Government Parameters that have been assumed to apply at the time when the case study is set.

4.4   If you have studied payroll for AAT Foundation level Unit 3, you should recognise the figures shown on the following screen.

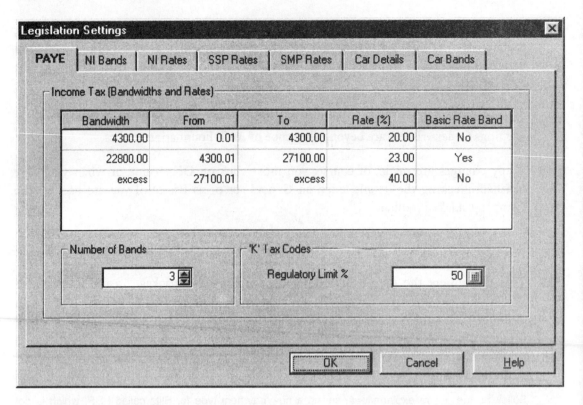

4.5   Look at this option if you like, and see what happens when you click on the various buttons, but *do not change* any of the figures or details when you are working on an assignment because this will make the results from your work different from the results given in this book.

4.6   Although there is no need for you to do anything with the **Government Legislation** icon and options, you will quickly come to appreciate the fact that all this information is stored in and available for use by Sage. What this means, of course, is that with a computerised payroll system you do not need to worry about tables and rates and endless calculations. The system does it all for you.

Activity 10.4

As we say, you should not change any of the government details when you are actually doing an assignment, because this will affect your answers.

However, just to try out the feature, assume that the government have introduced a new higher rate of tax of 60% for taxable earnings over £100,000.

Can you make these changes to the Government parameters in your Payroll 4 package?

---

5   SELECTING EMPLOYEES

5.1   Now we can move back to the Payroll stacked toolbar and look at the first two icons here. Click on the Payroll button to get back to a screen like the one shown at the beginning of this chapter.

5.2   If you select an employee name in the main part of the window and click on the **Employee Record** icon (or alternatively click on **Open** at the top of the screen) you will get a window that looks quite similar to a Customers or Suppliers record in the Sage Sterling accounting package.

5.3   This allows you:

   (a)   to add a new employee;

(b) to amend employee records; and

(c) to record that an employee has left the company.

These topics are the subject of the next chapter.

5.4 As an introduction to employee records and payroll processing with Sage, however, it is important that you learn to use the **Outline** button, in the row of buttons at the top of the screen. (The **Criteria** button in this row serves a similar function.)

The Outline button

5.5 Click on the **Outline** button. The window display changes to the following, which is known as the *Tree View*.

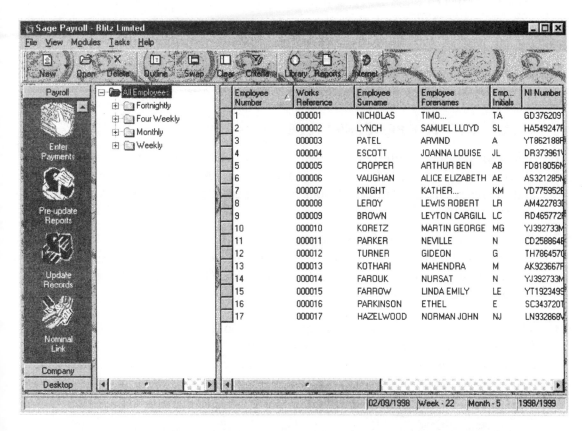

5.6 As you can see a column appears that looks like a portion of File Manager or Explorer. Clicking on one of the folders changes the list of employees that is shown so that it includes only those in the chosen category.

5.7 Suppose you wanted to change the *records* of all employees who are paid *weekly* (for example, if all such employees had just had a pay rise). Rather than having to remember which employees fitted this category or to go through all the records one by one you could use the **Outline** button and the folders that are displayed when you do so.

(a) Click on Outline to get the tree view.

(b) If all you see is a folder saying All Employees, double-click on it, until the sub-categories appear.

(c) Click on the Weekly folder.

(d) The result will be that only weekly paid employees are shown in the main list.

To get back to a list of *all* the employees, just click on the All Employees folder again.

5.8   The Outline facility is also available when you are processing *payments* for employees, so you can avoid accidentally including monthly paid employees in a payroll run when you only wanted to process weekly paid employees. Obviously the monthly paid employees won't mind if you pay them their monthly salary every *week*, but your employer won't exactly thank you for it!

5.9   Practise using the **Outline** button and **Clear** and **Swap** buttons until you are sure you understand how they work. In some cases the result will be that no employees at all are displayed.

Activity 10.5

Load Assignment 7.

Using the criteria button as explained above, find out which employees are set up to be paid monthly and which to be paid weekly. How many are paid in cash? Make a note of their employee numbers in each case.

At the end of this activity make sure that *all* employees are shown on the screen.

---

6   CHANGING THE PROCESS DATE

6.1   When processing payroll, it is necessary to specify the Process Date. You will know already, if you have started to study payroll, that the PAYE system is a cumulative one and the figures used in the calculations depend a great deal on what week or month of the year it is.

6.2   We saw at the beginning of this chapter that when you enter the Payroll 4 package the first thing you have to do is **OK** the Process Date. By default this is set at 'today's' date – the date according to the clock and calendar in your PC. However, you can change this date at any time.

6.3   The assignments in this book will always instruct you to reset the Process Date after you have processed the payroll for a week or month. You *must* do this, otherwise your answers will be wrong.

Changing the Process Date

6.4   To specify a Process Date of your choice, simply click on the Change Process Date icon in the Payroll stacked toolbar. When you do this the following window appears.

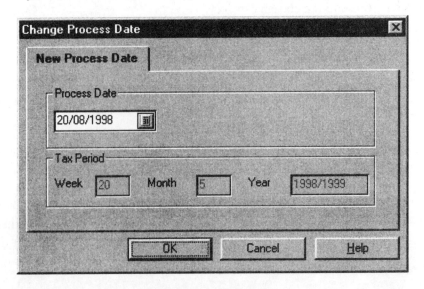

6.5   A date will already be shown in this field, but you can replace this with the date you want to specify. Do this, and press Tab, or click on OK or press Enter. The Tax Week, Month and Year boxes will change accordingly.

6.6   Check that the date you entered is indeed in the Tax Week or Month required. It is very easy at certain times of the year to key in, say, 97 when you mean 98, so be careful about this.

Activity 10.6

Load Assignment 7 (it should already be loaded from the previous activity, in which case there is no need to load it again.)

Using trial and error (or knowledge of the right ranges of dates if you happen to have it), change the process date so that it is:

(a)   tax week 44, 1998/99;
(b)   tax week 48, 1998/99;
(c)   tax month 12, 1998/99;
(d)   tax week 12, 1999/00;
(e)   tax month 11, week 46, 1997/98.

---

7   QUITTING THE PROGRAM

7.1   To leave the Payroll 4 package click on **File** and choose **Exit** from the menu that appears or *double-click* in the symbol in the top left hand corner of the screen or on the **X** in the top right corner.

7.2   This is one of several points in the Payroll package when you will be encouraged to back-up your data. In real life it is good practice to do so.

7.3   In the assignment work in this book, however, you do not *have to* back up your data; therefore you can specify No when given a screen prompt asking whether you want to back up. Your work up until this point will be retained in the system until different data is loaded up - when you or somebody else using the system want to do another assignment, say.

Answers to activities_____

Answer 10.2

There should be 17, corresponding to the list at the beginning of this chapter.

Answer 10.4_____

You should end up with a bandwidth of £72,900 taxed at 40% and the excess taxed at 60%. You never need to type *excess*: the program will do this for you.

Answer 10.5

Monthly paid employees are numbers 1 to 11 and 17. Weekly paid are numbers 12 to 16. None are paid in cash.

Answer 10.6

Just to start you off, tax week 44, 1998/99 is in the range 01/02/99 to 07/02/99.

Chapter 11 Adding and removing employees

Chapter topic list

1 Adding a new employee

2 Pay elements

3 Amending employee details

4 Leavers

5 Conclusion

Learning objectives

On completion of this chapter you will be able to:

	Performance criteria	Range statement
• add new employees to a computerised payroll file	19.1.1 to 19.1.8	19.1.1 to 19.1.5
• amend details of existing employees	1.1.1 to 19.1.8, 19.2.1 to 19.2.4	1.1.1 to 19.1.5, 19.2.1 to 19.2.6
• remove the details of an employee who has left the organisation	1.1.1 to 19.1.8, 19.2.1 to 19.2.4	1.1.1 to 19.1.5, 19.2.1 to 19.2.6
• print out reports for government returns	19.3.1 to 19.3.8	19.3.1 to 19.3.4

1   ADDING A NEW EMPLOYEE

1.1   Details of a new employee must be added to the payroll file whenever an employee joins the organisation.

1.2   To add a new employee to the payroll file, click on the **Payroll** button in the stacked toolbar and then click on the **New** button at the top left of the screen. (Alternatively, click on the **Employee Record** icon in the main stacked toolbar and then on the **New** button in the **Employee Record** window that appears.)

1.3   When you click on one of these **New** buttons a special help facility called the **Employee Wizard** appears.

The Wizard makes it simple to enter all the correct details for a new employee, but we shall explain the entries in some detail because it provides a good reminder of some of the key points from your Unit 3 studies.

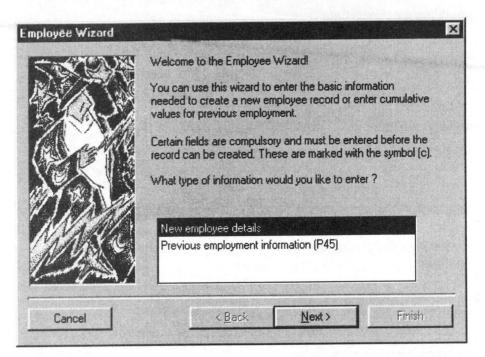

1.4   Your first task is to choose whether or not to enter the new employee's P45 details at this time. You can enter them later if you like, but if you have them to hand it is best to do so know, so click on **Previous employment information (P45)** to highlight it and then click on **Next>**. A series of on-screen forms will now appear, and you have to fill in the details, just like filling in a questionnaire. At any point you can click on **<Back** to go back to the previous screen, for example if you realise that you made a mistake, or if you left something blank because you couldn't immediately find the relevant information.

1.5   The first screen looks like this. Note that some items (marked (c) for compulsory) *must* be entered before you can move on.

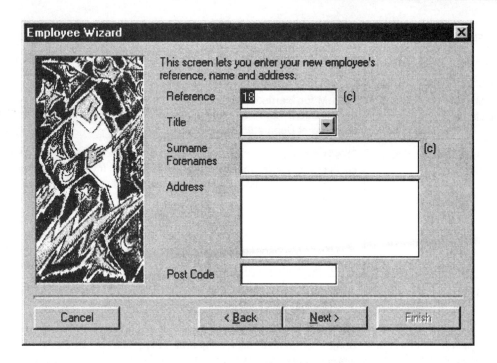

Field name	Comp?	What to enter
Reference	Yes	The program automatically assigns the new employee the next unused number in sequence, although you can change this if you wish the employee to have a number of your own choosing. You will not be allowed to continue on to the next screen unless there is an entry here. Press Tab to move to the next field
Title		If you click on the downward pointing arrow at the side of this box you are given the choice of Mr, Mrs, Miss, Ms and Dr. Click on whichever applies or else type in your own entry, such as Sir, Rev, Mme. Press Tab to move to the next field.
Surname	Yes	Key in the surname/family name of the employee. Press Tab.
Forenames		Key in the forenames of the employee. You are allowed up to 30 characters, including spaces, so there is room for several names. Press Tab.
Address/ Post Code		Enter the employee's address as indicated. If you want to leave a line blank, just press Tab to move on the next line.

1.6 When you have entered the necessary details click on **Next** to get to the next screen which asks for the following important information.

Field name	Comp?	What to enter
Male/ Female	Yes	Type M or F (although strictly the answer to the question on screen is Yes!). The word Male or Female will appear.
Marital status	Yes	Type M for Married or S for Single. As you know, this affects people's tax situation, so it is a compulsory field. There are no options for Divorced or Separated.
Date of birth	Yes	This is not just to remind you to send the employee a birthday card or so that you know when there are likely to be free drinks about. It is necessary information for the operation of the PAYE and National Insurance systems. Make sure you enter a date here and make sure it is the correct one. The date of birth should be entered as a six-digit item, in the format DDMMYY (eg 050659 for 5 June 1959). Alternatively, use the Calendar button or press function key F4, just like in SFW3 and SFW4.
Date began work	Yes	Again this is essential information, to allow the authorities to ascertain an individual's tax position and benefit entitlements.
Holiday scheme		Some companies allow different categories of employee different amounts of holiday and have various different arrangements for matters such as days brought forward from previous years. Details of different schemes can be set up using the Company Settings options that we looked at briefly in the last chapter. If this has been done, you can simply press F4 to get a list of schemes and click on the one that applies. This facility is not used in the Blitz case study.
Pension scheme		Again, different categories of employee may belong to different company pension schemes, and these would be set up using the Company settings option. If so press F4 to find the appropriate scheme.

1.7   The next two screens ask for essential PAYE and National Insurance information.

Field name	Comp?	What to enter
Tax code	Yes	Key in the employee's tax code, eg 523H or 404L etc, if you have it. If not the P46 information at the bottom of the screen is relevant.
Week 1/ Month1?		This is a simple Y or N option.
P46		Hopefully you remember about these from Unit 3 studies. This field will go dull if you have keyed in a Tax code, because it is not relevant. Otherwise you have a number of choices which drop down when you press F4 or click on the downward pointing arrow: P46 not completed, Certificate A signed, Certificate B signed, Neither certificate signed. Depending upon which of these options you choose, the Sage program allocates the correct tax code. In other words it saves you the bother of having to remember what to do in each set of circumstances. It allocates the code when you click on Next>, but you can then go <Back to see what it has done if you like.

Field name	Comp?	What to enter
National Insurance Number	Yes	Key in the employee's National Insurance number, then press Tab. The NI number should be a nine-digit code in the format LLNNNNNNL (L = a letter, N = a number).
		The *last* letter is always A, B, C or D (though this has nothing to do with NI Table letters). If it does not, the Sage package rejects it as an invalid number and offers to make up a temporary number. This is worth remembering if you are practising by making up your own details.
National Insurance Category	Yes	This will usually be Category A, the most common NI category, but you cannot just key in A. You must click on the arrow to the right of the box (or press F4) to make a drop down menu appear, offering you the choice of A, B, C, C (con/out), D (con/out), E (con/out), F, G, S or X (the abbreviation con/out means 'contracted out'). Scroll down to the appropriate letter (nearly always A) and click on it or press Tab when it is highlighted.

1.8   Next you get some questions about how the employee should be paid, and how he or she fits into the organisation.

Field name	Comp?	What to enter
How will payments be made?		Payments may be made by cash, by cheque, by credit transfer, by Giro or by electronic transfer (BACS). The system needs to know this so that it includes the relevant employees in cheque runs or sends the right details to BACS. Press F4 as usual to select the right option.
How often?		Options are Weekly, Monthly, Four Weekly or Fortnighlty. Press F4 to choose the right one for this employee.
Director?		If the employee is a Director of the company type Y. Otherwise leave the No where it is and Tab on to the next box. This information is needed because directors' National Insurance contributions are worked out on a different basis to those of other employees, to prevent abuse of the system.
Dept		An entry can be made here for the purposes of analysing payroll information by different department, such as Sales staff and Production staff. This feature is not used in the Blitz case study.
Cost centre		Again this is an optional field for the purposes of analysing payroll information. No entry is necessary in the Blitz case study. The term cost centre will make more sense when you have studied Unit 6 at intermediate level.

1.9   The next few screens require very little input from you.

Field name	Comp?	What to enter
Payment types		We looked at these in the previous chapter, so you may remember that Blitz has various types such as Hourly pay, Salaries, Bonuses.
		In the Blitz case study **do nothing** here: just click on **Next**. We shall deal with the Pay Elements separately, later in this chapter.

Field name	Comp?	What to enter
Deduction types		Various deductions may be set up on a payroll system such fees for as membership of a trade union or social club, charitable giving, SAYE and so on. None of these are relevant to Blitz, so just click on **Next**.

1.10 The next screen tells you about how to enter attachment of earnings details (beyond the scope of AAT studies) and also mentions Pay Elements, which we are going to cover later in this chapter. Read this now so it doesn't scare you when you see it in practice.

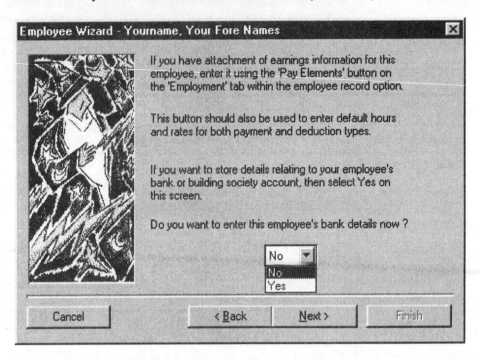

1.11 There is only one choice to be made here. If you want to enter details of the bank or building society to which the employee's wages or salary should be paid you can do so now. This is an optional item because new employees often forget to bring these details with them when they first start work, and so the information will not yet be available.

1.12 Assuming you say Yes at this point you will be asked (on the next two screens) to give the following details.

Field name	Comp?	What to enter
Type of Account		Choose bank or building society.
Branch Name		Provide this information if possible (although if it is a bank account the sort code, provided on the next screen is enough)
Branch Address/ Post Code		Enter the information you are given. You don't have to fill in every line, if it is a short address.

Field name	Comp?	What to enter
Account Name		This may be different from the employee's name. For instance it may be an account in joint names, husband and wife, or in a married woman's maiden name.
Account Number		You should take especial care in entering the account number and sort code. A mistake here will result in the employee's wages or salary going astray.
Sort Code		When you enter the bank sort code, there is no need to key in the hyphens as well as the figures: they will be added automatically (like the slashes in dates).
BACS Reference		This is only needed if payments are made by electronic transfer (as they generally are these days, though not in the case of Blitz).

1.13 There are two possibilities now.

(a) If you did not click on **Previous employment information (P45)** in the very first screen you will be told that you have finished entering the necessary details. If you forgot to choose the P45 option but now want to enter the details you can click on **<Back** until you get to the first screen again, select the P45 option and then click on **Next>** until you get to the relevant screen. You *will not lose any of the information* you have already entered if you do this, so feel free to do so.

(b) Alternatively you will see a screen that once again begins with the item Tax Code. For a new employee there are two additional entries to make.

Field name	Comp?	What to enter
Tax Code		This shows the tax code you entered earlier. You cannot alter it from this screen, although you could click Back to the original Tax Code screen and change it.
Taxable Gross Pay		This is the gross amount of taxable pay earned by the new employee in his or her previous employment in the year to date. (This is the gross pay before deducting free pay to date.) Enter this amount. It is shown on the P45.
Total Tax paid		This is the amount of tax paid by the new employee (in pounds and pence) in his or her previous employment in the year to date. Again this comes straight from the P45.

1.14 Once you have entered these details you get the following screen, which reminds you of *some* (but not all) of the other information that you may still have to enter. Just click on **Finish**.

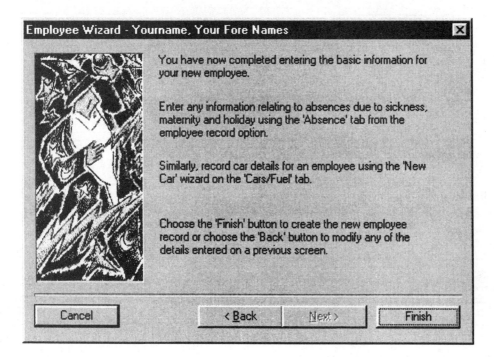

Employee Wizard - Yourname, Your Fore Names ✕

You have now completed entering the basic information for your new employee.

Enter any information relating to absences due to sickness, maternity and holiday using the 'Absence' tab from the employee record option.

Similarly, record car details for an employee using the 'New Car' wizard on the 'Cars/Fuel' tab.

Choose the 'Finish' button to create the new employee record or choose the 'Back' button to modify any of the details entered on a previous screen.

| Cancel | | < Back | Next > | Finish |

Activity 11.1

Load a fresh copy of Assignment 7 and, following the instructions above, set up an employee record using your own personal details unless otherwise specified.

Employee no	18
Name and title	Your name and title
Address	Your address

Start date	1st February 1999
Nat Ins no	PQ 12 43 65 D
Payment	Monthly, by cheque
Date of birth	Your date of birth
NI category	A
Marital status	Your marital status
Tax code	470T
Sex	Your sex

If an item of information is not specified you can assume it does not apply, or it will be entered later. Just click on Next to move on.

Click on **Finish** when you have entered the details. You will need them for the next exercise.

Looking at the record

1.15 You can now look at the entries you have made in a more usual form. You will see the new employee at the bottom of the list in the main window. Select the employee and either double-click, click on the **Employee Record** icon, or click the **Open** button at the top of the screen. This is what you will see.

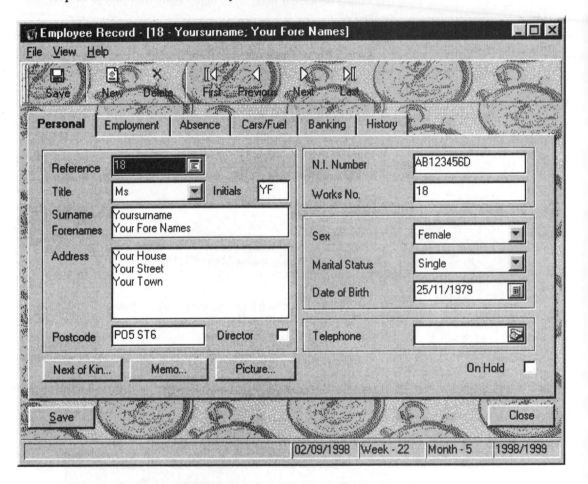

On Hold

1.16 The only additional point to note here is the **On Hold** box in the bottom right hand corner. If a check mark is entered in this box (by clicking on it) the employee is automatically **excluded** from any payroll processing routines, although any payments made to them during the year are included in the year end figures. This is useful if an employee has an extended **unpaid** period of absence for any reason, but does not actually leave the company. The check mark can be removed when the employee comes back to work by clicking on it again.

Other index tabs and P11 details

1.17 The Absence and Cars/Fuel index tabs in the Employee Record are not relevant because they are beyond the scope of AAT Foundation Payroll.

1.18 However it is worth having a look at the **History** tab. This gives you some brief details about what has happened so far, but more interestingly it offers you the option of looking at the information in **P11 form**, which should be very familiar from Unit 3 studies.

2   PAY ELEMENTS

2.1 Although you have clicked on **Finish,** actually you have not finished yet. You have not yet entered what is the most important information of all from the point of view of the employee – the **rate of pay!**

2.2 You do this by calling up the new employee record, as explained in paragraph 1.15. This time you click on the **Employment** tab to make the following window appear.

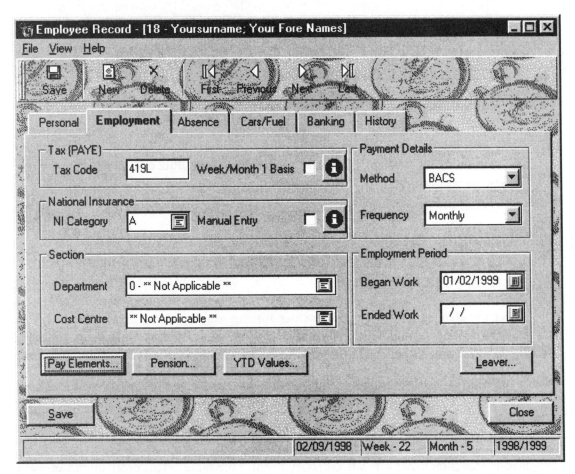

2.3 This contains some more of the details you entered with the Wizard, but what we are really interested in is the **Pay Elements** button at the bottom left of the screen. Click on this and you get the following.

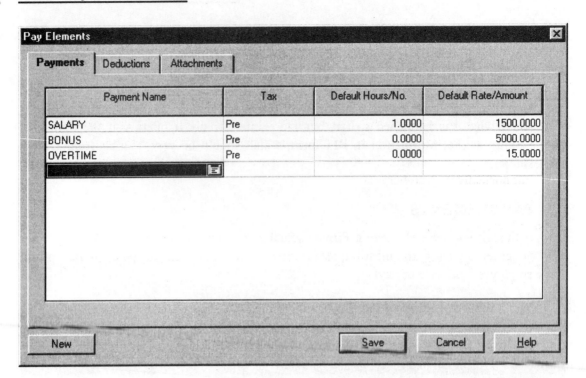

2.4   Some entries have already been made here for illustrative purposes. With a new employee record the screen would be blank to begin with.

Payment Name

2.5   The cursor begins in the Payment Name column. If you click on the button at the side of this or press F4 a list of Pay Elements drops down. In the Blitz case study there are five of these, as we saw in the previous chapter.

    1   BASIC RATE
    2   SALARY
    3   HOURLY RATE
    4   BONUS
    5   OVERTIME

2.6   Select the element that you want to enter for this employee and press Tab. The **Tax** column is filled in automatically, depending upon your Company Settings. If you have set up Salary as a Pay Element to be paid **Pre** tax, for instance (as you would, of course) then Pre appears here. If not, the word Post would appear.

Default Hours/No.

2.7   The cursor now moves on to the **Default Hours/No.** column. This is a very useful facility that means that it is not necessary to enter the same details every month or week for each employee.

Default hours

2.8   For instance, if employees are employed to work 35 hours per week then almost invariably they will be paid for 35 hours of work per week at a certain hourly rate, whatever other elements there may be in their pay in particular weeks. The Sage package therefore assumes by default that this is what will happen *whenever* the payroll is processed. If a employee only worked 30 hours one week you can change the entry for that week when you run the payroll. If it is a normal week there is practically nothing more to do, once you have set this default.

Default No.

2.9   In the illustration above the Salary default is set to the number 1. This simply means that the employee will get one chunk of monthly salary each time the payroll is run – every month in this case. Bonus and Overtime are set to 0, because the employee would not normally be paid these.

Default Rate/Amount

2.10   As you should now realise, the **rate of pay** that you enter is the rate of pay *per payment period*.

(a)   If the employee receives a fixed weekly wage or monthly salary, enter the weekly or monthly amount (*not* the annual equivalent).

(b)   If the employee is paid a rate per hour enter the hourly rate in pounds (and pence, if appropriate).

(c)   If the employee might receive a bonus enter an amount given to you by your supervisor.

(d)   If the employee might receive overtime payments enter the rate per hour for overtime.

Activity 11.2

(a)   How much is the employee paid per annum in the illustration of the Pay Elements screen above?

(b)   What would you enter in the Default rate column if the employee's annual salary were £20,000 per annum?

(c)   How would you pay the employee a bonus of £2,500?

Activity 11.3

Using the record you have been setting up in the exercises in this chapter, enter a salary of £48,000 per annum and an overtime rate of £40 per hour. (You should enjoy this bit, assuming this is more than you get paid at the moment!)

Roughly how much net pay do you think you would receive in a typical month with no overtime?

More elements

2.11   A separate entry is made for each element that the employee is likely to receive. There is no need to key in £ signs. Use **Tab** to move between lines.

2.12   If the employee were entitled to a completely new pay element, such as a special rate for working in unpleasant conditions, you could set this up for the company as a whole from this screen by clicking on the **New** button at the bottom of the screen.

Exiting from Pay Elements

2.13   Once you are happy that you have made the right entries, click on **Save** in the **Pay Elements** window. (If you are not happy you may wish to click on Cancel, in which case you will be asked to confirm that you do not want to save the changes you have made.)

Year to date information

2.14   If you did not enter P45 information when you were using the new employee Wizard, you can do so later by choosing the **Employment** tab and clicking on the **YTD Values...** button at the foot of the screen. A new widow will appear and the column you want is the *first* one, headed **Previous (P45) Employment**. Click in the Gross pay for tax field in this column and enter the details on the P45. Then move down to the Tax Paid box and enter the details.

Activity 11.4

The details on the P45 for the new employee record you have been creating are:

Gross pay for tax   £12,500.00
Tax paid   £1,864.75

Enter these as appropriate and Save the record.

Activity 11.5

Now for the fun. Close your record, having saved all the details. Change the process date to 28/02/99. Select your own record only (using the swap and clear facilities as appropriate. Now click on Enter Payments. Key in the number 1 in the Hours box for SALARY (we shall explain this fully in the next chapter) and press Tab. How much is net pay?

---

3   AMENDING EMPLOYEE DETAILS

3.1   The details that have been input and posted for any employee can be amended at a future time.

3.2   To amend the details for an employee or a range of employees, select the employee or employees by highlighting them in the list in the main screen and then click on **Employee Record** (or on Open, or just double-click on them).

3.3   The Employee Record screen will reappear showing all the existing details. To make an amendment, simply find the appropriate index tab (eg Banking to change bank details) move to the item you wish to alter and key in the new details. Then click on **Save.** If you forget to do this the system will remind you with a prompt.

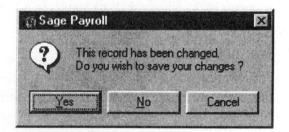

3.4   Unless you have decided *not* to make the amendment after all, click on **No**, then click on **Yes** to save your changes, then close the window.

Activity 11.6

Enter the following banking details for the record you have been setting up.

Barclays Bank, 60 High Street, Doncaster, DR3 5PU. Sort code is 40-02-08.

The account name is your name. The account number is 11482826.

Activity 11.7

Load up assignment 7. Amend the tax codes of any employee who currently has a tax code of 419L to 432L.

4   LEAVERS

4.1   When employees leave your organisation:

    (a)   the last payroll run applying to them must be posted (see the next chapter);

    (b)   their record must be flagged to show that they have left; and

    (c)   a P45 form must be produced for them.

4.2   Select the relevant employee or employees in the main window and then click on the **Employee Record** button. When the record appears click on the **Employment** index tab. At the foot of the screen is a button labelled **Leaver ....** Click on this and you will start up a Leaver Wizard. This generates information that you can copy straight onto a P45 if you wish.

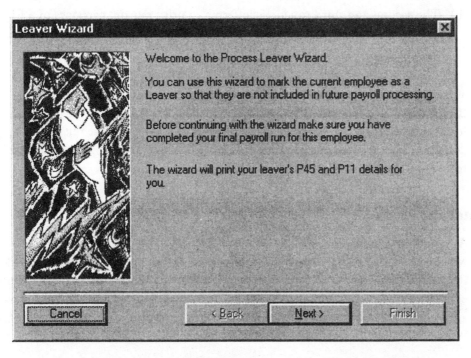

4.3   If you click on **Next>** you are asked to confirm the name of the employee who is leaving and the date of leaving (the current system date is entered as a default, but you can change this).

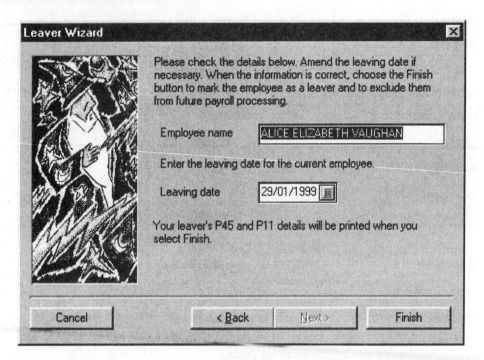

4.4   If you click on **Finish** the **Print** screen will appear allowing you to specify the number of copies you want, the printer to use and so on.

Note that even after you have clicked on OK the *first* time the Print screen will appear several more times with no apparent explanation!

(a)   The first time it is offering to print the P45 details.

(b)   The second and third times it is offering to print out the two sides of a P11 for the employee. If you don't want a P11, click on **Cancel**.

4.5   When you are returned to the Employee record Employment window you will see that the Leaver ... button is dulled. There is no need to Save what you have done: once you have run the Wizard it is saved already. You therefore need to use this option with care: don't play with it when you are mid-way through an assignment, for instance, unless you really do want to record that the employee has left.

Maintaining a record for leavers

4.6   Although an employee might be removed from the payroll, his or her details are not wiped off the file. The employee's details are kept on file, but with the word Leaver (instead of OK) now recorded in the status column of the main employee list window.

4.7   You will not be allowed by the program to add a new employee with the same payroll reference number as an employee who has been removed from the payroll.

4.8   Your employee's record will only be completely wiped off the file after the end of the tax year and after you have completed the year-end payroll routines.

The Delete button

4.9   You may have noticed that there is a button labelled **Delete** at the top of the main screen. Most of the time this just bring up a message telling you that the employee cannot be deleted until the year end. The only time that you can use it is:

(a)   *after* you have set up some details for a new employee; but

(b) *before* any payments have been processed and posted for the employee.

4.10 This might be useful if, say, you set up a new record for an employee who was due to start next Monday and then found on Monday morning that the employee had not bothered to turn up and had no intention of ever doing so.

Getting some practice

4.11 You can also use it for practice purposes. Feel free to set up (and save) any details you like for a new employee in order to find your way round the system. So long as you don't post any actual payments (we have not told you how to do so yet), you can delete any records you create.

4.12 In any case, even if you forget to delete a made up record you have added to Blitz data, it will disappear if you load a fresh copy of the assignment.

Activity 11.8

Load up Assignment 7. Change the payroll run date to 31/01/99. Joanna Louise Escott left on that day. What is the amount of tax paid in this employment, according to her P45?

---

5   CONCLUSION

5.1 It is a bit frustrating that we have not yet dealt with any numbers and seen the great advantages of computerised payroll processing. However the housekeeping aspects of payroll are also very important, so please be patient.

5.2 You should now be ready to tackle **Assignment 7**.

Answers to activities

Answer 11.1

You should not have selected the option to enter P45 details when you started. You should have left blank the holiday details, said No to the director status, left blank the department and cost centre fields and the deduction details screen, and said No you did not want to enter banking details.

Answer 11.2

(a) £1,500 per month = £18,000 per annum

(b) £20,000 ÷ 12 = £1666.6667. (The use of four decimal places helps to minimise rounding differences.)

(c) In the month when the bonus was to be paid at the time you ran the payroll you would set the Default number to 0.5 (£5000 • 0.5 = £2,500). This will become clearer in the next chapter.

Answer 11.3

Your answer should be around £3,000. We shall use the Sage package to calculate the exact amount later in this chapter.

Answer 11.5

You should get the answer £3,016.05. Not bad, just for reading a chapter! Unfortunately we cannot arrange for Blitz to send you a cheque.

Answer 11.8

You should get the answer £803.79.

Chapter 12   Payroll processing

Chapter topic list

1   Payroll routines

2   Preparing to enter payments

3   Entering payments

4   Reports and payslips

5   Update records

6   Holiday pay and pensions

7   Paying the Inland Revenue

8   End of the tax year

9   Conclusion

Learning objectives

On completion of this chapter you will be able to:

	Performance criteria	Range statement
enter gross payments for employees for the period	19.1.1 to 19.1.8	19.1.1 to 19.1.5
produce a payments report	19.3.1 to 19.3.8	19.3.1 to 19.3.4
obtain information for the net amount of pay due to each employee, and for produce payslips	19.2.1 to 19.2.4	19.2.1 to 19.2.6
update the payroll file data for payments and deductions in the week or month	19.1.1 to 19.1.8	19.1.1 to 19.1.5
pay advances of holiday pay and make pensions deductions	19.1.1 to 19.1.8	19.1.1 to 19.1.5
obtain information to include in the payslip that is sent to the Collector of Taxes each month with a cheque for the PAYE and NIC deductions;	19.2.1 to 19.2.4	19.2.1 to 19.2.6
produce yearly summaries of information for the Inland Revenue and set up the payroll for a new tax year	19.3.1 to 19.3.8	19.3.1 to 19.3.4

1   PAYROLL ROUTINES

1.1   Within every organisation, there should be established routines for processing the payroll. When there are weekly-paid staff, there will be weekly payroll procedures. Similarly, for monthly-paid staff, there should be procedures for how and when to process the monthly payroll. In the Blitz case study, weekly-paid employees are paid on Fridays, and monthly-paid employees are paid on the last Friday of the calendar month. The monthly payroll procedures therefore occur on the same day as a weekly payroll.

1.2   There are several basic procedures that you should carry out before starting.

(a)   Check that you have added to the file any new employees who will expect to be paid in the payroll run, and that you have removed any employees who have left since the previous payroll run.

(b)   Make sure that you are using the correct government parameters. Has the Inland Revenue informed you of any new changes to income tax rates or NI contribution rates, or to individual's tax codes, for example? If so, check the date for implementing the new rates and codes. This will be specified in information sent to you by the Inland Revenue.

(c)   Make sure that you have all the data you need for entering payments to employees. Do you have the correct rates of pay? For hourly-paid workers, do you have details of the number of hours worked by each of them? Do you have all the information you need about overtime hours, commission payments and bonuses?

1.3   Sage Payroll 4 allows you to process the payroll quickly, easily and accurately, provided you have the correct parameters on file and all the necessary input data to hand.

2   PREPARING TO ENTER PAYMENTS

Process Date

2.1   Before you begin any payroll processing session check that you have specified the correct Process Date. We looked at this feature in Chapter 10. Click on the **Change Process Date** icon to specify the correct date.

2.2   This *must* be a date *after* the date that the payroll was last updated. There is a **Last Updated** column in the list of employees in the main window. Simply scroll across using the horizontal scroll bar at the bottom of the screen or the → arrow key until you find it. The dates shown will sometimes be different for different employees: except at the end of a month, weekly paid employees will have a more recent date than monthly paid employees.

Select employees

2.3   The next step is to select the employee records that you want to process. The best way to do this is to use the **Outline** button. As you should recall from Chapter 10, clicking on this button brings up the following window.

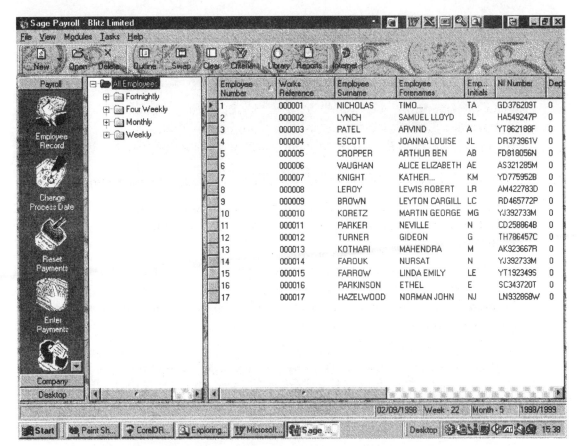

(*Note.* If you can't get this there is something wrong with your **Criteria** settings. Click on the Criteria button and make sure that all types of Payment Period have a tick in the box next to them. You should not normally need to do this.)

2.4   Usually the selection of employees you want to process will be either:

(a)   all weekly paid employees; or
(b)   all monthly paid employees; or
(c)   all employees.

In the Blitz case study for three (or four) weeks of each month you will process weekly paid employees only, and for the fourth (or fifth) week you will process both weekly and monthly paid employees together.

2.5   To select all weekly paid employees, simply click on the ⬜ **Weekly** folder. Only weekly paid employees will now be shown. Then click on the **Swap** button at the top of the screen. This highlights all the employees. (You may need to click on **Clear** before you do this, if any employees were already selected. This is just like the accounting package, so you should be used to this feature by now.)

Activity 12.1

Following these procedures make sure you can also select all Monthly paid employees, one individual employee and All employees.

Selecting non-eligible employees

2.6   It may have occurred to you that if you follow this procedure you will end up selecting employees who are recorded as having left the company. This need not concern you because Sage spots whether you have selected anyone who is not eligible for payment and, when you try to enter payments of them, it displays a message such as the following.

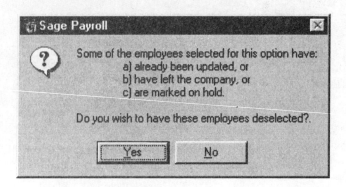

2.7   In this case Sage has spotted that you tried to select someone who had left the company so you should click on **Yes.**

Activity 12.2

Load the data for Assignment 8. Change the process date to 05/02/99. Select all weekly paid employees for processing, as instructed above. Click on **Enter Payments**. Accept any message you get about deselecting employees. Click on close to complete this exercise (since you don't know what to do next, yet.

What do you see now in the main employee list window?

---

3   ENTERING PAYMENTS

3.1   Having selected the employees you wish to pay you have the *option* of clicking on an icon in the button labelled **Reset Payments.** We shall explain what this does, but as a rule we recommend that you *do not use it!*

The Reset Payments icon

3.2   This icon relates to a feature of the Sage Payroll 4 program, which is that the last payments made to the employees in the previous payroll run were *saved* on file. So if last month all monthly paid employees were paid an amount of 1 × their monthly salary rate and 0 × their Bonus rate then these values will be retained. This is normally what you would want to happen.

3.3   However, if, say, last month was bonus month and all employees got a bonus of 0.8 × their bonus rate then 0.8 is the value that the system has retained. This month they may be due the remaining 0.2 × their bonus rate, but the system will pay them 0.8 × the rate again if you do not do something about it.

3.4   Clicking on the Reset Payments icon starts up a **Reset Payments Wizard** that allows you to make the necessary adjustment (or even clear away of the previous month's retained entries) *before* you start processing payments.

3.5   In many cases (certainly in the case of Blitz) this is not any quicker than resetting amounts as necessary when you are entering payments, and so we shall not explore this topic any further.

The Enter Payments icon

3.6   You are now ready to start entering payments. Click on the **Enter Payments** icon in the **Payroll** stacked toolbar. The following window appears.

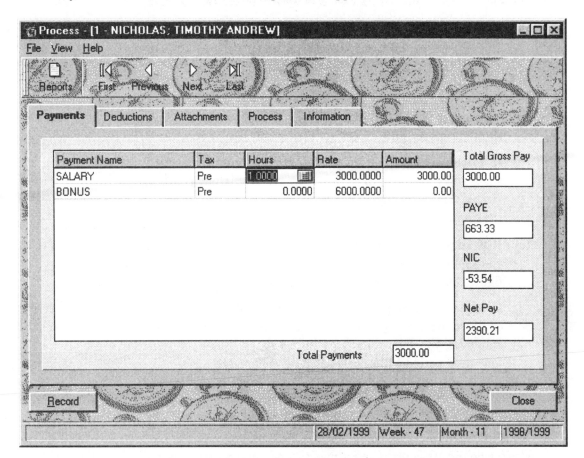

3.7   This window will allow you to enter the payment details for every employee who is to receive pay in this payroll run (that is, according to whether you specified weekly-paid, monthly-paid or all employees). As you can see, as long as you did not use the Reset Payments icon, the details from the last payroll run are included: 1 × the monthly Salary rate and 0 × the Bonus rate.

   (*Note for tutors*. Tutors who are used to previous versions of the Sage Payroll package may wish to note that it is very much *easier* to do so with Payroll 4.)

3.8   The window will list all the **elements of pay** that the employee might receive, for example basic pay, overtime, commission, bonus, etc. These are the payment types that are held as part of the employee record, as described in the previous chapter.

3.9   The record already holds a record of the employee's **rate of pay** for each particular payment type.

How to enter payments

3.10   The *only* thing you have to do, on most occasions, is accept *one* number. In other words, most often, you do nothing!

3.11   When the window opens the first line in the column headed **Hours** is highlighted. In the example above, it is in the box corresponding to SALARY and when the window appears it *already* has the entry: 1.0000. If this is correct you have *already* processed the payroll for this employee and you can just accept it and move onto the next. If not, change it.

3.12   Although this column is headed **Hours**, this is not necessarily what it means. For each payment type, you should key in, not necessarily 'hours', but the *multiple* of the rate of pay that the employee is due to receive. You have probably realised this by now, and some examples should clarify what you have to do.

(a)   If an employee is paid £800 gross **salary** every month, the employee details on file will include a record of £800.00 as his rate of pay for monthly salary. Against the payment type for monthly salary, in the column headed **Hours** you should therefore key in 1 then press Tab. This is because the employee is due to receive one month's salary. The employee's gross salary of 800.00 (1 × 800) will appear automatically on the same line of the screen, in the **Amount** column. (You cannot alter the rate through this screen.)

(b)   If an employee is paid £3 per hour at an **hourly rate,** and works **50** hours, you should key in 50 against the payment type Hourly Pay in the column headed **Hours.** The gross pay of 150.00 (3 × 50) will appear automatically in the column to the right.

(c)   If an employee is to receive a **bonus** of £250, and his rate of pay for a bonus is £500, you should key in 0.5 against the payment type Bonus in the HOURS column. The figure 250.00 (0.5 × 500) will appear automatically in the column to the right.

(d)   If an employee is paid *every four weeks*, and receives £100 per week, his or her employee details might record a **basic rate** of pay 100.00. To process the pay for the employee, you should key in 4 then Tab, and the total gross pay of 400.00 for the four-week period will be calculated by the program.

Example: Entering payments

3.13   An illustrative entry is shown below, for an employee earning a fixed wage of £180 per week, who did six hours of overtime at £5 per hour and who is getting a £600 bonus at a bonus 'rate of pay' of £400.

Payment Name	Tax	Hours	Rate	Amount
BASIC RATE	Pre	1.0000	180.0000	180.00
OVERTIME	Pre	6.0000	5.0000	30.00
BONUS	Pre	1.5000	400.0000	600.00

Your keystrokes to produce all this are simply those highlighted: 1, 6 and 1.5, pressing Tab to move down a line. All the other entries, including the zeros, are added by the program. If you want to leave a line blank (the bonus line would usually be left blank, for instance) just press Tab to pass it by.

Calculating PAYE and NI

3.14   As you key in details in this column notice that the fields for Total Gross Pay, PAYE, National Insurance and Net Pay are calculated and recalculated *automatically*, with no effort from you. How much easier this is than Payroll for Unit 3!

3.15   The program does this by reference to the Employee Record details and the Government Parameters that are held on file.

Moving on to the next employee

3.16   Once you have accepted or changed the Hours column entry you can move on to the next employee that you selected for payment entry.

3.17   To do this simply click on the **Next** button at the top of the screen. Any changes that you have entered so far *will be retained*, though they will *not yet be posted* to the system.

Tax refunds

3.18   If the employee is entitled to a tax refund because he or she has paid too much tax so far in the year, a screen message will appear when first you click on **Next**.

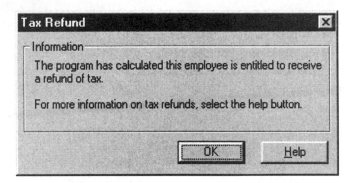

3.19   Sometimes you get the message the moment you move on to the next employee. This is because the details saved from *last* period will give rise to a refund if they are left unchanged *this* period.

3.20   Your only option is to click on **OK** (the other option, Help, just tells you things you should know from Unit 3 studies already), but make a note that the message arose, and check with your supervisor whether the employee should be paid the tax refund: it may have arisen because the details you have been given are incorrect.

Finishing the payroll run

3.21   When you have accepted or entered the payments for every employee selected, you can click on **Close** to return to the main window.

Activity 12.3

Load up **Assignment 9**. Change the date to 05/03/99. Enter the following payments and note down the net pay of each employee. Click on the **Next** button at the top of the screen to take you on to the next employee. Exit by clicking on **Close**.

	Week 48 (6 March)	
	Overtime Hours	Basic Hours
Mahendra Kothari	6	
Nursat Farouk	4½	
Linda Farrow	5	
Ethel Parkinson		14
Caroline Stanley		44

---

4   REPORTS AND PAYSLIPS

4.1   You can now produce a variety of reports, summarising the pay run. You do this *before* you update the records, so you can check a hard copy and correct any mistakes you might have made. Do this by scrolling down to the **Pre-update Reports** icon in the

Payroll stacked toolbar. The most important of the many options you get are shown in the illustration below.

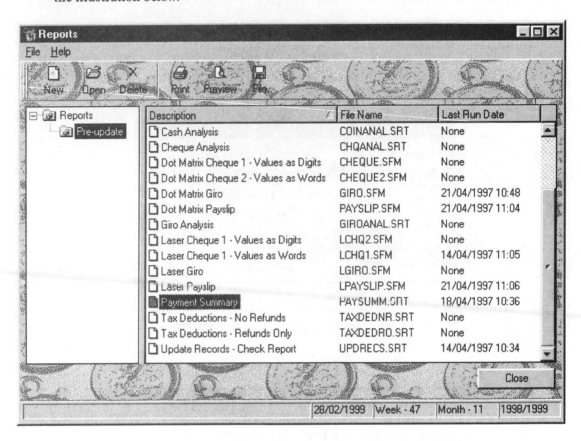

Payments Summary

4.2 The Payments Summary is the most useful document for checking purposes. An illustrative Payments Summary is not shown here, because it is a quite a lengthy document. You will be able to produce one in an assignment. In broad terms, however, the summary shows gross pay, deductions and net pay for the payroll period and for the year to date. A separate summary is provided for weekly and monthly-paid employees.

Cash analysis, cheque analysis, giro analysis

4.3 There are also options to produce an analysis of payments to employees paid in cash, by cheque and by bank giro transfer respectively. All three options are very similar.

4.4 To produce a Cheque Analysis, for example, click on Cheque Analysis to highlight it and then choose how you want the report to be Output using the Print, Preview or File buttons at the top of the screen.

4.5 In early versions of Payroll 4 there does not appear to be any way of specifying the cheque number - that is, the number of the cheques that has been/will be written to pay an employee, but this may have been corrected in later versions.

4.6 An illustrative example of a cheque analysis is shown below.

Blitz Limited	Cheque Analysis	Page: 1
Date: 31/03/99	Tax Month: 12 Week: -42	

Emp Ref	Employee name	Nett pay	Cheque Number
12	G TURNER	84.88	
13	M KOTHARI	92.13	
14	N FAROUK	75.88	
15	L FARROW	85.81	
16	E PARKINSON	32.20	
	Grand Total:-	370.90	

Payslips

4.7 The program can print payslips for employees. There are some default 'templates' for the layout of payslips, with filename PAYSLIP.SFM (for Dot Matrix printers) and LPAYSLIP.SFM (for Laser printers). Your college may have devised its own layout. Check with your tutor.

4.8 To print (or view) payslips, click on the **Pre-update Reports** icon.

4.9 A sample payslip is shown below. In this example, the employee will receive a cheque for £115.92, and the payslip will be enclosed in the pay packet with the cheque.

			Payment method -Cheque		Payment Period - Weekly	
1.00	147.2000	147.20	PAYE Tax	21.17	Total Gross Pay Td	5554.00
			National Insurance	10.11	Gross for Tax TD	5554.00
			Pension	-	Tax paid TD	701.11
				-	Earnings for NI TD	2059.00
				-	National Insurance .TD	141.27
				-	Pension TD	-
				-	-------------	
				-	Earnings for NI	147.00
				-	Gross for Tax	147.20
			Rounding B/F	0.00	Total Gross Pay	147.20
			Rounding C/F	0.00	Nat. Insurance Number	AK9232345A
03/1999		0		12 Mr. G TURNER		

Activity 12.4

Load up Assignment 7 and change the process date to 26/02/99.

Do a payroll run for monthly paid employees and obtain a payments summary. Also prepare a payslip for the employee Norman Hazelwood only.

What is the total net pay for monthly employees? What is the total employer's national insurance?

How much tax is paid by Norman Hazelwood?

---

5   UPDATE RECORDS

5.1   When you have entered payments for each employee and obtained any reports or payslips that you want, you must update the payroll records. It is only when you *update* the payroll that the new pay figures for each employee will be added to the existing figures in the payroll files that hold the P11 data for each employee. The records must be updated before you can do the next payroll run.

5.2   Do not update the payroll, however, until you have finished processing. If you wish to produce a payments summary, payslips, a cheque analysis or any similar output for the payroll run, do this first and update the records afterwards.

5.3   You can only update *one type of employee (weekly, monthly etc) at a time*. If you try to update All Employees at once you will get a message telling you to do different types separately.

Therefore first *select* the monthly or weekly employees whose records you wish to update, and then Click on the **Update Records** icon in the Payroll stacked toolbar. A warning message will appear telling you to print out any reports you need first and also to re-select any employees who are currently recorded as on holiday (see later). Click on **Yes** if all is well. Then an **Update Records Wizard** swings into action.

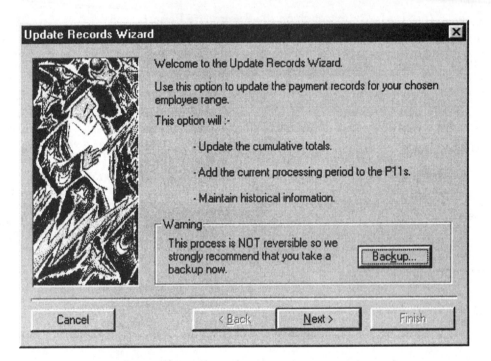

5.4   The Wizard strongly recommends that you do a **Back up** *before* updating the records so that you can recreate the previous records if you later find that you have made a mistake when processing the current batch of entries.

In real life this is very good practice, but it is not necessary for the purposes of the Blitz case study (you can recreate the old records by loading up the assignment you are doing again). Back up if you wish to (you will need a floppy disk or an appropriate directory and some space on your computer's hard disk). Otherwise click on **Next>.**

5.5   You will now get the following window.

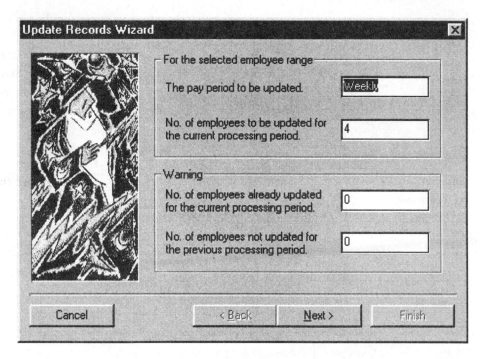

5.6 This shows you how many records of each type you are about to update. If you are happy with what you see, click on OK (if not click on Cancel). A box appears showing you graphically that the relevant amounts are being calculated. You then get an option to de-select any employees that you do not wish to update. Assuming you don't wish to do this, just click on **Finish.** A window appears telling you that the updating is taking place and then you get a window confirming that the records have been updated. Just click on OK.

Activity 12.5

There is not much more to say: you have now covered the main areas for processing payroll by computer. There is a lot of detail to absorb before you can really start to use the system properly, but once you get the hang of it a computerised payroll system should be much easier to operate than a manual system.

If you would like to put some of your new skills to practice before reading on, you are now in a position to attempt Assignment 8. We strongly recommend that you do so.

---

6 HOLIDAY PAY AND PENSIONS

Holidays

6.1 As you probably remember from your studies for Unit 3, weekly paid employees might ask for an advance of holiday pay, in which case they will be paid for the week just gone and a week (or more) ahead. This causes complications in manual payroll because the PAYE system is cumulative but the NI system is not.

6.2 Sage Sterling copes with this very easily. You may have noticed that the Enter Payments window has four other index tabs besides the main Payments tab that we have looked at already. Look back at the illustrations above.

(a) The ones dealing with **Deductions** (eg fees for trade union membership) and **Attachments** (beyond the scope of AAT Foundation) need not concern us.

(b) The one labelled **Information** gives you details from the employee's record like tax code, cumulative earnings to date and so on.

(c) The one labelled **Process** does several things that are useful to us.

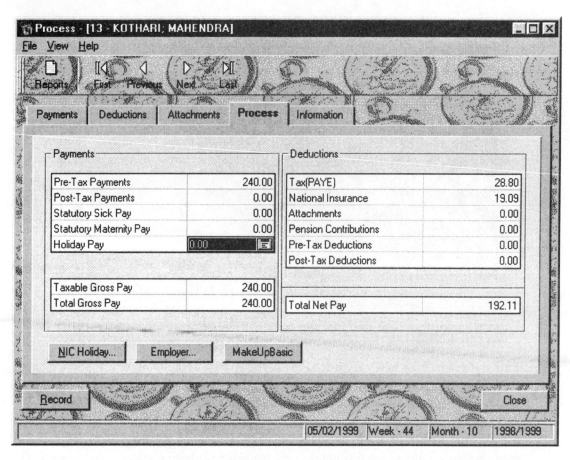

6.3   When an employee is to be paid an advance of holiday pay, proceed as follows.

(a)   Process the current week's payment to that employee in the normal way, but before moving on to the next employee, click on the **Process** index tab, and click on the Finder button in the Holiday Pay box (see the illustration above).

The following pops up.

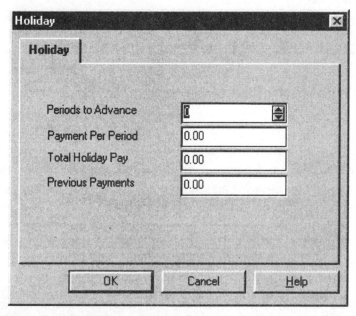

(b)   In the **Periods to Advance** box type in the number of periods pay to be advanced. For a weekly paid employee taking one week off type in 1. If the employee wants an advance of two weeks holiday pay, type in 2, and so on.

(c)   When you have done this click on OK. A new Enter Payments screen will appear, solely for the holiday pay. The cursor will be flashing in the BASIC RATE line, where there is usually a 1.0000. Here, though, it will be blank and you have to type in the same entry as you made in the Periods to Advance box in (b) above. The package will then automatically do all the necessary payroll calculations that apply to the holiday payment.

(d)   Click on OK and you will be returned to the **Process** index tab. The current week's pay will now have had the holiday advance added to it. You can see this in the Taxable Gross Pay line just under the Holiday Pay line. If a normal week's pay is £185.20 and a week's holiday pay is to be advanced, this will now say £370.40.

(e)   Move on to the next employee.

Note. There is no need to move back to the **Payments** index tab before moving on. If you do so the **Hours** column entry will still say 1.0000, but you can see from the Net Pay figure that the Holiday Pay has been taken account of, so *do not* alter this.

Pensions

6.4   Setting up a pension payment for an employee is very much like setting up Pay Elements and pay rates for salary or wages. It is a two part process, if the pension scheme is a new one.

6.5   The first task, before you begin entering payments, is to click on the **Company** button in the stacked toolbar and then on **Company Settings.** This gives you a series of index cards, one of which says **Pension.** If you click on this another window will appear. This allows you to set up the details for up to ten different pension schemes.

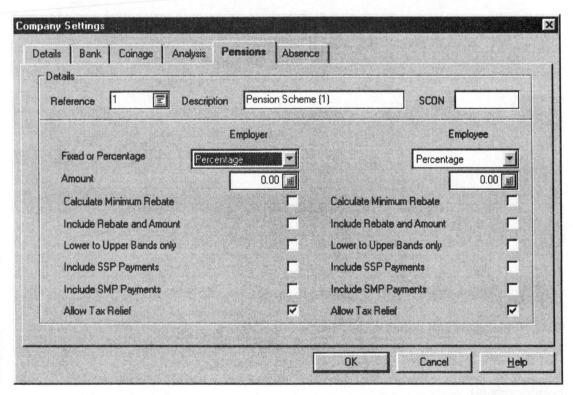

6.6   Here we are setting up Pension Scheme 1, as you can see from the **Description** box. You can change the description to whatever is most appropriate, for example 'Pension Scheme: Over 5 years service' or 'Directors' Pension Scheme'.

6.7   In the Blitz case study you will leave the **Percentage** box as it is and in the **Amount** box below type in the percentage of employees' pay that will be contributed to the pension scheme by the employer (if it is 10% type in 10). (Alternatively, a scheme might have contributions of a fixed amount, say £50 per month.)

6.8 You can ignore the tick boxes(these deal with matters beyond the scope of your studies), but the ones labelled **Allow Tax Relief** should be ticked (normally they will be automatically). Tab through these to get to the Employee Percentage Amount box and type in the percentage of employees' gross pay that will be contributed, if any. Then click on OK.

6.9 The second step is to change the Records of employees who will be members of this pension scheme.

6.10 Click on the **Payroll** button in the stacked toolbar, select the employees concerned and then click on **Employee Record** or **Open**. You then want the **Employment** index tab, which has a button labelled **Pensions ...** at the bottom, next to the Pay Elements button.

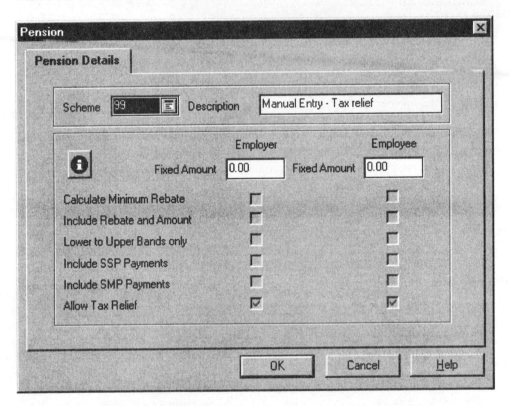

6.11 All you have to do is press F4 or click on the Finder button beside the **Scheme** box and select the right number for the pension scheme that applies to this employee. The other details will be filled in automatically. Then click on OK and Save and move on to the next Record that you need to modify.

6.12 When you next process payments the pensions deductions will be calculated automatically and shown on the relevant employees' Enter Payments screens.

Employer's NI

6.13 Finally, notice that there is a button at the bottom of the **Process** tab that says **Employer ....** If you click on this you get information about how much the employer will pay in National Insurance contributions and pension contributions.

Activity 12.6

Load up assignment 8 and change the date to 27/02/99.

Set up a pension scheme whereby the employer and employee each contribute 2% of employee's pay.

Leyton Brown is to be a member of this pension scheme. Process his pay for February 1999. How much does he contribute to the pension scheme and what is his net pay?

Activity 12.7

Load up Assignment 7 and change the date to 5 February 1999.

Process a (gross) payment for the week just passed to Gideon Turner (only) of £215.25 and, following the instructions above, pay him an advance of 1 week's holiday pay.

How much does he receive in net pay?

7   PAYING THE INLAND REVENUE

7.1   Employers in the UK are required pay the Collector of Taxes the PAYE and National Insurance contributions they have deducted from their employees. This payment must be made within 14 days of the end of a tax month (by the 19th of each calendar month, for the previous tax month), and the cheque should be accompanied by a payslip. Special payslips are provided to employers by the Inland Revenue.

7.2   The Sage Payroll 4 program includes an option to produce the information to enter on the payslip. The information required includes the total amount of PAYE and National Insurance contributions deducted in the month, tax refunds, and SSP and SMP payments.

Form P32

7.3   To produce this information, you should have *already* processed and updated the payroll for the tax month. When you have done this, proceed as follows.

(a)   Make **All Employees** appear in the main window (using the Outline button and the folders as necessary). Then click on **Clear** to make sure no individual employees are selected (a P32 includes details for everyone) and then **Swap** to select all of them.

(b)   Click on the **Reports** button which is the last but one at the top right of the main window. This gives you a large number of types of report covering Employees, Absence and so on, as well as Company wide reports.

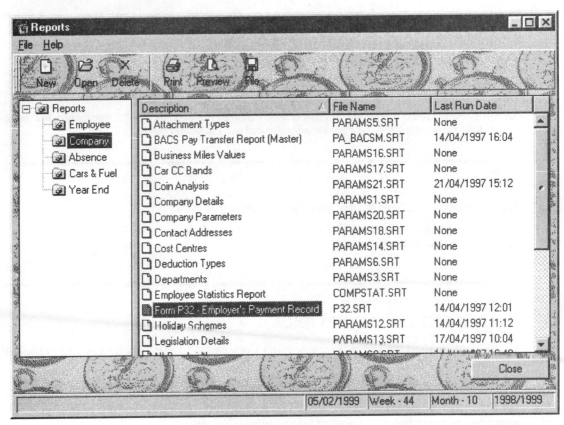

7.4   For a P32, select the **Company** folder, as illustrated above and look down the list until you see Form P32 (highlighted above). Select this and then click on **Print** or **Preview** at the top of the screen.

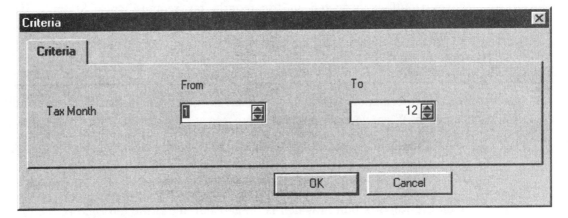

7.5   You simply have to specify the month range for which you want a P32. If it were month 11 you would type 11 in both the From and To boxes. Then click on OK and your P32 details will be produced.

P11 deductions sheet

7.6   Organisations with a manual payroll system must maintain a cumulative record for each employee for the year to date on a P11. A P11 deductions sheet contains information for the tax year to date about an employee's payments, deductions for PAYE and NI, and SSP and SMP payments.

7.7   A computer-produced version of a P11 that is acceptable to the Inland Revenue can be obtained from the Sage Payroll 4 system. To produce a paper copy of the two halves (NIC and PAYE) of a P11 (or several P11s for a range of employees), select the employee or employees for whom you want a P11 and then click on **Reports**. This time you want the **Employee** folder. Scroll down the list of available reports until you find the two entries for **P11** (almost the last items in the list). **Print or Preview** as before.

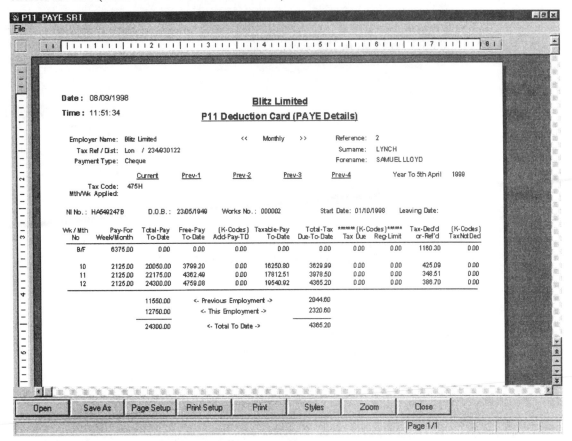

Activity 12.8

Load up Assignment 7. Change the date to 5 February 1999. Produce a P32 for month 10.

What is the Total Amount Due to the authorities?

---

8   END OF THE TAX YEAR

8.1   At the end of each tax year, an employer must submit an annual return to the Inland Revenue, on forms P14 and P35. The P14 form, one for each employee, contains details that include the employee's name, NI number, NI category, date of birth, earnings in the year, NI contributions, tax code, PAYE, SSP, SMP etc. The P35 is a total summary of the information on the individual P14s.

8.2   The Sage Payroll 4 program has a facility for producing information for these reports automatically.

8.3   You must also clear the year-to-date totals for gross pay and deductions, and re-set these to zero for the new tax year.

Year end reports

P35 Form

8.4   Begin by setting the Process Date to 5th April, the end of the tax year.

8.5   Make sure **All Employees** are shown in the main window and that all are selected (just as you did for a P32)

8.6   Then click on **Reports** and this time select the **Year End** folder. Select the option for a P35 and click on Print or Preview.

P11 deduction forms

8.7   You can produce the two halves of P11 deduction forms by selecting this option. You can pre-select individual employees or produce a P11 for each employee, filled in up to the end of the tax year. The data is extensive, and it is easier (but potentially time-consuming and paper-consuming) to Print the forms than to Preview them.

P14/P60 certificate

8.8   There are several options for P14s depending on the layout you want and the type of printer you have. You can print P14s for individual employees if you pre-select them.

Clearing the year-to-date

8.9   You must clear the year-to-date totals after the end of a tax year, before you process the first payroll for the new tax year. Click on the word **Tasks** in the menu bar at the top of the screen.

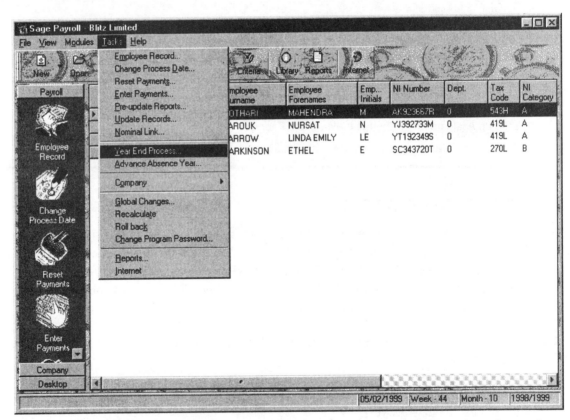

Note that this menu offers you another way of selecting many of the options that we have been using via icons and buttons. If you prefer to use the **Tasks** menu to start up any of these options feel free to do so.

8.10   In this instance the option you want is **Year End Process**. When you click on this you are recommended to take a back-up and asked to specify or confirm the tax year. Click on OK if the screen shows the correct tax year. Enter the correct year and click on OK if the year shown on the screen prompt is incorrect. Then click on **Clear.**

8.11   A **Clear Year End Wizard** appears telling you exactly what the consequences of clearing the year to date figures are. All you have to do is to read what the Wizard says, clicking on **Next>** and then **Finish**, if you accept what is going to happen.

8.12   The year end totals on file will be then be cleared automatically. You can now process the payroll for the new tax year.

Tax codes and tax rates

8.13   Early in the new tax year, many employees are given a new tax code. New tax codes should be entered on file, when notification is received. This can be done using the normal facilities for amending employee records. Alternatively, if there are lots of employees with the same tax code (for example lots with the standard single persons' and married persons' codes) you can use the **Global Changes** option in the **Tasks** menu. Yet another Wizard appears.

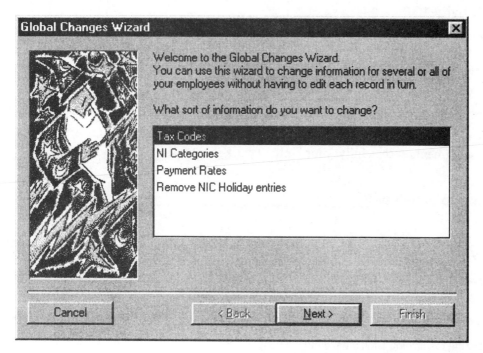

8.14   At least once each year, the government is likely to alter tax bands and National Insurance bands, and possibly income tax rates and National Insurance contribution rates. The Inland Revenue should indicate to all employers when new bands or new rates should become effective.

8.15   Sage send out an update disk for a modest sum which will amend the rates and bands for you and make any other changes necessary to the software.

8.16   Failing this, though, you yourself will have to enter the new bands and rates, before making the first payroll run to which the new details should apply.

Pay rises

8.17   An employer will usually review wages and salaries once a year, possibly at different dates for different grades of employee. There might also be an annual bonus.

8.18   It is common for pay rises and bonuses to coincide with the end of the company's accounting year or the end of the calendar year (31 December). They can occur, however, at any time.

8.19 Payment rate changes can be entered on file using the normal facilities for amending employee records or else via the **Global Changes Wizard.**

End-of-year bonuses

8.20 Bonuses should be paid in a normal payroll run, using the Enter Payments window. To pay a bonus in the Sage Payroll 4 system, you need to know the amount of the employee's bonus, as recorded in the employee details.

8.21 For example, suppose an employee's bonus *rate* of pay (in the employee record on file) is £2,000. The *actual* bonus payable is £1,500, just 75% of the £2,000. To pay a bonus of £1,500, 0.75 should be entered against Bonus. By pressing Enter, the program will then calculate the bonus as £1,500 ($0.75 \times £2,000$).

Activity 12.9

You should be ready to attempt Assignment 8 (if you have not done it already) and Assignments 9 and 10.

---

9   CONCLUSION

9.1 You have now completed Part C of this book, and if you have done all of the Assignments successfully, your Unit 19 work is complete. Well done!

Answers to activities_____

Answer 12.2

Five out of six employees should be highlighted. Employee 12 should not be highlighted, since he has left.

Answer 12.3_____

These are the results you should have got.

	Net pay
Mahendra Kothari	221.51
Nursat Farouk	188.49
Linda Farrow	189.77
Ethel Parkinson	55.20
Caroline Stanley	217.81

Answer 12.4_____

Total net pay is £12,711.97. Total employer's national insurance (from the second page of the payments summary) is £1,582.06

Norman Hazelwood pays £303.66 in tax.

Answer 12.6_____

His pension contribution is £22.00 (click on the Process tab to find this). Net pay is £858.62.

Answer 12.7

Enter the payment as usual and then click on the Process tab and the button at the end of the Holiday Pay line. Follow the instructions given above.

The answer you get should be £332.91.

Answer 12.8

You should get the answer £6,887.67.

Part D
Assignments

Assignment
1 Supplier invoices and credit notes

Performance criteria

The following performance criteria are covered *at an easy level* in this Assignment.

Element 19.1 Input information from source documents into a computer system

1   All vital fields are completed

3   All errors in inputting and coding are identified and corrected

4   Correct part of the computer system is used for inputting

5   New unique reference codes are generated as necessary

6   Inputting is completed to agreed deadline

8   Risks to the information technology environment are minimised at all times

Element 19.2 Locate and retrieve recorded details of requested items from a computer system

1   Correct details are retrieved

2   Search facilities are used optimally

4   Risks to the information technology environments are minimised at all times

Element 19.3 Generate and print standard reports on a computer system

1   Required range and report correctly specified

2   Printed information is correct and complete

3   Hard copy is clean, clearly printed and aligned correctly

4   Efforts are made to minimise the wastage of paper

5   Printer area is kept clean and tidy

6   Work is produced to agreed deadline

8   Risks to the information technology environment are minimised at all times

ASSIGNMENT 1: SUPPLIER INVOICES AND CREDIT NOTES

Loading and carrying out the assignment

For instructions on how to load the data for assignments using the BPP Blitz program, refer to the online Help or to Section 7 of Chapter 2 and Section 3 of Chapter 3. Check with your tutor in case special instructions apply to your college's system.

If you need to break off from this assignment part-way through, back-up your entries so far on a floppy disk, following the instructions given on screen when you quit the Sage program. You can then restore your entries when you start work again. (See Appendix 3)

If you want to keep a permanent copy of your finished work, back it up and save the back-up file in a separate suitably named sub-directory on your floppy disk such as A:\ASMT01.

Purpose

Assignment 1 tests your ability to set up accounts for new suppliers in the purchase ledger, to process invoices and credit notes from suppliers, to post the entries to the appropriate accounts in the suppliers and nominal ledgers, to produce reports and to check the current balance on the creditors control account.

The **Tasks** for this assignment will be found follwing the **Information.** Read the information and all the tasks *before* commencing work.

Information

Your supervisor asks you to process eight invoices and two credit notes received from suppliers. Today's date is 2 October 1998. Details are as follows.

Invoices from existing suppliers

Invoice No	Supplier	A/C Ref	Details	Nominal ledger account	£	Net amount (excluding VAT) £
C6147	AA1 Mini Cabs	AA1MIN	Taxi fares	Travelling		38.40
26187	Newlite Cleaning Fluids	NEWLIT	Cleaning materials	Materials purchases		168.70
435796	Flooring Supplies Ltd	FLOORI	Cleaning materials	Materials purchases	202.36	
			Equipment	Plant and machinery	620.00	
						822.36
4821	First Steps Ladder Hire	FIRSTS	Ladder hire	Equipment hire		126.75

All these invoices are subject to VAT at the standard rate of 17.5%. All invoices are dated 1 October 1998.

Invoices from new suppliers (Inv no = invoice number. Inv date = invoice date)

(a)   Samurai Insurance Brokers
15 Osnabruck Street
London EC3 5JG
Tel: 0171-488 1066

A/C ref	Inv no	Inv date	Nominal ledger account	Net amount £	VAT
SAMURA	02381	1 Oct 98	Premises insurance	1,650.00	
			Vehicle insurance	1,125.00	
			Miscellaneous insurance	430.00	
				3,205.00	

This invoice has a Post-It note attached by your supervisor saying 'NB - insurance is exempt from VAT - code T2.'

(b)   3D Technical Bookshops
116 Albert Road
Wood Green
London N22 7RB
Tel: 0181-889 3539
Contact: Adrian

A/C ref	Inv no	Inv date	Nominal ledger account	Net amount £	VAT
3DTECH	001462	30 Sep 98	Books	179.95	0%

(c)   Thames Water
Umbrella House
Weather Street
London WC1 9JK
Tel: 0171-837 4411

A/C ref	Inv no	Inv date	Nominal ledger account	Net amount £	VAT
THAMES	132157	1 Oct 98	Water rates	420.00	0%

(d)   ANS Newspaper Group
19 Cecil Road
London NW10 4PP
Tel: 0181-453 2926
Contact: Mandy Walker

A/C ref	Inv no	Inv date	Nominal ledger account	Net amount £	VAT
ANSNEW	621014	29 Sep 98	Advertising	750.00	17.5%

For all invoices, you have been given details of the item purchased, and you have been instructed to allocate each item to an appropriate nominal ledger account. Refer to the nominal ledger codes in Appendix 1 of this book if necessary.

Credit Notes from Suppliers

Credit note no	Supplier	A/C ref	Net amount £	VAT
K0320	B L Office Furnishing	BLOFFI	150.00	17.5%
C0259	Trojan Secretarial Service	TROJAN	60.00	17.5%

Both credit notes are dated 1 October 1998.

The credit note from B L Office Furnishing is for the return of office furniture supplied in damaged condition. The credit note from the Trojan Secretarial Service is for overcharging; a temporary secretary had been employed for two days, but Trojan, the agency supplying the secretary, had charged for three days.

Your supervisor has asked you to identify the nominal ledger accounts for the credit note transactions, but has told you that the credit note for B L Office Furnishing relates to fixed assets (furniture and fixtures) and the credit note for Trojan Secretarial Service relates to casual wages.

Tasks

(a)   Enter these transactions in the Suppliers Ledger and post the details. Use the tax code T0 for items with 0% VAT.

(b)   Print a detailed suppliers invoices day book listing and suppliers credits day books listing covering *only* the transactions you have posted. If you do not have access to a printer, you should display these listings (one at a time) on your screen. Check that the number of entries in the system so far is 83. What is the total amount of transactions in each day book listing?

(c)   Obtain the balance on the Creditors Control Account, after all the entries have been posted. (This is the total amount currently owed to suppliers for goods or services obtained on credit.) The nominal ledger code for this account is 2100. You can obtain the balance on the account either by looking at an appropriate screen display or by printing a copy of the Activity for the account.

Assignment
2 Customer invoices and credit notes

Performance criteria

The following performance criteria are covered *at a basic level* in this Assignment.

Element 19.1 Input information from source documents into a computer system

1   All vital fields are completed

2   Incomplete or unauthorised source documents are referred for clarification

3   All errors in inputting and coding are identified and corrected

4   Correct part of the computer system is used for inputting

5   New unique reference codes are generated as necessary

6   Inputting is completed to agreed deadline

8   Risks to the information technology environment are minimised at all times

Element 19.2 Locate and retrieve recorded details of requested items from a computer system

1   Correct details are retrieved

2   Search facilities are used optimally

3   Confidential information is not disclosed to unauthorised people

4   Risks to the information technology environments are minimised at all times

Element 19.3 Generate and print standard reports on a computer system

1   Required range and report correctly specified

2   Printed information is correct and complete

3   Hard copy is clean, clearly printed and aligned correctly

4   Efforts are made to minimise the wastage of paper

5   Printer area is kept clean and tidy

6   Work is produced to agreed deadline

7   Documents are correctly collated and distributed as directed

8   Risks to the information technology environment are minimised at all times

ASSIGNMENT 2: Customer invoices and credit notes

Loading and carrying out the assignment

For instructions on how to load the data for assignments using the BPP Blitz program, refer to the online Help or to Section 7 of Chapter 2 and Section 3 of Chapter 3. Check with your tutor in case special instructions apply to your college's system.

NB. If you want to do the Windows exercise you will need a blank floppy disk.

If you need to break off from this assignment part-way through, back-up your entries so far on a floppy disk, following the instructions given on screen when you quit the Sage program. You can then restore your entries when you start work again. (See Appendix 3)

If you want to keep a permanent copy of your finished work, back it up and save the back-up file in a separate suitably named sub-directory on your floppy disk such as A:\ASMT02.

Purpose

Assignment 2 tests your ability to set up accounts for new customers in the customers ledger, to process invoices and credit notes to customers, to post the entries to the appropriate accounts in the customers and nominal ledgers, to produce listings and to answer queries from customers by searching the ledger files. If you have access to a printer, the assignment also tests your ability to produce invoices and credit notes.

The **Tasks** for this assignment will be found following the **Information**. Read the information and all the tasks *before* commencing work.

Information

It is now 8 October 1998. You have been asked to process a batch of invoices and credit notes.

The invoice details and credit note details that you are asked to process are received in the accounts section of Blitz Limited on customer order forms, illustrated on the next page.

Invoices

The invoice details for processing are as follows. All invoices are subject to VAT at the standard rate (17.5%): code T1.

(1)	*Customer Name*	R P Marwood
	New Customer?	Yes
	Address	17 Eton Villas
		Harrow Road
		London NW3 0JS
	Telephone	0171-722 4488
	Contact	Mr Marwood
	Credit Limit?	No

	Details	*Net Amount*
	Domestic services	£66.00

(2)	*Customer Name*	School of Dance
	New Customer?	Yes
	Address	10 Underwood Street
		London N1 6SD
	Telephone	0171-490 2449
	Contact	Bernice
	Credit Limit?	Yes, £600

	Details	*Net Amount*
	Cleaning school property	£250.00

(3)	*Customer Name*	B & T Fashions Ltd
	New Customer?	Yes
	Address	8 Green Lanes
		London N16 4LM
	Telephone	0171-226 2703
	Contact	Peter Bruce
	Credit Limit?	No

	Details	*Net Amount*
	Window cleaning	£144.00

(4)   *Customer Name*   The Keith Group
     New Customer?   Yes
     Address   3 Sheringham Avenue
                                 London N14 2TT
     Telephone   0181-360 7723
     Contact   Pat Walker
     Credit Limit?   Yes, £2,500

	Net Amount
Details	
Office cleaning at Grants Parade	£1,420.00
London N14 and Spur House, Watford	

(5)   *Customer Name*   Rapid Pizzas
     New Customer?   Yes
     Address   90 Upper Street
                                   London N10 4ZX
     Telephone   0181-444 4136
     Contact   Luciano Palmarozza
     Credit Limit?   No
     Settlement discount   5%

Details
5 cases of Flame detergent at £12 per case
3 boxes of Bream cleaner at £30.40 per box
50 pairs of cleaning gloves at £0.84 per pair

(6)   *Customer Name*   Bridgford & Co
     New Customer?   No

	Net Amount
Details	
Office cleaning at invoice	£420.00
address	

(7)   *Customer Name*   D J Hargreaves
     New Customer?   No

	Net Amount
Details	
Domestic services	£43.50

(8)   *Customer Name*   Elite Caterers
     New Customer?   No

	Net Amount
Details	
Kitchen cleaning	£644.00
In addition, supply of materials	
10 boxes of oven cleaner at £6.10 per box	
6 cases of Flame detergent at £12 per case	
7 brushes at £3.42 each	

(9)   *Customer Name*   Meakin Media Services Ltd
      New Customer?   No

      Details   *Net Amount*
      Window cleaning   £249.00

(10)   *Customer Name*   A Rose Ltd
      New Customer?   Not sure
      Address   8 Mill Mead Road
                                 London N17 7HP
      Telephone   0181-808 4204
      Credit Limit?   No

      Details   *Net Amount*
      Window cleaning   £125.00

(11)   *Customer Name*   Gardeners Delight
      New Customer?   Not sure
      Invoice Address   212 Spa Road
                                   London NW3 3DQ
      Delivery Address   Gardeners Delight Centre
                                   Buckmans Road
                                   London NW3
      Telephone   0181-368 2115
      Contact   Joe Grundy
      Credit Limit?   No
      Settlement discount   5%

      Details
      30 cases of window cleaning fluid at £21.00 per case

(12)   *Customer Name*   Payne Properties Ltd
      New Customer?   Yes
      Address   18 Caledonian Road
                                   London N1 9PN
      Telephone   0171-837 3442
      Contact   Carl Megson
      Credit Limit?   Yes, £2,500
      Settlement discount   5%

      Details   *Net Amount*
      Office cleaning at invoice address and 8 Richardson Street   £1,210.00

(13)   *Customer Name*   T P Paul
              New Customer?   Yes
              Address   1 Arcola Street
                                 London N8 1QB
              Telephone   0181-348 5453
              Contact   Mrs Paul
              Credit Limit?   No

Details	*Net Amount*
Domestic services	£60.00

(14)   *Customer Name*   Siddall Wallis
              New Customer?   No

Details	*Net Amount*
Window cleaning	£182.00

(15)   *Customer Name*   Norris Hydraulics Ltd
              New Customer?   No

Details	*Net Amount*
Factory and office cleaning	£816.40

Credit Notes

The following credit notes are to be produced. Make sure these are numbered 1, 2 and 3, and all dated 8 October 1998.

(1)   *Customer*   Gelling Private Bank
              Details   Credit note for £250 (plus VAT), following a customer complaint about the poor quality of cleaning at one of the office premises.

(2)   *Customer*   Royal Properties Ltd
              Details   Credit note for £300 (plus VAT), following an agreement with the customer that the scale of the office cleaning service provided was less than originally anticipated.

(3)   *Customer*   DCS Roofing
              Details   Credit note for £150.00 (plus VAT), after customer complaint about a window broken by a Blitz window cleaner.

Tasks

(a) Enter the invoice and credit note details in the system. Make sure that the first invoice in the series is numbered 10036, changing the invoice number shown on screen if necessary. Where appropriate, establish new customer accounts.

Use the invoice and credit note options in the Invoicing window if you have access to a printer. Use the Batch Invoices option in the Customers window if you do not have access to a printer and are unable to print out data. Check the nominal ledger accounts used by Blitz Limited to account for sales. These are included in the list in Appendix 1.

(b) Print the invoices and credit notes. If you can, back-up your work *before* posting the invoices, so that you can correct any errors discovered later without re-entering all the data.

(c) Post the invoice and credit note details to the appropriate accounts in the customers ledger and nominal ledger.

(d) Produce day book listings of customer invoices and customer credits for these transactions. Print the listings if you have access to a printer. Otherwise, display each listing on screen.

(e) Your supervisor wants to know the current balance on the Debtors Control Account in the nominal ledger. Find out what this is. If you have access to a printer, print out the details of this account.

(f) Your supervisor also wants to know the current debit, credit and net total balances on each of the four sales accounts (codes 4000, 4001, 4002 and 4100 in the nominal ledger). After you have entered the invoice and credit note details, find out what these balances are.

(g) *This task can only be carried out if you have access to a printer.*

The invoice you have produced for the School of Dance has been damaged accidentally. Coffee has been spilled over it. Produce another invoice for sending to the customer.

(h) You receive a telephone call from your contact at CCC Engineering Limited. They have not yet received an invoice for factory cleaning services, but need to know what the cost will be, for a management meeting that afternoon. Find out the amount of the invoice.

(i) *Windows exercise*

Use the Blitz program to unload the Blitz Windows Exercises onto a blank floppy disk. (see Chapter 2 for more detailed instructions). (If you have not done Exercise 5 in Chapter 2, do this first.)

Without closing Sage switch to the word processing application on your computer (Microsoft Word or whatever). Open the document A2FAX which will now be on your floppy disk and *save* it with another appropriate name.

Prepare a fax to send to CCC Engineering in time for their management meeting this afternoon. The fax number is 01923 354071. Other details can be found from CCC Engineering's customer record or from an audit trail report. Copy from Sage and Paste into your word processing document if you wish to, and can work out how.

Note. To switch between applications use Alt + Tab.

(j) *Windows exercise*

The missing invoice was one of an early batch that was prepared manually, not using the Sage system. Unfortunately there is no copy.

Open the document A2INV and prepare a duplicate invoice for CCC Engineering. The invoice details are those you found for the previous task.

Mention the duplicate invoice in your fax produced for the previous task. (Alter it if you have saved and closed it already.)

If you have access to a printer, print out the fax and the duplicate invoice.

Assignment
3 Payments to suppliers

Performance criteria

The following performance criteria are covered *at a moderate level* in this Assignment.

Element 19.1 Input information from source documents into a computer system

1 All vital fields are completed

2 Incomplete or unauthorised source documents are referred for clarification

3 All errors in inputting and coding are identified and corrected

4 n is used for inputting

   ....nerated as necessary

   ....adline

   ....source documents are followed

   ....environment are minimised at all times

....recorded details of requested

   ....ed to unauthorised people

   ....vironments are minimised at all times

....andard reports on a computer

   ....ecified

   ....lete

   ....ligned correctly

4 Efforts are made to minimise the wastage of paper

5 Printer area is kept clean and tidy

6 Work is produced to agreed deadline

7 Documents are correctly collated and distributed as directed

8 Risks to the information technology environment are minimised at all times

ASSIGNMENT 3: PAYMENTS TO SUPPLIERS

Loading and carrying out the assignment

For instructions on how to load the data for assignments using the BPP Blitz program, refer to the online Help or to Section 7 of Chapter 2 and Section 3 of Chapter 3. Check with your tutor in case special instructions apply to your college's system.

NB. If you want to do the Windows exercise you will need a blank floppy disk.

If you need to break off from this assignment part-way through, back-up your entries so far on a floppy disk, following the instructions given on screen when you quit the Sage program. You can then restore your entries when you start work again. (See Appendix 3)

If you want to keep a permanent copy of your finished work, back it up and save the back-up file in a separate suitably named sub-directory on your floppy disk such as A:\ASMT03.

Purpose

Assignment 3 tests your ability to process payments to suppliers, to post the transactions to the appropriate accounts in the purchase ledger and nominal ledger, to deal with part payments, credit notes, settlement discounts and payments in advance, to deal with payments for cheque requisitions, to produce reports for payments, and to check the current balance on the bank account and creditors control account in the nominal ledger. If you have access to a printer, the Assignment also tests your ability to produce remittance advices.

The **Tasks** for this assignment will be found folowing the **Information.** Read the information and all the tasks *before* commencing work.

Information

It is now 9 October 1998. You have been asked to process a batch of payments.

(1) Your supervisor has asked you to record the following payment transactions.

Supplier	Ref code	Amount	Cheque no
AA1 Mini Cabs	AA1MIN	£117.50	000100
British Telecom plc	BTELEC	£540.50	000101
Capital Radiopaging	CAPITA	£376.00	000102
B L Office Furnishing	BLOFFI	£1,493.78	000103
First Steps Ladder Hire	FIRSTS	£332.23	000104
Samurai Insurance Brokers	SAMURA	£3,205.00	000105
3D Technical Bookshops	3DTECH	£179.95	000106
The Ironcliffe Group	IRONCL	£3,000.00	000107
Trojan Secretarial Services	TROJAN	£141.00	000108
Muswell Hill Council	MUSWEL	£1,240.00	000109
North London Advertiser	NORTHL	£1,175.00	000110
Sterling Supplies	STERLI	£642.37	000111
Uniform Workerwear	UNIFOR	£763.75	000112
Van Centre	VANCEN	£19,059.44	000113

The payments to B L Office Furnishing and Trojan Secretarial Services are net of credit notes outstanding on these accounts.

(2) You have also been asked to process a newly-received credit note of £235 (£200 plus VAT of £35) from the Chieftain Newspaper Group (because of an error in an advertisement printed in a newspaper), and a cheque (number 000114) to this supplier for the balance outstanding on the account of £1,175. The credit note number is SC0108. The nominal account code is 6201.

(3) You have been given the following note by your supervisor.

> We have received full credit notes and revised invoices from three suppliers because they offered us early settlement discounts over the phone but did not reflect this on their original invoices, which have already been posted.
>
> The suppliers and the relevant Nominal Codes are:
>
> Floorsanders (Equipment) (FLOORS)   0020
> Harrow Cleaning Supplies (HARROW)   5000
> Matthias Scaffolding (MATTHI)   0020
>
> Please proceed as follows.
>
> (a) Post the credit notes, which are each for the full amount currently shown as outstanding on these accounts. Use the reference 'Disc'.
>
> (b) Set up early settlement discounts for these three suppliers: 3% from Harrow Cleaning Supplies and 5% from the other two.
>
> (c) Post the revised invoices. Use code T3 and post VAT manually.
>
> (d) Pay the invoices taking advantage of the discounts.

The revised invoice details are as follows.

Supplier	Invoice no	Gross	VAT	Net
FLOORS	34005	1,005.31	143.31	862.00
HARROW	HC1213	2,840.62	412.22	2,428.40
MATTHI	63041	3,335.48	475.48	2,860.00

(4) Blitz Limited will be purchasing more equipment from Highpile Cleaning Supplies (code HIGHPI). It has been agreed with the supplier that Blitz should make a payment of

£3,500, to settle its outstanding debt and as a payment in advance for future purchases. You have been asked to record the payment. The cheque number is 000118.

(5) You have also been asked to prepare cheques and record the payments for the following cheque requisitions. The supplier names will be filled in manually.

Cheque no	Amount	Purpose	Nominal code
000119	£258.50 (inc VAT at 17.5%)	Training course	8203
000120	£105.50 (no VAT)	Train ticket	7400
000121	£98.70 (inc VAT at 17.5%)	Refreshments	8205

Tasks

(a) Post these transactions to the appropriate ledger accounts. Read task (b) before you do this.

(b) Print a remittance advice for Samurai Insurance Brokers and B L Office Furnishing. (You need access to a printer to do this.) Remember that you must do this *before* you post the payment transactions.

(c) Print a report for the payments to suppliers and the bank transaction payments. If you do not have access to a printer, produce a screen display for the report. What is the total amount of payments?

(d) Print a copy of the bank account transactions (nominal ledger code 1200) to date (9 October 1998), and establish how much money, according to the records, is remaining in this account. If you do not have access to a printer, obtain a screen display of the account to establish the remaining cash balance.

(e) Establish the current balance on the creditors control account (nominal ledger account code 2100).

(f) *Windows exercise*

You can do this exercise if you have a spreadsheet package such as Microsoft Excel or Lotus 1-2-3 available. However spreadsheets are a topic for Intermediate level, so you don't *have* to do it if you are a bit frightened of them at the moment. (Coward!)

If you have not already done so, unload the Blitz Windows exercises onto a floppy disk, as explained in Chapter 2. Then start up your spreadsheet package, and open the spreadsheet file named A3SPRSHT which will now be on the floppy disk, and save it with a new name.

(If you are not using Microsoft Excel accept any prompts you get from another package about converting the file.)

As you can see, your supervisor has extracted some information from the Sage package and entered it into a spreadsheet.

(i) Explain the meaning of the numbers in the columns headed No. and Ref.

(ii) Your supervisor cannot understand why the totals do not match those shown in your payments report. Can you work out why? Alter the spreadsheet so that it produces the correct totals. The *totals* are calculated automatically, but you can alter the other amounts.

(iii) Use the skills you have acquired in working with word processors to improve the appearance of this document. (If you are using both Word and Excel you will see strong similarities in the features available.)

(iv) If you have access to a printer, print out your revised version of the spreadsheet.

Assignment
4   Receipts from customers

Performance criteria

The following performance criteria are covered *at a moderate level* in this Assignment.

Element 19.1 Input information from source documents into a computer system

1   All vital fields are completed

2   Incomplete or unauthorised source documents are referred for clarification

3   All errors in inputting and coding are identified and corrected

4   Correct part of the computer system is used for inputting

5   New unique reference codes are generated as necessary

6   Inputting is completed to agreed deadline

7   Organisational procedures for filing source documents are followed

8   Risks to the information technology environment are minimised at all times

Element 19.2 Locate and retrieve recorded details of requested items from a computer system

1   Correct details are retrieved

2   Search facilities are used optimally

3   Confidential information is not disclosed to unauthorised people

4   Risks to the information technology environments are minimised at all times

Element 19.3 Generate and print standard reports on a computer system

1   Required range and report correctly specified

2   Printed information is correct and complete

3   Hard copy is clean, clearly printed and aligned correctly

4   Efforts are made to minimise the wastage of paper

5   Printer area is kept clean and tidy

6   Work is produced to agreed deadline

7   Documents are correctly collated and distributed as directed

8   Risks to the information technology environment are minimised at all times

ASSIGNMENT 4: RECEIPTS FROM CUSTOMERS

Loading and carrying out the assignment

For instructions on how to load the data for assignments using the BPP Blitz program, refer to the online Help or to Section 7 of Chapter 2 and Section 3 of Chapter 3. Check with your tutor in case special instructions apply to your college's system.

If you need to break off from this assignment part-way through, back-up your entries so far on a floppy disk, following the instructions given on screen when you quit the Sage program. You can restore your entries when you start work again. (See Appendix 3)

If you want to keep a permanent copy of your finished work, back it up and save the back-up file in a separate, suitably named sub-directory on your floppy disk such as A:\ASMT04.

Purpose

The purpose of this assignment is to test your ability to enter details of payments received from customers and to post these details to the appropriate ledgers. The transactions include payments in full and part payments, receipts with a deduction for a credit note, receipts with a deduction for an early settlement discount, payments on account, payments with order, writing off small unpaid balances on a customer account and a customer refund. The completeness and accuracy of your input will be checked by a further test of your ability to produce reports and listings, and to find the current balance on the bank current account and the debtors control account.

The **Tasks** for this assignment will be found following the **Information**. Read the information and all the tasks *before* commencing work.

Information

You are asked by your supervisor to process the following transactions. The transactions are for processing on 12 October 1998, unless otherwise indicated.

(1) You have been given the following two customer invoices to process. You have been asked to enter and post the invoice details. If you have access to a printer, you should also produce invoices for these customers, as well as posting the invoice details to the ledgers.

Customer name	Bradley Fashions Ltd
A/C Reference Code	BRADLE
New Customer?	Yes
Address	18 Hospital Bridge Road
	St Albans, Herts
	SA5 9QT
Telephone	01727 532678
Credit Limit?	Yes, £2,500
Contact	Lee

Details

For contract cleaning services, £820 plus VAT at the standard rate

Customer name	A Rathod
A/C Reference Code	RATHOD
New Customer?	Yes
Address	200 West Road
	London N17 4GN
Telephone	0181-808 7814
Credit Limit?	No

Details

For domestic services, £75 plus VAT at the standard rate

(2) The following payments have been received from existing customers. You have been asked to post the details to the ledgers. Your supervisor instructs you that you must use the relevant invoice number as the reference (or the first invoice number if several are being paid).

Customer	*A/C ref code*	*Amount* £
E T Adams	ADAMSE	143.35
Farrar Air Tools Ltd	FARRAR	940.00
D J Hargreaves	HARGRE	51.11
A Rose Ltd	ROSEAL	141.00
CCC Engineering	CCCENG	1527.50
Bridgford and Co	BRIDGF	981.13
Goodman Brickworks Ltd	GOODMA	141.47
Townend Angus Ltd	TOWNEN	1087.70
P Wood	WOODPX	166.85
P Leyser & Co	LEYSER	96.59
A Wyche	WYCHEA	88.13
D C Sherry	SHERRY	49.35

(3) You have been asked to cancel an unpaid invoice of £70.50 for T P Paul and clear this account. This was an invoice for domestic cleaning services, nominal account code 4002.

(4) You have also been asked to post details of the following payments from customers, for which each customer has taken advantage of an early settlement discount of 5%.

Customer	A/C ref code	Cheque amount £	Discount taken £
Payne Properties	PAYNEP	1350.66	60.50
Rapid Pizzas	RAPIDP	215.66	9.66

(5) The following payments have been received, where the customer has reduced the payment to allow for a credit note.

Customer	A/C ref code	Amount paid(cheque amount) £
Gelling Private Bank	GELLIN	1727.25
DCS Roofing	DCSROO	82.25

Note. It may be advisable to take a back-up at this point, if you are happy with all the entries you have made, in case you make an error in posting the remaining transactions.

(6) The following part-payments have been received:

Customer	A/C ref code	Amount paid (cheque amount) £
Elite Caterers	ELITEC	200.00
Campbell Consultants	CAMPBE	70.00

(7) You have been asked to enter and post details of a payment of £828.75 by Clough and Partners. This payment is partly to settle an outstanding invoice and partly a payment in advance for services not yet provided by Blitz Limited.

(8) A payment on account has been received from the following new customer.

Customer name	M Zakis Ltd
A/C Reference Code	MZAKIS
Address	43 Ballards Lane
	London N12 0DG
Telephone	0181-445 2993
Credit Limit?	No
Amount of payment on account:	£500

(9) The following payments have been received:

Customer	A/C ref code	Amount paid(cheque amount) £
A T Haslam	HASLAM	42.00
R P Marwood	MARWOO	77.50

In each case, the customer has not paid the full invoice amount, but it has been decided to write off the small unpaid amount in each case. Post the details of the amounts to be written off. (Hint. Take a note of the unpaid amount in each case. If you forget to do this, can you think of a way of searching for this information in the Customers ledger?)

(10) Immediate payments have been received (by cheque) for the following items, without a requirement to supply an invoice or give credit to the customer. Payments *include* VAT at the standard rate of 17.5% in each case.

Item	Amount received	Paying-in slip number
	£	
Window cleaning	47.00	500000
Domestic services	101.05	500001
Domestic services	61.10	500002
Materials sales	117.50	500003
Window cleaning	86.95	500004

These receipts must be entered and posted to the appropriate accounts.

Tasks

(a) Enter and post the transactions as described in information items (1) to (10) above. Make all the necessary entries, including the set up of new customer accounts where appropriate.

(b) Produce a report for:

(i) amounts received from credit customers on 12 October 1998

(ii) bank receipts (ie amounts received from sources other than credit customers) on 12 October 1998.

Print the report if you have access to a printer; otherwise produce a screen display. What is the total amount received?

(c) After you have printed these reports, you are asked to process a refund of £96.59 to P Leyser for a payment already received. The refund has been agreed by the chief accountant with the customer.

(d) As at the end of processing, establish the total debits, credits and overall balances on the following accounts in the nominal ledger

	Account Code
Bank current account	1200
Debtors control account	1100

(e) Your supervisor wants to know how much is still owed by the customer Elite Caterers. What is the outstanding balance on this account?

Assignment
5 Other cash transactions

Performance criteria

The following performance criteria are covered *at an advanced level* in this Assignment.

Element 19.1 Input information from source documents into a computer system

1   All vital fields are completed

2   Incomplete or unauthorised source documents are referred for clarification

3   All errors in inputting and coding are identified and corrected

4   Correct part of the computer system is used for inputting

5   New unique reference codes are generated as necessary

6   Inputting is completed to agreed deadline

7   Organisational procedures for filing source documents are followed

8   Risks to the information technology environment are minimised at all times

Element 19.2 Locate and retrieve recorded details of requested items from a computer system

1   Correct details are retrieved

2   Search facilities are used optimally

3   Confidential information is not disclosed to unauthorised people

4   Risks to the information technology environments are minimised at all times

Element 19.3 Generate and print standard reports on a computer system

1   Required range and report correctly specified

2   Printed information is correct and complete

3   Hard copy is clean, clearly printed and aligned correctly

4   Efforts are made to minimise the wastage of paper

5   Printer area is kept clean and tidy

6   Work is produced to agreed deadline

7   Documents are correctly collated and distributed as directed

8   Risks to the information technology environment are minimised at all times

ASSIGNMENT 5: OTHER CASH TRANSACTIONS

Loading and carrying out the assignment

For instructions on how to load the data for assignments using the BPP Blitz program, refer to the online Help or Section 7 of Chapter 2 and Section 3 of Chapter 3. Check with your tutor in case special instructions apply to your college's system.

If you need to break off from this assignment part-way through, back-up your entries so far on a floppy disk, following the instructions given on screen when you quit the Sage program. You can restore your entries when you start work again. (See Appendix 3)

If you want to keep a permanent copy of your finished work, back it up and save the back-up file in a separate, suitably named sub-directory on your floppy disk such as A:\ASMT05.

Purpose

The purpose of Assignment 5 is to test your ability to post entries for petty cash in the nominal ledger and to make a small number of journal entries, and to carry out a bank reconciliation. In addition, the assignment includes a further test of your ability to post transactions for customer and supplier invoices, and customer and supplier payments.

The **Tasks** for this assignment will be found following the **Information**. Read the information and all the tasks *before* commencing work.

Information

(1)   On 13 October 1998, Blitz Limited's directors decided to set up a petty cash system with a float of £300. A cheque (number 000122) for £300 in cash was drawn on the company's bank account that day.

(2)   The following invoices have been received from suppliers.

Supplier	New supplier	Invoice number	Date	Details	Net amount £	VAT £
Hardin & Nobbs Chapel Place White Hart Lane London N17 4HA 0181-801 1907 A/C Ref HARDIN	Yes	2641	12 Oct 1998	Legal fees (N/C 7600)	1200.00	210.00
Flooring Supplies Ltd	No	435850	8 Oct 1998	Cleaning materials (N/C 5000)	762.00	133.35
Trojan Secretarial Services	No	03012	12 Oct 1998	Casual labour (N/C 7005)	210.00	36.75
AA1 Mini Cabs	No	C6281	15 Oct 1998	Taxis (N/C 7401)	134.70	23.57
Great North Hotel 75 Park Road Ealing London W5 6RU 0181-997 6005 A/C Ref GREATN	Yes	6601	7 Oct 1998	Hotel room (N/C 7402)	110.00	19.25
				Hotel meal (N/C 7406)	26.00	4.55
				Hotel telephone (N/C 7502)	3.40	0.60
				Total	139.40	24.40
Lerwick Cleaning Co Ryelands Road Norwich, NH7 4DB 01603 590624	Yes	S4031	14 Oct 1998	Cleaning materials (N/C 5000)	1400.00	245.00
				Carriage (N/C 5100)	20.00	3.50
A/C Ref LERWIC				Total	1420.00	248.50
First Steps Ladder Hire	No	5024	8 Oct 1998	Ladder hire (N/C 7700)	81.00	14.18
Prairie Couriers Ltd	No	T34228	14 Oct 1998	Couriers (N/C 7501)	92.50	16.19
Amin Launderers 16 Southey Road London N15 3AK 0181-802 2541 A/C Ref AMINLA	Yes	0877	8 Oct 1998	Laundry (N/C 7802)	145.00	25.38

Part D: Assignments

(3) The following invoices are to be sent out to customers, all dated 16 October 1998, with VAT charged at the standard rate.

Customer	New customer?	Invoice number	Details	Net amount £
Aspinall & Co	No	10053	Window cleaning	90.00
Elite Caterers	No	10054	Kitchen cleaning	190.00
S T Chana 78 Katherine Road London N9 8UL 0181-803 0147 No credit limit A/C Ref CHANAS	Yes	10055	Domestic services	135.00
L Haynes & Co 14 Millmead Road London N17 2XD 0181-885 3731 No credit limit A/C Ref HAYNES	Yes	10056	Window cleaning Materials sales Total	82.00 45.20 127.20
Brookes Acoustics Ltd	No	10057	Warehouse cleaning	670.00
CCC Engineering	No	10058	Factory cleaning	850.00
Tek Systems 115 Cricklewood Broadway London NW2 5ES 0181-452 9442 Credit limit £2,000 A/C Ref TEKSYS	Yes	10059	Contract cleaning Materials sales Total	450.00 63.00 513.00
Telefilm Latinamerica 100 Tower Bridge Road London SE1 6FJ 0171-403 2144 Credit limit £2,500 A/C Ref TELEFI	Yes	10060	Contract cleaning	830.00
GHH Commercial Bank	No	10061	Contract cleaning	950.00
The Keith Group	No	10062	Office cleaning	850.00
Owen of London 19 Piccadilly London W1 9CD 0171-734 2043 Credit limit £3,000 A/C Ref OWENLO	Yes	10063	Contract cleaning Window cleaning Materials sales Total	750.00 130.00 55.40 935.40
Biophysica Orbit Court 33 Fairfax Road London NW6 4LL 0171-624 2002 No credit limit A/C Ref BIOPHY	Yes	10064	Window cleaning Domestic services Total	63.00 45.00 108.00

(4) The following payments to suppliers were made on 16 October 1998.

Date	Supplier	Cheque number	Amount £	Details
16 Oct 1998	Ace Telephone Answering	000123	250.00	Part payment of invoice
16 Oct 1998	ANS Newspaper Group	000124	1200.00	Payment of invoice plus payment on account
16 Oct 1998	Wells Business Systems	000125	1516.50	Payment of invoice, net of credit note CN4245 for £387 (gross) dated 14/10/98. Nominal code 0030.

(5) The following payments have been received from customers.

Date	Supplier	Amount £	Details
14 Oct 1998	Campbell Consultants	70.00	Part payment of invoice
15 Oct 1998	Brookes Acoustics Ltd	1000.00	Part payment of invoice
16 Oct 1998	Gardeners Delight	703.24	Payment of invoice, discount of £31.50 taken

(6) The company has received a cheque from Mr V J Richardson, a relative of one of the directors, for £10,000. The money was banked on 12 October 1998. It represents a loan from Mr Richardson to the company. A journal voucher has been prepared as follows:

JOURNAL VOUCHER			J02
	N/C	Debit £	Credit £
Cash	1200	10,000	
Loan account	2300		10,000
Loan from Mr V J Richardson			

(7) In the period to 16 October 1998, petty cash vouchers for expenditure items were as follows. (VAT is only shown where the company has obtained a valid VAT invoice.)

Ref	Date	Item	N/C code	Net amount £	VAT £	Gross amount £
PC001	13/10/98	Postage stamps	7501	24.00	0	24.00
PC002	13/10/98	Biscuits, coffee	8205	32.49	0	32.49
PC003	13/10/98	Milk	8205	15.20	0	15.20
PC004	13/10/98	Taxis	7400	25.00	0	25.00
PC005	14/10/98	Train fares	7400	9.20	0	9.20
PC006	14/10/98	Washing up liquid	8205	1.75	0	1.75
PC007	14/10/98	Photocopying	7500	24.00	4.20	28.20
PC008	15/10/98	Stationery	7504	37.24	6.52	43.76
PC009	15/10/98	Taxis	7400	15.00	0	15.00
PC010	16/10/98	Sandwiches, cakes	8205	38.26	0	38.26
PC011	16/10/98	Parking	7304	7.00	0	7.00
PC012	16/10/98	Train fares	7400	8.40	0	8.40

Notes and coin totalling £72.00 were paid into petty cash on 16 October. This was money received for various small window cleaning jobs, for which VAT should be recorded at the standard rate.

(8) Blitz Limited has not yet set up a computerised payroll system. Wages were paid by bank transfer on 16 October 1998, and the following transactions need to be accounted for.

	Code	Debit £	Credit £
Bank account	1200		4133.04
PAYE	2210		2217.96
National Insurance	2211		975.20
Directors salaries	7001	1350.80	
Staff salaries	7003	475.75	
Wages – regular	6000	4859.65	
Employers NI	7006	640.00	
		7326.20	7326.20

(9) On 19 October 1998, the following bank statement was received from the company's bank.

Account 11765444

Centre Bank
Apple Road Branch
38 Apple Road
London N22

BLITZ LIMITED
25 APPLE ROAD
LONDON N12 3PP

Particulars	Date	Withdrawn £	Paid in £	Balance £
BGC	21 AUG		20000.00	
BGC	21 AUG		20000.00	40000.00
BAC	16 SEP	6053.93		
				33946.07
000100	12 OCT	117.50		
000103	12 OCT	1493.78		
000104	12 OCT	332.23		
000105	12 OCT	3205.00		
000107	12 OCT	3000.00		
000111	12 OCT	642.37		
000113	12 OCT	19059.44		
000114	12 OCT	1175.00		4920.75
000101	13 OCT	540.50		
000102	13 OCT	376.00		
000106	13 OCT	179.95		
000108	13 OCT	141.00		
000109	13 OCT	1240.00		
000112	13 OCT	763.75		
000116	13 OCT	2767.77		1088.22DR
BGC	13 OCT		143.35	
BGC	13 OCT		51.11	
BGC	13 OCT		1527.50	
BGC	13 OCT		981.13	
BGC	13 OCT		940.00	
BGC	13 OCT		1087.70	
BGC	13 OCT		88.13	
BGC	13 OCT		141.00	
BGC	13 OCT		141.47	
BGC	13 OCT		166.85	

BGC	13 OCT		49.35	
BGC	13 OCT		96.59	
BGC	13 OCT		1350.66	
BGC	13 OCT		215.66	
BGC	13 OCT		1727.25	
BGC	13 OCT		200.00	
BGC	13 OCT		70.00	
BGC	13 OCT		828.75	
BGC	13 OCT		82.25	
BGC	13 OCT		101.05	
BGC	13 OCT		42.00	
BGC	13 OCT		500.00	
BGC	13 OCT		47.00	
BGC	13 OCT		77.50	
BGC	13 OCT		86.95	
BGC	13 OCT		61.10	
BGC	13 OCT		117.50	9833.63
000110	13 OCT	1175.00		
000115	13 OCT	962.21		
000118	13 OCT	3500.00		
000119	13 OCT	258.50		
000120	13 OCT	105.50		
000121	13 OCT	98.70		
CASH WITHDRAWAL	16 OCT	300.00		
TRANSFER-LEYSER	16 OCT	96.59		3337.13
BGC	16 OCT		70.00	
BGC	16 OCT		10000.00	13407.13
BANK CHARGES	16 OCT	25.60		13381.53

Tasks

(a) Post the transaction for withdrawing cash from the company's bank account to set up a petty cash system. Use the cheque number as a reference for the transaction (information item [1]).

(b) Post the transactions for invoices received from suppliers (information item [2]).

(c) Post the transactions for invoices sent out to customers (information item [3]). For the purpose of this assignment, you are not required to produce invoices.

(d) Post the payments to suppliers (information item [4]).

(e) Post the receipts from customers (information item [5]).

(f) Post the receipt of the money as a loan from Mr V J Richardson, using the journal voucher as your source document. The transaction reference should be the journal voucher number. The tax reference code should be T9.

(g) Post the petty cash transactions to the nominal ledger, for both expenditure and income items. Enter the income items as a single transaction, with reference PCR001. Produce a listing for the petty cash payments. Print the listing if you have access to a printer.

(h) The company uses an imprest system for petty cash. On 16 October 1998, the money in petty cash should be topped up to £300. A cheque (number 000126) is to be drawn on the bank account to withdraw cash.

    (i)   What should be the cheque amount?

    (ii)   Assume that a cheque for this amount is drawn, and petty cash is restored to £300. Post this cash withdrawal transaction. Give it a reference code 000126 and a tax code T9.

(i) Post the wages and salaries transactions, shown in information item (8), to the appropriate nominal ledger accounts. Post the transactions by means of a journal entry. Give the transaction a reference of J04. Use tax code T9.

(j)   Your supervisor wishes to know the balances on the following nominal ledger accounts after you have dealt with tasks (a) to (i).

	Nominal ledger account code
Debtors control account	1100
Bank - current account	1200
Creditors control account	2100
Staff salaries	7003
Travelling	7400
Equipment hire	7700
Sales - contract cleaning	4000
Sales - window cleaning	4001
Sales - domestic services	4002
Sales - materials	4100
Petty cash	1230
Discounts allowed	4009

Report the balances on these accounts.

(k)   Carry out a bank reconciliation on 19 October 1998, after you have completed tasks (a) to (j). How many unreconciled transactions are there and what are the amounts for:

(i)   statement balance;
(ii)   uncleared items;
(iii)   trial balance?

(l)   Are there any discrepancies that have come to light during this assignment that you think should be reported to your supervisor?

Assignment
6 Other credit transactions

Performance criteria

The following performance criteria are covered *at an advanced level* in this Assignment.

Element 19.1 Input information from source documents into a computer system

1   All vital fields are completed
2   Incomplete or unauthorised source documents are referred for clarification
3   All errors in inputting and coding are identified and corrected
4   Correct part of the computer system is used for inputting
5   New unique reference codes are generated as necessary
6   Inputting is completed to agreed deadline
7   Organisational procedures for filing source documents are followed
8   Risks to the information technology environment are minimised at all times

Element 19.2 Locate and retrieve recorded details of requested items from a computer system

1   Correct details are retrieved
2   Search facilities are used optimally
3   Confidential information is not disclosed to unauthorised people
4   Risks to the information technology environments are minimised at all times

Element 19.3 Generate and print standard reports on a computer system

1   Required range and report correctly specified
2   Printed information is correct and complete
3   Hard copy is clean, clearly printed and aligned correctly
4   Efforts are made to minimise the wastage of paper
5   Printer area is kept clean and tidy
6   Work is produced to agreed deadline
7   Documents are correctly collated and distributed as directed
8   Risks to the information technology environment are minimised at all times

ASSIGNMENT 6: OTHER CREDIT TRANSACTIONS

Loading and carrying out the assignment

For instructions on how to load the data for assignments using the BPP Blitz program, refer to the online Help or to Section 7 of Chapter 2 and Section 3 of Chapter 3. Check with your tutor in case special instructions apply to your college's system.

You will need a blank floppy disk to do the Windows exercise, if you did not save the Windows data you unloaded earlier.

If you need to break off from this assignment part-way through, back-up your entries so far on a floppy disk, following the instructions given on screen when you quit the Sage program. You can restore your entries when you start work again. (See Appendix 3)

If you want to keep a permanent copy of your finished work, back it up and save the back-up file in a separate, suitably named sub-directory on your floppy disk such as A:\ASMT06.

Purpose

This assignment tests your ability to post contra entries and write-offs for bad debts and to correct errors. It also tests your ability to deal with a variety of customer problems: customers who exceed their credit limit and late payers, and chasing customers for payment by producing an aged debtors list, statements and reminder letters.

The **Tasks** for this assignment will be found following the **Information**. Read the information and all the tasks *before* commencing work.

Information

Tim Nicholas and Maria Green, the directors of Blitz Limited, are quite pleased with the first few weeks of trading by the company. They are very aware, however, that the company must continue to win more sales if it is to be successful. This could mean having to take the risk of selling services to customers who might not be creditworthy. In addition, cash flow could be a problem. The company has already borrowed £10,000 from Mr V Richardson, and has used a bank overdraft facility. The directors have therefore recognised a need to collect money from debtors efficiently, to make sure that cash keeps coming into the business.

(1) Credit limits have been set for some of Blitz Limited's customers. If a customer exceeds his credit limit, however, the company's policy from now onwards will be to supply the goods or services and increase the customer's credit limit by £1,000. However, the directors wish to be informed of any such change.

(2) On 21 October 1998, you have been asked to process the following transactions. All sales are subject to VAT at the standard rate.

Credit Sales

Customer	New customer?	Invoice number	Details	Net amount £
ANS Newspaper Group 19 Cecil Road London NW10 5CD 0181-453 2926 No credit limit A/C code ANSNEW	Yes	10065	Window cleaning	150.00
Brookes Acoustics Ltd	No	10066	Window cleaning	120.00
CCC Engineering Ltd	No	10067	Contract cleaning	630.00
R C Chadwick	No	10068	Domestic services	50.00
South Sea Airtours Girton House 62 Appendale Road London N17 1RA 0181-885 5553 Credit limit £2,500 A/C code SOUTHS	Yes	10069	Contract cleaning Materials sales Total	480.00 75.00 555.00
Clough & Partners	No	10070	Window cleaning	70.00
GHH Commercial Bank	No	10071	Contract cleaning	500.00
The Keith Group	No	10072	Contract cleaning Window cleaning Total	350.00 140.00 490.00
D J Hargreaves	No	10073	Domestic services	60.00
Meakin Media	No	10074	Window cleaning	100.00
Norris Hydraulics Ltd	No	10075	Contract cleaning	620.00
K Ogden Property Co	No	10076	Contract cleaning	480.00
Owen of London	No	10077	Window cleaning	150.00

School of Dance	No	10078	Contract cleaning	320.00
R I Tepper	No	10079	Contract cleaning	250.00
B Walton & Co	No	10080	Window cleaning	150.00
WRW Catering	No	10081	Contract cleaning	370.00
The Lapsley Agency	Yes	10082	Window cleaning	144.00
105 Thetford Road			Domestic services	105.00
London N9 0PB			Total	249.00
0181-803 0147				
No credit limit				
A/C code LAPSLE				

Cash sales

The following amounts were received from cash sales to customers.

Date	Details	Gross amount (including VAT) £	Method of payment	Paying in slip
21 October 1998	Domestic services	51.70	Cheque	500005
21 October 1998	Domestic services	44.00	Cheque	500006
21 October 1998	Materials sales	37.60	Cheque	500007
22 October 1998	Materials sales	25.38	Notes and coin	
23 October 1998	Domestic services	35.25	Notes and coin	
23 October 1998	Materials sales	52.88	Cheque	500008

The cheque payments were banked on 23 October 1998. The two receipts in notes and coin were put into petty cash (with reference codes PCR002 and PCR003 respectively).

Invoices from suppliers

The following invoices were received from suppliers. All three suppliers are also credit customers of the company.

Supplier	New supplier?	Invoice number	Date	Details	Net amount £	VAT £
ANS Newspaper Group	No	621347	20 Oct 1998	Advertising (N/C 6201)	471.28	82.47
Elite Caterers 85B Crowland Road London N15 9KW 0181-800 2069 A/C ref ELITEC	Yes	2046	20 Oct 1998	Catering (N/C 7403)	250.00	43.75
Meakin Media Ltd 4 Nursery Road Ashford Middlesex, AF8 5TS 01784 358452 A/C ref MEAKIN	Yes	10035	20 Oct 1998	Advertising (N/C 6201)	200.00	35.00

Receipts from customers

The following receipts from customers were obtained on 22 October 1998.

Customer	A/C ref	Amount £	Details
A Rathod	RATHOD	88.13	
A Rose Ltd	ROSEAL	146.88	
S T Chanas	CHANAS	158.00	
Biophysica	BIOPHY	52.88	To settle a part of an invoice relating to domestic services
Aspinall & Co	ASPINA	105.75	
Elite Caterers	ELITEC	1427.31	
Meakin Media Ltd	MEAKIN	350.16	

Tasks

(a) Post the credit sales transactions. You are not required to print out invoices, and you can use the Customers window Invoice option if you wish, although this may not give you warning messages.

    (i)   Prepare a list of customers who have exceeded their current credit limit.

    (ii)   Increase the credit limit for each of these customers by £1,000 each.

(b) Post the cash sales transactions (both the bank transactions and the petty cash transactions).

(c) Post the three invoices received from suppliers.

(d) Post the receipts from customers. The accounts of Elite Caterers and Meakin Media should be settled by means of *contra entries*.

(e) A cheque is being prepared to settle the account with ANS Newspaper group (cheque number 000127, dated 22 October 1998). The amount owed by ANS Newspaper Group should be offset against amounts owed to ANS, and the amount of the cheque should be for the difference.

    (i)   What is the amount of the cheque?

    (ii)   Post this cheque, and settle the accounts in the Suppliers and Customers ledgers by means of a contra entry.

(f) On 23 October 1998, you are instructed to write off small unpaid balances in any customer's account. Unpaid balances of £1 or less should be written off.

    (i)   Write off these small unpaid balances.

    (ii)   What is the total amount of bad debts written off in this exercise?

(g) Information has been received that the following customers have gone out of business.

Name	A/C ref
E T Adams	ADAMSE
L Haynes & Co	HAYNES

You are instructed that if there are any unpaid debts outstanding on the account of E T Adams or L Haynes & Co, the debts should be written off.

(h) A credit note (reference 004) was issued to Owen of London on 22 October 1998 for £150 (plus VAT). Post this transaction, giving it a N/C code of 4000. (You are not required to produce the credit note itself.)

(i) (*Note.* In Sterling Plus 2 this task will not produce an accurate answer if the *actual* date when you do it is before 23 October 1998. In SFW3 you can change the date by clicking on Defaults and picking the appropriate item from the menu.)

    (i)   If you have access to a printer, produce a statement showing all transactions to date for GHH Commercial Bank.

(ii) If you have access to a printer, produce a fairly stern reminder letter for WRW Catering Ltd.

(j) An invoice from AA1 Mini Cabs for £158.27 in October was entered in the accounts with a nominal ledger account code of 7401. Your supervisor tells you that the code should have been 7400. You are required to alter the code.

(k) A badly printed invoice from Newlite Cleaning Fluids dated 12 September was entered in the accounts incorrectly as £473.91 including VAT. The net amount, which is all that can be seen on the invoice, was actually £403. You are required to correct the error. What is the corrected figure?

(l) What are the current balances on the following nominal ledger accounts?

	Code
Bank current account	1200
Debtors control account	1100
Creditors control account	2100
Bad debt write off account	8100
Advertising account	6201
Sales - contract cleaning	4000
Sales - window cleaning	4001
Sales - domestic services	4002
Sales - materials	4100

(m) *Windows exercise: Aged Debtors Analysis*

Suppose that no more payments are received from customers before 5 November 1998. On 5 November, it is decided to review the current state of debtors, and take action to chase late payers.

However, due to a small fire which affected some of Blitz's computer hardware, it proves impossible to use the Sage system on 5 November.

Fortunately, the data from a print-out of an aged debtors analysis dated 4 November has been copied by your supervisor into a spreadsheet. A copy of this can be inspected using the BPP Blitz program. If you still have the floppy disk onto which you unloaded the Blitz Windows exercises earlier you will find a file named A6AGED. (If you don't have the disk you used earlier, unload a fresh copy of the Windows data using the Blitz program. See Chapter 2.)

(i) Open A6AGED.XLS using your spreadsheet program and save it with a new name.

(ii) Check that the total value of debtors outstanding agrees with the value on your Sage system now that you have posted all the transactions for this assignment.

(iii) Sort the data in order of value of overall balance: largest first. Which five customers owe the largest amounts? (See the note below if you don't know how to sort the data.)

(iv) Sort the data in order of largest balance outstanding for over 30 days. Make a list of customers with a balance of over £1,000 that has been outstanding for more than 30 days.

(v) Resort the data into customer account code order.

(*Hint.* In Microsoft Excel you can sort data by clicking on the word **Data** at the top of the screen and then on **Sort** in the menu that drops down. In Lotus 1-2-3 you click on **Range** and then **Sort**. The trick is to find the word 'sort': once you have done so, just follow the instructions given by the spreadsheet package.)

Assignment
7 Adding and removing employees

Performance criteria

The following performance criteria are covered *at an easy level* in this Assignment.

Element 19.1 Input information from source documents into a computer system

1 All vital fields are completed

2 Incomplete or unauthorised source documents are referred for clarification

3 All errors in inputting and coding are identified and corrected

4 Correct part of the computer system is used for inputting

5 New unique reference codes are generated as necessary

6 Inputting is completed to agreed deadline

8 Risks to the information technology environment are minimised at all times

Element 19.2 Locate and retrieve recorded details of requested items from a computer system

1 Correct details are retrieved

2 Search facilities are used optimally

4 Risks to the information technology environments are minimised at all times

Element 19.3 Generate and print standard reports on a computer system

1 Required range and report correctly specified

2 Printed information is correct and complete

3 Hard copy is clean, clearly printed and aligned correctly

4 Efforts are made to minimise the wastage of paper

5 Printer area is kept clean and tidy

6 Work is produced to agreed deadline

8 Risks to the information technology environment are minimised at all times

ASSIGNMENT 7: ADDING AND REMOVING EMPLOYEES

Loading and carrying out the assignment

For instructions on how to load the data for assignments using the BPP Blitz program, refer to Section 7 of Chapter 2 and Section 3 of Chapter 3. Check with your tutor in case special instructions apply to your college's system.

Don't forget that the data must unload into the PAYDATA directory (or possibly COMPANY.001\PAYDATA) for assignments 7 to 10. Change the default settings in the Blitz program if necessary. The initial Payroll Run Date (Process Date) will be 050299, although this is not strictly relevant for this assignment.

If you need to break off from this assignment part-way through, back-up your entries so far on a floppy disk, following the instructions given on screen when you quit the Sage program. You can restore your entries when you start work again. (See Appendix 3)

If you want to keep a permanent copy of your finished work, back it up and save the back-up file in a separate, suitably named sub-directory on your floppy disk such as A:\ASMT07.

Purposes

The purpose of this assignment is to test your ability to add new employees to the payroll file and remove an employee who has left, and to amend employee details on the payroll file.

The **Tasks** for this assignment will be found following the **Information**. Read the information and all the tasks *before* commencing work.

Information

The assignment begins in February 1999. You have been given the following information to process.

New employees

Three new employees will join the company in February. Their details are listed below.

Employee no	18	19	20
Name	Caroline Ann Stanley	Ms Sheila Jane Babcock	Donald Coombs
Address	15 Wedmore Street London N19	2 Crawford Avenue Wembley, Middlesex	47 Galsworthy Road London N22
Start date	1 February 1999	3 February 1999	8 February 1999
Nat Ins no	WR 48 27 61 B	PT 19 35 40 D	CS 47 41 66 A
Payment	Weekly, by cheque	Monthly, by cheque	Monthly, by cheque
Rate of pay	£6.50 per hour	£11,800 per annum	£13,800 per annum
Bonus scheme?	No	Yes. Maximum bonus £1,000	Yes. Maximum bonus £1,200
Date of birth	31 May 1944	12 November 1952	18 April 1968
NI category	A	B	A
Marital status	Single	Married	Single
Banking details			
Bank	Fallans Bank	Crofts Bank	Centre Bank
Address	6 Acre Street London N19	Lingfield Road Wembley	4 St Lawrence Street London N20
Sort code	42-00-03	20-16-73	82-11-52
Account no	11739268	24932879	75839429
Account name	C A Stanley	R & S J Babcock	D Coombs
P45 details			
Tax code	419T Wk1/Mth1	360L	K15
Gross pay to date	£8,440.32	£7,002.00	£10,684.80
Tax paid to date	£1,028.93	£811.12	£2380.41

None of the new employees is a director of the company.

Leaver

A weekly paid employee, Gideon Turner, left on 29 January. This day (a Friday) was his last working day with the company. His employee reference number is 12.

Amendments

Arvind Patel, one of the company's employees, has moved home. His new address is 51 Dysons Road, London N18.

Another employee, Norman Hazelwood has changed his bank. His new banking details are as follows:

Bank	Fallans Bank
Address	8 Woodside Lane
	Wembley, Middlesex
Sort code	42-08-16
Account no	62749835
Account name	N J & S L Hazelwood

Overtime

From 1 February 1999, the company has introduced overtime payments for staff who are paid a fixed weekly wage. The employees affected are:

Employee no	Name
13	Mahendra Kothari
14	Nursat Farouk
15	Linda Farrow

The overtime rate of pay will be £7.20 per hour.

Tasks

When you start up Sage Payroll specify a Payroll Run Date (Process Date) of 5 February 1999.

(a) Add the three new employees..

(b) Make the amendments to the payroll records of Arvind Patel and Norman Hazelwood.

(c) Amend the employee details for the weekly-paid workers who are entitled to overtime pay from 1 February. These are employees 13, 14 and 15.

(d) Remove the employee who has left (Gideon Turner) and obtain the details that were entered on his P45. What are his P45 details?

Assignment
8 Processing payroll

Performance criteria

The following performance criteria are covered *at a moderate level* in this Assignment.

Element 19.1 Input information from source documents into a computer system

1   All vital fields are completed
2   Incomplete or unauthorised source documents are referred for clarification
3   All errors in inputting and coding are identified and corrected
4   Correct part of the computer system is used for inputting
5   New unique reference codes are generated as necessary
6   Inputting is completed to agreed deadline
7   Organisational procedures for filing source documents are followed
8   Risks to the information technology environment are minimised at all times

Element 19.2 Locate and retrieve recorded details of requested items from a computer system

1   Correct details are retrieved
2   Search facilities are used optimally
4   Risks to the information technology environments are minimised at all times

Element 19.3 Generate and print standard reports on a computer system

1   Required range and report correctly specified
2   Printed information is correct and complete
3   Hard copy is clean, clearly printed and aligned correctly
4   Efforts are made to minimise the wastage of paper
5   Printer area is kept clean and tidy
6   Work is produced to agreed deadline
7   Documents are correctly collated and distributed as directed
8   Risks to the information technology environment are minimised at all times

ASSIGNMENT 8: PROCESSING PAYROLL

Loading and carrying out the assignment

For instructions on how to load the data for assignments using the BPP Blitz program, refer to Section 7 of Chapter 2 and Section 3 of Chapter 3. Check with your tutor in case special instructions apply to your college's system.

The initial Payroll Run Date (Process Date) is 050299.

You will need a blank floppy disk to do the Windows exercise, if you did not save the Windows data you unloaded earlier.

If you need to break off from this assignment part-way through, back-up your entries so far on a floppy disk, following the instructions given on screen when you quit the Sage program. You can restore your entries when you start work again. (See Appendix 3)

If you want to keep a permanent copy of your finished work, back it up and save the back-up file in a separate, suitably named sub-directory on your floppy disk such as A:\ASMT08.

Purpose

The purpose of this assignment is to test your ability to process weekly and monthly payroll. The test of your ability to process the payroll includes a requirement to print (or display) payroll reports and payslips.

The **Tasks** for this assignment will be found following the **Information**. Read the information and all the tasks *before* commencing work.

Information

The assignment begins on Friday 5 February 1999, week 44 of the 1998/99 tax year, when you are about to process the payroll for the week. You have been given the following information to process.

Week 44 payroll

Weekly paid employees are paid on 6 February 1999. Details of hours worked for hourly paid staff and of overtime hours are as follows.

Employee	Hours worked	Overtime hours
Ethel Parkinson	8½	
Caroline Stanley	38	
Mahendra Kothari		4½
Nursat Farouk		6
Linda Farrow		7½

Week 45 payroll

Weekly paid employees are paid on 12 February. Details of hours worked and overtime hours are as follows:

Employee	Hours worked	Overtime hours
Ethel Parkinson	10	
Caroline Stanley	40	
Mahendra Kothari		3
Nursat Farouk		4
Linda Farrow		0

Week 46 payroll

Weekly paid employees are paid on 19 February. Details of hours worked and overtime hours are as follows.

Employee	Hours worked	Overtime hours
Ethel Parkinson	14½	
Caroline Stanley	46½	
Mahendra Kothari		7½
Nursat Farouk		8
Linda Farrow		5½

Week 47 and Month 11 payroll

There is a weekly and monthly payroll run on 26 February. Allow tax refunds where appropriate. Details of hours worked by hourly-paid staff and overtime hours of other weekly-paid staff are as follows.

Employee	Hours worked	Overtime hours
Ethel Parkinson	12½	
Caroline Stanley	40	
Mahendra Kothari		0
Nursat Farouk		0
Linda Farrow		2

Tasks

(a) *Week 44*

Ensure that the Payroll Run Date (Process Date) is 5 February 1999.

(i) Process the payroll for Week 44. Allow a tax refund, where appropriate.

(ii) Print or display a payments summary for the week, and establish (in total) the gross pay for the week, PAYE, employees' National Insurance contributions and net pay. What is the amount of employer's NI?

(iii) Update the payroll file.

(b) *Week 45*

Change the Payroll Run Date (Process Date) to 12 February 1999.

(i) Process the payroll for Week 45. Print or display a cheque analysis and establish the pay cheque amounts for each employee for the week. The first cheque number in the cheque run is 0002069 (PLUS2 only).

(ii) Update the payroll file.

(c) *Week 46*

Change the Payroll Run Date (Process Date) to 19 February 1999. Process the payroll for Week 46. Establish for each employee the gross pay for the week, PAYE, NI contributions and net pay. Update the payroll file.

(d) *Week 47 and Month 11*

Change the Payroll Run Date (Process Date) to 26 February 1999.

(i) Process the payroll for Week 47 and Month 11. It has been agreed that Sheila Babcock will receive a gross salary equal to 92% of her normal monthly salary, and Donald Coombs will receive 75% of his normal monthly salary. This is because they joined after 1 February.

(ii) Print or display a payment summary to establish, for weekly-paid employees and for monthly-paid employees, the gross pay, PAYE, employees' National Insurance contributions, net pay and employer's National Insurance contributions for the week/month.

(iii) Print (or display) a payslip for employees 2 and 3. Then update the payroll file.

(e) *Windows exercise*

Tim Nicholas would like a memo giving details of total gross pay, total National Insurance, and total overall payroll cost for the month, and any differences from the previous months totals. A similar memo was prepared last month.

On 26 February 1999 your supervisor collects the information shown on the next page from P11 print outs and has asked you to prepare the memo.

Unload the Blitz Windows exercises onto a blank floppy disk if you have not already done so. Open the file A8MEMO with your word processor and A8SPSHT with your spreadsheet package. Save each file with a different name.

(i) Enter this month's figures and details in the appropriate columns. The totals will be calculated automatically.

(ii) Copy the spreadsheet into the memo and make any other changes that you think are appropriate.

(iii) If possible, print out a copy of the memo.

Month 11

		Total Gross	Employers Nat. Ins.
1	T. NICHOLAS	3,000.00	300.00
2	S. LYNCH	2,125.00	212.50
3	A. PATEL	1,650.00	165.20
4	J. ESCOTT	1,500.00	150.00
5	A. CROPPER	850.00	59.64
6	A. VAUGHAN	875.00	61.32
7	K. KNIGHT	900.00	63.00
8	L. LEROY	1,083.33	108.40
9	L. BROWN	1,100.00	110.00
10	M. KORETZ	1,083.33	108.40
11	N. PARKER	1,083.33	108.40
12	G. TURNER	0.00	0.00
13	M. KOTHARI	1,067.00	106.90
14	N. FAROUK	968.00	97.00
15	L. FARROW	927.00	86.73
16	E. PARKINSON	182.00	0.00
17	N. HAZELWOOD	1,350.00	135.20
18		1069.00	107.10
19		983.33	63.28
20		1,150.00	60.48

Assignment
9 Payroll routine

Performance criteria

The following performance criteria are covered *at an advanced level* in this Assignment.

Element 19.1 Input information from source documents into a computer system

1   All vital fields are completed
2   Incomplete or unauthorised source documents are referred for clarification
3   All errors in inputting and coding are identified and corrected
4   Correct part of the computer system is used for inputting
5   New unique reference codes are generated as necessary
6   Inputting is completed to agreed deadline
7   Organisational procedures for filing source documents are followed
8   Risks to the information technology environment are minimised at all times

Element 19.2 Locate and retrieve recorded details of requested items from a computer system

1   Correct details are retrieved
2   Search facilities are used optimally
3   Confidential information is not disclosed to unauthorised people
4   Risks to the information technology environments are minimised at all times

Element 19.3 Generate and print standard reports on a computer system

1   Required range and report correctly specified
2   Printed information is correct and complete
3   Hard copy is clean, clearly printed and aligned correctly
4   Efforts are made to minimise the wastage of paper
5   Printer area is kept clean and tidy
6   Work is produced to agreed deadline
7   Documents are correctly collated and distributed as directed
8   Risks to the information technology environment are minimised at all times

ASSIGNMENT 9: PAYROLL ROUTINE

Loading and carrying out the assignment

For instructions on how to load the data for assignments using the BPP Blitz program, refer to Section 7 of Chapter 2 and Section 3 of Chapter 3. Check with your tutor in case special instructions apply to your college's system.

If you need to break off from this assignment part-way through, back-up your entries so far on a floppy disk, following the instructions given on screen when you quit the Sage program. You can restore your entries when you start work again. (See Appendix 3)

If you want to keep a permanent copy of your finished work, back it up and save the back-up file in a separate, suitably named sub-directory on your floppy disk such as A:\ASMT09.

Purpose

You probably found Assignment 8 slow going if you were wise and took a great deal of care with your entries. Now you have a bit of experience try dealing with March 1999. Assignment 9 re-tests your ability to add a new employee to the payroll, and asks you to process the payroll for weeks 48-51 and month 12 of the tax year.

The **Tasks** for this assignment will be found following the **Information**. Read the information and all the tasks *before* commencing work.

Information

(1) A new employee joined the company on 1 March 1999. Her details are as follows:

Employee number	*21*
Name	*Miss Sarah Romain*
Address	10 Dean Road, London N20
Nat Ins number	LC 40 63 11 B
Nat Ins category	A
Date of birth	30 June 1947
Tax code	423T Week 1/Month 1
Payment	Weekly, by cheque
Payment type	Rate per hour
Payment rate	£7 per hour, no overtime or bonus
Marital status	Single
Banking details	Bank of Wales
Address	50 Meldon Way, London N22
Sort code	07-22-24
A/C number	13925398
A/C name	S Romain

P45 details	£
Gross earnings in year to date	3,885.00
Tax paid in year to date	0.00

(2) You receive notification that the tax code for Lewis Leroy should be 395L for 1998/99.

(3) Neville Parker and Linda Farrow are going on holiday to Playa de Las Americas from 6 to 20 March 1999. Weekly paid employees receive an advance of basic pay for holiday periods.

(4) Tim Nicholas is now a member of a special company pension scheme. He pays 5% of his monthly gross salary into this scheme and Blitz Ltd pays a further 10%. The first payment is to be on 26 March 1999.

Weekly payroll, weeks 48-51

The payroll run for weeks 48-51 took place on Friday 5, 12, 19, and 26 March respectively. Details for weekly-paid and hourly-paid staff of overtime and hours worked are as follows.

| | Week 48 (5 March) | | Week 49 (12 March) | | Week 50 (19 March) | |
	O'time Hours	Basic Hours	O'time Hours	Basic Hours	•'time Hours	Basic Hours
Mahendra Kothari	5½		8		6	
Nursat Farouk	5		6		4½	
Linda Farrow	2		0		0	
Ethel Parkinson		7		11		12
Caroline Stanley		41½		21		38
Sarah Romain		16		33		22½

| | Week 51 (26 March) | |
	O'time Hours	Basic Hours
Mahendra Kothari	5	
Nursat Farouk	7½	
Linda Farrow	7	
Ethel Parkinson		4
Caroline Stanley		43½
Sarah Romain		31½

Monthly payroll, Month 12

The payroll run for March takes place on 26 March.

Tasks

When you enter the Sage program, record a Payroll Run Date (Process Date) of 5 March 1999.

(a) *Week 48*

    (i) Amend the tax code for L Leroy.

    (ii) Insert the details of the new employee on the payroll file.

    (iii) Process the payroll for Week 48. If an employee is entitled to a tax refund or an advance of holiday pay, this should be paid.

    (iv) Establish in total the gross pay, PAYE, employees' National Insurance contributions, net pay and employer's NI contributions for the week.

    (v) Update the payroll file, being sure to reselect any employees on holiday.

(b) *Week 49*

Change the Payroll Run Date (Process Date) to 12 March 1999.

    (i) Process the Payroll for Week 49.

    (ii) Establish the amount of the payroll cheque for each employee. The first cheque number should be 0002074.

    (iii) Produce information for the P32 payment record (and for the monthly payslip to the Collector of Taxes) for the tax month 6 February to 5 March 1999 (Month 11).

    (iv) Update the payroll file.

(c) *Week 50*

Specify a Payroll Run Date (Process Date) of 19 March 1999.

    (i) Process the payroll for Week 50 and update the payroll file.

    (ii) Establish for each employee and in total the gross pay, PAYE, employees' National Insurance contributions, net pay and employer's NI contributions for the week.

    (iii) Update the payroll file.

(d) *Week 51*

Specify a Payroll Run Date (Process Date) of 26 March 1999.

(i) Set up the pension scheme for Tim Nicholas.

(ii) Process the payroll for Week 51 and month 12. Any tax refund due should be paid.

(iii) What is the gross pay and net pay of employees in Week 51?

(iv) Establish the total gross salaries for the month of the current monthly-paid employees, the total deductions for PAYE, employees' National Insurance contributions, and the total employer's National Insurance contributions.

(v) Print (or display) payslips for Tim Nicholas and Leyton Brown. If your printer uses A4 sized paper you may well need to reset your printer to its 'landscape' option to do this.

(vi) Update the payroll file.

(e) Tim Nicholas is very pleased to be paying so little National Insurance this month.

(i) Can you suggest why the system has produced the figure that it has done for his National Insurance?

(ii) Can you tell Tim Nicholas how much is paid in employer's National Insurance with regard to him in Month 12?

Assignment
10 End of the tax year

Performance criteria

The following performance criteria are covered *at an advanced level* in this Assignment.

Element 19.1 Input information from source documents into a computer system

1   All vital fields are completed

2   Incomplete or unauthorised source documents are referred for clarification

3   All errors in inputting and coding are identified and corrected

4   Correct part of the computer system is used for inputting

5   New unique reference codes are generated as necessary

6   Inputting is completed to agreed deadline

7   Organisational procedures for filing source documents are followed

8   Risks to the information technology environment are minimised at all times

Element 19.2 Locate and retrieve recorded details of requested items from a computer system

1   Correct details are retrieved

2   Search facilities are used optimally

3   Confidential information is not disclosed to unauthorised people

4   Risks to the information technology environments are minimised at all times

Element 19.3 Generate and print standard reports on a computer system

1   Required range and report correctly specified

2   Printed information is correct and complete

3   Hard copy is clean, clearly printed and aligned correctly

4   Efforts are made to minimise the wastage of paper

5   Printer area is kept clean and tidy

6   Work is produced to agreed deadline

7   Documents are correctly collated and distributed as directed

8   Risks to the information technology environment are minimised at all times

ASSIGNMENT 10: END OF THE TAX YEAR

Loading and carrying out the assignment

For instructions on how to load the data for assignments using the BPP Blitz program, refer to Section 7 of Chapter 2 and Section 3 of Chapter 3. Check with your tutor in case special instructions apply to your college's system.

If you need to break off from this assignment part-way through, back-up your entries so far on a floppy disk, following the instructions given on screen when you quit the Sage program. You can restore your entries when you start work again. (See Appendix 3)

If you want to keep a permanent copy of your finished work, back it up and save the back-up file in a separate, suitably named sub-directory on your floppy disk such as A:\ASMT10.

Purpose

The aim of this assignment is to provide a final test of your ability to deal with payroll processing. It also takes you from one tax year (1998/99) into the next (1999/2000) and tests your ability to deal with year-end payroll routines.

The **Tasks** for this assignment will be found following the **Information**. Read the information and all the tasks *before* commencing work.

Information

(1) An hourly-paid employee, Ethel Parkinson, left the company on 2 April 1999.

(2) A new employee joined on 6 April 1999. His details are as follows:

Employee number	22
Name	M. Jean-Baptiste Bannister
Address	46 Broadwick Street, London N18
Nat Ins number	WE 27 40 63 C
Nat Ins category	A
Date of birth	24 October 1977
Tax code	290H
Status	Married - male
Payment	Monthly, by cheque
Payment type	Fixed salary plus annual bonus
Payment rate	£12,750 per annum salary. Maximum bonus £1,500.

Banking details	Crofts Bank
Address	Station Parade, London N18
Sort code	20-01-20
A/C number	11924272
A/C name	J-B BANNISTER

P45 details (Month 12 1998/99)	
Taxable gross pay	£9,850.00
Tax paid	£1,467.20

Week 52 payroll, 1998/99

The payroll data for weekly-paid staff for week 52 is as follows. The payroll run takes place on Friday 2 April 1999.

	Week 52 (2 April)	
	O'time Hours	*Basic Hours*
Ethel Parkinson		5
Caroline Stanley		35
Sarah Romain		34
Mahendra Kothari	5½	
Nursat Farouk	6½	
Linda Farrow	3	

Weeks 1-3 payroll, 1999/2000

The payroll data for weekly-paid staff for weeks 1-3 of the new tax year are as follows:

	Week 1 (9 April)		Week 2 (16 April)		Week 3 (23 April)	
	O'time Hours	Basic Hours	O'time Hours	Basic Hours	O'time Hours	Basic Hours
Caroline Stanley		42		25		32½
Sarah Romain		28½		31		27
Mahendra Kothari	6		7		3	
Nursat Farouk	3		8		4	
Linda Farrow	2½		4		0	

Pay increases

The annual salary of several employees was increased from 1 April 1999, as follows:

Employee	Number	New annual salary £
T Nicholas	1	40,000
S Lynch	2	30,000
A Patel	3	22,000
J Escott	4	19,000
A Vaughan	6	12,000
L Leroy	8	15,000
M Koretz	10	14,000

Bonuses

The company's directors are extremely pleased with the results of the Blitz A Team division, and have decided to pay a bonus on 23 April 1999 to all employees who are entitled to a bonus in their pay arrangements. The bonus will be 40% of the 'maximum' bonus. The 'maximum' is the amount recorded in employee details as the employee's rate of pay for a bonus.

Tasks

(a) *Week 52*

Enter the Sterling Payroll program, specifying 2 April 1999 as the Payroll Run Date (Process Date).

(i) Process the payroll for Week 52 of the tax year 1998/99.

(ii) Print (or display) a payment summary. What are the amounts for total gross pay, tax paid, employees' National Insurance and net pay?

(iii) Update the payroll file.

(iv) Remove Ethel Parkinson from the payroll. What are her P45 details?

(v) Print a statement of the information for inclusion in the payslip to the Collector of Taxes for the month 6 March to 5 April 1999. What are the total amounts of tax and National Insurance contributions payable to the Collector of Taxes for the month?

(vi) Produce a P35 report for the tax year ended 5 April 1999.

(vii) Clear the year end totals on the payroll file.

(b) *Week 1*

Specify 9 April as the Payroll Run Date (Process Date).

(i) Add the new employee, J-B Bannister, to the payroll as employee number 22.

(ii)   Process the weekly payroll for Week 1. What is the total net pay for all employees for the week? Update the payroll file.

(iii)   Search the employee file for the employee record of Nursat Farouk. What are the amounts shown in his records for gross pay to date, PAYE, and employee's National Insurance contributions to date?

(c) *Week 2*

Specify a Payroll Run Date (Process Date) of 16 April 1999.

(i)   Process the payroll for Week 2.

(ii)   What is the net pay of each employee for the week?

(iii)   Update the payroll file.

(d) *Week 3/month 1*

Specify a Payroll Run Date (Process Date) of 23 April 1999.

(i)   Amend the salaries of the employees receiving an increase in pay.

(ii)   Process the payroll for Week 3 and Month 1. The bonuses for the previous year should be paid, but the new employee, J-B Bannister, is not entitled to any bonus and only gets 25 days pay.

(iii)   Print (or display) a payment summary for this payroll run. What is the total gross pay, PAYE, employees' National Insurance contributions, net pay and employer's National Insurance contributions for the month, for monthly-paid staff?

(iv)   What is the total value of payroll cheques to employees, for both weekly- and monthly-paid staff?

(v)   Update the payroll file.

Part E
Solutions

SOLUTION TO ASSIGNMENT 1: SUPPLIER INVOICES AND CREDIT NOTES

You can enter the new supplier accounts in the Suppliers Ledger using either the Invoices button or the Record button.

If you use the Record button, as suggested in Chapter 4, you should set up accounts for the four new suppliers before entering any invoice details. Having set up the new accounts, you can switch to the Invoices window to process the 8 invoices.

Having processed and posted the invoice details, you should then close the Invoices window and open the Credits window to process and post the details of the 2 credit notes.

(*Plus2*: Batch Credits = Supplier Credit Note.)

(*SFW3*: Invoices = Batch Invoices; Record = Supplier Record; Credits = Batch Credits.)

Points to check

You should check the following points.

Date

For each invoice (or credit note) you should enter the date of the invoice (or credit note). You should *not* enter today's date, 2 October.

Nominal ledger codes

Carefully check transaction details shown below in the two listings. These list the entry details for the transactions. Make sure that you have specified the correct nominal ledger code for each transaction. To find the correct N/C codes for the credit notes, you should have looked for the account codes for Furniture and Fixtures (0040) and Wages - Casual (7005).

When an invoice is for purchases or items of expense for more than one nominal ledger account, you should enter each part of the invoice separately. This means that you should have entered:

(a) 2 lines of details for the invoice from Flooring Supplies Ltd, one for the purchase of cleaning materials (code 5000) and one for the purchase of plant and machinery (code 0020); and

(b) 3 lines of details for the invoice from Samurai Insurance Brokers, one for the premises insurance (code 7104), one for the vehicle insurance (code 7303) and one for miscellaneous items of insurance (code 8204).

Listings

When you have entered and posted the details of the invoices and credit notes, you can print the 'day book' listings.

Use the Reports button in the *Suppliers ledger* window and select Day Books: Supplier Invoices (detailed) and then Day Books: Supplier Credits (detailed).

(*Plus2*: click on the Reports button in the *main* Sage window, and then select the Supplier Invoices option and then the Supplier Credits option.)

Part E: Solutions

You should specify the date ranges 290998 to 021098 for supplier invoices and 011098 to 011098 for credit notes.

The printouts should appear as follows, with 11 entries in the purchases day book and 2 entries in the purchases returns day book. (However, the sequence of transactions and the transaction numbers can vary, according to the order in which you entered them in the system.) The gross value of transactions is shown at the bottom of each listing.

Blitz Limited

Day Books : Supplier Invoices (Detailed)

Date from: 29/09/98
Date to: 02/10/98

Supplier From:
Supplier To: ZZZZZZZZ

Trans From: 1
Trans To: 83

N/C From:
N/C To: 99999999

Dept From: 0
Dept To: 999

No	Tp	A/c	N/C	Date	Ref.	Details	Net	T/C	VAT	Total
71	PI	AA1MIN	7400	011098	C6147	Taxi fares	38.40	T1	6.72	45.1
72	PI	NEWLIT	5000	011098	26187	Cleaning materials	168.70	T1	29.52	198.2
73	PI	FLOORI	5000	011098	435796	Cleaning materials	202.36	T1	35.41	237.7
74	PI	FLOORI	0020	011098	435796	Equipment	620.00	T1	108.50	728.5
75	PI	FIRSTS	7700	011098	4821	Ladder hire	126.75	T1	22.18	148.9
76	PI	SAMURA	7104	011098	02381	Premises insurance	1650.00	T2	0.00	1650.0
77	PI	SAMURA	7303	011098	02381	Vehicle insurance	1125.00	T2	0.00	1125.0
78	PI	SAMURA	8204	011098	02381	Misc insurance	430.00	T2	0.00	430.0
79	PI	3DTECH	7505	300998	001462	Books	179.95	T0	0.00	179.9
80	PI	THAMES	7102	011098	132157	Water rates	420.00	T0	0.00	420.0
81	PI	ANSNEW	6201	290998	621014	Advertising	750.00	T1	131.25	881.2
						Totals	5711.16		333.58	6044.7

Blitz Limited

Day Books : Supplier Credits (Detailed)

Date from: 01/10/98
Date to: 01/10/98

Supplier From:
Supplier To: ZZZZZZZZ

Trans From: 1
Trans To: 83

N/C From:
N/C To: 99999999

Dept From: 0
Dept To: 999

No	Tp	A/c	N/C	Date	Ref.	Details				
82	PC	BLOFFI	0040	011098	K0320	Damaged furniture	150.00	T1	26.25	17
83	PC	TROJAN	7005	011098	C0259	Temp overcharge	60.00	T1	10.50	7
						Totals :	210.00		36.75	24

Creditors control account

The balance on the creditors control account is £50,517.10.

	£
Total credits (invoices)	50,763.85
Total debits (credit notes)	246.75
Balance	50,517.10

This can be obtained by Escaping from the Suppliers Ledger to the main screen, and clicking on the Nominal Ledger button. In the Nominal Ledger window, click on Clear to ensure that no accounts are selected, then scroll down to account 2100 and select it by clicking on it. Then click on the Activity button and accept the defaults you are offered. For output you can display the account on screen and at the bottom of the screen you will find the total balances. Alternatively, you can select the account as before, click on Report in the Nominal ledger window and print out an Activity report.

(*Plus2*: click on Activity and then on History.)

SOLUTION TO ASSIGNMENT 2: CUSTOMER INVOICES AND CREDIT NOTES

The solution here is written on the assumption that you have access to a printer and are producing invoices (the invoice and credit note options in the *Invoicing* window). If you are using the Batch Invoice option in the Customers window, however, and do not intend to print invoices, the task of entering and posting the transaction details should be simpler, because you do not have to worry about the text and layout of the invoices.

Invoices

If you use the Invoicing window options, you should *save* each transaction when you have input the details, then print the invoices in batches, and then update the ledgers.

Make sure you specify the nominal account code correctly for each item in each invoice.

Code	Account
4000	Sales - contract cleaning
4001	Sales - window cleaning
4002	Sales - domestic services
4100	Sales - materials

Where appropriate, enter new customer details, following the screen prompts. The default tax code is T1 if you choose to set this (we recommend you do). The suggested reference codes to use are as follows:

Customer	Ref code
R P Marwood	MARWOO
School of Dance	SCHOOL
B & T Fashions Ltd	BTFASH
The Keith Group	KEITHG
Rapid Pizzas	RAPIDP
Gardeners Delight	GARDEN
Payne Properties	PAYNEP
T P Paul	PAULTP

You must decide whether invoices (or credit notes) should be entered using the Product button or the Service button. We suggest you use the Product option for the invoices for Rapid Pizzas, Elite Caterers and Gardeners Delight. Use the stock code S1.

When entering product invoices orer details, DO NOT enter a figure for discount. This box would be used for *additional* discount (eg a bulk order discount) *on top of* the early settlement discount that you set up in the customer record.

Order details

You should insert order details into an invoice where appropriate. Clicking on the Order Details index tab (Order button in Plus2) will give you a pop-up window for adding information about the delivery address. In this assignment, you need to add order details for the invoice to Gardeners Delight - ie you need to add details of the delivery address, which is different from the invoice address.

Details

You should add details for the invoice, based on the information given in the assignment. When you use the (Invoicing) invoice options, the program will calculate the amount owed for each stock item from the quantity and price per unit. If you prepared a Service invoice that includes materials (the Elite Caterers invoice), you should have calculated yourself the amount payable (net of VAT) for materials, and entered this amount in the invoice.

Use tax code T1 for every invoice. The VAT and total amount payable are calculated automatically.

Footer

There is no requirement on any invoice for footer details, and you will not need to use the Footer index tab (or button).

Printing

To print the invoices, you must first select the invoices and then click on the Print Invoices button in the Invoicing window. To print invoices for stock items, you should select those of type *Inv* and use the appropriate size (11" or A4) of the layout INVPFUL (Plus2: INVOICE.LYT) for the invoice layout (unless your tutor tells you otherwise). To print Service invoices, select those of the type *Srv* and use the SRVNEW layout (Plus2 INVTEXT.LYT).

If you do not wish to print all the invoices, you can select individual ones of each type to print.

Posting

When you use the (Invoicing window) invoice options, you must post the transactions to the ledgers using the Update Ledgers button in the Invoicing window. Select all of the items listed in the Invoicing window: you can do this by clicking on Clear and then on Swap. Decide whether you want a print-out when the Update Ledgers window appears, and then simply click on OK. Follow the screen prompt for printing. A part of a printed listing of the invoices that might be produced is shown below. The invoice numbers may not be the same as yours, depending on the order in which you entered the data. Columns for Stock Code and Quantity have been omitted for lack of space.

Blitz Limited

Update Ledgers Report

Inv/Crd	Audit	Date	A/C	N/C	Details	Net	VAT	Total
2	85	081098	ROYALP	4000	Services	−300.00	−52.50	−352.50
					Invoice Totals:	−300.00	−52.50	−352.50
10041	94	081098	BRIDGF	4000	Services	420.00	73.50	493.50
					Invoice Totals:	420.00	73.50	493.50
10042	95	081098	HARGRE	4002	Services	43.50	7.61	51.11
					Invoice Totals:	43.50	7.61	51.11
10043	96	081098	ELITEC	4000	KITCHEN CLEANING	644.00	112.70	756.70
	97			4100	10 BOXES OF OVEN CLEANER	61.00	10.68	71.68
	98			4100	6 CASES OF FLAME DETERGENT	72.00	12.60	84.60
	99			4100	7 BRUSHES	23.94	4.19	28.13
					Invoice Totals:	800.94	140.17	941.11
10044	100	081098	MEAKIN	4001	Services	249.00	43.58	292.58
					Invoice Totals:	249.00	43.58	292.58

Credit notes

In Line 50 and SFW4 use the SrvCredit (SFW3:Service Credit Note) option and process the credit notes just like the service invoices.

In Plus2 the credit notes have to be processed in a similar way to the invoices for materials if you have Sterling Plus 2. Use 'stock code' S1 and specify 1 for the quantity.

Listings

In Line 50, SFW4 and SFW3 click on the reports button in the *Customers* window.

(a) Use the Day Books: Customer Invoices (Detailed) option to preview or print the sales day book listing for invoices.

(b) Use the Day Books: Customer Credits (Detailed) option to preview or print the sales day book listing for credit notes.

In Plus 2 click on the Reports button in the *main* Sage window and use the Customer Invoices option and then the Customer Credits option.

In selecting the items for listing, you can specify the date range from 081098 to 081098.

Extracts from the listings are shown below. (The Dept column is omitted.)Check the totals shown. You should have obtained these same *totals* yourself (invoice numbers for particular customers may be different: it depends on the order in which you post the details.)

Blitz Limited

Day Books : Customer Invoices (Detailed)

Date from: 08/10/98
Date to: 08/10/98

Supplier From:
Supplier To: ZZZZZZZZ

Trans From: 1
Trans To: 106

N/C From:
N/C To: 99999999

Dept From: 0
Dept To: 999

No.	Tp	A/c	N/C	Date	Refn.	Details	Net	VAT	T/c	Total
87	SI	MARWOO	4002	081098	10036	Services	66.00	11.55	T1	77.55
88	SI	SCHOOL	4000	081098	10037	Services	250.00	43.75	T1	293.75
89	SI	BTFASH	4001	081098	10038	Services	144.00	25.20	T1	169.20
90	SI	KEITHG	4000	081098	10039	Services	1420.00	248.50	T1	1668.50
91	SI	RAPIDP	4100	081098	10040	FLAME DETERGENT	60.00	9.98	T1	69.98
92	SI	RAPIDP	4100	081098	10040	BREAM CLEANER	91.20	15.16	T1	106.36
93	SI	RAPIDP	4100	081098	10040	CLEANING GLOVES	42.00	6.98	T1	48.98
94	SI	BRIDGF	4000	081098	10041	Services	420.00	73.50	T1	493.50
95	SI	HARGRE	4002	081098	10042	Services	43.50	7.61	T1	51.11
96	SI	ELITEC	4000	081098	10043	KITCHEN CLEANING	644.00	112.70	T1	756.70
97	SI	ELITEC	4100	081098	10043	OVEN CLEANER	61.00	10.68	T1	71.68
98	SI	ELITEC	4100	081098	10043	FLAME DETERGENT	72.00	12.60	T1	84.60
99	SI	ELITEC	4100	081098	10043	BRUSHES	23.94	4.19	T1	28.13
100	SI	MEAKIN	4001	081098	10044	Services	249.00	43.58	T1	292.58
101	SI	ROSEAL	4001	081098	10045	Services	125.00	21.88	T1	146.88
102	SI	GARDEN	4100	081098	10046	WIND. CLEAN FLUID	630.00	104.74	T1	734.74
103	SI	PAYNEP	4000	081098	10047	Services	1210.00	201.16	T1	1411.16
104	SI	PAULTP	4002	081098	10050	Services	60.00	10.50	T1	70.50
105	SI	SIDDAL	4001	081098	10048	Services	182.00	31.85	T1	213.85
106	SI	NORRIS	4000	081098	10049	Services	816.40	142.87	T1	959.27
	:					Totals	6610.04	1138.98		7749.02

Blitz Limited

Day Books : Customer Credits (Detailed)

Date from: 08/10/98
Date to: 08/10/98

Supplier From:
Supplier To: ZZZZZZZZ

Trans From: 1
Trans To: 106

N/C From:
N/C To: 99999999

Dept From: 0
Dept To: 999

No.	Tp	A/c	N/C	Date	Refn.	Details	Net	VAT	T/c	Total
84	SC	GELLIN	4000	081098	1	Services	250.00	43.75	T1	293.75
85	SC	ROYALP	4000	081098	2	Services	300.00	52.50	T1	352.50
86	SC	DCSROO	4001	081098	3	Services	150.00	26.25	T1	176.25
	:					Totals	700.00	122.50		822.50

Balance on the debtors control account

Escape to the main window, and click on the Nominal Ledger button. Then select the Debtors Control Account (code 1100) and click on Activity (and then History in Plus2). Accept the default transaction range you are offered. If you check the totals at the foot of the account, you should find that they are as follows.

	Debit	Credit
Totals:	30369.45	822.50
Balance:	29546.95	

Sales accounts

You can find the balances for each sales account using the Nominal Ledger Activity window (use the History option in Plus2). Click on the Nominal Ledger button, scroll down to the accounts concerned and highlight them, then click on Activity. Accept the defaults you are offered. Use the < and > buttons at the bottom of the screen to move from one account to the next.

The current balances shown in the box at the foot of each account's Activity window should be as follows:

Account		Debit	Credit	Balance
		£	£	£
4000	Sales - contract cleaning	550.00	21,357.80	20,807.80
4001	Sales - window cleaning	150.00	2,670.40	2,520.40
4002	Sales - domestic services	0.00	853.10	853.10
4100	Sales – materials	0.00	980.14	980.14

School of Dance

(a) One method is to use the Criteria button in the Invoicing window and set the Customer A/C field's sign to 'equals' and first box to SCHOOL. If you click on Criteria On and Close this will give you a window that includes only the relevant invoice.

(b) Select this invoice and click on the Print Invoices button in the Invoicing window.

(*Plus2:* Activity = Activity + History; Criteria On + Close = Criteria On; Print Invoices = Print Batch.)

CCC Engineering

Click on Customers and select the CCCENG account. Then click on the Activity button. You can find the amount currently owed by the customer, but not whether an invoice has been printed. The invoice amount is £1,527.50.

Windows exercises

The next two pages show suggested solutions to the two Windows exercises in this assignment. Your versions will probably look different, especially if you used a word processor other than Word.

For your duplicate invoice you will need to know the original invoice details including the VAT. An audit trail report for transaction number 40 is the best source. Use the Reports button in the main window and specify a transaction range 40 to 40 (and a date range ending on or after 8/10/98). Alternatively you can look at CCC Engineering's transaction history and calculate the VAT manually.

To copy from one application to the other, select (highlight) the item press Ctrl + C to copy, switch to the other application and position your cursor, then press Ctrl + V. (This is probably more trouble than it is worth in this example, but it is a very useful trick to know.)

Blitz Limited

25 Apple Road
London N12 3PP

Fax Cover Sheet

DATE:	October 8, 1998	**TIME:**	11:15
TO:	V Cockcroft CCC Engineering Ltd	**PHONE:** **FAX:**	01923 354022 01923 354071
FROM:	Your name Blitz Limited	**PHONE:** **FAX:**	0181 912 2013 0181 912 6387
RE:	Invoice number 10005		

Number of pages including cover sheet: Two

Message

This is in response to your telephone call earlier this morning.

The amount due is £1,527.50 (including VAT of £227.50). For your reference a copy of the invoice accompanies this cover note. Payment is due within 30 days of the date of the invoice.

Blitz Limited

25 Apple Road
London
N12 3PP
Tel: 0181 912 2013
Fax: 0181 912 6387

INVOICE

INVOICE NO: 10005
DATE: 22 September, 1998

To:

CCC Engineering Limited
28 Gardener Road
Watford
WF3 7GH

Deliver To:
Invoice address

QUANTITY	DESCRIPTION	UNIT PRICE	AMOUNT
	Factory cleaning	N/A	1300.00

SUBTOTAL	1300.00
VAT	227.50
SHIPPING & HANDLING	-
TOTAL DUE	**1527.50**

Make all cheques payable to: Blitz Limited
If you have any questions concerning this invoice, call: Your name, 0181 912 2013

THANK YOU FOR YOUR BUSINESS!

SOLUTION TO ASSIGNMENT 3: PAYMENTS TO SUPPLIERS
Remittance advice notes

If you have access to a printer, and you intend to print the remittance advice notes (Task (b) of the assignment), you *must* produce the remittance advice notes before you save the payments in question. (This is to help prevent fraud.)

Payments to suppliers

You should now process the payment transactions for the 14 payments shown in paragraph (1) in Assignment 3. Click on Bank in the main Sage window and then on the Supplier button. Follow the procedures described in Chapter 6.

It is simpler to use the Pay in Full button for these payments, rather than typing in the amount of the cheque (though it is worth trying both methods to see the difference). In the former case, press Tab when you reach the £ sign box. Click on Pay in Full when the cursor is in the Payment boxes until the £ sign box shows the correct amount.

Save each transaction only after you have printed a remittance advice if required.

Chieftain Newspaper Group

To process the payment to the Chieftain Newspaper group, you must first post the credit note transaction to the relevant account in the Suppliers Ledger. There is no need to close down the Bank option and return to the main Sage window if you do not want to. Just click on Suppliers and then Credits (SFW3: Batch Credits) to input the credit note details – as explained in Chapter 4.

When you have entered and posted the credit note transaction, press Esc to return to the Supplier payments window (or open it up again if you closed it). You can then process the payment to the supplier, using the credit note to reduce the cheque payment to £1,175.

Credit notes and early settlement discounts

You will first need to find out the amount of the credit notes by looking at the Activity for each of the accounts mentioned. The amounts you should have posted are as follows.

Account	Gross	VAT	Net
FLOORS	1,012.85	150.85	862.00
HARROW	2,853.37	424.97	2,428.40
MATTHI	3,360.50	500.50	2,860.00

Post the new invoices as you have done in previous assignments except that instead of accepting tax code T1 and letting the program calculate VAT at 17.5% on the full amount, use code T3 and type in the amount of VAT shown on the invoice.

To pay the new invoices, you will have to calculate the discount to establish what the amount of each cheque payment should be. You should have produced the following results:

Supplier code	Net amount £	Discount %	Discount £	Cheque payment £
FLOORS	862.00	5%	43.10	962.21
HARROW	2,428.40	3%	72.85	2767.77
MATTHI	2,860.00	5%	143.00	3192.48

To enter the payment details, Tab past the £ sign box and click on Pay in Full when you reach the Payment box. Then type in the amount of the discount in the Discount box.

Highpile Cleaning Supplies

Here, you are paying an invoice and also making a payment on account for invoices not yet received. Type 3500 in the £ sign box and then when you reach the Payment box click on Pay in Full.

Now click on Save. You will be told that there is an unallocated cheque balance of £1,135.31. Click on Yes to post it as a payment on account.

Bank transaction payments

To make the payments for the cheque requisitions, press Esc until you reach the Bank Accounts window and then click on Payment. For each payment that includes VAT (cheques 000119 and 000121) you can enter the gross payment in the Net column and then click on Calc Net. The VAT will be calculated automatically, and the Net amount adjusted to exclude VAT. The tax code for the train ticket (cheque 000120) should be T0.

Listing (Line 50, SFW4 and SFW 3)

You have processed payments to suppliers (Suppliers Ledger) and for three bank transactions (Nominal Ledger). There are several ways of doing this in Line 50, SFW4 and SFW3. (For Plus2, see the next page.) We suggest that you click on Reports in the Bank accounts window and select:

(a) Day Books: Bank Payments (Summary); and also

(b) Day Books: Supplier Payments (Summary).

Enter 091098 as the date in both date boxes, when making your specifications for the listing.

The output in printed form should be as follows. (Check that your totals match the totals shown here.)

Blitz Limited

Day Books: Supplier Payments (Summary)

Date from: 09/10/98
Date to: 09/10/98

Bank From:
Bank To: 99999999

Transaction From: 1
Transaction To: 133

Supplier From:
Supplier To: ZZZZZZZZ :

No.	Bank	A/c	Date	Refn.	Details	Net	VAT	Total
107	1200	AA1MIN	091098	000100	Purchase Payment	117.50	0.00	117.50
108	1200	BTELEC	091098	000101	Purchase Payment	540.50	0.00	540.50
109	1200	CAPITA	091098	000102	Purchase Payment	376.00	0.00	376.00
110	1200	BLOFFI	091098	000103	Purchase Payment	1493.78	0.00	1493.78
111	1200	FIRSTS	091098	000104	Purchase Payment	332.23	0.00	332.23
112	1200	SAMURA	091098	000105	Purchase Payment	3205.00	0.00	3205.00
113	1200	3DTECH	091098	000106	Purchase Payment	179.95	0.00	179.95
114	1200	IRONCL	091098	000107	Purchase Payment	3000.00	0.00	3000.00
115	1200	TROJAN	091098	000108	Purchase Payment	141.00	0.00	141.00
116	1200	MUSWEL	091098	000109	Purchase Payment	1240.00	0.00	1240.00
117	1200	NORTHL	091098	000110	Purchase Payment	1175.00	0.00	1175.00
118	1200	STERLI	091098	000111	Purchase Payment	642.37	0.00	642.37
119	1200	UNIFOR	091098	000112	Purchase Payment	763.75	0.00	763.75
120	1200	VANCEN	091098	000113	Purchase Payment	19059.44	0.00	19059.44
122	1200	CHIEFT	091098	000114	Purchase Payment	1175.00	0.00	1175.00
129	1200	FLOORS	091098	000115	Purchase Payment	962.21	0.00	962.21
131	1200	HARROW	091098	000116	Purchase Payment	2767.77	0.00	2767.77
133	1200	MATTHI	091098	000117	Purchase Payment	3192.48	0.00	3192.48
135	1200	HIGHPI	091098	000118	Purchase Payment	2364.69	0.00	2364.69
136	1200	HIGHPI	091098	000118	Payment on Account	1135.31	0.00	1135.31

| | Totals | : | | | | 43,863.98 | 0.00 | 43,863.98 |

Blitz Limited

Day Books: Bank Payments (Summary)

Date from: 09/10/98
Date to: 09/10/98

Bank From:
Bank To: 99999999

Transaction From: 1
Transaction To: 133

N/C From:
N/C To: ZZZZZZZZ :

Dept From: 0
Dept To: 999

No	Tp	A/C	Date	Chq. No	Details	Net	VAT	T/c	
137	BP	8203	091098	000119	Training course	220.00	38.50	T1	258.50
138	BP	7400	091098	000120	Train ticket	105.50	0.00	T0	105.50
139	BP	8205	091098	000121	Refreshments	84.00	14.70	T1	98.70
					Totals	409.50	53.20		462.70

Listing (Plus2)

In *Plus2* you can produce (in printed form or as a screen display) a listing that includes *both* types of payment. Click on Reports in the main Sage window and select the **Payments Report** option. The totals will be the sum of the totals of the two reports shown above:

Net	£44,273.48
VAT	£53.20
Total	£44,326.68

Bank balance

You can print or display the Activity on the bank current account by selecting it in the Nominal Ledger (code 1200). Accept the default 'From' date and specify a 'To' date of 09/10/98. You should get a credit balance of £10,380.61.

(Note: the Tp column indicates bank receipt [BR], purchase payment [PP], payment in advance [PA], or bank payment [BP]).

Nominal Activity

Date from: 09/10/98						N/C **1200**	
Date to: 09/10/98						N/C To: **1200**	

Transaction From: 1
Transaction To: 133

No.	Tp	Date	Refn	Details	Value	Debit	Credit
1	BR	190898		M Green - shares	20000.00	20000.00	
2	BR	190898		T Nicholas - shares	20000.00	20000.00	
8	JC	160998	xxxxx	Wages and salaries	6053.93		6053.93
107	PP	091098	100	Purchase Payment	117.50		117.50
108	PP	091098	101	Purchase Payment	540.50		540.50
109	PP	091098	100102	Purchase Payment	376.00		376.00
110	PP	091098	103	Purchase Payment	1493.78		1493.78
111	PP	091098	104	Purchase Payment	332.23		332.23
112	PP	091098	105	Purchase Payment	3205.00		3205.00
113	PP	091098	106	Purchase Payment	179.95		179.95
114	PP	091098	107	Purchase Payment	3000.00		3000.00
115	PP	091098	108	Purchase Payment	141.00		141.00
116	PP	091098	109	Purchase Payment	1240.00		1240.00
117	PP	091098	110	Purchase Payment	1175.00		1175.00
118	PP	091098	111	Purchase Payment	642.37		642.37
119	PP	091098	112	Purchase Payment	763.75		763.75
120	PP	091098	113	Purchase Payment	19059.44		19059.44
122	PP	091098	114	Purchase Payment	1175.00		1175.00
129	PP	091098	115	Purchase Payment	962.21		962.21
131	PP	091098	116	Purchase Payment	2767.77		2767.77
133	PP	091098	117	Purchase Payment	3192.48		3192.48
135	PP	091098	118	Purchase Payment	2364.69		
136	PA	091098	118	Payment on Account	1135.31		3500.00
137	BP	091098	119	Training course	258.50		258.50
138	BP	091098	120	Train ticket	105.50		105.50
139	BP	091098	121	Refreshments	98.70		98.70
				Totals :		40000.00	50380.61
				History Balance :			10380.61

Balance on the creditors control account

You should repeat the same exercise as for the bank account balance, selecting account code 2100 for the creditors control account. The balance on the account is now £6,113.86.

Spreadsheet

If you did this exercise you should fairly easily have been able to explain that the No. column lists the number of the transaction – the number allocated by the Sage package to each consecutive transaction that you post. The Ref column shows either the cheque number or the credit note number or, in the case of discounts, the original invoice number.

The problem with the totals is that some items have been included that should not have been included and one item has been omitted. To put things right you should have deleted the amounts shown in boxes ('cells') 16, 19, 21 and 23 in columns G and I, and you should have entered the amount 1,135.31 in cell J25.

As part of your tidying up exercise you could have changed the lines in capitals to small letters, made the headings italic, given the spreadsheet a title, and so on. No 'answer' is shown because many 'answers' are acceptable, although they will be different in appearance. Would you be ashamed to give yours to a senior person in your organisation? Alternatively, is it *so* beautiful that it is obvious that you don't have enough other work to take up your time?

SOLUTION TO ASSIGNMENT 4: RECEIPTS FROM CUSTOMERS

The assignment requires you to process a variety of transactions. However, you might by this stage be using the software with greater confidence, as you become more familiar with it.

Posting new invoices

The procedures for entering details of new customer accounts and producing invoices were described in Chapter 5. If you have access to a printer, you should use the Invoicing option in the main window, and:

(a) the Service window to produce the invoice;
(b) the Print Invoices button to print the invoices; and
(c) the Update Ledgers button to post the transactions to the ledgers.

The nominal account code should be 4000 for the invoice to Bradley Fashions (contract cleaning) and 4002 for the invoice to A Rathod (domestic services).

One of the two invoices is reproduced on the next page. If you have forgotten how to produce invoices, look again at Chapter 5.

If you do not have access to a printer, you should enter and post the invoice using the Invoices (SFW3: Batch Invoices) button in the Customers window.

Receipts - payment in full for invoices

Posting the 12 receipts transactions listed in item (2) in the information for the assignment should not present any difficulties. Click on the Bank button and then on the Customer button.

These are all payments in full for one or more outstanding invoices. In every case, you can use the Pay in Full button for allocating the receipt to an invoice. Make sure you include references for each receipt or they will all be lumped together in some of the reports that you might want to print out.

Click on Save when you have posted the details for each customer and move on to the next customer.

In the case of two customers (D J Hargreaves and A Rose Ltd) the amount received is in payment for just one invoice, when there are two outstanding invoices on the account. In cases where it is not clear what is being paid you should always allocate the payment to the earliest invoices on the account.

Invoice   Page 1
10051
12/10/98

Blitz ltd

25 Apple Road
London
N12 3PP

BRADLEY FASHIONS LTD
18 HOSPITAL BRIDGE
ROAD
ST ALBANS
HERTS

BRADLE

Service Details	Discount%	Net Amount	VAT Amount
CONTRACT CLEANING	0.00	820.00	143.50

Total Net Amount	820.00
Total VAT Amount	143.50
Carriage	0.00
Invoice Total	963.50

T P Paul

The invoice of £70.50 for T P Paul is unpaid. This can be cancelled by creating a credit note for £70.50. You can do this, for the purpose of this assignment, by using the Credits (Plus2: Credit Note; SFW3: Batch Credits) option in the Customers window.

To *clear* the account you then need to click on the Bank button and open the Customer window. Specify PAULTP as the account code and enter the date then Tab to the Receipt box (Plus2: Paid box). Click on Pay in Full for both transactions which will cancel each other out.

Discounts

Begin by checking that the discount has been correctly calculated. If you disagree with the customer's calculation, you would have to speak to your supervisor or (if authorised to do so) telephone the customer to query the mistake.

To check the calculation you first need to find out the transaction number(s) by looking up the customers' Activity and then the net amount due by looking at thse transactions in the Financials listing.

The transactions are numbers 103 and numbers 91, 92 and 93. In the case of Rapid Pizzas, the discount of £9.66 must be divided into three chunks.

Transaction no	Net amount	Discount (5%)
103	1210.00	60.50
91	60.00	3.00
92	91.20	4.56
93	42.00	2.10
		9.66

Post this by returning to the Bank Customer receipts window and entering the relevant account code. In each case (Payne Properties and Rapid Pizzas) you should remember to follow these procedures.

(a) Make sure you enter a reference for the invoice being paid.

(b) Tab through the Amount box leaving it blank.

(c) In Line 50, SFW4 and SFW3 tab through the Receipt box leaving it blank. (In Plus2, click on Pay in Full for each item and press Tab.)

(d) Enter the amount of the discount in the appropriate box. The amount in the Receipt box will automatically be calculated. (In Plus2 the Paid box will automatically be recalculated.)

Deductions for credit notes

Stay in the Bank Customer window. For each customer account, enter the invoice as the reference number. Leave the Amount box blank and Tab to the Receipt box. Click on Pay in Full in each case.

Part payments

The part payments by Elite Caterers and Campbell Consultants should be processed either:

(a) by *keying in* the amount of the payment in the Amount box, and then Tabbing to the Receipt box of the first invoice listed and clicking on Pay in Full; *or*

(b) by Tabbing through the Amount box and then *keying in* the amount of the payment in the first Receipt box you come to. Then you can just click on Save.

(In Plus2 Receipt box = Paid box.)

Clough and Partners

This payment of an invoice plus a payment on account must be processed by *typing* the amount received in the Amount box. When you click on Save after entering the receipt details, accept the Post as a Payment on Account message.

M Zakis Ltd

Before you process the receipt from M Zakis, you must set up an account for the (new) customer in the Customers ledger. Type in the code MZAKIS and press Tab. Click on **New** when the Customer Account window appears.

When you have set up and saved the account, return to the Bank Customer window (in the Bank Accounts part of the program). The receipt can then be processed by typing it into the Amount box and clicking on Save. Accept the prompt that appears.

Writing off small unpaid balances

Process the payments from A T Haslam and R P Marwood in the same way as the part payments from other customers. There will be unpaid balances of £0.18 and £0.05 respectively. (If you forgot to take a note of these amounts you can find the unpaid balance by searching the list in the Customers window.)

In Line 50 and SFW4 click on Tools (SFW3: Data) at the top of the screen, then on Write Off, Refund, Return. Choose the Sales Ledger amendments option. From the area list pick Write off Customer Transactions below a value. To be safe a good value to enter is 0.50, although you could put in a higher amount – say 1 (£1.00) – if you wish. Select both the accounts by highlighting them and click on Next. Confirm that you are writing off 23p by clicking on Finish.

(In Plus2 Click on Features right at the top of the screen, and then on Customer Features and then Write off Transactions on the menus that drop down. The maximum write off value you should now enter is 0.18. (Although you could put in a higher amount if you wish, say 1.00 for £1. Select both accounts by highlighting them and then click on Write Off. A message will appear asking you to confirm the write off. Click on Yes.)

Bank receipts

The five items of bank receipts from non-credit customers should be entered by using the Receipt button in the Bank Accounts window.

For each transaction, select the correct nominal ledger code (N/C). This should be 4001 for window cleaning, 4002 for domestic services and 4100 for materials sales. Enter the five transactions separately. Just key in the single number 4 and then click on the Finder button (or press F4) if you forget which nominal Sales account is which.

Reports

You should print, preview or display a *Day Books: Customer Receipts* report and a *Day Books: Bank Receipts* report, using the reports button in the Bank window. (In Plus2 you want a Deposits Report.)

The Reports window will allow you to specify the parameters for items to be listed. Specify a Date Range 121098 to 121098. Don't forget to specify what sort of Output you require.

The total amount for the report is as follows.

	Net £	Tax £	Gross £
Customer Receipts	10,508.25	0.00	10,508.25
Bank Receipts	352.00	61.60	413.60
Total	10,860.25	61.60	10,921.85

(There is no tax shown for receipts from credit customers, since the VAT is accounted for when the invoice is issued, not when it is paid.)

P Leyser refund

In Line 50 and SFW4 click on Tools (SFW3: Data) at the top of the screen, then on Write Off, Refund, Return, and choose the Sales Ledger option. Choose Customer Invoice Refund from the list that appears as you click on Next. Scroll down to the LEYSER account and click on Next. The payment will appear in the window. Select it and click on Next again. You are asked which account you want to post the refund to: in this case it is account 1200. Select this and click on Next. If the information given in the next window is correct, click on Finish.

In Plus2, click on Features at the top of the screen, then Customer Features, then Invoice Refunds. Enter the account reference code (LEYSER) and press Tab. The invoice will appear on screen. Click on it to highlight it and then click on the Refund button. Click on Yes when you get a message asking you to confirm.

Account balances - nominal ledger

You can establish these using the Activity button (then the History button in Plus2) in the Nominal window. You will need to do two searches of the ledger, one for each account. The balances should be:

Account	N/C code	Debit entries	Credit entries	Balance
Bank current account	1200	50,921.85	50,477.20	444.65
Debtors control account	1100	31,517.67	11,568.23	19,949.44

Account balances - sales ledger

Click on the Customers button and scroll down until you find the account ELITEC. You should find that the balance outstanding on this account is £1,497.81.

SOLUTION TO ASSIGNMENT 5: OTHER CASH TRANSACTIONS

Many of the tasks for this assignment are similar to tasks that were set in Assignments 1-4. There are invoices from new and existing suppliers, invoices to new and existing customers, and payments and receipts. In addition, however, some of the tasks relate to petty cash transactions, journal transactions and a bank reconciliation. Assignment 5 is therefore a wide-ranging test of your competence with Sage.

Setting up the petty cash system

The petty cash system is set up by withdrawing £300 in cash from the bank. This bank-cash transaction should be recorded in the nominal ledger as a journal entry. Click on the Journals button in the Nominal Ledger window. The fields should be completed as follows.

(a) Reference. Use the cheque number as a reference for the transaction. This is 000122.

(b) Date 131098.

(c) The double entry is as follows. (It doesn't matter whether you do the debit or the credit entry first.)

N/C	Details	T/c	Debit £	Credit £
1200	To petty cash	T9		300.00
1230	From bank account	T9	300.00	

Save the transaction, then press Esc or click on Close.

Invoices from suppliers

The invoices from suppliers can be entered using the Invoices button in the Suppliers window. This allows you to enter new supplier details, where appropriate. The transaction date should be the invoice date, not the date on which you are processing the transactions. Some invoices relate to different items of expense, and so different nominal ledger account codes. For example, the invoice from Great North Hotel should be recorded on three lines, for nominal ledger account codes 7402, 7406 and 7502 respectively. All the purchase invoice transactions should have a tax code T1. Your accuracy in entering the transactions is tested by a later task in the assignment. If you cannot remember how to process supplier invoices, check back to Chapter 4.

Customer invoices

For this assignment, there is no requirement to produce invoices, and you can enter the details using the Invoices option in the Customers window. You need to assign each sales item to the appropriate nominal ledger account code - 4000 for contract cleaning, 4001 for window cleaning, 4002 for domestic services and 4100 for materials sales. All transactions should have a T1 tax code, and a date of 161098.

This method of posting customer invoices is similar to posting supplier invoices. When an invoice is for several items, each with a different nominal ledger sales account code, enter each part of the invoice on a separate line.

Payments to suppliers

To record the payments to suppliers, Click on Bank and then on the Supplier button in the Bank Accounts window. Look up the supplier account reference codes if you need to, using the Finder button or the F4 function key to display the supplier accounts on screen.

For the Ace Telephone Answering and ANS Newspaper Group invoices, *key in* the amount paid in the Amount box, then Tab to the Payment box and click on Pay in Full. With the ANS Newspaper Group payment, confirm that the payment on account should be posted.

Before you record the payment from Wells Business Systems you should post the credit note. Use the Calc Net option to allocate the amount correctly.

Receipts from customers

Click on the Customer button in the Bank Accounts window. The receipts from the three customers can be processed in a similar way to the payments to suppliers. Don't forget that there *must* be a reference number. Use the number of the invoice being paid.

V J Richardson cheque

This transaction can be posted as a journal entry. Click on the Journals button in the Nominal Ledger window. The entries in the main part of the screen should be:

N/C	Details	T/c	Debit £	Credit £
1200	Loan - V J Richardson	T9	10000.00	
2300	To bank account	T9		10000.00

Alternatively, you can post the transaction as a bank receipt, using the Receipt button in the Bank Accounts window. The N/C code for the receipt should be 2300, the net amount 10000 and the tax code T9.

Petty cash transactions

In Line 50, SFW4 and SFW3 click on the Bank button and then select account 1230 Petty Cash.

In Plus2 click on the Cash button in the main Sage window. To post the payments out of petty cash, just click on the Payments button and a window that will be familiar by now will appear. To post the receipt into petty cash the N/C code 4001 should be used (for window cleaning sales). Enter 72 as the Net amount, then click on the Calc Net button to calculate the VAT automatically. The final entry should be for a net cash receipt of £61.28 and VAT of £10.72.

To produce reports of Cash Payments (or Receipts), click on the Reports button in the Bank window (Plus2: main Sage window) and scroll down the list until you find the appropriate option. Select the date range 131098 to 161098. Print the listing if you have access to a printer. Otherwise, display the listing on screen. An extract from the listing is shown below.

Blitz Limited

Cash Payments (Summary)

Date from: 13/10/98
Date to 16/10/98

Bank From:
Bank To: 99999999

Transaction from: 1
Transaction To: 235

No.	Tp	A/C	Date	Refn	Details	Net	VAT	Total
223	CP	7501	131098	PC001	POSTAGE STAMPS	24.00	0.00	24.00
224	CP	8205	131098	PC002	BISCUITS, COFFEE	32.49	0.00	32.49
225	CP	8205	131098	PC003	MILK	15.20	0.00	15.20
226	CP	7400	131098	PC004	TAXIS	25.00	0.00	25.00
227	CP	7400	141098	PC005	TRAIN FARES	9.20	0.00	9.20
228	CP	8205	141098	PC006	WASHING UP LIQUID	1.75	0.00	1.75
229	CP	7500	141098	PC007	PHOTOCOPYING	24.00	4.20	28.20
230	CP	7504	151098	PC008	STATIONERY	37.24	6.52	43.76
231	CP	7400	151098	PC009	TAXIS	15.00	0.00	15.00
232	CP	8205	161098	PC010	SANDWICHES, CAKES	38.26	0.00	38.26
233	CP	7304	161098	PC011	PARKING	7.00	0.00	7.00
234	CP	7400	161098	PC012	TRAIN FARES	8.40	0.00	8.40
					Totals	237.54	10.72	248.26

Topping up petty cash

Check the balance on the Petty Cash account (N/C 1230) by looking at the list of accounts in and balances in the main Nominal Ledger window. This should show a balance of £123.74.

A cheque for £176.26 cash (£300 - £123.74) must be drawn to top up the petty cash balance to £300.

To post this entry, click on the Journals button in the Nominal Ledger window. The main part of the entry is as follows:

N/C	Details	T/c	Debit £	Credit £
1200	To petty cash	T9		176.26
1230	From bank account	T9	176.26	

Check that the balance on the petty cash account (N/C 1230) is now £300 (look again at the list in the Nominal Ledger window).

Wages and salaries

These transactions can be entered in the nominal ledger accounts as a single journal entry. Click on Journals in the Nominal Ledger window. Key in the date 161098 and (as instructed) reference J04. The remaining entries should be as follows:

N/C	Description	T/c	Debit	Credit
			£	£
1200	Cash for wages	T9		4133.04
2210	PAYE, 16 Oct	T9		2217.96
2211	Nat Ins, 16 Oct	T9		975.20
7001	Directors salaries	T9	1350.80	
7003	Staff salaries	T9	475.75	
6000	Wages	T9	4859.65	
7006	Employers NI	T9	640.00	

The total debits equal the total credits, therefore you can post these transactions as a single journal entry.

Account balances

You can just scroll through the Nominal Ledger window to search for the account balances required by your supervisor. Check that you have the following balances.

N/C		Debit	Credit
		£	£
1100	Debtors control account	25486.83	
1200	Bank – current account	4642.09	
2100	Creditors control account		7677.28
7003	Staff salaries	951.50	
7400	Travelling	301.50	
7700	Equipment hire	503.75	
4000	Sales – contract cleaning		27167.80
4001	Sales – window cleaning		3060.68
4002	Sales – domestic services		1103.90
4100	Sales – materials		1243.74
1230	Petty cash	300.00	
4009	Discounts allowed	101.66	
5009	Discounts taken		258.95

Bank reconciliation

Doing a bank reconciliation can seem a fairly complex task, and you need to be thorough. Your source document is the bank statement itself. You must match every item on the bank statement against a corresponding entry in the nominal ledger bank account.

If you have access to a printer, print out a listing of activity on the Bank Account. In Line 50, SFW4 and SFW3 you can use the Statements button to do this, accepting the default dates you are offered. In Plus2 do this through the Report option in the Nominal ledger window.

Now click on the Bank Reconciliation (Plus2: Reconcile) button in the Bank Accounts window. A listing of transactions in the nominal ledger bank account will appear on screen. It is probably best to *maximise* the window for this sort of detailed screen work: click on the upward-pointing triangle in the top right hand corner of the Bank Reconciliation window.

The matching process can now begin. When you match a transaction in the nominal ledger bank account with an item on the statement sent by the bank, you must note the match. Do this by clicking on the transaction on screen. The matched transaction will be highlighted in a different colour. Use the Page Down and Page Up keys, the ↑ and ↓ cursor keys, or the scroll bar to search through the list of transactions on screen.

You should be able to match nearly every item on the bank's statement against a transaction in the nominal ledger account. In this exercise, there is an additional item on the bank statement for bank charges. You should post this item to the nominal ledger (N/C code 7901 for bank charges) and you can do this by:

(a) clicking on the Adjustment button;
(b) completing the relevant fields in the window that pops up.

When you have matched *every* transaction on the bank's statement against the nominal ledger transactions on screen and you have also entered the bank charges details, you are nearing the end of the bank reconciliation exercise.

Check the balance in the Reconcile Balance (or Statement Balance) field on the screen. This should equal the balance on the bank statement itself (13,381.53). If you have achieved this reconciliation, click on Save.

You can now display or print out a list of reconciled and unreconciled transactions. In Line 50, SFW4 and SFW3 click on Reports in the Bank window and obtain reports of Unreconciled Payments and Unreconciled Receipts. Extracts from these are shown below.

In Plus2 click on the Statement button in the Bank window. You will be asked to specify your output requirements: Printer, Preview or File. Click on Printer if you have a printer available. Click on Preview if not. If you get a Preview you may need to Zoom in or out to see it properly. Use the Page Down key to search to the bottom of the listing, if you are looking at a preview. At the end of the list you should see 7 unreconciled payments and 2 unreconciled receipts, as follows.

Blitz Limited

Unreconciled Payments

Date From: 01/01/80
Date To: 31/12/99

Bank From:
Bank To: 99999999

Transaction From: 1
Transaction To: 245

No.	Tp	Date	Refn.	Details	Amount
133	PP	091098	000117	Purchase Payment	3192.48
213	PP	161098	000123	Purchase Payment	250.00
214	PP	161098	000124	Purchase Payment	881.25
215	PA	161098	000124	Payment on Account	318.75
216	PP	161098	000125	Purchase Payment	1516.50
236	JC	161098	000126	TO PETTY CASH	176.26
238	JC	161098	J04	CASH FOR WAGES	4133.04
					10468.28

Unreconciled Receipts

No.	Tp	Date	Refn.	Details	Receipts
218	SR	151098	10004	Sales Receipt	1000.00
219	SR	161098	10046	Sales Receipt	703.24
					1703.24

Overall the position is as follows.

	£
Statement balance	13,381.53
Unreconciled payments	(10,468.28)
Unreconciled receipts	1,703.24
Trial balance	4,616.49

The trial balance figure is different (by £25.60) from the account balance figure you gave your supervisor earlier. This is because you have now posted the bank charges.

Discrepancies

Your answer to this will depend partly upon how accurately you have posted the data.

You should have had alert messages when posting the sales invoices for Brookes Acoustics and The Keith Group. (You may not have if you are using an early version of Sterling for Windows 3. However, balances which are over the credit limit are shown in red in the Customers window.) In real life you should have drawn this to the attention of your supervisor. Presumably the services had already been provided, but there may be occasion to refuse further orders from these customers. The position will become clearer when you tackle the next assignment.

SOLUTION TO ASSIGNMENT 6: OTHER CREDIT TRANSACTIONS

Posting credit sales transactions

The credit sales transactions should be entered using the Invoices option in the Customers window. Remember to code each item for the correct sales account in the nominal ledger, and use tax code T1 for every transaction. Whenever a customer exceeds the existing credit limit, make a note of the name, but continue to process the transaction.

The customers who have exceeded their existing credit limit are:

GHH Commercial Bank
The Keith Group
Norris Hydraulics Ltd
School of Dance
R I Tepper Ltd

The Keith Group has already exceeded its credit limit, even before you post the current transaction. In Plus2, or in any package if you use the Invoicing option, there should be a warning message telling you that the customer is over the credit limit. Click on OK, but make a note of this.

Their credit limit should be increased by £1,000 in each case. To do this as soon as you get a warning message (ie without closing the Customers Invoice window) click on the Customers button again, select the relevant customer account and click on the Record button. The customer details will then appear on screen. Move to the credit limit field (on the Defaults tab in Line 50, SFW4 and SFW3) and key in a new credit limit (overwriting the old limit) by adding 1000 to the limit. Then click on Save and press Esc twice.

Alternatively you can post all the invoices first and then alter the credit limits of the Customers shown on the list you made as you went through. This is the best option if your version of the package is not giving you warning messages.

Cash sales

The cheques received should be posted as Receipts in the Bank Accounts window. Enter each transaction in turn selecting the correct N/C code. The four entries should be as follows, if the tax code is entered as T1.

Deposit No.	N/C	Date	Amount	Description	Amount and tax code
500005	4002	211097	–	Domestic services	51.7 then Calc Net button
500006	4002	211097	–	Domestic services	44 then Calc Net
500007	4100	211097	–	Materials sales	37.6 then Calc Net
500008	4100	231097	–	Materials sales	52.88 then Calc Net

Save each transaction when you have entered the details. You then get a blank window for the next transaction.

The cash receipts should be posted in account 1230 as Petty Cash Receipts. (In Plus2 click on the Cash button in the main Sage window and then the Receipts button.) The two entries should be:

Ref	Date	N/C	Details	Net and Tax
PCR002	221097	4100	Materials sales	25.38 then Calc Net
PCR003	231097	4002	Domestic services	35.25 then Calc Net

Click on Save each time.

Invoices received from suppliers

Click on the Invoices button in the Suppliers Ledger window. Enter the three transactions, setting up new supplier accounts where appropriate. The tax code is T1 for all three transactions. Check the instructions in Chapter 4 if you have forgotten how to post supplier invoices to the ledgers.

Receipts from customers

Click on the Customer button in the Bank Accounts window. Post the seven transactions. Check the instructions in Chapter 7 if you have forgotten how to do this.

Tab through the main Amount box if you can see at a glance which invoice(s) are being settled. Just click on Pay in Full when you get to the relevant Receipt box (Plus2: Paid box). If it is not clear how the payment should be allocated, *type in* the amount received in the main Amount box and then click on Pay in Full in each of the Receipt boxes. When there is no more money to allocate, click on Save.

You should type in the amounts for S T Chanas, Elite Caterers,, and Meakin Media.

Contra entries

The accounts of Elite Caterers and Meakin Media can now be settled by contra entries. Take each customer/supplier in turn.

In Line 50 and SFW4 click on Tools (SFW3: Data), then on Contra Entries. (In Plus2 click on Features, then Customer Features, then Contra Entries.)

(a) For Elite Caterers, enter both the Sales Ledger A/C and the Purchase Ledger A/C as ELITEC. The screen will display the unpaid invoice balances in the customer account (left-hand side) and the supplier account (right-hand side) for Elite Caterers. Click on each transaction in the sales account and then click on the supplier account transaction. The totals should be the same, and can therefore be set off in full against each other, so just click on OK to post the contra entry.

(b) For Meakin Media, repeat the procedure. The A/C code is MEAKIN for both the Customers Ledger account and the Suppliers Ledger account. The *first* entry in the customer account and the entry in the supplier account should be selected.

ANS Newspaper Group

Click your way into the Contra Entries window again. Start to post a contra entry transaction, by entering ANSNEW as the Sales Ledger A/C and Purchase Ledger A/C codes. The window should then display unpaid invoices as follows:

	£
In the customer account for ANSNEW	176.25
In the supplier account for ANSNEW	553.75
Difference	377.50

The difference in amounts owing is £377.50, and a cheque should be drawn up for this amount.

Click on Bank, then on Supplier. Post a payment to ANSNEW for £377.50, dated 22 October 1997, cheque number 000127. Key the amount 377.50 into the £ sign box, then tab down to the *invoice* for advertising (amount £553.75) and click on Pay in Full. Then Save this transaction.

Return to the Contra Entries window. You can now process a contra entry for ANS Newspaper Group, in the same way as for Elite Catering and Meakin Media.

Writing off small unpaid balances

In Line 50 and SFW4 click on Tools (SFW3: Data), then on Write Off, Refund, Return and opt for the Sales Ledger. Choose Write Off Customer transaction below a value. (In Plus2 click on Features, then Customer Features, then the Write off transaction option.)

Enter a value of 1.01 (£1.01). The screen will display two unpaid balances.

CAMPBE 1.00
CHANAS 0.63

Click on both of these and then click on Next (on the Write Off button in Plus2). Confirm the write offs when asked to do so. The total amount written off is £1.63.

Writing off accounts

Look at the Customers window to find the balances on the accounts ADAMSE and HAYNES. You should do this to establish that E T Adams currently owes nothing to Blitz.

With L Haynes & Co, however, there is an unpaid balance on the account. This must be written off as a bad debt.

To write off the bad debt for L Haynes & Co, click on Tools (SFW3: Data) then on Write Off, Refund, Return, then on the Sales Ledger (Plus2: Features and Customer Features). This time select the Write off Customer Accounts option. Choose the account reference HAYNES. Two lines are shown, but both relate to the same invoice. When you click on the Next button (Write Off button in Plus2), *both* will be written off.

Credit note

The sales credit note to Owen of London should be posted using the Credits (Plus2: Credit Note; SFW3: Batch Credits) button in the Customers window. (Check the instructions in Chapter 5 if you have forgotten how to do this). The entry should be:

A/C	Date	Ref	N/C	Description	Amount	T/c
OWENLO	221097	004	4000	Credit note	150.00	T1

GHH Commercial Bank - Statement

Select the GHHCOM account in the Customers window and the click on Statements. Enter the dates as a range that cannot help but include all transactions to date: given that Blitz was set up in August 1997, a range 010897 to the end of the actual current month at the time when you are doing this assignment would certainly cover everything. Then make your choice of Output option and stationery (to suit your printer, if applicable) and click on Run (OK in Plus2).

The printed statement is shown on the next page, as it would appear on blank stationery (ie stationery that is not pre-printed). The statement is duplicated in two columns. The right hand column is for the customer to use as a remittance advice note. The left hand column is the customer's statement of account. Only one column is shown here.

**BLITZ LTD
25 APPLE ROAD
LONDON
N12 3PP**

GHH COMMERCIAL BANK   GHHCOM
50 GRESHAM ST   311097
LONDON EC2

                                                                                    1

220997	10020	Office cleaning	1733.13
161097	10061	Contract cleaning	1116.25
211097	10071	Contract cleaning	587.50

Current	30 Days	60 Days	90 Days	120+ Days
1703.75	1733.13	0.00	0.00	0.00

                                                              Amount Due

                                                                 3436.88

WRW Catering - Reminder letter

Select WRWCAT in the Customer window (remembering to clear any other highlighting first)
and then click on Letter. In Line 50, SFW4 and SFW3 choose the option Payment Reminder
(v2) (or include a contact name if you like). (In Plus2 accept the OVERDUE.SAL option as the
File Name.) Choose whatever form of output you want. The reminder letter you should
produce is shown below. Which letter do you think is most suitable in the circumstances?

W R W CATERING LTD
11 STATION PARADE
BARNET
HERTS
BT5 2KC

4th November 1997

Dear Ms H C VERNON

Re : Overdue account   :   £ 756.70

According to our records we have not yet received payment on your overdue account,
now totalling   £ 756.70

I trust that this matter has been an oversight on your part, but now that the matter has been
brought to your attention we would ask you to forward a cheque in settlement.

If you have any outstanding queries, please do not hesitate to contact us.

Should payment have crossed in the post please disregard this letter.

Yours sincerely,

Blitz Limited

Line 50, SFW4 and SFW3 letter

W R W CATERING LTD
11 STATION PARADE
BARNET
HERTS
BT5 2KC

Dear Sir/Madam

We have written to your Payables Manager requesting payment of our overdue account. Unfortunately the account remains unpaid and we would now appreciate your assistance in avoiding a suspension of deliveries, a step which we must reluctantly take if payment is not received by return.

Yours sincerely,

Blitz Limited

Correcting the N/C code

A correction to an account code is an accounting error. You must first find the transaction reference number. Open the Suppliers window and select the account AA1MIN. Click on Activity (and then History in Plus2). The transaction history of the account will show the October invoice for £158.27. (This includes VAT.) The transaction number is 186.

In Line 50 and SFW4 click on File, then on Maintenenance then on Corrections (SFW3: Data ... Disk Doctor ... Correct). In the window that appears scroll to transaction number 186 and click on Edit.

In Line 50, SFW4 and SFW3 click on Edit again and alter the N/C code. Then click on Close, then on Save and confirm that you wish to post he changes. If you scroll down to the end of the list you can see that the correction has been posted.

In Plus2 tab to N/C and correct the code, then click on OK and confirm that you want to post the changes. If you scroll down to the end of the transaction list you will see that an Error correction has been posted automatically. Press Esc or click on Close.

Newlite Cleaning Fluids

Check the Activity (History) for NEWLIT in the Suppliers window. You should take a note of the transaction number (17) and the details of the invoice that has been posted incorrectly. Then use File ... Maintenance (SFW3 and Plus2: Disk Doctor) to correct the transaction as just explained.

The details should be:

A/C	NEWLIT
Date	120997
Inv No	26115
N/C	5000
Details	Cleaning materials
Net Amount	403.00
T/c	T1

The corrected invoice figure is £403.00 net plus VAT of £70.53 giving a total invoice amount of £473.53. In Line 50, SFW4 and SFW3 you can use the calculator button in the Edit Transaction Split Record screen to calculate the correct amount.

Current balances

To find the current balances on the nominal ledger accounts, simply call up the Nominal Ledger window. Scroll through each account in turn and copy down the balances shown. These should be as follows.

	Code	Balance £	
Bank current account	1200	6754.28	(debit)
Debtors control account	1100	28369.34	(debit)
Creditors control account	2100	7676.90	(credit)
Bad debt write off account	8100	151.32	(debit)
Advertising account	6201	3421.28	(debit)
Sales - contract cleaning	4000	31017.80	(credit)
Sales - window cleaning	4001	4084.68	(credit)
Sales - domestic services	4002	1430.35	(credit)
Sales - materials	4100	1417.34	(credit)

Aged debtors list

In some versions of Sage Sterling software, though not within Sage Sterling Plus 2, it is possible to produce an aged Debtors Listing as at a certain date, whatever the real date. If you had the facility within Sage Plus 2 to produce such a listing as at 4 November 1997 it would give the following totals, assuming also that you had posted everything correctly.

Balance	Current	30 days	60 days
28,369.34	15,816.05	12,553.29	0.00

This shows that £12,553.29 of invoices have been unpaid for between 30 and 60 days. The total value of unpaid invoices (debtors) is £28,369.34

In Plus2 you would have the same overall balance but it is likely that you will get a different aged breakdown, depending on the actual date on which you try to run the report (it is the Balances report in the Customers Report window).

Windows exercise

The customers owing the five largest amounts are:

A/C	Balance
GHHCOM	3,436.88
OGDENK	3,278.25
KEITHG	3,243.00
NORRIS	2,775.47
ROYALP	1,762.50

In Line 50, SFW4 and SFW3 you can do this exercise simply by clicking on the word Balance in the main Customers window. This re-sorts the data (smallest balance first).

Customers with a balance of over £1,000 that has been outstanding for more than 30 days are as follows. In Line 50, SFW4 and SFW3 you can do this using the Change Program Date option (in the Settings menu in Line 50 and SFW4; in the Defaults menu in SFW3) and the Criteria button.

A/C	Balance	Current	30 days
OGDENK	3,278.25	564.00	2,714.25
ROYALP	1,762.50	−352.50	2,115.00
GHHCOM	3,436.88	1,703.75	1,733.13
HARVEY	1,715.50	0.00	1,715.50
NORRIS	2,775.47	1,687.77	1,087.70

SOLUTION TO ASSIGNMENT 7: ADDING AND REMOVING EMPLOYEES

If there are significant differences between the procedures to follow in Plus 2 and Payroll 4 they are dealt with separately. If the difference is small the Payroll 4 procedure or term is shown in brackets.

You should specify a Payroll Run Date (Process Date) of 050299, even though this is not strictly necessary for this assignment.

Adding new employees

In Plus 2, click on the Employee button in the main Payroll window, then click on the Clear button to ensure that none are selected. Now click on Record.

In Payroll 4 ensure that the Payroll toolbar stack is selected, if necessary, and click on the New button at the top of the screen.

The first blank record available will be for employee number 18.

In Plus 2, when you have finished entering details for one employee, click on save and the next numbered blank record will appear. Press Esc or click on Close when you have entered and posted all the new details. Don't forget that you can drag out the borders of some windows to re-size them.

In Payroll 4 the Wizard will take you through the necessary steps.

The details to enter (or accept) for each employee in turn are as follows. Press Tab to move between fields. Fields not listed should be left with their default values (as, for example the employee number is) or left blank.

In Payroll 4 use Mr, Mrs or Miss for the Title, unless otherwise specified (or unless your organisation is strongly opposed to the use of Miss). You were not told this: you should know from common sense and from Unit 21 - 25 studies.

Employee no	18	19	20
Surname	Key in the name given in the assignment.		
Forenames	As given		
Address	Key in the information given in the assignment.		
Date of birth	310544	121152	180468
Works number	Accept the value given, 000018, 000019 and 000020 respectively.		
Payment type	Cheque Weekly	Cheque Monthly	Cheque Monthly
Employment began	010299	030299	080299
Tax code	419TW1	360L	K15
Effective from	010299	030299	080299
NI category	A	B	A
Effective from	010299	030299	080299
NI number	WR 48 27 61 B	PT 19 35 40 D	CS 47 41 66 A
Marital status	Single	Married	Single
Male/female	Female	Female	Male

Plus2 users

Tables button

When you have input these details for an employee, click on the Tables button and then on Edit Payment 1. Choose from Basic Rate, Salary, Hourly Rate, Bonus or Overtime. In these cases, employee 18 gets an hourly rate and employees 19 and 20 a salary.

Both Sheila Babcock and Donald Coombs should also have a second payment type. When you have OK'd the first type select the second line in the Payment Description box and click on Edit Payment 2 to set up the bonus. Click on Close or press Esc when you have finished.

PayRates button

Next click on the PayRates button and simply key in the amount detailed in the assignment for each Payment Type.

Don't forget that this is a rate per *period of payment*: per hour or per month, not per year. You have to divide the salaries by twelve. Your entries should be as follows.

Employee no	Payment Type 1		Payment Type 2	
18	Rate:	6.5000	None	
19	Rate:	983.3333	Rate:	1000.0000
20	Rate:	1150.0000	Rate:	1200.0000

Main YTD button

Tab to the Previous (P45) column and enter the Gross Pay for Tax and Tax Paid as given in the assignment. All other fields should be left as they are.

Bank button

Simply click on the Bank button and enter the banking details as given in the assignment.

Posting the records

When you have finished with these four buttons you can click on Save and move on to the next new record. You can delete a new record at any time before transactions are posted to it.

Payroll 4 users

Once the Employee Wizard has done its job, select the new employee from the list in the main window and click on Employee Record or Open. Click on the Employment tab and then on the Pay Elements button.

In these cases, employee 18 gets an hourly rate and employees 19 and 20 a salary. Both Sheila Babcock and Donald Coombs should also have a second payment type.

Your entries should be as follows.

Employee no	1st pay element		2nd pay element	
18	Rate:	6.5000	None	
19	Rate:	983.3333	Rate:	1000.0000
20	Rate:	1150.0000	Rate:	1200.0000

Amendments to employee details

Select each employee in turn and click on Record (Employee Record). That employee's current details will appear.

Change the address of Arvind Patel and the banking details of Norman Hazelwood, as set out in the assignment. The quickest way is to Tab between fields and press the delete button when an item you are going to have to retype is highlighted (the whole line disappears in one keystroke). Take care not to delete anything you shouldn't though).

Save any changes you make by clicking on the Save button. If you try to close an amended employee record without doing this you may be asked to confirm that you want to do so. If you click on Yes, your changes will not be saved. If you click on No you are just returned to where you were (to save your changes or make further ones).

Overtime

The employees entitled to overtime pay are numbers 13 to 15. Click on Clear (get into the habit of always doing this before selecting a new range of employees). Select these employees and then click on Record (Employee Record).

In Plus2 use the Tables button to set up the new payment type for these employees. When you have done this click on PayRates and enter 7.2000 for each employee.

In Payroll 4 use the Employment index card and the Pay Elements button.

To move between records (when you select more than one to look at or change):

(a) in Plus2 use the 'forward' and 'fast-forward' type buttons at the bottom of the screen (next to Leaver);

(b) in Payroll 4 use the Next button at the top of the screen.

Leaver: P45

You should not remove an employee from file until after his or her final wage/salary payment has been made. Since Gideon Turner is earning no money in February you can remove him from the file before the first payroll run in February.

Clear any highlighting from the list of employees, then select Gideon Turner (employee 12). Click on Record (Employment Record and then Employment in Payroll 4), then click on Leaver at the bottom of the screen. Ensure the date of leaving is shown as 290199. Click on Print P45 details (Finish) and choose your Output type.

The main elements of his P45 details are shown on the next page.

Date: 05/02/99

Blitz Limited
25 Apple Road
London
N12 3PP

P45 Details

Company PAYE Reference

Employee Details

Employee's Surname	TURNER
Employee's Forenames	GIDEON

Works Number	000012
Department	NO DEPARTMENT

Date of leaving   29/01/1999

Employee's Address   211 FRANCIS ROAD
                                      LONDON N17

N.I. Number   TH 78 64 57 C

Tax Code   330L

Last entry on P11 Deduction card

Tax Week	43
Total pay to date	7748.25
Total tax to date	1045.85

Current Employment

Total pay to date	2798.25
Total tax to date	421.08

Click on Save when you are returned to the Employee Record window (you will be prompted to do so if you forget) and then close this window.

You can now close Sage. Back-up your data on a floppy disk if all of your entries are correct and you wish to save your own work.

SOLUTION TO ASSIGNMENT 8: PROCESSING PAYROLL

If there are significant differences between the procedures to follow in Plus 2 and Payroll 4 they are dealt with separately. If the difference is small the Payroll 4 procedure or term is shown in brackets.

Payroll, Week 44

Plus2

Click on the Process button in the main Payroll window. To set the Payroll Run Date (Process Date), click on the Date button. The Payroll Run Date (Process Date) window will appear, showing today's date if you did not change the date when you first loaded up the Payroll package. Change the date to 050299 if necessary and then click on OK. Confirm that the tax year is 1998/99.

In the Process Payroll List window you should now click on Criteria, then clear all the check boxes except Weekly, Cash, Giro and Cheque. Now click on Criteria On. You will be returned to a window showing only six employees. Click on Swap to highlight them all.

It is probably more convenient for payroll processing if you do *not* use the Clear button at the *top* of the window to clear the payments file. This should make processing the payroll easier, because the program will display the previous gross pay of each employee, which you can then accept or amend, as required. If you clear the file, you will have far more keying in to do.

Next, therefore, click on the Payments button. You will get a message telling you that leavers will not be processed. This is what you want so click on OK. The details for the first employee will be displayed.

Payroll 4

Click on Payroll in the stacked toolbar if necessary and then on Change Process Date to set the date as 050299.

Click on Outline and select the Weekly folder. Select all of the weekly-paid employees using the Clear and Swap buttons. Then click on Enter Payments. You will get a message telling you that some employees (ie Gideon Turner, who has left) will be de-selected. This is OK.

Entering payments

The 'quantities' to enter should be:

(a) 1 for a fixed weekly wage;

(b) the number of overtime hours worked for overtime (4.5, 6 or 7.5); and

(c) the hours worked for hourly paid staff (8.5 or 38).

In Plus2, click on Save when you have entered the details for an employee and then click on the 'forward' button at the bottom left of the window to move on to the next.

In Payroll 4 click on Next to move on.

Select the Yes or OK option when you receive a screen prompt about a tax refund for Ethel Parkinson, Employee 16.

When you have entered all the payments click on Close. Click on Reports (Pre-Update Reports) and select the Payment Summary option. Choose Display (Preview) or Printer to view/display the details, then click on Run.

The details requested should be as follows for Week 44. (Full details are given at the end of this solution.)

	£	£
Total gross pay		1,065.60
PAYE	141.36	
Nat Ins	82.82	
		224.18
Nett pay		841.42
Employer's Nat Ins		103.30

You must not forget to update the payroll file. Close the File View (Preview) window if you chose the Display (Preview) option and click on Update (Update Records). Follow the screen prompts. When you get the prompt for backing up your files, you do not have to do so, but if you want to make sure you have a blank floppy disk standing by.

In Plus 2 click on Yes in the Update Records window. When the update is finished it should show that five employees have been updated.

In Payroll 4 simply work through the Wizard.

Week 45 payroll

The new Payroll Run Date (Process Date) should be 120299. Processing the payroll should be done in a similar way to the Week 44 payroll processing. When Ethel Parkinson's record appears you will immediately be asked to allow a tax refund. Click on No, post the new hours, then click on Save. You are then asked to allow a refund (of a different amount). Say Yes this time.

Don't forget to Update the Records after you have entered the payments.

To produce a cheque analysis, select the Cheque Analysis option in the Process Reports window.

In Plus2 specify the first cheque number (0002069) at the screen prompt. The cheque amounts you print or display should be:

	£
M Kothari	206.94
N Farouk	186.21
L Farrow	164.77
E Parkinson	42.40
C Stanley	200.39
	800.71

Week 46 payroll

Change the Payroll Run Date (Process Date) to 190299. Process the payroll and update the records, using the information provided, in the same way as for Weeks 44 and 45. Deal with tax refunds as before: Ethel Parkinson should pay some tax this week.

A Payment Summary should give you the following details:

Employee		Gross pay £	PAYE £	Employee's NI £	Net pay £
13	M Kothari	294.00	40.99	24.33	228.68
14	N Farouk	267.60	40.53	21.63	205.44
15	L Farrow	244.60	32.80	19.33	192.47
16	E Parkinson	58.00	1.00	0.00	57.00
18	C Stanley	302.25	48.34	25.13	228.78
		1166.45	163.66	90.42	912.37

Week 47/Month 11 payroll

Change the Payroll Run Date (Process Date) to 260299.

In Plus2 click on Criteria and place an X mark in the Monthly box as well as the Weekly box. Click on Criteria On, then on Swap to highlight all employees.

In Payroll 4 use the Outline button, clear and Swap to select all employees. (Alternatively you can process weekly and monthly paid employees separately.)

For most monthly-paid staff, you just need to check that there is a 1.0000 for the salary of each person, then simply click on the forward button (Next) to move on to the next employee.

In Plus2 there is no need (or opportunity) to Save, because the details that will be used when you update are already saved from the previous run. Once you get used to this, the processing should therefore be very rapid.

The only exceptions are the monthly-paid employees who joined in the month. Instead of 1.0000, salary entitlements should be 0.92 for Sheila Babcock and 0.75 for Donald Coombs. Deal with tax refunds as before.

Your output from a Payments Summary should include the following figures.

	Weekly	Monthly
No of employees	5	14
	£	£
Gross pay	979.40	18367.16
PAYE	(121.87)	(3121.07)
Nat Ins	(72.62)	(1184.79)
Nett pay	784.91	14,061.30
Employer's NI	93.10	1705.82

Pay-slips

For pay-slips, you are only required to print (or view) pay-slips for employees 2 and 3.

In Plus2 select them and then click on the Layouts button. Select the Payslips option in the Layouts window. If you intend to print the pay-slips it is best to change the page orientation to Landscape. You should be able to do this via the Options button in the Print window that will appear.

In Payroll 4, select the two employees and click on the Pre-update Reports icon to get your pay-slips.

The pay-slips should show net pay for Samuel Lynch of £1,347.41 and for Arvind Patel of £1,058.54.

Further checking

Here are extracts from payments summaries for the periods not given in full above.

Week 44

Employee		Gross pay	PAYE	Employee's NI	Net pay
		£	£	£	£
13	M Kothari	272.40	36.16	22.13	214.11
14	N Farouk	253.20	37.31	20.23	195.66
15	L Farrow	259.00	35.80	20.83	202.37
16	E Parkinson	34.00	-3.60	0.00	37.60
18	C Stanley	247.00	35.69	19.63	191.68
		1,065.60	141.36	82.82	841.42

Week 45

Employee		Gross pay	PAYE	Employee's NI	Net pay
		£	£	£	£
13	M Kothari	261.60	33.63	21.03	206.94
14	N Farouk	238.80	33.86	18.73	186.21
15	L Farrow	205.00	24.80	15.43	164.77
16	E Parkinson	40.00	-2.40	0.00	42.40
18	C Stanley	260.00	38.68	20.93	200.39
		1,005.40	128.57	76.12	800.71

Week 47

Employee		Gross pay	PAYE	Employee's NI	Net pay
		£	£	£	£
13	M Kothari	240.00	28.80	18.93	192.27
14	N Farouk	210.00	27.19	15.93	166.88
15	L Farrow	219.40	27.60	16.83	174.97
16	E Parkinson	50.00	-0.40	0.00	50.40
18	C Stanley	260.00	38.68	20.93	200.39
		979.40	121.87	72.62	784.91

Month 11

Employee	Gross pay £	PAYE £	Employee's NI £	Net pay £
1	3000.00	663.33	3.50	2333.17
2	2125.00	348.51	187.96	1588.53
3	1650.00	288.25	142.96	1218.79
4	1500.00	268.01	127.76	1104.23
5	850.00	104.25	62.96	682.79
6	875.00	135.76	33.73	705.51
7	900.00	115.75	67.76	716.49
8	1083.33	177.84	86.16	819.33
9	1100.00	136.68	87.76	875.56
10	1083.33	134.15	86.16	863.02
11	1083.33	126.00	86.16	871.17
17	1350.00	303.66	112.96	933.38
19	904.67	128.16	34.80	741.71
20	862.50	190.72	64.16	607.62
	18,367.16	3,121.07	1,184.79	14,061.30

Windows exercise

This sort of task is very common day to day work for an accountant in a modern office. A suggested solution is shown on the next page.

Delete the figures from the previous month's memo, and alter the wording as appropriate. You should have included some explanation of the differences.

To copy from one application to the other, simply highlight the material you want to copy, press Ctrl + C, then switch to the other application, position the cursor and press Ctrl + V. (In Microsoft Word it will come out as a 'table', which is a little like a spreadsheet, except that it doesn't do very sophisticated calculations. You can convert the table to text if you like, though there is little reason to do so.)

We have changed the font of the copied material to make it consistent with the memo style.

MEMO

To: Mr Nicholas
From: Senior Accountant
Subject: Payroll costs, February 1999
Date: 26 February 1999

Here, as agreed, is the monthly list showing total payroll costs for February 1999.

The differences are due to the introduction of overtime payments from 1 February 1999 and to the addition of three new employees to the payroll. Gideon Turner left the company at the end of January 1999.

	Month 11	*February*	*1999*			
		Total	*Employers*	*Total*	*Previous*	
		Gross	*Nat.Ins.*	*Cost*	*month*	*Difference*
1	T. NICHOLAS	3,000.00	300.00	3,300.00	3,300.00	0.00
2	S. LYNCH	2,125.00	212.50	2,337.50	2,337.50	0.00
3	A. PATEL	1,650.00	165.20	1,815.20	1,815.20	0.00
4	J. ESCOTT	1,500.00	150.00	1,650.00	1,650.00	0.00
5	A. CROPPER	850.00	59.64	909.64	909.64	0.00
6	A. VAUGHAN	875.00	61.32	936.32	936.32	0.00
7	K. KNIGHT	900.00	63.00	963.00	963.00	0.00
8	L. LEROY	1,083.33	108.40	1,191.73	1,191.73	0.00
9	L. BROWN	1,100.00	110.00	1,210.00	1,210.00	0.00
10	M. KORETZ	1,083.33	108.40	1,191.73	1,191.73	0.00
11	N. PARKER	1,083.33	108.40	1,191.73	1,191.73	0.00
12	G. TURNER	0.00	0.00	0.00	946.20	(946.20)
13	M. KOTHARI	1,067.00	106.90	1,173.90	1,056.20	117.70
14	N. FAROUK	968.00	97.00	1,065.00	924.20	140.80
15	L. FARROW	927.00	86.73	1,013.73	877.52	136.21
16	E. PARKINSON	182.00	0.00	182.00	212.00	(30.00)
17	N. HAZELWOOD	1,350.00	135.20	1,485.20	1,485.20	0.00
18	C STANLEY	1,069.00	107.10	1,176.10	0.00	1,176.10
19	S BABCOCK	983.33	63.28	1,046.61	0.00	1,046.61
20	D COOMBS	1,150.00	60.48	1,210.48	0.00	1,210.48
		22,946.32	2,103.55	25,049.87	22,198.17	2,851.70

SOLUTION TO ASSIGNMENT 9: PAYROLL ROUTINE

Remember to start the assignment by specifying a Payroll Run Date (Process Date) of 050399.

New tax code

Amend the tax code for L Leroy to 395L by calling up his Employee Record. His reference number is 8. Tab to the old tax code and press delete. Save the new details when you have finished.

New employee

If you were able to add new employee details in Assignment 7, adding details for Sarah Romain should be straightforward. Her payment type is hourly, and the payment rate is 7.00. The method of payment is Cheque Weekly, and her tax code 423TWI.

Payroll processing, Weeks 48-50

If you attempted Assignment 8 successfully, you should be able to process the payroll and update the records for Weeks 48, 49 and 50.

Holiday pay

Plus2

When you get to Linda Farrow proceed as follows.

(a) Enter her overtime details as usual. Net pay should say £174.77 at this point.

(b) Click on the HOL button at the foot of the screen.

(c) Linda is to be advanced two weeks pay, so type in 2 in the Periods to advance box, press Tab and click on OK.

(d) A new payments screen will appear with the cursor flashing in the Basic Rate field. Key in 2 and press Tab. Net pay on this screen should say £329.54. Click on OK.

(e) You are returned to the main payments screen where Linda's net pay is now shown as the week 48 net pay (£174.77) plus the advance for weeks 49 and 50 (£329.54) = £504.31.

(f) Neville Parker will be paid his monthly salary in the normal way.

Payroll 4

When you get to Linda Farrow proceed as follows.

(a) Enter her overtime details as usual. Net pay should say £174.77 at this point.

(b) Click on the Process index tab and Tab down to the Holiday Pay line.

(c) Press F4 or click on the Finder button.

(d) Linda is to be advanced two weeks pay, so type in 2 in the Periods to advance box and click on OK.

(e) A new payments screen will appear. Key in 2 and press Tab. Click on OK.

(f) You are returned to the Process screen where Linda's net pay is now shown as the week 48 net pay (£174.77) plus the advance for weeks 49 and 50 (£329.54) = £504.31.

Confidentiality

If you assumed that Linda and Neville are going to Tenerife *together* and checked up on things like their marital status and age, you should not be so nosy. If you actually *commented* about this to your colleagues you have abused your position as a payroll assistant. No marks for confidentiality (though you may be a highly competent office gossip!)

The output you should produce each week is as follows. Full details are given at the end of this solution.

Week 48 (from a Payment Summary, parts 1 and 2)

	£	£
Gross pay		1,564.75
PAYE	192.82	
Employees' Nat Ins	118.01	
		310.83
Net pay		1,253.92
Employer's Nat Ins		135.88

Week 49 (from a Cheque Analysis report)

Tax (Week-49 Month-12)

Ref	Employee name	Nett pay
13	M KOTHARI	231.06
14	N FAROUK	195.66
16	E PARKINSON	45.60
18	C STANLEY	116.97
21	S ROMAIN	181.19
	Grand Total:-	770.48

P32 Payment Record

Use the Criteria (Outline, Clear, Swap) button to select *all* employees, both weekly and monthly paid. Then click on the Reports button (and then the Company folder in Payroll 4). Select the Form P32 option. Specify the month range as 11 to 11.

The total payment due is £7,406.08, shown in the extract below.

Employer's Payment Record (Form P32)

	(7) Net NI	(8) PAYE tax	(9) Total Due
	3,678.09	3,727.99	7,406.08

Date range

Week: 060299 – 050399
Month: 060299 – 050399

Week 50 (from a Payment Summary)

BLITZ Tax week 50	PAYMENTS SUMMARY – PART 1 << Weekly >>			Page: 1	
Ref	Taxable Gross Pay	PAYE	Nat Ins	Nett Pay	Employer's Nat Ins
13	283.20	38.46	23.23	221.51	28.35
14	242.40	34.55	19.13	188.72	24.25
16	48.00	-0.80	0.00	48.80	0
18	247.00	35.69	19.63	191.68	24.75
21	157.50	15.00	10.63	131.87	11.02
	978.10	122.90	72.62	782.58	88.37

Week 51 and Month 11

Pension

Set up Tim Nicholas's pension as follows.

(a) Click on Company (Company Settings).

(b) Click on Pension.

(c) In the window that appears ensure that Scheme 1 is highlighted. In Plus2 click on Edit.

(d) Specify 10 as the Employer percentage and 5 as the Employee percentage. Ignore everything else on the screen. Then click on OK and (in Plus2) Save.

(e) Click on Employee (Employee Record) and call up the record of Tim Nicholas.

(f) Finally:

   (i) in Plus2 click on Tables and then click on the magnifying glass symbol to the right of the Pension scheme field at the foot of the screen. Select Scheme 1 and click on OK. Then click on Close and Save;

   (ii) in Payroll 4 click on the Employment tab and then on the Pensions button. Select Scheme 1 and then Save.

Processing

You should then use the Criteria button to select both Weekly and Monthly paid employees for processing. Remember that S J Babcock and D Coombs are entitled to a *full month's salary* in March (unlike February).

The output you should obtain from a payment summary is as follows.

	Monthly-paid employees		*Weekly -paid employees*	
	£	£	£	£
Gross pay		18,733.32		1,314.65
Pension	150.00			
PAYE	2,999.60		177.71	
Employees' NI	<u>1,213.17</u>		<u>104.35</u>	
		<u>4,362.77</u>		<u>282.06</u>
Net pay		14,370.55		1032.59
Employers' NI		1,795.66		129.95

Payslips

The pay-slip details for Tim Nicholas and Leyton Brown are shown below.

TIMOTHY ANDREW NICHOLAS — BLITZ — 26/03/99

SALARY:	1.0000	3000.0000	3000.00
BONUS:	-	6000.0000	-
PAYE Tax	603.34		
National Ins	-		
Pension	150.00		
Sick Pay:			-
Maternity Pay:			-
Holiday Pay:			-
Rounding B/F			-
Rounding C/F			-

TOTAL GROSS PAY TD	38850.00
Gross for tax TD	38800.00
Tax paid TD	8280.00
Earnings for NI TD	15035.00
National Ins TD	1344.78
Pension TD	150.00
Earnings for NI	-
Gross for tax	2850.00
TOTAL GROSS PAY	3000.00
	2246.66

425L 0 QM 12 1

LEYTON CARGILL BROWN — BLITZ — 26/03/99

SALARY:	1.0000	1100.3300	1100.33
BONUS:	-	1400.0000	-
PAYE Tax	136.46		
National Ins	87.76		
Pension	-		
Sick Pay:			-
Maternity Pay:			-
Holiday Pay:			-
Rounding B/F			-
Rounding C/F			-

TOTAL GROSS PAY TD	12375.00
Gross for tax TD	12375.00
Tax paid TD	1449.95
Earnings for NI TD	5494.00
National Ins TD	438.80
Pension TD	-
Earnings for NI	-
Gross for tax	1098.00
TOTAL GROSS PAY	1100.00
	875.78

550H 0 QM 12 9

Tim Nicholas's NI

You might find it useful to print out a P11 Deduction Card (NIC) for Tim Nicholas (employee number 1) or look at his P11 using the View P11 button in the Employee List menu. You need to click on the Employee (Employee Record) button and then on Reports (Information) to find this option.

(a) Tim Nicholas pays no NI because he is a director and his NI contributions are worked out on a cumulative basis. He is appointed as a director when there are 31 weeks left in the tax year and therefore his maximum contributions are based on 31 times the upper earnings limit of £485 = £15,035. He had been paid a total of 5 x £3,000 = £15,000 by the beginning of month 11, so only £(15,035 - 15,000) = £35 was subject to NI in month 11, and none of his month 12 salary is subject to NI.

This is a difficult point. Have full marks if you simply found out that he is set up on the system as a director and knew that director's NICs are not calculated in the same way as for other employees. If you thought this had something to do with Tim's pension, lose a mark and do some more study for Unit 3!

(b) Your answer should be £300.00 (obtained from the payment summary that you have already produced).

Further checking

Full details not given above are as follows.

Week 48

Employee		Gross pay £	PAYE £	Employee's NI £	Net pay £
13	M Kothari	279.60	37.77	22.83	219.00
14	N Farouk	246.00	35.47	19.53	191.00
15	L Farrow	629.40	77.40	47.69	504.31
16	E Parkinson	28.00	-4.80	0.00	32.80
18	C Stanley	269.75	40.98	21.83	206.94
21	S Romain	112.00	6.00	6.13	99.87
		1,564.75	192.82	118.01	1,253.92

Week 49

Employee		Gross pay £	PAYE £	Employee's NI £	Net pay £
13	M Kothari	297.60	41.91	24.63	231.06
14	N Farouk	253.20	37.31	20.23	195.66
16	E Parkinson	44.00	-1.60	0.00	45.60
18	C Stanley	136.50	11.00	8.53	116.97
21	S Romain	231.00	31.78	18.03	181.19
		962.30	120.40	71.42	770.48

Week 51

Employee		Gross pay	PAYE	Employee's NI	Net pay
		£	£	£	£
13	M Kothari	276.00	37.08	22.53	216.39
14	N Farouk	264.00	39.61	21.33	203.06
15	L Farrow	255.40	35.00	20.43	199.97
16	E Parkinson	16.00	-7.20	0.00	23.20
18	C Stanley	282.75	43.97	23.13	215.65
21	S Romain	220.50	29.25	16.93	174.32
		1,314.65	177.71	104.35	1,032.59

Month 12

Employee	Gross pay	Pension	PAYE	Employee's NI	Net pay
	£	£	£	£	£
1	3,000.00	150.00	603.34	0.00	2,246.66
2	2,125.00	0.00	386.70	187.96	1,550.34
3	1,650.00	0.00	288.26	142.96	1,218.78
4	1,500.00	0.00	268.02	127.76	1,104.22
5	850.00	0.00	104.26	62.96	682.78
6	875.00	0.00	135.77	33.73	705.50
7	900.00	0.00	115.76	67.76	716.48
8	1,083.33	0.00	-6.13	86.16	1,003.30
9	1,100.00	0.00	136.46	87.76	875.78
10	1,083.33	0.00	134.16	86.16	863.01
11	1,083.33	0.00	126.00	86.16	871.17
17	1,350.00	0.00	303.90	112.96	933.14
19	983.33	0.00	146.35	37.88	799.10
20	1,150.00	0.00	256.75	92.96	800.29
	18,733.32	150.00	2,999.60	1,213.17	14,370.55

SOLUTION TO ASSIGNMENT 10: END OF THE TAX YEAR

Week 52

The payments summary you should produce is as follows. (Several columns are omitted here, for reasons of space.)

Tax (Week-52)

Ref	Employee's Name	Taxab-Gross	P.A.Y.E.	Nat Ins	Nett Pay
13	MAHENDRA KOTHARI	279.60	37.77	22.83	219.00
14	NURSAT FAROUK	256.80	38.23	20.53	198.04
15	LINDA EMILY FARROW	226.60	29.20	17.53	179.87
16	ETHEL PARKINSON	20.00	-6.40	0.00	26.40
18	CAROLINE ANN STANLEY	227.50	31.09	17.63	178.78
21	SARAH ROMAIN	238.00	33.39	18.73	185.88
		1,248.50	163.28	97.25	987.97

To remove Ethel Parkinson from the payroll (once you have updated the records), you should now call up her Employee Record (then click on the Employment tab in Payroll 4) and click on the Leaver button. Her P45 details are as follows.

Date: 02/04/99

Blitz Limited
25 Apple Road
London
N12 3PP

P45 Details

Company PAYE Reference	London (North) 234/930122

Employee Details

Employee's Surname	PARKINSON
Employee's Forenames	ETHEL
Works Number	000016
Department	NO DEPARTMENT
Date of leaving	02/04/1999
Employee's Address	FLAT 12
	MASONS HOUSE
	219 ROBERTS ROAD
	LONDON N17
N.I. Number	SC 34 37 20 C
Tax Code	270L

Last entry on P11 Deduction card

Tax Week	52
Total pay to date	3077.50
Total tax to date	73.60
Current Employment	
Total pay to date	1510.00
Total tax to date	-0.20

Collector of Taxes (P32 Payment Record)

Select *all* employees. Then click on Reports (and then choose the Company folder in Payroll 4). Select the Form P32 option. Produce a report for month 12.

The total amounts of tax payable are as follows:

	Net NI £	PAYE tax £	Total due £
Totals	3780.71	3583.89	7364.60

P35

In Plus 2 click on Period End at the top of the screen and then on Year End. Then click on the P35 Form button. The tax year ending is 5 April 1999. The P35 (substitute) form can be printed, as shown below.

In Payroll 4 begin by setting the Process Date to 5th April, the end of the tax year. Make sure **All Employees** are shown in the main window and that all are selected. Then click on **Reports** and select the **Year End** folder. Select the option for a P35 and click on Print or Preview.

Blitz Limited
25 Apple Road
London

N12 3PP

FORM P35 (CS) (SUBSTITUTE) - Deductions Workings Sheets

N.I.C. (1)	S.S.P.	S.M.P.	Employee Name	Income Tax (5)	
3444.78	0.00	0.00	TIMOTHY ANDREW NICHOLAS	4583.33	
2428.86	0.00	0.00	SAMUEL LLOYD LYNCH	2320.60	
1540.80	0.00	0.00	ARVIND PATEL	1441.25	
1388.80	0.00	0.00	JOANNA LOUISE ESCOTT	1339.82	
490.40	0.00	0.00	ARTHUR BEN CROPPER	417.00	
475.25	0.00	0.00	ALICE ELIZABETH VAUGHAN	678.57	
653.80	0.00	0.00	KATHERINE MURIE KNIGHT	578.75	
778.24	0.00	0.00	LEWIS ROBERT LEROY	527.40	
988.80	0.00	0.00	LEYTON CARGILL BROWN	683.17	
778.24	0.00	0.00	MARTIN GEORGE KORETZ	536.83	
972.80	0.00	0.00	NEVILLE PARKER	611.40	
493.74	0.00	0.00	GIDEON TURNER	421.08	
966.78	0.00	0.00	MAHENDRA KOTHARI	675.37	
844.38	0.00	0.00	NURSAT FAROUK	651.02	
761.05	0.00	0.00	LINDA EMILY FARROW	610.40	
0.00	0.00	0.00	ETHEL PARKINSON	-0.20	R
992.64	0.00	0.00	NORMAN JOHN HAZELWOOD	1215.10	
393.99	0.00	0.00	CAROLINE ANN STANLEY	324.12	
234.36	0.00	0.00	SHEILA JANE BABCOCK	274.51	
332.80	0.00	0.00	DONALD COOMBS	447.47	
156.14	0.00	0.00	SARAH ROMAIN	115.42	
19,116.65	0.00	0.00	Grand Totals	18,452.41	

Clear year-to-date

In Plus2 select all employees and click on the Clear YTD button in the Year End window. Ensure that 1999 is shown as the tax year. Then click on OK.

In Payroll 4 Click on Tasks, choose Year End Process and follow the Wizard.

Week 1, New employee

Specify a Payroll Run Date (Process Date) 090499. You should be able to add the new employee details from the information given in the assignment. However, *do not* add P45 details, because these relate to the previous tax year.

The new employee number should be 22, according to your instructions. (In Plus2 if you clear any highlighting and click on Record the program may give you a window with the number 12, the first unused record. Change this if so. You do not have to be a slave to everything the computer suggests.)

The details include:

Payment type	Cheque monthly
Rates of pay:	

Salary: 1062.50 (12,750 ÷ 12)

Bonus: 1,500

Week 1 payroll run

The total net pay for the week, from the payment summary, is £948.03. Remember to update the payroll file.

Nursat Farouk

Select Nursat Farouk.

In Plus2 click on Employee Record and then on Main YTD. You should find the following information.

In Payroll 4 click on Employee Record, then on History, then on View P11 to find this information.

	£
Total gross pay	231.60
Tax paid	32.01
NI contribution	18.03

Week 2

Remember to update the payroll file after you have entered the payments. The net pay of each employee (from the payment summary) is as follows:

	£
M Kothari	226.17
N Farouk	205.44
L Farrow	182.86
C Stanley	135.17
S Romain	171.81
	921.45

Salary increases

In Plus 2 click on Employee, select the employees receiving a rise by clicking on them to highlight them and click on the Employee Record button.

In Plus2 you can then choose the PayRates button. For each employee key in the new *monthly* salary. Close the PayRates window and Save the changes. Use the 'forward' button to move on to the next employee in the range.

In Payroll 4 select the employees receiving a rise, click on Employee Record, then on the Employment tab , then on the Pay Elements button.

The amounts to enter are:

T Nicholas	3333.3333	(40000 ÷ 12)
S Lynch	2500.0000	(30000 ÷ 12)
A Patel	1833.3333	(22000 ÷ 12)
J Escott	1583.3333	(19000 ÷ 12)
A Vaughan	1000.0000	(12000 ÷ 12)
L Leroy	1250.0000	(15000 ÷ 12)
M Koretz	1166.6667	(14000 ÷ 12)

Week 3/Month 1

The new Payroll Run Date (Process Date) should be 230499.

Process the month-end payroll in the same way as in Assignments 8 and 9. Remember, however, to include a bonus payment. For all employees entitled to a bonus, enter 0.4 in the appropriate field (since the bonus is 40% of the amount recorded on file). Enter 0 for the new employee, J-B Bannister, in this field, because he is not entitled to a bonus.

(You should also check the basic salary amounts for employees who have received a pay rise this month.)

(a) For employees 1 to 10, 17, 19 and 20, your input should be 1 (Salary) and 0.4 (Bonus).

(b) For employees 13-15, who are on a fixed weekly wage with overtime, enter the basic rate as 1 and the enter the number of hours of overtime worked.

(c) For employees 18 and 21, who are hourly paid, key in the number of hours worked.

(d) For employee 22, the salary entry should be $25/30 = 0.83$ and the bonus entry 0.

The total gross pay and deductions for monthly-paid staff can be obtained from a payment summary. (Use the Payments Summary option.)

The figures should be as follows.

	Weekly £	Monthly £
Gross pay	1,105.65	31,805.20
Pension		286.67
PAYE	143.06	6,808.67
Nat Ins (employees)	85.05	2,189.84
Net pay	877.54	22,520.02
Nat Ins (employer's)	98.79	2,868.27

The total value of cheques can be obtained from a cheque summary. You can print or display this information, using the Cheque Analysis option in the Process Reports window. Don't worry about the specification of cheque numbers. The total value of cheques should be **£23,397.56**.

Don't forget to update the payroll file.

Further checking

Here are the full payment summaries not given above, in case you want to check your work in detail.

Week 1

Employee		Gross pay	PAYE	Employee's NI	Net pay
		£	£	£	£
13	M Kothari	283.20	38.45	23.23	221.52
14	N Farouk	231.60	32.01	18.03	181.56
15	L Farrow	223.00	30.17	17.23	175.60
18	C Stanley	273.00	41.67	22.23	209.10
21	S Romain	199.50	24.42	14.83	160.25
		1,210.30	166.72	95.55	948.03

Week 2

Employee		Gross pay	PAYE	Employee's NI	Net pay
		£	£	£	£
13	M Kothari	290.40	40.30	23.93	226.17
14	N Farouk	267.60	40.53	21.63	205.44
15	L Farrow	233.80	32.71	18.23	182.86
18	C Stanley	162.50	16.20	11.13	135.17
21	S Romain	217.00	28.56	16.63	171.81
		1,171.30	158.30	91.55	921.45

Week 3

Employee		Gross pay	PAYE	Employee's NI	Net pay
		£	£	£	£
13	M Kothari	261.60	33.63	21.03	206.94
14	N Farouk	238.80	33.86	18.73	186.21
15	L Farrow	205.00	26.04	15.43	163.53
18	C Stanley	211.25	27.41	16.03	167.81
21	S Romain	189.00	22.12	13.83	153.05
		1,105.65	143.06	85.05	877.54

Month 1

Employee		Gross pay £	Pension £	PAYE £	Employee's NI £	Net pay £
1	T Nicholas	5,733.33	286.67	1,641.73	307.09	3,497.84
2	S Lynch	4,100.00	0.00	1,086.53	187.96	2,825.51
3	A Patel	2,833.33	0.00	598.53	187.96	2,046.84
4	J Escott	2,183.33	0.00	425.09	187.96	1,570.28
5	A Cropper	1,350.00	0.00	219.24	112.96	1,017.80
6	A Vaughan	1,500.00	0.00	279.27	57.75	1,162.98
7	K Knight	1,420.00	0.00	235.34	119.76	1,064.90
8	L Leroy	1,810.00	0.00	329.64	158.96	1,321.40
9	L Brown	1,660.00	0.00	265.24	143.76	1,251.00
10	M Koretz	1,726.67	0.00	282.03	150.56	1,294.08
11	N Parker	1,643.33	0.00	262.94	142.16	1,238.23
17	N Hazelwood	1,950.00	0.00	441.65	172.96	1,335.39
19	S Babcock	1,383.33	0.00	238.10	53.28	1,091.95
20	D Coombs	1,630.00	0.00	367.13	140.96	1,121.91
22	J Bannister	881.88	0.00	136.21	65.76	679.91
		31,805.20	286.67	6,808.67	2,189.84	22,520.02

Part F
Appendices

APPENDIX 1: THE BLITZ NOMINAL LEDGER - ACCOUNTS AND CODES

The following is a list of the accounts in the nominal ledger of Blitz Limited.

Fixed assets

0010	FREEHOLD PROPERTY
0011	LEASEHOLD PROPERTY
0020	PLANT AND MACHINERY
0021	PLANT AND MACHINERY DEPRECIATION
0030	OFFICE EQUIPMENT
0031	OFFICE EQUIPMENT DEPRECIATION
0040	FURNITURE AND FIXTURES
0041	FURNITURE AND FIXTURES DEPRECIATION
0050	MOTOR VEHICLES
0051	MOTOR VEHICLES DEPRECIATION

Current assets

1001	STOCK
1002	WORK IN PROGRESS
1003	FINISHED GOODS
1100	DEBTORS CONTROL ACCOUNT
1101	SUNDRY DEBTORS
1102	OTHER DEBTORS
1103	PREPAYMENTS
1200	BANK CURRENT ACCOUNT
1210	BANK DEPOSIT ACCOUNT
1220	BUILDING SOCIETY ACCOUNT
1230	PETTY CASH

Current liabilities

2100	CREDITORS CONTROL ACCOUNT
2101	SUNDRY CREDITORS
2102	OTHER CREDITORS
2109	ACCRUALS
2200	TAX CONTROL ACCOUNT
2201	VAT LIABILITY
2210	PAYE
2211	NATIONAL INSURANCE
2230	PENSION FUND
2300	LOANS
2310	HIRE PURCHASE
2320	CORPORATION TAX
2330	MORTGAGES

Financed by

3000	ORDINARY SHARES
3001	PREFERENCE SHARES
3100	RESERVES
3101	UNDISTRIBUTED RESERVES
3200	PROFIT AND LOSS ACCOUNT

Sales

4000	SALES - CONTRACT CLEANING
4001	SALES - WINDOW CLEANING
4002	SALES - DOMESTIC SERVICES
4009	DISCOUNTS ALLOWED
4100	SALES MATERIALS
4101	SALES TYPE E
4200	SALES OF ASSETS
4900	MISCELLANEOUS INCOME
4901	ROYALTIES RECEIVED
4902	COMMISSIONS RECEIVED
4903	INSURANCE CLAIMS
4904	RENT INCOME
4905	DISTRIBUTION AND CARRIAGE

Purchases

5000	MATERIALS PURCHASES
5001	MATERIALS IMPORTED
5002	MISCELLANEOUS PURCHASES
5003	PACKAGING
5009	DISCOUNTS TAKEN
5100	CARRIAGE
5101	DUTY
5102	TRANSPORT INSURANCE
5200	OPENING STOCK
5201	CLOSING STOCK

Direct expenses

6000	PRODUCTIVE LABOUR
6001	COST OF SALES LABOUR
6002	SUB-CONTRACTORS
6100	SALES COMMISSIONS
6200	SALES PROMOTIONS
6201	ADVERTISING
6202	GIFTS AND SAMPLES
6203	PUBLIC RELATIONS (LIT & BROCHURES)
6900	MISCELLANEOUS EXPENSES

Overheads

7001	DIRECTORS SALARIES
7002	DIRECTORS REMUNERATION
7003	STAFF SALARIES
7004	WAGES - REGULAR
7005	WAGES - CASUAL TEMPORARY STAFF
7006	EMPLOYERS NI
7007	EMPLOYERS PENSIONS
7008	RECRUITMENT EXPENSES
7100	RENT
7102	WATER RATES
7103	GENERAL RATES
7104	PREMISES INSURANCE
7200	ELECTRICITY
7201	GAS
7202	OIL
7203	OTHER HEATING COSTS

Overheads
(continued)

7300	FUEL AND OIL
7301	REPAIRS AND SERVICING
7302	LICENCES
7303	VEHICLE INSURANCE
7304	MISCELLANEOUS MOTOR EXPENSES
7400	TRAVELLING
7401	CAR HIRE
7402	HOTELS
7403	UK ENTERTAINMENT
7404	OVERSEAS ENTERTAINMENT
7405	OVERSEAS TRAVELLING
7406	SUBSISTENCE
7500	PRINTING
7501	POSTAGE AND CARRIAGE
7502	TELEPHONE
7503	TELEX/TELEGRAM/FACSIMILE
7504	OFFICE STATIONERY
7505	BOOKS ETC
7600	LEGAL FEES
7601	AUDIT & ACCOUNTANCY FEES
7602	CONSULTANCY FEES
7603	PROFESSIONAL FEES
7700	EQUIPMENT HIRE
7701	OFFICE MACHINE MAINTENANCE
7800	REPAIRS AND RENEWALS
7801	CLEANING
7802	LAUNDRY
7803	PREMISES EXPENSES (MISC)
7900	BANK INTEREST PAID
7901	BANK CHARGES
7902	CURRENCY CHARGES
7903	LOAN INTEREST PAID
7904	HP INTEREST
7905	CREDIT CHARGES

Miscellaneous

8000	DEPRECIATION
8001	PLANT & MACHINERY DEPRECIATION
8002	FURNITURE/FIX/FITTINGS DEPRECIATION
8003	VEHICLE DEPRECIATION
8004	OFFICE EQUIPMENT DEPRECIATION
8100	BAD DEBT WRITE OFF
8102	BAD DEBT PROVISION
8200	DONATIONS
8201	SUBSCRIPTIONS
8202	CLOTHING COSTS
8203	TRAINING COSTS
8204	INSURANCE
8205	REFRESHMENTS
9998	SUSPENSE ACCOUNT
9999	MISPOSTINGS ACCOUNT

APPENDIX 2: FUNCTION KEYS

The table below shows the various functions assigned in the Sage Sterling packages to the F keys along the top of the keyboard.

	Line 50 and Sterling for Windows 3 & 4	Plus2	Payroll
F1	Help	Help	Help
F2	System calculator	System calculator	System calculator
F3	For nominal a/c details when invoicing a customer		
F4	Finder search list, calculator or calendar	Finder search list	Finder search list
F5	Pastes current system date into a field	Pastes current system date into a field	
F6	Copies a field	Deletes a line	Deletes a line
F7	Inserts a row	Adjustments in Bank reconciliations	
F8	Deletes a row		
F9	Calculate Net		
F10			
F11	User definable key	User definable key	User definable key
F12	User definable key	User definable key	User definable key

APPENDIX 3: MANAGING BLITZ AND SAGE

This appendix contains some general advice on running the BPP Blitz case study and Sage on your computer system. It is intended primarily for those working alone or for college lecturers setting up the system for the first time.

This Appendix does not supersede the Sage manuals.

If you are setting up the case study on a network or a larger system, please consult the system manager of your organisation to find out the best way of running it on your system.

Topics covered here are as follows.

(a) Setting up Sage
(b) Company defaults
(c) The Plus 2 Help facility
(d) Backing up and restoring data
(e) Running the BPP Blitz program
(e) Reading data from the A:\drive

Setting up Sage

If you are installing Sage for the first time and you wish to use it exclusively for the BPP Blitz case study, or if you are reinstalling it for use with this book, proceed as follows.

(a) Follow the instructions in the Sage manuals for installing the software. You can accept all the defaults that you are offered.

(b) The Blitz Company 'personal' details are shown below, though it is not essential that you enter these. You may prefer to use your own or your college's details.

(b) Accept the default options for Group (Sage) and Program Directory and Data Directory (probably C:\SFW, C:\PLUS2, or similar).

*Please **make a note** of the directory into which Sage is installed: you will need to know this when you set up the Blitz program.*

(c) Blitz Limited's Financial Year begins in August 1998.

Company defaults

These can be set by clicking on the word **Defaults** at the top of the main Sage screen and choosing Company Preferences from the menu that drops down.

Address

Blitz's address is:

> Blitz Limited
> 25 Apple Road
> London
> N12 3PP

Password

If you decide to use a password, make sure you can remember what it is! LETMEIN is commonly used.

Plus 2 Help facility

Sterling Plus 2 provides quite detailed 'speech bubble' prompts for new users. These appear on screen when the mouse pointer is allowed to hover over a button or a field.

This facility *may* be useful for beginners, but it soon starts to slow down their work and becomes intrusive for those who have had a little experience. This book makes no use of these prompts. They are not, in any case, available in the more recently released Line 50, Sterling for Windows 4 or Sterling for Windows 3.

We recommend that this facility be turned off after the first session of using the program. This is done in the following way.

(a) In the Company Preferences window, click on the **Defaults** button. A Company Preferences Defaults window will appear.

(b) Just above the OK and Cancel buttons is a Help section. To turn off the prompts ensure that there is not check mark in the Toolbar Help box or the Field Help box. (Just click on the box to insert or remove the check mark.)

(c) Click on OK.

(d) Click on Save.

Backing up and restoring data using Sage

Backing up

The Sage package offers you the chance to back up your data onto a floppy disk or into another directory whenever you exit the program. You can also do this at other times by clicking on the word **Data** at the top of the main window and choosing the Backup option. It is not a difficult procedure: it is very similar to the Save and Save As options in any other Windows program.

If you read the information shown in the window that appears when you choose the Backup option, you will see that by default Sage will back up into the main (A:\) directory of a floppy disk in drive A. However it can back up to *any* drive or directory you choose. Click on the **Setup** button in this window to find the appropriate directory.

Note the following points.

(a) The accounting package makes back-up files called SAGEBACK.001 (or 002 etc if more than one disk is needed).

> *If you want to keep a copy of, say, your finished versions of Assignments 1 and 2 in back up form you will need to save the individual backup files in separate **directories** on your floppy disk. You cannot rename the files: the program will not recognise them if you do.*

(b) The payroll package makes backups coded by week and tax year. For example SAGE4498.001 is a back-up file of Week 44 1998/99 payroll data.

A single 1.44 MB floppy disk is large enough to store backups of all ten Sage assignments in this book.

Restoring data

You restore data by clicking on **Data** in the main window and choosing the restore option.

The procedure is just like backing up, except in reverse. It is very similar to the Open file procedure in any other Windows application. However, remember that restoring data has the effect of overwriting any data that is presently in the system, so make sure that this is what you want to do.

Backing up and restoring data using Blitz

Blitz 98 has a **Tools** menu that offers a quick back up and restore facility. This was still being finalised at the time of publication of this book See the documentation accompanying the Blitz 98 disk and the online Help.

Running the BPP Blitz program

Blitz simply unzips data from the BLITZ98 subdirectory into the ACCDATA sub-directory (Assignments 1 to 6) or PAYDATA sub-directory (Assignments 7 to 10) of your Sage software.

Instructions for setting up the BPP Blitz program are included with the disk. See also Chapters 2 and 3 of this book and please refer to the online Help. **Please do NOT ring BPP unless you have read all the documentation and help provided.** If you do ring, the first question we will ask is whether you have read this information.

Blitz can only run *outside* Payroll version 4 and early versions of the Sterling for Windows 3 package . In other words you must load up the Blitz data *before* starting up SFW3 version 3.0 or Payroll 4 version 4.0.

Blitz can run *inside* the Plus2 package and SFW version 3.11 onwards up to Line 50. In other words you can load up the Blitz data before or after you have started up Sage. To access the Blitz program from within Sage you need to set a default. Click on the word **Defaults** at the top of the main window, then on Company Preferences, then on the **Defaults** button. You will then see a Company Preferences Defaults window, with a section labelled Function Keys.

In the F11 box delete the entry CONTROL.EXE (which brings up the Windows Control Panel) and type in C:\BLITZ98\BLITZ98.EXE.

Reading data from the A:\drive

In practice the Sage package would work from data files held on the *hard drive*. (For any but the smallest company the files would soon become too big for there to be any other option.)

However, for the purposes of the Blitz case study it is possible to set up the system to read data from the A:\drive. Some colleges may prefer this option.

(a)   Close the Sage program if it is open.

(b)   Click once on the Sage icon to highlight its name and then click on the word **File** at the top of the Sage group window. In the menu that appears choose the Properties option.

(c)   In the Program Item Properties window that appears the command line will presently be one or other of the following, depending which version you are using.

     C:\SFW\SFW.EXE C:\SFW   or   C:\PLUS2\FINCON.EXE C:\PLUS2

(d)   To make the program read data from the A:\ drive, change the final element of this statement as follows (EXE should be followed by a single space).

     C:\SFW\SFW.EXE A:\   or   C:\PLUS2\FINCON.EXE A:\

(e)   To start up the program you will now always need to have a floppy disk in the A:\ drive containing a directory called ACCDATA. This is then the destination directory for Blitz data.

To make the payroll program perform in this way you should follow the same procedure. The new command line will be something like this:

C:\PLUS2\PAYROLL.EXE A:\

Windows 95

To do this in Windows 95, you first need to create Sage and Sage Payroll 'Shortcuts'. Then you can click on them with your *right* mouse button and choose Properties from the menu that appears. The Target line on the Shortcut index card is the one to change, as described above.

ORDER FORM

Any books from our AAT range can be ordered by telephoning 0181-740 2211. Alternatively, send this page to our Freepost address or fax it to us on 0181-740 1184, or email us at **publishing@bpp.co.uk**. Or look us up on our Website: http://www.bpp.co.uk

All books are sent out within 48 hours of receipt of your order, subject to availability.

To: BPP Publishing Ltd, Aldine House, Aldine Place, London W12 8AW

Tel: 0181-740 2211   **Fax: 0181-740 1184**   **Email: publishing@bpp.co.uk**

Mr / Ms (full name): _____

Day-time delivery address: _____

_____

Postcode: _____   Daytime Tel: (for queries only):_____

Please send me the following quantities of books:	5/98 Interactive Text	8/98 DA Kit	8/98 CA Kit
FOUNDATION			
Unit 1 Cash Transactions	☐	(5/98) ☐	☐
Unit 2 Credit Transactions	☐		
Unit 3 Payroll Transactions	(6/98) ☐	☐	
Unit 19 Data Processing (Windows) *	(8/98) ☐		
Unit 21-25 Business Knowledge	☐		

* Contains hands-on tuition and assignments; you will need access to Sage accounting software and BPP data disks

	Interactive Text	DA Kit	CA Kit
INTERMEDIATE			
Unit 4 Financial Records and Accounts	☐	(5/98) ☐	☐
Unit 5 Cost Information	☐		
Unit 6 Reports and Returns	☐	(5/98) ☐	
Unit 20 Information Technology	☐		
Unit 22: see below			
TECHNICIAN			
Unit 7/8 Core Managing Costs and Allocating Resources	☐		☐
Unit 9 Core Managing Accounting Systems		(5/98) ☐	
Unit 10 Option Drafting Financial Statements			☐
Unit 14 Option Cash Management and Credit Control		☐	
Unit 15 Option Evaluating Activities			
Unit 16 Option Implementing Auditing Procedures			
Unit 17 Option Business Taxation Computations	(8/98) ☐	date TBC	
Unit 18 Option Personal Taxation Computations	(8/98) ☐	date TBC	

TOTAL BOOKS   ☐ + ☐ + ☐ = ☐

                                                    @ £9.95 each = £ ☐

Postage and packaging:

UK: £2.00 for each book to maximum of £10

Europe (inc ROI & CI): £4.00 for each book   P & P   £ ☐

Rest of the World: £6.00 for each book

Unit 22 Maintaining a Healthy Workplace Interactive Text (postage free)   Quantity ☐ @ £3.95   £ ☐

GRAND TOTAL £ ☐

I enclose a cheque for £ _____ (cheques to BPP Publishing Ltd) or charge to Access/Visa/Switch

Card number ☐☐☐☐ ☐☐☐☐ ☐☐☐☐ ☐☐☐☐ ☐☐☐

Start date _____   Expiry date _____   Issue no. (Switch only)___

Signature _____

REVIEW FORM & FREE PRIZE DRAW

All original review forms from the entire BPP range, completed with genuine comments, will be entered into one of two draws on 31 January 1999 and 31 July 1999. The names on the first four forms picked out on each occasion will be sent a cheque for £50.

Name: _____   Address: _____

_____

_____

How have you used this Interactive Text?
(Tick one box only)

☐ Home study (book only)

☐ On a course: college _____

☐ With 'correspondence' package

☐ Other _____

Why did you decide to purchase this Interactive Text? *(Tick one box only)*

☐ Have used BPP Texts in the past

☐ Recommendation by friend/colleague

☐ Recommendation by a lecturer at college

☐ Saw advertising

☐ Other _____

During the past six months do you recall seeing/receiving any of the following?
(Tick as many boxes as are relevant)

☐ Our advertisement in *Accounting Technician* Magazine

☐ Our advertisement in *PASS*

☐ Our brochure with a letter through the post

Which (if any) aspects of our advertising do you find useful?
(Tick as many boxes as are relevant)

☐ Prices and publication dates of new editions

☐ Information on Text/Workbook content

☐ Facility to order books off-the-page

☐ None of the above

Your ratings, comments and suggestions would be appreciated on the following areas

	Very useful	Useful	Not useful
Introductory section (How to use this Text, etc)	☐	☐	☐
Coverage of elements of competence	☐	☐	☐
Windows coverage	☐	☐	☐
The Blitz program	☐	☐	☐
Explanation of accounting software (Sage)	☐	☐	☐
Cash and credit transactions assignments (1 - 6)	☐	☐	☐
Payroll assignments (7 - 10)	☐	☐	☐

	Excellent	Good	Adequate	Poor
Overall opinion of this Text	☐	☐	☐	☐

Do you intend to continue using BPP Interactive Texts/Assessment Kits? ☐ Yes ☐ No

Would you like to use a more advanced BPP book on computerised accounting (covering stock, prepayments and accruals, reporting etc)? ☐ Yes ☐ No

Please note any further comments and suggestions/errors on the reverse of this page

Please return to: Clare Donnelly, BPP Publishing Ltd, FREEPOST, London, W12 8BR

REVIEW FORM & FREE PRIZE DRAW (continued)

Please note any further comments and suggestions/errors below

FREE PRIZE DRAW RULES

1   Closing date for 31 January 1999 draw is 31 December 1998. Closing date for 31 July 1999 draw is 30 June 1999.

2   Restricted to entries with UK and Eire addresses only. BPP employees, their families and business associates are excluded.

3   No purchase necessary. Entry forms are available upon request from BPP Publishing. No more than one entry per title, per person. Draw restricted to persons aged 16 and over.

4   Winners will be notified by post and receive their cheques not later than 6 weeks after the relevant draw date. Lists of winners will be published in BPP's *focus* newsletter following the relevant draw.

5   The decision of the promoter in all matters is final and binding. No correspondence will be entered into.